Maven: The Definitive Guide

Maven: The Definitive Guide

Sonatype

O'REILLY®

Beijing · Cambridge · Farnham · Köln · Sebastopol · Tokyo

Maven: The Definitive Guide

by Sonatype

Copyright © 2008 Sonatype. All rights reserved.
Printed in the United States of America.

Published by O'Reilly Media, Inc., 1005 Gravenstein Highway North, Sebastopol, CA 95472.

O'Reilly books may be purchased for educational, business, or sales promotional use. Online editions are also available for most titles (*http://safari.oreilly.com*). For more information, contact our corporate/institutional sales department: 800-998-9938 or *corporate@oreilly.com*.

Editor: Mike Loukides

Production Editor: Sarah Schneider

Production Services: Appingo, Inc.

Cover Designer: Karen Montgomery

Interior Designer: David Futato

Illustrator: Robert Romano

Printing History:

August 2008: First Edition.

ISBN: 978-0-596-51733-5

[LSI]   [2011-05-13]

1304944188

Table of Contents

Part III.   Maven Reference

Preface

Although there are a number of references for Maven online, there is no single, well-written narrative for introducing Maven that can serve as both an authoritative reference and an introduction. What we've tried to do with this effort is provide such a narrative coupled with useful reference material.

Maven... What Is It?

The answer to this question depends on your own perspective. The great majority of Maven users are going to call Maven a "build tool": a tool used to build deployable artifacts from source code. Build engineers and project managers might refer to Maven as something more comprehensive: a project management tool. What is the difference? A build tool such as Ant is focused solely on preprocessing, compilation, packaging, testing, and distribution. A project management tool such as Maven provides a superset of features found in a build tool. In addition to providing build capabilities, Maven can also run reports, generate a web site, and facilitate communication among members of a working team.

Here is a more formal definition of Apache Maven (*http://maven.apache.org*): Maven is a project management tool that encompasses a Project Object Model, a set of standards, a project lifecycle, a dependency management system, and logic for executing plugin goals at defined phases in a lifecycle. When you use Maven, you describe your project using a well-defined Project Object Model, Maven can then apply cross-cutting logic from a set of shared (or custom) plugins.

Don't let the fact that Maven is a "project management" tool scare you away. If you are just looking for a build tool, Maven will do the job. In fact, the first few chapters of Part II will deal with the most common use case: using Maven to build and distribute your project.

Font Conventions

This book follows certain conventions for font usage. Understanding these conventions upfront makes it easier to use this book:

Italic
> Used for filenames, file extensions, URLs, application names, emphasis, and new terms when they are first introduced.

`Constant width`
> Used for Java™ class names, methods, variables, properties, data types, database elements, and snippets of code that appear in text.

`Constant width bold`
> Used for commands you enter at the command line and to highlight new code inserted in a running example.

`Constant width italic`
> Used to annotate output.

Maven Writing Conventions

The book follows certain conventions for naming and font usage in relation to Apache Maven. Understanding these conventions upfront makes it easier to read this book:

Compiler plugin
> Maven plugins are capitalized.

`create` goal
> Maven goal names are displayed in a constant width font.

plugin
> Maven revolves around the heavy use of plugins, but you won't find *plugin* defined in the dictionary. This book uses "plugin" without a hyphen because it is easier to read and write and because it is a standard throughout the Maven community.

Maven Lifecycle, Maven Standard Directory Layout, Project Object Model
> Core Maven concepts are capitalized whenever they are referenced in the text.

`goalParameter`
> A Maven goal parameter is displayed in a constant width font.

`compile` phase
> Lifecycle phases are displayed in a constant width font.

 This icon signifies a tip, suggestion, or general note.

This icon indicates a warning or caution.

Using Code Examples

This book is here to help you get your job done. In general, you may use the code in this book in your programs and documentation. You do not need to contact us for permission unless you're reproducing a significant portion of the code. For example, writing a program that uses several chunks of code from this book does not require permission. Selling or distributing a CD-ROM of examples from O'Reilly books does require permission. Answering a question by citing this book and quoting example code does not require permission. Incorporating a significant amount of example code from this book into your product's documentation does require permission.

We appreciate, but do not require, attribution. An attribution usually includes the title, author, publisher, and ISBN. For example: "*Maven: The Definitive Guide* by Sonatype. Copyright 2008 Sonatype, 978-0-596-51733-5."

If you feel your use of code examples falls outside fair use or the permission given above, feel free to contact us at *permissions@oreilly.com*.

Safari® Books Online

 When you see a Safari® Books Online icon on the cover of your favorite technology book, that means the book is available online through the O'Reilly Network Safari Bookshelf.

Safari offers a solution that's better than e-books. It's a virtual library that lets you easily search thousands of top tech books, cut and paste code samples, download chapters, and find quick answers when you need the most accurate, current information. Try it for free at *http://safari.oreilly.com*.

How to Contact Us

Please address comments and questions concerning this book to the publisher:

O'Reilly Media, Inc.
1005 Gravenstein Highway North
Sebastopol, CA 95472
800-998-9938 (in the United States or Canada)
707-829-0515 (international/local)
707-829-0104 (fax)

O'Reilly's web page for this book, where we list errata, examples, or any additional information. You can access this page at:

http://www.oreilly.com/catalog/9780596517335

To comment or ask technical questions about this book, send email to:

bookquestions@oreilly.com

For more information about our books, conferences, Resource Centers, and the O'Reilly Network, see our web site at:

http://www.oreilly.com

Acknowledgments

Sonatype would like to thank the following contributors who have provided feedback that improved the quality of this book. Thanks to Chad Gorshing, Marcus Biel, Brian Dols, Mangalaganesh Balasubramanian, Marius Kruger, and Mark Stewart. Special thanks to Joel Costigliola for helping debug and correct the Spring web chapter. Stan Guillory was practically a contributing author given the number of corrections he posted to the book's Get Satisfaction page. Thank you, Stan. Special thanks to Richard Coasby of Bamboo for acting as the provisional grammar consultant.

Sarah Schneider and Marlowe Shaeffer of O'Reilly Media, and Mark Jewett of Appingo, should receive medals for the extreme patience they displayed as this book continued to miss schedule after schedule. Thank you, Sarah, and the entire production department for making this book a success. Thanks to Mike Loukides and Mike Hendrickson for providing the necessary editorial oversight to make sure that we were given enough time and feedback to publish a book that will remain relevant in the months and years to come.

Thanks to all of the authors, especially Bruce Snyder, Brian Fox, John Casey, Jason van Zyl, and Eugene Kuleshov. Everyone at Sonatype played a part in the content of this book, and everyone worked together to help us create a foundation for this documentation.

Thanks to all of our contributing authors, especially Eric Redmond.

Tim O'Brien would like to thank his perfect wife, Susan, and child, Josephine.

## PART I

Introduction

The two chapters in this brief introduction describe Maven, explain how it stacks up to and improves on other build tools throughout time, and show you how to install and run it on all platforms. If you've already installed Maven and are familiar with the core concepts of the tool, you might want to skip ahead to Part II. Then again, even if you are already somewhat familiar with Maven, you might want to peruse some of the propaganda in this introduction so you're prepared when people start asking you why your organization or project should use Maven. After this section, you should have a better idea of what Maven is, what makes it different from some of the other options out there, and how to install it and learn more from the built-in help facilities.

## CHAPTER 1

Introducing Apache Maven

Convention over Configuration

Convention over configuration is a simple concept. Systems, libraries, and frameworks should assume reasonable defaults without requiring that unnecessary configuration systems should "just work." Popular frameworks such as Ruby on Rails and EJB3 have started to adhere to these principles in reaction to the configuration complexity of frameworks such as the initial Enterprise JavaBeans™ (EJB) specifications. An illustration of convention over configuration is something like EJB3 persistence. All you need to do to make a particular bean persistent is to annotate that class with `@Entity`. The framework will then assume table names and column names from the name of the class and the names of the properties. Hooks are provided for you to override these names if the need arises, but, in most cases, you will find that using the framework-supplied defaults results in a faster project execution.

Maven incorporates the concept by providing sensible default behaviors for projects. Without customization, source code is assumed to be in *${basedir}/src/main/java* and resources are assumed to be in *${basedir}/src/main/resources*. Tests are assumed to be in *${basedir}/src/test*, and a project is assumed to produce a JAR (Java ARchive) file. Maven assumes that you want to compile byte code to *${basedir}/target/classes* and then create a distributable JAR file in *${basedir}/target*. Although this might seem trivial, consider the fact that most Ant-based builds have to define the locations of these directories in every subproject. Maven's adoption of convention over configuration goes further than just simple directory locations; Maven's core plugins apply a common set of conventions for compiling source code, packaging distributions, generating web sites, and many other processes. Maven's strength comes from the fact that it is "opinionated." It has a defined lifecycle and a set of common plugins that know how to build libraries and web applications. If you follow the convention, Maven will require almost zero effort—just put your source in the correct directory, and Maven will take care of the rest.

One side effect of using systems that follow "convention over configuration" is that end users might feel that they are forced to use a particular setup. While it is certainly true that Maven has some central opinions that shouldn't be challenged, most of the defaults can be customized. For example, the location of a project's source code and resources can be customized, names of JAR files can be customized, and through the development of custom plugins, almost any behavior can be tailored to your specific environment's requirements. If you don't follow convention, Maven will allow you to customize defaults in order to adapt to your requirements.

A Common Interface

Before Maven provided a common interface for building software, every single project had someone dedicated to managing a completely custom build system, and developers had to take time away from developing software to learn about the idiosyncrasies of each new project they wanted to contribute to. In 2001, you'd take a completely different approach to building a project such as Apache Turbine (*http://turbine.apache.org/*) than you would to building a project such as Tomcat (*http://tomcat.apache.org*). If a new source analysis tool came out that would perform static analysis on source code, or if someone developed a new unit testing framework, everyone would have to drop what they were doing and figure out how to fit it into each project's custom build environment. How would you run unit tests? There were a thousand different answers. This environment was characterized by endless arguments about tools and build procedures. The age before Maven was an age of inefficiency—the age of the "Build Engineer."

Today, most open source developers have used or are currently using Maven to manage new software projects. This transition is less about developers moving from one build tool to another and more about developers starting to adopt a common interface for project builds. As software systems have become more modular, build systems have become more complex, and the number of projects has skyrocketed. Before Maven, when you wanted to check out a project such as Apache ActiveMQ (*http://activemq.apache.org*) or Apache ServiceMix (*http://servicemix.apache.org*) from Subversion and build it from source, you really had to set aside about an hour to figure out the build system for each particular project. What does the project need to build? What libraries do I need to download? Where do I put them? What goals can I execute in the build? In the best case, it took a few minutes to figure out a new project's build, and in the worst cases (like the old Servlet API implementation in the Jakarta Project), a project's build was so difficult it would take many hours just to get to the point where a new contributor could edit source and compile the project. These days, with Maven, you check it out from source, and you run *mvn install*.

Although Maven provides an array of benefits, including dependency management and reuse of common build logic through plugins, the core reason it has succeeded is that it has defined a common interface for building software. When you see that a project such as Apache Wicket (*http://wicket.apache.org*) uses Maven, you can assume that you'll be able to check it out from source and build it with *mvn install* without much hassle. You know where the ignition key goes, and you know that the gas pedal is on the right and the brake is on the left.

Universal Reuse Through Maven Plugins

The core of Maven is pretty dumb; it doesn't know how to do much beyond parsing a few XML documents and keeping track of a lifecycle and a few plugins. Maven has been designed to delegate most responsibility to a set of Maven plugins that can affect the Maven lifecycle and offer access to goals. Most of the action in Maven happens in plugin goals that take care of things like compiling source, packaging bytecode, publishing sites, and any other task that needs to happen in a build. The Maven you download from Apache doesn't know much about packaging a WAR file or running JUnit tests; most of Maven's intelligence is implemented in the plugins, and the plugins are retrieved from the Maven repository. In fact, the first time you run something like *mvn install* with a brand new Maven installation, it retrieves most of the core Maven plugins from the central Maven repository. This is more than just a trick to minimize the download size of the Maven distribution; this is behavior that allows you to upgrade a plugin to add capability to your project's build. The fact that Maven retrieves both dependencies and plugins from the remote repository allows for universal reuse of build logic.

The Maven Surefire plugin is responsible for running unit tests. At some point between version 1.0 and the version that is in wide use today, someone decided to add support for the TestNG unit testing framework in addition to the support for JUnit. This happened in a way that didn't break backward compatibility—if you were using the Surefire plugin to compile and execute JUnit 3 unit tests, and you upgraded to the most recent version of the Surefire plugin, your tests continued to execute without fail. You also gained new functionality, so if you wanted to execute unit tests in TestNG, you now had that ability, thanks to the efforts of the maintainers of the Surefire plugin. You also gained the ability to run annotated JUnit 4 unit tests. You gained all of these capabilities without having to upgrade your Maven installation or install new software. Most importantly, nothing about your project had to change aside from a version number for a plugin in a POM.

It is this mechanism that affects much more than the Surefire plugin: projects are compiled with a Compiler plugin, projects are turned into JAR files with a Jar plugin, and there are plugins for running reports, plugins for executing JRuby and Groovy code, as well as plugins to publish sites to remote servers. Maven has abstracted common build tasks into plugins that are maintained centrally and shared universally. If the state of the art changes in any area of the build, if some new unit testing framework is released or if some new tool is made available, you don't have to be the one to hack your project's custom build system to support it. You benefit from the fact that plugins are downloaded from a remote repository and maintained centrally. This is what is meant by universal reuse through Maven plugins.

Conceptual Model of a "Project"

Maven maintains a model of a project: you are not just compiling source code into bytecode, you are developing a description of a software project and assigning a unique set of coordinates to a project. You are describing the attributes of the project. What is the project's license? Who develops and contributes to the project? What other projects does this project depend on? Maven is more than just a "build tool"; it is more than just an improvement on tools such as *make* and Ant; it is a platform that encompasses a new semantics related to software projects and software development. This definition of a model for every project enables such features as:

Dependency management
> A project is defined as unique coordinates that consists of a group identifier, artifact identifier, and version. Projects can now use these coordinates to declare dependencies.

Remote repositories
> Related to dependency management, we can use the coordinates defined in the Maven Project Object Model (POM) to create repositories of Maven artifacts.

Universal reuse of build logic
> Plugins are coded to work with the POM; they are not designed to operate on specific files in known locations. Everything is abstracted into the model—plugin configuration and customization happens in the model.

Tool portability and integration
> Tools such as Eclipse, NetBeans, and IntelliJ now have a common place to find information about a project. Before the advent of Maven, every integrated development environment (IDE) had a different way to store what was essentially a custom POM. Maven has standardized this description, and although each IDE continues to maintain custom project files, they can be easily generated from the model.

Easy searching and filtering of project artifacts
> Tools such as Nexus allow you to index and search the contents of a repository using the information stored in the POM.

Maven has provided a foundation for the beginnings of a consistent semantic description of a software project.

Is Maven an Alternative to XYZ?

So, sure, Maven is an alternative to Ant, but Apache Ant (*http://ant.apache.org*) continues to be a great, widely used tool. It has been the reigning champion of Java builds for years, and you can integrate Ant build scripts with your project's Maven build very easily. This is a common usage pattern for a Maven project. On the other hand, as more and more open source projects move to Maven as a project management platform, working developers are starting to realize that Maven not only simplifies the task of build management, it is helping to encourage a common interface between developers and software projects. Maven is more of a platform than a tool. Although you can consider Maven an alternative to Ant, you are comparing apples to oranges. "Maven" includes more than just a build tool.

This is the central point that makes all of the Maven versus Ant, Maven versus Buildr, Maven versus Gradle arguments irrelevant. Maven isn't totally defined by the mechanics of your build system. It isn't about scripting the various tasks in your build as much as it is about encouraging a set of standards, a common interface, a lifecycle, a standard repository format, a standard directory layout, etc. It certainly isn't about what format the POM happens to be in, i.e., XML versus YAML versus Ruby. Maven is much larger than that, and Maven refers to much more than the tool itself. When this book talks about Maven, it is referring to the constellation of software, systems, and standards that support it. Buildr, Ivy, Gradle—all of these tools interact with the repository format that Maven helped create, and you could just as easily use a tool such as Nexus to support a build written entirely in Buildr. Nexus is introduced in Chapter 16.

Although Maven is an alternative to many of these tools, the community needs to evolve beyond seeing technology as a zero-sum game between unfriendly competitors in a contest for users and developers. This might be how large corporations relate to one another, but it has very little relevance to the way that open source communities work. The headline "Who's winning? Ant or Maven?" isn't very constructive. If you force us to answer this question, we're definitely going to say that Maven is a superior alternative to Ant as a foundational technology for a build; at the same time, Maven's boundaries are constantly shifting and the Maven community is constantly trying to seek out new ways to become more ecumenical, interoperable, and cooperative. The core tenets of Maven are declarative builds, dependency management, repository managers, and universal reuse through plugins, but the specific incarnation of these ideas at any given moment is less important than the sense that the open source community is collaborating to reduce the inefficiency of "enterprise-scale builds."

Comparing Maven and Ant

Although the previous section should convince you that the authors of this book have no interest in creating a feud between Apache Ant and Apache Maven, we are cognizant of the fact that most organizations have to make a decision between Ant and Maven. In this section, we compare and contrast the tools.

Ant excels at build process; it is a build system modeled after *make* with targets and dependencies. Each target consists of a set of instructions that are coded in XML. There is a `copy` task and a `javac` task as well as a `jar` task. When you use Ant, you supply it with specific instructions for compiling and packaging your output. Look at the simple *build.xml* file shown in Example 1-1.

Example 1-1. A simple Ant build.xml file

```xml
<project name="my-project" default="dist" basedir=".">
    <description>
        simple example build file
    </description>
    <!-- set global properties for this build -->
    <property name="src" location="src/main/java"/>
    <property name="build" location="target/classes"/>
    <property name="dist"  location="target"/>

    <target name="init">
      <!-- Create the time stamp -->
      <tstamp/>
      <!-- Create the build directory structure used by compile -->
      <mkdir dir="${build}"/>
    </target>

    <target name="compile" depends="init"
          description="compile the source " >
      <!-- Compile the java code from ${src} into ${build} -->
      <javac srcdir="${src}" destdir="${build}"/>
    </target>

    <target name="dist" depends="compile"
          description="generate the distribution" >
      <!-- Create the distribution directory -->
      <mkdir dir="${dist}/lib"/>

      <!-- Put everything in ${build} into the MyProject-${DSTAMP}.jar file -->
      <jar jarfile="${dist}/lib/MyProject-${DSTAMP}.jar" basedir="${build}"/>
    </target>

    <target name="clean"
          description="clean up" >
      <!-- Delete the ${build} and ${dist} directory trees -->
      <delete dir="${build}"/>
      <delete dir="${dist}"/>
    </target>
</project>
```

In this simple Ant example, you can see how you have to tell Ant exactly what to do. There is a compile goal that includes the javac task, which compiles the source in the *src/main/java* directory to the *target/classes* directory. You have to tell Ant exactly where your source is, where you want the resulting bytecode to be stored, and how to package this all into a JAR file. Although some recent developments help make Ant less procedural, a developer's experience with Ant is in coding a procedural language written in XML.

Contrast the previous Ant example with a Maven example. In Maven, to create a JAR file from some Java source, all you need to do is create a simple *pom.xml*, place your source code in *${basedir}/src/main/java*, and then run *mvn install* from the command line. The example Maven *pom.xml* that achieves the same results as the simple Ant file listed in Example 1-1 is shown in Example 1-2.

Example 1-2. A simple Maven pom.xml

```
<project>
  <modelVersion>4.0.0</modelVersion>
  <groupId>org.sonatype.mavenbook</groupId>
  <artifactId>my-project</artifactId>
  <version>1.0</version>
</project>
```

That's all you need in your *pom.xml*. Running *mvn install* from the command line will process resources, compile source, execute unit tests, create a JAR, and install the JAR in a local repository for reuse in other projects. Without modification, you can run *mvn site* and then find an *index.html* file in *target/site* that contains links to Javadoc and a few reports about your source code.

Admittedly, this is the simplest possible example project: a project that contains only source code and produces a JAR; a project that follows Maven conventions and doesn't require any dependencies or customization. If we want to start customizing the behavior, our *pom.xml* is going to grow in size, and in the largest of projects, you can see collections of very complex Maven POMs that contain a great deal of plugin customization and dependency declarations. But even when your project's POM files become more substantial, they hold an entirely different kind of information from the build file of a similarly sized project using Ant. Maven POMs contain declarations: "This is a JAR project," and "The source code is in *src/main/java*." Ant build files contain explicit instructions: "This is project," "The source is in *src/main/java*," "Run javac against this directory," "Put the results in *target/classses*," "Create a JAR from the ....", etc. Where Ant has to be explicit about the process, there is something "built-in" to Maven that just knows where the source code is and how it should be processed.

The differences between Ant and Maven in this example are:

Apache Ant

- Ant doesn't have formal conventions such as a common project directory structure; you have to tell Ant *exactly* where to find the source and where to put the output. Informal conventions have emerged over time, but they haven't been codified into the product.

- Ant is procedural; you have to tell Ant exactly what to do and when to do it. You have to tell it to compile, then copy, then compress.

- Ant doesn't have a lifecycle; you have to define goals and goal dependencies. You have to attach a sequence of tasks to each goal manually.

Apache Maven

- Maven has conventions: in the example, it already knew where your source code was because you followed the convention. It put the bytecode in *target/classes*, and it produced a JAR file in target.

- Maven is declarative; all you had to do was create a *pom.xml* file and put your source in the default directory. Maven took care of the rest.

- Maven has a lifecycle, which you invoked when you executed *mvn install*. This command told Maven to execute a series of sequence steps until it reached the lifecycle. As a side effect of this journey through the lifecycle, Maven executed a number of default plugin goals that did things such as compile and create a JAR.

Maven has built-in intelligence about common project tasks in the form of Maven plugins. If you want to write and execute unit tests, all you need to do is write the tests, place them in *${basedir}/src/test/java*, add a `test`-scoped dependency on either TestNG or JUnit, and run *mvn test*. If you want to deploy a web application and not a JAR, all you need to do is change you project type to WAR and put your docroot in *${basedir}/src/main/webapp*. Sure, you could do all of this with Ant, but you would be writing the instructions from scratch. In Ant, you would first have to figure out where the JUnit JAR file should be, and then you would have to create a classpath that includes the JUnit JAR file, and then you would tell Ant where it should look for test source code, write a goal that compiles the test source to bytecode, and execute the unit tests with JUnit.

Without supporting technologies such as antlibs and Ivy (and even with these supporting technologies), Ant has the feeling of a custom procedural build. An efficient set of Maven POMs in a project that adheres to Maven's assumed conventions has surprisingly little XML compared to the Ant alternative. Another benefit of Maven is the reliance on widely shared Maven plugins. Everyone uses the Maven Surefire plugin for unit testing, and if someone adds support for a new unit testing framework, you can gain new capabilities in your own build just by incrementing the version of a particular Maven plugin in your project's POM.

The decision to use Maven or Ant isn't a binary one, and Ant still has a place in a complex build. If your current build contains some highly customized process, or if you've written some Ant scripts to complete a specific process in a specific way that cannot be adapted to the Maven standards, you can still use these scripts with Maven. Ant is made available as a core Maven plugin. Custom Maven plugins can be implemented in Ant, and Maven projects can be configured to execute Ant scripts within the Maven project lifecycle.

Summary

This introduction has been kept purposefully short. We have covered a basic outline of what Maven is and how it stacks up to and improves on other build tools throughout time. The next chapter will explain how to install and run Maven, and Chapter 3 will dive into a simple project and show how Maven can perform phenomenal tasks with the smallest amount of configuration.

## CHAPTER 2

Installing and Running Maven

This chapter contains very detailed instructions for installing Maven on a number of different platforms. Instead of assuming a level of familiarity with installing software and setting environment variables, we've opted to be as thorough as possible to minimize any problems that might arise due to a partial installation. The only thing this chapter assumes is that you've already installed a suitable Java Development Kit (JDK). If you are just interested in installation, you can move on to the rest of the book after reading through the "Downloading Maven" and "Installing Maven" sections. If you are interested in the details of your Maven installation, this entire chapter will give you an overview of what you've installed and the Apache Software License.

Verify Your Java Installation

Although Maven can run on Java 1.4, this book assumes that you are running at least Java 5. Go with the most recent stable JDK available for your operating system. Either Java 5 or Java 6 will work with all of the examples in this book:

```
% java -version
java version "1.6.0_02"
Java(TM) SE Runtime Environment (build 1.6.0_02-b06)
Java HotSpot(TM) Client VM (build 1.6.0_02-b06, mixed mode, sharing)
```

Maven works with all certified Java-compatible development kits, and a few noncertified implementations of Java. The examples in this book were written and tested against the official Java Development Kit releases downloaded from the Sun Microsystems web site. If you're working with a Linux distribution, you may need to download Sun's JDK yourself and make sure it's the version you're invoking (by running *java -version*, as shown earlier). Now that Sun has open sourced Java, this will hopefully improve in the future, and we'll get the Sun Java Runtime Environment (JRE) and JDK by default even in purist distributions. Until that day, you may need to do some of your own downloading.

Downloading Maven

You can download Maven from the Apache Maven project web site by going to *http://maven.apache.org/download.html*.

When downloading Maven, make sure you choose the latest version of Apache Maven from the web site. The latest version of Maven at the time of this writing is Maven 2.0.9. If you are not familiar with the Apache Software License, you should get acquainted with the terms of the license before you start using the product. More information on the Apache Software License can be found in "About the Apache Software License," later in this chapter.

Installing Maven

There are wide differences between operating systems such as Mac OS X and Microsoft Windows, and there are subtle differences between different versions of Windows. Luckily, the process of installing Maven on all of these operating systems is relatively painless and straightforward. The following sections outline the recommended best-practice for installing Maven on a variety of operating systems.

Installing Maven on Mac OS X

You can download a binary release of Maven from *http://maven.apache.org/download .html*. Download the current release of Maven in a format that is convenient for you to work with. Pick an appropriate place for it to live, and expand the archive there. If you expanded the archive into the directory */usr/local/maven-2.0.9*, you may want to create a symbolic link to make it easier to work with and to avoid the need to change any environment configuration when you upgrade to a newer version:

```
/usr/local % ln -s maven-2.0.9 maven
/usr/local % export M2_HOME=/usr/local/maven
/usr/local % export PATH=${M2_HOME}/bin:${PATH}
```

Once Maven is installed, you need to do a couple of things to make it work correctly. You need to add its *bin* directory in the distribution (in this example, */usr/local/maven/bin*) to your command path. You also need to set the environment variable M2_HOME to the top-level directory you installed (in this example, */usr/local/maven*).

 Installation instructions are the same for both OS X Tiger and Leopard. It has been reported that Maven 2.0.6 is shipping with a preview release of Xcode. If you have installed XCode, run *mvn* from the command line to check availability. XCode installs Maven in */usr/share/maven*. We recommend installing the most recent version of Maven 2.0.9, as there have been a number of bug fixes and improvements since Maven 2.0.9 was released.

You'll need to add both `M2_HOME` and `PATH` to a script that will run every time you log in. To do this, add the following lines to *.bash_login*:

```
export M2_HOME=/usr/local/maven
export PATH=${M2_HOME}/bin:${PATH}
```

Once you've added these lines to your own environment, you will be able to run Maven from the command line.

 These installation instructions assume that you are running *bash*.

Installing Maven on Microsoft Windows

Installing Maven on Windows is very similar to installing Maven on Mac OS X, the main differences being the installation location and the setting of an environment variable. This book assumes a Maven installation directory located at *c:\Program Files \maven-2.0.9*, but it won't make a difference if you install Maven in another directory as long as you configure the proper environment variables. Once you've unpacked Maven in the installation directory, you will need to set two environment variables—`PATH` and `M2_HOME`. To set these environment variables from the command line, type in the following commands:

```
C:\Users\tobrien > set M2_HOME=c:\Program Files\maven-2.0.9
C:\Users\tobrien > set PATH=%PATH%;%M2_HOME%\bin
```

Setting these environment variables on the command line will allow you to run Maven in your current session, but unless you add them to the system environment variables through the control panel, you'll have to execute these two lines every time you log into your system. Set both `M2_HOME` and `PATH` to point to your Maven installation.

Installing Maven on Linux

To install Maven on a Linux machine, follow the exact procedure outlined in "Installing Maven on Mac OS X," earlier in this chapter.

Installing Maven on FreeBSD or OpenBSD

To install Maven on a FreeBSD or OpenBSD machine, follow the exact procedure outlined in "Installing Maven on Mac OS X," earlier in this chapter.

Testing a Maven Installation

Once Maven is installed, you can see if it is installed properly by running *mvn -v* from the command line. If Maven has been installed, you should see something resembling the following output:

```
~/examples $ mvn -v
Maven 2.0.9
```

If you see this output, you know that Maven has been successfully installed. If you do not see this output and your operating system cannot find the *mvn* command, make sure that your PATH and M2_HOME environment variables have been properly set.

Maven Installation Details

Maven's download measures in at roughly 1.5 MiB.* It has attained such a slim download size because the core of Maven has been designed to retrieve plugins and dependencies from a remote repository on demand. When you start using Maven, it will start to download plugins to a local repository as described in the section "User-Specific Configuration and Repository," later in this chapter. In case you are curious, let's take a quick look at what is in Maven's installation directory:

```
/usr/local/maven $ ls -p1
LICENSE.txt
NOTICE.txt
README.txt
bin/
boot/
conf/
lib/
```

LICENSE.txt contains the software license for Apache Maven. This license is described in some detail later in the section "About the Apache Software License." *NOTICE.txt* contains some notices and attributions required by libraries that Maven depends on. *README.txt* contains some installation instructions. *bin/* contains the *mvn* script that executes Maven. *boot/* contains a JAR file (*classwords-1.1.jar*) that is responsible for creating the Class Loader in which Maven executes. *conf/* contains a global *settings.xml* that can be used to customize the behavior of your Maven installation. If you need to customize Maven, it is customary to override any settings in a *set tings.xml* file stored in *~/.m2*. *lib/* contains a single JAR file (*maven-core-2.0.9-uber.jar*) that contains the core of Maven.

---

* Ever purchased a 200 GB hard drive only to realize that it showed up as less than 200 GiB when you installed it? Computers understand Gibibytes, but retailers sell products using Gigabytes. MiB stands for Mebibyte, which is defined as 2^{20} or 1024^2. These binary prefix standards are endorsed by the Institute of Electrical and Electronics Engineers (IEEE), the International Committee for Weights and Measures (CIPM), and the International Electrotechnical Commission (IEC). For more information about Kibibytes, Mebibytes, Gibibytes, and Tebibytes, see *http://en.wikipedia.org/wiki/Mebibyte*.

User-Specific Configuration and Repository

Once you start using Maven extensively, you'll notice that Maven has created some local user-specific configuration files and a local repository in your home directory. In ~/.m2, there will be:

settings.xml
A file containing user-specific configuration for authentication, repositories, and other information to customize the behavior of Maven.

repository/
This directory contains your local Maven repository. When you download a dependency from a remote Maven repository, Maven stores a copy of the dependency in your local repository.

In Unix (and OS X), your home directory will be referred to using a tilde (i.e., ~/bin refers to /home/tobrien/bin). In Windows, we will also be using ~ to refer to your home directory. In Windows XP, your home directory is C:\Documents and Settings\tobrien, and in Windows Vista, your home directory is C:\Users\tobrien. From this point forward, you should translate paths such as ~/m2 to your operating system's equivalent.

Upgrading a Maven Installation

If you've installed Maven on a Mac OS X or Unix machine according to the details given in "Installing Maven on Mac OS X" and "Installing Maven on Linux," it should be easy to upgrade to newer versions of Maven when they become available. Simply install the newer version of Maven (*/usr/local/maven-2.future*) next to the existing version of Maven (*/usr/local/maven-2.0.9*). Then, switch the symbolic link */usr/local/maven* from */usr/local/maven-2.0.9* to */usr/local/maven-2.future*. Since you've already set your M2_HOME variable to point to */usr/local/maven*, you won't need to change any environment variables.

If you've installed Maven on a Windows machine, simply unpack Maven to *c:\Program Files\maven-2.future* and update your M2_HOME variable.

Getting Help with Maven

Although this book aims to be a comprehensive reference, there are going to be topics we miss and special situations and tips that are not covered. The core of Maven is very simple, but the real work in Maven happens in the plugins, and there are too many plugins available to cover them all in one book. When you encounter problems and features that are not covered in this book, we suggest searching for answers at the following locations:

http://maven.apache.org

This is the first place you should look; the Maven web site contains a wealth of information and documentation. Every plugin has a few pages of documentation, and it provides a series of "quick start" documents that will be helpful in addition to the contents of this book. Although the Maven site contains plenty of information, it can also be a frustrating, confusing, and overwhelming. A custom Google search box on the main Maven page will search known Maven sites for information. This provides better results than a generic Google search.

Maven user mailing list

The Maven user mailing list is the place for users to ask questions. Before you ask a question on the user mailing list, you will want to search for any previous discussion that might relate to your question. It is bad form to ask a question that has already been asked without first checking to see whether an answer already exists in the archives. There are a number of useful mailing list archive browsers; we've found Nabble to be the most useful. You can browse the user mailing list archives here: *http://www.nabble.com/Maven---Users-f178.html*. You can join the user mailing list by following the instructions available here: *http://maven.apache.org/mail-lists.html*.

http://www.sonatype.com

Sonatype maintains an online copy of this book and other tutorials related to Apache Maven.

 Despite the best efforts of some very dedicated Maven contributors, the Maven web site is poorly organized and full of incomplete (and sometimes misleading) snippets of documentation. Throughout the Maven community there is a lack of a common standards for plugin documentation. Some plugins are heavily documented, whereas others lack even the most basic instructions for usage. Often your best bet is to search for a solution in the archives of the user mailing list. If you really want to help, submit a patch to the Maven site (or this book).

Using the Maven Help Plugin

Throughout the book, we will be introducing Maven plugins and talking about Maven Project Object Model (POM) files, settings files, and profiles. There are going to be times when you need a tool to help you make sense of some of the models that Maven is using and what goals are available on a specific plugin. The Maven Help plugin allows you to list active Maven profiles, display an effective POM, print the effective settings, or list the attributes of a Maven plugin.

For a conceptual overview of the POM and plugins, see Chapter 3.

The Maven Help plugin has four goals. The first three goals—`active-profiles`, `effective-pom`, and `effective-settings`—describe a particular project and must be run in the base directory of a project. The last goal—`describe`—is slightly more complex, showing you information about a plugin or a plugin goal. The following commands provide some general information about the four goals:

`help:active-profiles`
> Lists the profiles (project, user, global) that are active for the build.

`help:effective-pom`
> Displays the effective POM for the current build, with the active profiles factored in.

`help:effective-settings`
> Prints out the calculated settings for the project, given any profile enhancement and the inheritance of the global settings into the user-level settings.

`help:describe`
> Describes the attributes of a plugin. This need not run under an existing project directory. You must give at least the `groupId` and `artifactId` of the plugin you wish to describe.

Describing a Maven Plugin

Once you start using Maven, you'll spend most of your time trying to get more information about plugins. You'll want to know: How do plugins work? What are the configuration parameters? What are the goals? The `help:describe` goal is something you'll use very frequently to retrieve this information. With the `plugin` parameter, you can specify a plugin you wish to investigate, passing in either the plugin prefix (e.g., `maven-help-plugin` as `help`) or the *groupId:artifact[:version]*, where *version* is optional. For example, the following command uses the Help plugin's `describe` goal to print out information about the Maven Help plugin:

```
$ mvn help:describe -Dplugin=help
...
Group Id:  org.apache.maven.plugins
Artifact Id: maven-help-plugin
Version:    2.0.1
Goal Prefix: help
Description:

The Maven Help plugin provides goals aimed at helping to make sense out of
    the build environment. It includes the ability to view the effective
    POM and settings files, after inheritance and active profiles
    have been applied, as well as a describe a particular plugin goal to give
```

```
      usage information.
  ...
```

Executing the `describe` goal with the plugin parameter prints out the Maven coordinates for the plugin, the goal prefix, and a brief description of the plugin. Although this information is helpful, you'll usually be looking for more detail than this. If you want the Help plugin to print a full list of goals with parameters, execute the `help:describe` goal with the parameter `full` as follows:

```
$ mvn help:describe -Dplugin=help -Dfull
...
Group Id:    org.apache.maven.plugins
Artifact Id: maven-help-plugin
Version:     2.0.1
Goal Prefix: help
Description:

The Maven Help plugin provides goals aimed at helping to make sense out of
    the build environment. It includes the ability to view the effective
    POM and settings files, after inheritance and active profiles have been
    applied, as well as a describe a particular plugin goal to give usage
    information.

Mojos:


================================================
Goal: 'active-profiles'
================================================
Description:

Lists the profiles which are currently active for this build.

Implementation: org.apache.maven.plugins.help.ActiveProfilesMojo
Language: java

Parameters:
-----------------------------------------------

[0] Name: output
Type: java.io.File
Required: false
Directly editable: true
Description:

This is an optional parameter for a file destination for the output of
this mojo...the listing of active profiles per project.


-----------------------------------------------

[1] Name: projects
Type: java.util.List
Required: true
Directly editable: false
Description:
```

```
This is the list of projects currently slated to be built by Maven.


------------------------------------------------

This mojo doesn't have any component requirements.
================================================

... remove the other goals ...
```

This option is great for discovering all of a plugin's goals as well as their parameters. But sometimes this gives you far more information than you need. To get information about a single goal, set the `mojo` parameter as well as the `plugin` parameter. The following command lists all of the information about the Compiler plugin's `compile` goal:

```
$ mvn help:describe -Dplugin=compiler -Dmojo=compile -Dfull
```

 What's a Mojo? In Maven, a plugin goal is known as a Mojo.

About the Apache Software License

Apache Maven is released under the Apache License, version 2.0. If you want to read this license, you can look at *${M2_HOME}/LICENSE.txt* or read it on the Open Source Initiative's web site at *http://www.opensource.org/licenses/apache2.0.php*.

Chances are good that, if you are reading this book, you are not a lawyer. If you are wondering what the Apache License, version 2.0 means, the Apache Software Foundation has assembled a very helpful Frequently Asked Questions (FAQ) page about the license, available here: *http://www.apache.org/foundation/licence-FAQ.html*. Here's the answer to the frequently asked question "I am not a lawyer. What does it all mean?":

> *[This license] allows you to:*
>
> - Freely download and use Apache software, in whole or in part, for personal, company internal, or commercial purposes;
> - Use Apache software in packages or distributions that you create.
>
> *It forbids you to:*
>
> - Redistribute any piece of Apache-originated software without proper attribution;
> - Use any marks owned by the Apache Software Foundation in any way that might state or imply that the Foundation endorses your distribution;
> - Use any marks owned by the Apache Software Foundation in any way that might state or imply that you created the Apache software in question.
>
> *It requires you to:*
>
> - Include a copy of the license in any redistribution you may make that includes Apache software;

- Provide clear attribution to the Apache Software Foundation for any distributions that include Apache software.

It does not require you to:

- Include the source of the Apache software itself, or of any modifications you may have made to it, in any redistribution you may assemble that includes it;
- Submit changes that you make to the software back to the Apache Software Foundation (though such feedback is encouraged).

This ends the installation information. The next part of the book contains Maven examples.

## PART II

Maven by Example

The first Maven book was *Maven: A Developer's Notebook* (O'Reilly). That book introduced Maven in a series of steps via a conversation between you and a colleague who already knew how to use Maven. The idea behind the (now-retired) Developer's Notebook series was that developers learn best when they are sitting next to other developers and going through the same thought processes, learning to code by doing and experimenting. Although the series was successful, the Notebook format had limitations. Notebooks were designed to be "goal-focused" books that take you through a series of steps to achieve very specific goals. By contrast, larger reference books provide comprehensive material that covers the entirety of the topic.

If you read *Maven: A Developer's Notebook*, you'll learn how to create a simple project or a project that creates a WAR from a set of source files. But if you want to find out the specifics of something like the Assembly plugin, you'll hit an impasse. Because there is currently no well-written reference material for Maven, you have to hunt through plugin documentation on the Maven web site or cull from a series of mailing lists. Once you really dig into Maven, you end up reading through thousands of HTML pages on the Maven site written by hundreds of developers, each with a different idea of what it means to document a plugin. Despite the best efforts of well-meaning volunteers, reading through plugin documentation on the Maven site is frustrating at best, and at worst, it's a reason to abandon Maven. Quite often, Maven users get stuck because they just can't find an answer.

This lack of an authoritative (or definitive) reference manual has held Maven back for a few years, and it has been something of a dampening force on Maven adoption. With *Maven: The Definitive Guide,* we intend to change that situation by providing a comprehensive reference in Part III. In Part II, we're preserving the narrative progression of a Developer's Notebook; it is valuable material that helps people learn Maven by example. Thus, here we "introduce by doing," and in Part III, we fill in the blanks and dig into the details. Where Part III might use a reference table and a program listing detached from an example project, Part II is motivated by real examples.

After reading this part, you should have everything you need to start using Maven. You might need to refer to Part III only when you start customizing Maven by writing custom plugins or when you want more detail about specific plugins.

## CHAPTER 3

A Simple Maven Project

Introduction

In this chapter, we introduce a simple project created from scratch using the Maven Archetype plugin. This elementary application provides us with the opportunity to discuss some core Maven concepts while you follow along with the development of the project.

Before you can start using Maven for complex, multimodule builds, we have to start with the basics. If you've used Maven before, you'll notice that it does a good job of taking care of the details. Your builds tend to "just work," and you only really need to dive into the details of Maven when you want to customize the default behavior or write a custom plugin. However, when you do need to dive into the details, a thorough understanding of the core concepts is essential. This chapter aims to introduce you to the simplest possible Maven project and then presents some of the core concepts that make Maven a solid build platform. After reading it, you'll have an fundamental understanding of the build lifecycle, Maven repositories, dependency management, and the Project Object Model (POM).

Downloading This Chapter's Example

This chapter develops a very simple example that will be used to explore core concepts of Maven. If you follow the steps as described, you shouldn't need to download the examples to recreate the code produced by Maven. We will be using the Maven Archetype plugin to create this simple project, and in this chapter we won't modify the project in any way. If you would prefer to read this chapter with the final example source code, the example project may be downloaded with the book's example code at *http://www.sonatype.com/book/mvn-examples-1.0.zip* or *http://www.sonatype.com/book/mvn-examples-1.0.tar.gz*. Unzip this archive in any directory, and then go to the *ch03/* directory. There you will see a directory named *simple/*, which contains the source code for this chapter. If you wish to follow along with the example code in a web browser, go to *http://www.sonatype.com/book/examples-1.0* and click on the *ch03/* directory.

Creating a Simple Project

To start a new Maven project, use the Maven Archetype plugin from the command line:

```
$ mvn archetype:create -DgroupId=org.sonatype.mavenbook.ch03 \
                        -DartifactId=simple \
                        -DpackageName=org.sonatype.mavenbook
[INFO] Scanning for projects...
[INFO] Searching repository for plugin with prefix: 'archetype'.
[INFO] artifact org.apache.maven.plugins:maven-archetype-plugin: checking for \
       updates from central
[INFO] ------------------------------------------------------------------------
[INFO] Building Maven Default Project
[INFO]    task-segment: [archetype:create] (aggregator-style)
[INFO] ------------------------------------------------------------------------
[INFO] [archetype:create]
[INFO] artifact org.apache.maven.archetypes:maven-archetype-quickstart: \
       checking for updates from central
[INFO] Parameter: groupId, Value: org.sonatype.mavenbook.ch03
[INFO] Parameter: packageName, Value: org.sonatype.mavenbook
[INFO] Parameter: basedir, Value: /Users/tobrien/svnw/sonatype/examples
[INFO] Parameter: package, Value: org.sonatype.mavenbook
[INFO] Parameter: version, Value: 1.0-SNAPSHOT
[INFO] Parameter: artifactId, Value: simple
[INFO] * End of debug info from resources from generated POM *
[INFO] Archetype created in dir: /Users/tobrien/svnw/sonatype/examples/simple
```

mvn is the Maven 2 command. `archetype:create` is called a Maven goal. If you are familiar with Apache Ant, a Maven goal is analogous to an Ant target; both describe a unit of work to be completed in a build. The `-Dname=value` pairs are arguments that are passed to the goal and take the form of `-D` properties, similar to the system property options you might pass to the Java Virtual Machine via the command line. The purpose of the `archetype:create` goal is to quickly create a project from an archetype. In this context, an archetype is defined as "an original model or type after which other similar things are patterned; a prototype."* A number of archetypes are available in Maven for anything from a simple Swing application to a complex web application. In this chapter, we are going to use the most basic archetype to create a simple skeleton starter project. The plugin is the prefix `archetype`, and the goal is `create`.

Once we've generated a project, take a look at the directory structure Maven created under the simple directory:

```
simple/❶
simple/pom.xml❷
      /src/
      /src/main/❸
```

---

* *The American Heritage Dictionary of the English Language*

```
        /main/java
    /src/test/❹
        /test/java
```

This generated directory adheres to the Maven Standard Directory Layout. We'll get into more details later in this chapter, but for now, let's just try to understand these few basic directories:

❶ The Maven Archetype plugin creates a directory that matches the `artifactId`. Simple. This is known as the project's base directory.

❷ Every Maven project has what is known as a Project Object Model (POM) in a file named *pom.xml*. This file describes the project, configures plugins, and declares dependencies.

❸ Our project's source code and resources are placed under *src/main*. In the case of our simple Java project, this will consist of a few Java classes and some properties files. In another project, this could be the document root of a web application or configuration files for an application server. In a Java project, Java classes are placed in *src/main/java*, and classpath resources are placed in *src/main/resources*.

❹ Our project's test cases are located in *src/test*. Under this directory, Java classes such as JUnit or TestNG tests are placed in *src/test/java*, and classpath resources for tests are located in *src/test/resources*.

The Maven Archetype plugin generated a single class `org.sonatype.mavenbook.App`, which is a 13-line Java class with a static main function that prints out a message:

```
package org.sonatype.mavenbook;

/**
 * Hello world!
 *
 */
public class App
{
    public static void main( String[] args )
    {
        System.out.println( "Hello World!" );
    }
}
```

The simplest Maven archetype generates the simplest possible program: a program that prints "Hello World!" to standard output.

Building a Simple Project

Once you have created the project with the Maven Archetype plugin by following the directions from the previous section ("Creating a Simple Project") you will want to build and package the application. To do so, run *mvn install* from the directory that contains the *pom.xml*:

```
$ mvn install
[INFO] Scanning for projects...
[INFO] ------------------------------------------------------
[INFO] Building simple
[INFO]    task-segment: [install]
[INFO] ------------------------------------------------------
[INFO] [resources:resources]
[INFO] Using default encoding to copy filtered resources.
[INFO] [compiler:compile]
[INFO] Compiling 1 source file to /simple/target/classes
[INFO] [resources:testResources]
[INFO] Using default encoding to copy filtered resources.
[INFO] [compiler:testCompile]
[INFO] Compiling 1 source file to /simple/target/test-classes
[INFO] [surefire:test]
[INFO] Surefire report directory: /simple/target/surefire-reports


-------------------------------------------------------
 T E S T S
-------------------------------------------------------
Running org.sonatype.mavenbook.AppTest
Tests run: 1, Failures: 0, Errors: 0, Skipped: 0, Time elapsed: 0.105 sec

Results :

Tests run: 1, Failures: 0, Errors: 0, Skipped: 0

[INFO] [jar:jar]
[INFO] Building jar: /simple/target/simple-1.0-SNAPSHOT.jar
[INFO] [install:install]
[INFO] Installing /simple/target/simple-1.0-SNAPSHOT.jar to \
   ~/.m2/repository/org/sonatype/mavenbook/ch03/simple/1.0-SNAPSHOT/ \
   simple-1.0-SNAPSHOT.jar
```

You've just created, compiled, tested, packaged, and installed the simplest possible Maven project. To prove to yourself that this program works, run it from the command line:

```
$ java -cp target/simple-1.0-SNAPSHOT.jar org.sonatype.mavenbook.App
Hello World!
```

Simple Project Object Model

When Maven executes, it looks to the Project Object Model for information about the project. The POM answers such questions as: What type of project is this? What is the project's name? Are there any build customizations for this project? Example 3-1 shows the default *pom.xml* file created by the Maven Archetype plugin's create goal.

Example 3-1. Simple project's pom.xml file

```
<project xmlns="http://maven.apache.org/POM/4.0.0"
         xmlns:xsi="http://www.w3.org/2001/XMLSchema-instance"
         xsi:schemaLocation="http://maven.apache.org/POM/4.0.0
```

```
        http://maven.apache.org/maven-v4_0_0.xsd">
  <modelVersion>4.0.0</modelVersion>
  <groupId>org.sonatype.mavenbook.ch03</groupId>
  <artifactId>simple</artifactId>
  <packaging>jar</packaging>
  <version>1.0-SNAPSHOT</version>
  <name>simple</name>
  <url>http://maven.apache.org</url>
  <dependencies>
    <dependency>
      <groupId>junit</groupId>
      <artifactId>junit</artifactId>
      <version>3.8.1</version>
      <scope>test</scope>
    </dependency>
  </dependencies>
</project>
```

This *pom.xml* file is the most basic POM you will ever deal with for a Maven project. Usually a POM file is considerably more complex, defining multiple dependencies and customizing plugin behavior. The first few elements—groupId, artifactId, packaging, version—are known as the Maven coordinates, which uniquely identify a project. name and url are descriptive elements of the POM, providing a human-readable name and associating the project with a project web site. Lastly, the dependencies element defines a single, test-scoped dependency on a unit testing framework called JUnit. These topics will be further introduced in the next section, "Core Concepts," and in Chapter 9. All you need to know at this point is that the *pom.xml* is the file that makes Maven go.

Maven always executes against an effective POM, a combination of settings from this project's *pom.xml*, all parent POMs, a Super POM defined within Maven, user-defined settings, and active profiles. All projects ultimately extend the Super POM, which defines a set of sensible default configuration settings and which is fully explained in Chapter 9. Although your project might have a relatively minimal *pom.xml*, the contents of your project's POM are interpolated with the contents of all parent POMs, user settings, and any active profiles. To see this "effective" POM, run the following command in the simple project's base directory:

```
$ mvn help:effective-pom
```

When you run this, you should see a much larger POM that exposes the default settings of Maven. This goal can come in handy if you are trying to debug a build and want to see how all of the current project's ancestor POMs are contributing to the effective POM. For more information about the Maven Help plugin, see "Using the Maven Help Plugin" in Chapter 2.

Core Concepts

Now that we've just run Maven for the first time, this is a good point to introduce a few of the core concepts of Maven. In Example 3-1, you generated a project that consisted of a POM and some code assembled in the Maven Standard Directory Layout. You then executed Maven with a lifecycle phase as an argument that prompted Maven to execute a series of Maven plugin goals. Lastly, you installed a Maven artifact into your local repository. Wait—what is a "lifecycle"? What is a "local repository"? The following section defines some of Maven's central concepts.

Maven Plugins and Goals

In the previous section, we ran Maven with two different types of command-line arguments. The first command was a single plugin goal, the create goal of the Archetype plugin. The second execution of Maven was a lifecycle phase, install. To execute a single Maven plugin goal, we used the syntax *mvn archetype:create*, where arche type is the identifier of a plugin and create is the identifier of a goal. When Maven executes a plugin goal, it prints out the plugin identifier and goal identifier to standard output:

```
$ mvn archetype:create -DgroupId=org.sonatype.mavenbook.ch03 \
                        -DartifactId=simple \
                        -DpackageName=org.sonatype.mavenbook
...
[INFO] [archetype:create]
[INFO] artifact org.apache.maven.archetypes:maven-archetype-quickstart: \
        checking for updates from central
...
```

A Maven plugin is a collection of one or more goals (see Figure 3-1). Examples of Maven plugins can be simple core plugins such as the Jar plugin that contains goals for creating JAR files, the Compiler plugin that contains goals for compiling source code and unit tests, or the Surefire plugin that contains goals for executing unit tests and generating reports. Other, more specialized Maven plugins include the Hibernate3 plugin, for integration with the popular persistence library Hibernate, and the JRuby plugin, which allows you to execute Ruby as part of a Maven build or to write Maven plugins in Ruby. Maven also provides you with the ability to define custom plugins. A custom plugin can be written in any number of languages, including Java, Ant, Groovy, BeanShell, and, as previously mentioned, Ruby.

A goal is a specific task that may be executed as a standalone goal or along with other goals as part of a larger build. A goal is a "unit of work" in Maven. Examples of goals include the compile goal in the Compiler plugin, which compiles all of the source code for a project, or the test goal of the Surefire plugin, which can execute unit tests. Goals are configured via configuration properties that can be used to customize behavior. For example, the compile goal of the Compiler plugin defines a set of configuration parameters that allow you to specify the target JDK version or whether to use the

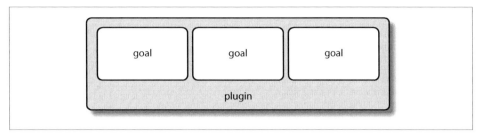

Figure 3-1. A plugin contains goals

compiler optimizations. In the previous example, we passed in the configuration parameters `groupId` and `artifactId` to the `create` goal of the Archetype plugin via the command-line parameters *-DgroupId=org.sonatype.mavenbook.ch03* and *-DartifactId=simple*. We also passed the `packageName` parameter to the `create` goal as `org.sonatype.mavenbook`. If we had omitted the `packageName` parameter, the package name would have defaulted to `org.sonatype.mavenbook.ch03`.

 When referring to a plugin goal, we frequently use the shorthand notation: *pluginId:goalId*. For example, when referring to the `create` goal in the Archetype plugin, we write `archetype:create`.

Goals define parameters that can define sensible default values. In the `archetype:create` example, we did not specify what kind of archetype the goal was to create on our command line; we simply passed in a `groupId` and an `artifactId`. This is our first brush with *convention over configuration*. The convention, or default, for the `create` goal is to create a simple project called Quickstart. The `create` goal defines a configuration property `archetypeArtifactId` that has a default value of `maven-archetype-quickstart`. The Quickstart archetype generates a minimal project shell that contains a POM and a single class. The Archetype plugin is far more powerful than this first example suggests, but it is a great way to get new projects started fast. Later in this book, we'll show you how the Archetype plugin can be used to generate more complex projects such as web applications, and how you can use the Archetype plugin to define your own set of projects.

The core of Maven has little to do with the specific tasks involved in your project's build. By itself, Maven doesn't know how to compile your code or even how to make a JAR file. It delegates all of this work to Maven plugins like the Compiler plugin and the Jar plugin, which are downloaded on an as-needed basis and periodically updated from the central Maven repository. When you download Maven, you are getting the core of Maven, which consists of a very basic shell that knows only how to parse the command line, manage a classpath, parse a POM file, and download Maven plugins as needed. By keeping the Compiler plugin separate from Maven's core and providing for an update mechanism, Maven makes it easier for users to have access to the latest options in the compiler. In this way, Maven plugins allow for universal reusability of common build logic. You are not defining the compile task in a build file; you are using a Compiler plugin that is shared by every user of Maven. If there is an improvement to the Compiler plugin, every project that uses Maven can immediately benefit from this change. (And, if you don't like the Compiler plugin, you can override it with your own implementation.)

Maven Lifecycle

The second command we ran in the previous section was *mvn install*. This command didn't specify a plugin goal; instead, it specified a Maven lifecycle phase. A phase is a step in what Maven calls the "build lifecycle." The build lifecycle is an ordered sequence of phases involved in building a project. Maven can support a number of different lifecycles, but the one that's most often used is the default Maven lifecycle, which begins with a phase to validate the basic integrity of the project and ends with a phase that involves deploying a project to production. Lifecycle phases are intentionally vague, defined solely as validation, testing, or deployment, and they may mean different things to different projects. For example, the package phase in a project that produces a JAR, means "package this project into a JAR"; in a project that produces a web application, the package phase may produce a WAR file. Figure 3-2 shows a simplified representation of the default Maven lifecycle.

Plugin goals can be attached to a lifecycle phase. As Maven moves through the phases in a lifecycle, it will execute the goals attached to each particular phase. Each phase may have zero or more goals bound to it. In the previous section, when you ran *mvn install*, you might have noticed that more than one goal was executed. Examine the output after running *mvn install* and take note of the various goals that are executed. When this simple example reached the package phase, it executed the jar goal in the Jar plugin. Since our simple Quickstart project has (by default) a jar packaging type, the jar:jar goal is bound to the package phase (see Figure 3-3).

We know that the package phase is going to create a JAR file for a project with jar packaging. But what of the goals preceding it, such as compiler:compile and surefire:test? These goals are executed as Maven steps through the phases preceding package in the Maven lifecycle; executing a phase will first execute all proceeding phases in order, ending with the phase specified on the command line. Each phase corresponds to zero or more goals, and since we haven't performed any plugin configuration or customization, this example binds a set of standard plugin goals to the default lifecycle. The following goals are executed in order when Maven walks through the default lifecycle ending with package:

resources:resources
> The resources goal of the Resources plugin is bound to the process-resources phase. This goal copies all of the resources from *src/main/resources* and any other configured resource directories to the output directory.

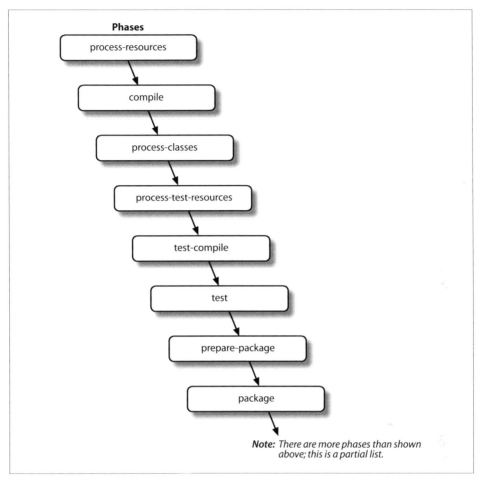

Figure 3-2. A lifecycle is a sequence of phases

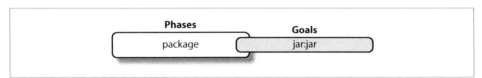

Figure 3-3. A goal binds to a phase

compiler:compile

> The compile goal of the Compiler plugin is bound to the compile phase. This goal compiles all of the source code from *src/main/java* or any other configured source directories to the output directory.

resources:testResources

> The testResources goal of the Resources plugin is bound to the process-test-resources phase. This goal copies all of the resources from *src/test/resources* and any other configured test resource directories to a test output directory.

compiler:testCompile

> The testCompile goal of the Compiler plugin is bound to the test-compile phase. This goal compiles test cases from *src/test/java* and any other configured test source directories to a test output directory.

surefire:test

> The test goal of the Surefire plugin is bound to the test phase. This goal executes all of the tests and creates output files that capture detailed results. By default, this goal will terminate a build if there is a test failure.

jar:jar

> The jar goal of the Jar plugin is bound to the package phase. This goal packages the output directory into a JAR file.

To summarize, when we run *mvn install*, Maven executes all phases up to install, and in the process of stepping through the lifecycle phases, it executes all goals bound to each phase (see Figure 3-4). Instead of executing a Maven lifecycle goal, you could achieve the same results by specifying a sequence of plugin goals as follows:

```
mvn resources:resources \
    compiler:compile \
    resources:testResources \
    compiler:testCompile \
    surefire:test \
    jar:jar
```

Executing the package phase is preferable to keeping track of all of the goals involved in a particular build. It also allows every project that uses Maven to adhere to a well-defined set of standards. The lifecycle is what allows a developer to jump from one Maven project to another without having to know very much about the details of each particular project's build. If you can build one Maven project, you can build them all.

Maven Coordinates

The Archetype plugin created a project with a file named *pom.xml*. This is the Project Object Model (POM), a declarative description of a project. When Maven executes a goal, each goal has access to the information defined in a project's POM. When the jar:jar goal needs to create a JAR file, it looks to the POM to find out what the JAR file's name is. When the compiler:compile task compiles Java source code into byte-code, it looks to the POM to see if there are any parameters for the compile goal. Goals execute in the context of a POM. Goals are actions we wish to take upon a project, and a project is defined by a POM. The POM names the project, provides a set of unique identifiers (coordinates) for a project, and defines the relationships between this project

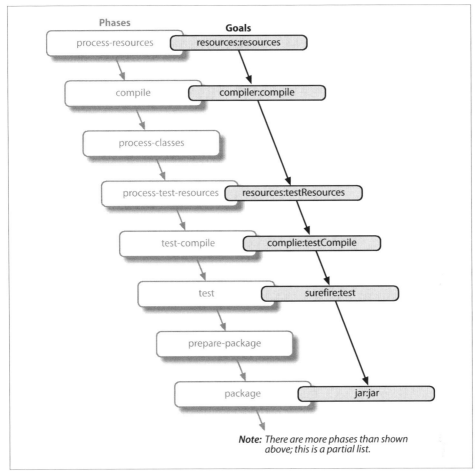

Phases

process-resources

compile

process-classes

process-test-resources

test-compile

test

prepare-package

package

Goals

resources:resources

compiler:compile

resources:testResources

complie:testCompile

surefire:test

jar:jar

Note: *There are more phases than shown above; this is a partial list.*

Figure 3-4. Bound goals are run when their phases execute

and others through dependencies, parents, and prerequisites. A POM can also customize plugin behavior and supply information about the community and developers involved in a project.

Maven coordinates define a set of identifiers that can be used to uniquely identify a project, a dependency, or a plugin in a Maven POM. Take a look at the POM shown in Figure 3-5.

We've highlighted the Maven coordinates for this project: `groupId`, `artifactId`, `version` and `packaging`. These combined identifiers make up a project's coordinates.[†] Just as in any other coordinate system, a Maven coordinate is an address for a specific

---

[†] There is a fifth, seldom-used coordinate named `classifier`, which we will introduce later in the book. You can feel free to ignore classifiers for now.

```
<project xmlns="http://maven.apache.org/POM/4.0.0"
  xmlns:xsi=http://www.w3.org/2001/XMLSchema-instance"
  xsi:schemaLocation="http://maven.apache.org/POM/4.0.0"
  http://maven.apache.org/maven-v4_0_0.xsd"
  <modelVersion>4.0.0</modelVersion>
  <groupId>mavenbook</groupId>
  <artifactId>my-app</artifactId>    coordinates
  <version>1.0-SNAPSHOT/<version>
  <name>Maven Quick Start Archetype</name>
  <url>http://maven.apache.org</url>
  <dependencies>
    <dependency>
      <groupId>junit</groupId>
      <artifactId>junit</artifactId>
      <version>3.8.1</version>
      <scope>test</scope>
    </dependency>
  </dependencies>
</project>
```

Figure 3-5. A Maven project's coordinates

point in "space": from general to specific. Maven pinpoints a project via its coordinates when one project relates to another, either as a dependency, a plugin, or a parent project reference. Maven coordinates are often written using a colon as a delimiter in the following format: `groupId:artifactId:packaging:version`. In the *pom.xml* file for our current project, its coordinate is represented as `mavenbook:my-app:jar:1.0-SNAPSHOT`. This notation also applies to project dependencies. Our project relies on JUnit version 3.8.1, and it contains a dependency on `junit:junit:jar:3.8.1`. Here is some more information about each part of the coordinate:

groupId

> The group, company, team, organization, project, or other group. The convention for group identifiers is that they begin with the reverse domain name of the organization that creates the project. Projects from Sonatype would have a `groupId` that begins with `com.sonatype`, and projects in the Apache Software Foundation would have a `groupId` that starts with `org.apache`.

artifactId

> A unique identifier under `groupId` that represents a single project.

version

> A specific release of a project. Projects that have been released have a fixed version identifier that refers to a specific version of the project. Projects undergoing active development can use a special identifier that marks a version as a `SNAPSHOT`.

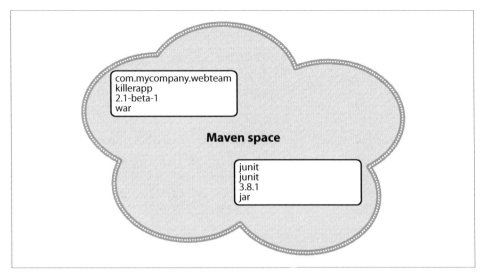

Figure 3-6. Maven space is a coordinate system of projects

The packaging format of a project is also an important component in the Maven co-ordinates, but it isn't a part of a project's unique identifiers. A project's *groupId:artifactId:version* make that project unique; you can't have a project with the same three `groupId`, `artifactId`, and `version` identifiers.

packaging
> The type of project, defaulting to `jar`, describing the packaged output produced by a project. A project with packaging `jar` produces a JAR archive; a project with packaging `war` produces a web application.

These four elements become the key to locating and using one particular project in the vast space of other "Mavenized" projects (see Figure 3-6). Maven repositories (public, private, and local) are organized according to these identifiers. When this project is installed into the local Maven repository, it immediately becomes locally available to any other project that wishes to use it. All you must do is add it as a dependency of another project using the unique Maven coordinates for a specific artifact.

Maven Repositories

When you run Maven for the first time, you will notice that Maven downloads a number of files from a remote Maven repository. If the simple project described in this chapter is the first time you run Maven, the first thing it will do is download the latest release of the Resources plugin when it triggers the `resources:resource` goal. In Maven, artifacts and plugins are retrieved from a remote repository when they are needed. One of the reasons the initial Maven download is so small (1.5 MiB) is that Maven doesn't ship with much in the way of plugins. Maven ships with the bare minimum and fetches from a remote repository when it needs to. Maven ships with a default remote repository location (*http://repo1.maven.org/maven2*), which it uses to download the core Maven plugins and dependencies.

Often you will be writing a project that depends on libraries that are neither free nor publicly distributed. In that case, you will either need to set up a custom repository inside your organization's network or download and install the dependencies manually. The default remote repositories can be replaced or augmented with references to custom Maven repositories maintained by your organization. Multiple products are available that allow organizations to manage and maintain mirrors of the public Maven repositories.

What makes a Maven repository? It's defined by structure. A repository is a collection of project artifacts stored in a structure and format that can be easily understood by Maven. Everything is stored in a directory structure that closely matches a project's coordinates. You can see this structure by opening up a web browser and going to the central Maven repository at *http://repo1.maven.org/maven2/*. You will notice that an artifact with the coordinates `org.apache.commons:commons-email:1.1` is available under the directory */org/apache/commons/commons-email/1.1/* in a file named *commons-email-1.1.jar*. The standard for a Maven repository is to store an artifact in a directory relative to the root of the repository:

```
/<groupId>/<artifactId>/<version>/<artifactId>-<version>.<packaging>
```

Maven downloads artifacts and plugins from a remote repository to your local machine and stores these artifacts in your local Maven repository. Once Maven has downloaded an artifact from the remote repository, it never needs to download that artifact again, as Maven will always look for the artifact in the local repository before looking elsewhere. On Windows XP, your local repository is likely in *C:\Documents and Settings\USERNAME\.m2\repository*, and on Windows Vista, your local repository is in *C:\Users\USERNAME\.m2\repository*. On Unix systems, your local Maven repository is available in *~/.m2/repository*. When you build a project such as the simple one you created in the previous section, the `install` phase executes a goal that installs your project's artifacts in your local Maven repository.

In your local repository, you should be able to see the artifact created by your simple project. If you run the *mvn install* command, Maven will install our project's artifact in your local repository. Try it:

```
$ mvn install
...
[INFO] [install:install]
[INFO] Installing .../simple-1.0-SNAPSHOT.jar to \
       ~/.m2/repository/org/sonatype/mavenbook/simple/1.0-SNAPSHOT/ \
       simple-1.0-SNAPSHOT.jar
...
```

As you can see from the output of this command, Maven installed our project's JAR file into our local repository. Maven uses the local repository to share dependencies across local projects. If you develop two projects—project-a and project-b—and project-b depends on the artifact produced by project-a, Maven will retrieve project-a's artifact from your local repository when it is building project-b. A Maven repository is both a local cache of artifacts downloaded from a remote repository and a mechanism for allowing your projects to depend on each other.

Maven's Dependency Management

In this chapter's simple example project, Maven resolved the coordinates of the JUnit dependency—junit:junit:3.8.1—to a path in a Maven repository: */junit/junit/3.8.1/ junit-3.8.1.jar*. The ability to locate an artifact in a repository based on Maven coordinates gives us the ability to define dependencies in a project's POM. If you examine the simple project's *pom.xml* file, you will see that there is a section that deals with dependencies, and that this section contains a single dependency—JUnit.

A more complex project would contain more than one dependency, or it might contain dependencies that depend on other artifacts. Support for transitive dependencies is one of Maven's most powerful features. Let's say your project depends on a library that, in turn, depends on 5 or 10 other libraries (Spring or Hibernate, for example). Instead of having to track down all of these dependencies and list them in your *pom.xml* explicitly, you can simply depend on the library you are interested in and Maven will add the dependencies of this library to your project's dependencies implicitly. Maven will also take care of working out conflicts between dependencies, and provides you with the ability to customize the default behavior and exclude certain transitive dependencies.

Let's take a look at a dependency that was downloaded to your local repository when you ran the previous example. Look in your local repository path under *~/.m2/reposi tory/junit/junit/3.8.1/*. If you have been following this chapter's examples, there will be a file named *junit-3.8.1.jar* and a *junit-3.8.1.pom* file, in addition to a few checksum files that Maven uses to verify the authenticity of a downloaded artifact. Note that Maven doesn't just download the JUnit JAR file, it also downloads a POM file for the JUnit dependency. The fact that Maven downloads POM files in addition to artifacts is central to Maven's support for transitive dependencies.

When you install your project's artifact in the local repository, you will also notice that Maven publishes a slightly modified version of the project's *pom.xml* file in the same directory as the JAR file. Storing a POM file in the repository gives other projects information about this project, most importantly what dependencies it has. If Project B depends on Project A, it also depends on Project A's dependencies. When Maven resolves a dependency artifact from a set of Maven coordinates, it also retrieves the POM and consults the dependencies POM to find any transitive dependences. These transitive dependencies are then added as dependencies of the current project.

A dependency in Maven isn't just a JAR file; it's a POM file that, in turn, may declare dependencies on other artifacts. These dependencies of dependencies are called transitive dependencies, and they are made possible by the fact that the Maven repository

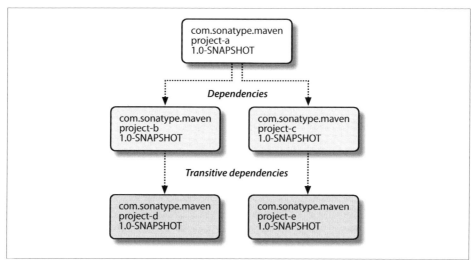

Figure 3-7. Maven resolves transitive dependencies

stores more than just bytecode; it stores metadata about artifacts. Figure 3-7 shows a possible scenario for transitive dependencies.

In this figure, project-a depends on project-b and project-c, project-b depends on project-d, and project-c depends on project-e. The full set of direct and transitive dependencies for project-a would be project-b, project-c, project-d, and project-e, but all project-a has to do is define a dependency on project-b and project-c. Transitive dependencies come in handy when your project relies on other projects with several small dependencies (such as Hibernate, Apache Struts, or the Spring Framework). Maven also provides you with the ability to exclude transitive dependencies from a project's classpath.

Maven also provides for different dependency scopes. The simple project's *pom.xml* contains a single dependency—junit:junit:jar:3.8.1—with a scope of test. When a dependency has a scope of test, it will not be available to the compile goal of the Compiler plugin. It will be added to the classpath for only the compiler:testCompile and surefire:test goals.

When you create a JAR for a project, dependencies are not bundled with the generated artifact; they are used only for compilation. When you use Maven to create a WAR or an EAR file, you can configure Maven to bundle dependencies with the generated artifact, and you can also configure it to exclude certain dependencies from the WAR file using the provided scope. The provided scope tells Maven that a dependency is needed for compilation, but should not be bundled with the output of a build. This scope comes in handy when you are developing a web application. You'll need to compile your code against the Servlet specification, but you don't want to include the Servlet API JAR in your web application's *WEB-INF/lib* directory.

Site Generation and Reporting

Another important feature of Maven is its ability to generate documentation and reports. In your simple project's directory, execute the following command:

```
$ mvn site
```

This will execute the `site` lifecycle phase. Unlike the default build lifecycle that manages generation of code, manipulation of resources, compilation, packaging, etc., this lifecycle is concerned solely with processing site content under the *src/site* directories and generating reports. After this command executes, you should see a project web site in the *target/site* directory. Load *target/site/index.html* and you should see a basic shell of a project site. This shell contains some reports under "Project Reports" in the lefthand navigation menu, and it also contains information about the project, the dependencies, and developers associated with it under "Project Information." The simple project's web site is mostly empty, since the POM contains very little information about itself beyond a coordinate, a name, a URL, and a single test dependency.

On this site, you'll notice that some default reports are available. A unit test report communicates the success and failure of all unit tests in the project. Another report generates Javadoc for the project's API. Maven provides a full range of configurable reports, such as the Clover report that examines unit test coverage, the JXR report that generates cross-referenced HTML source code listings useful for code reviews, the PMD report that analyzes source code for various coding problems, and the JDepend report that analyzes the dependencies between packages in a codebase. You can customize site reports by configuring which reports are included in a build via the *pom.xml* file.

Summary

In this chapter, we have created a simple project, packaged the project into a JAR file, installed that JAR into the Maven repository for use by other projects, and generated a site with documentation. We accomplished this without writing a single line of code or touching a single configuration file. We also took some time to develop definitions for some of the core concepts of Maven. In the next chapter, we'll start customizing and modifying our project *pom.xml* file to add dependencies and configure unit tests.

## CHAPTER 4

Customizing a Maven Project

Introduction

This chapter expands on the information introduced in Chapter 3. We're going to create a simple project generated with the Maven Archetype plugin, add some dependencies, add some source code, and customize the project to suit our needs. By the end of this chapter, you will know how to start using Maven to create real projects.

Downloading This Chapter's Example

We'll be developing a useful program that interacts with a Yahoo! Weather web service. Although you should be able to follow along with this chapter without the example source code, we recommend that you download a copy of the code to use as a reference. This chapter's example project may be downloaded with the book's example code at *http://www.sonatype.com/book/mvn-examples-1.0.zip* or *http://www.sonatype.com/book/mvn-examples-1.0.tar.gz*. Unzip this archive in any directory, and then go to the *ch04/* directory. There you will see a directory named *simple-weather/*, which contains the Maven project developed in this chapter. If you wish to follow along with the example code in a web browser, go to *http://www.sonatype.com/book/examples-1.0* and click on the *ch04/* directory.

Defining the Simple Weather Project

Before we start customizing this project, let's take a step back and talk about the simple weather project. What is it? It's a contrived example, created to demonstrate some of the features of Maven. It is an application that is representative of the kind you might need to build. The simple weather application is a basic command-line-driven application that takes a zip code and retrieves some data from the Yahoo! Weather RSS feed. It then parses the result and prints the result to standard output.

We chose this example for a number of reasons. First, it is straightforward. A user supplies input via the command line, the app takes that zip code, makes a request to

Yahoo! Weather, parses the result, and formats some simple data to the screen. This example is a simple main() function and some supporting classes; there is no enterprise framework to introduce and explain, just XML parsing and some logging statements. Second, it gives us a good excuse to introduce some interesting libraries such as Velocity, Dom4J, and Log4J. Although this book is focused on Maven, we won't shy away from an opportunity to introduce interesting utilities. Lastly, it is an example that can be introduced, developed, and deployed in a single chapter.

Yahoo! Weather RSS

Before you build this application, you should know something about the Yahoo! Weather RSS feed. To start with, the service is made available under the following terms:

> The feeds are provided free of charge for use by individuals and nonprofit organizations for personal, noncommercial uses. We ask that you provide attribution to Yahoo! Weather in connection with your use of the feeds.

In other words, if you are thinking of integrating these feeds into your commercial web site, think again—this feed is for personal, noncommercial use. The use we're encouraging in this chapter is personal educational use. For more information about these terms of service, see the Yahoo Weather! API documentation here: *http://developer .yahoo.com/weather/*.

Creating the Simple Weather Project

First, let's use the Maven Archetype plugin to create a basic skeleton for the simple weather project. Execute the following command to create a new project:

```
$ mvn archetype:create -DgroupId=org.sonatype.mavenbook.ch04 \
                                -DartifactId=simple-weather \
                                -DpackageName=org.sonatype.mavenbook \
                                -Dversion=1.0
[INFO] [archetype:create]
[INFO] artifact org.apache.maven.archetypes:maven-archetype-quickstart: \
      checking for updates from central
[INFO] ------------------------------------------------------------------------
[INFO] Using following parameters for creating Archetype: \
      maven-archetype-quickstart:RELEASE
[INFO] ------------------------------------------------------------------------
[INFO] Parameter: groupId, Value: org.sonatype.mavenbook.ch04
[INFO] Parameter: packageName, Value: org.sonatype.mavenbook
[INFO] Parameter: basedir, Value: ~/examples
[INFO] Parameter: package, Value: org.sonatype.mavenbook
[INFO] Parameter: version, Value: 1.0
[INFO] Parameter: artifactId, Value: simple-weather
[INFO] *** End of debug info from resources from generated POM ***
[INFO] Archetype created in dir: ~/examples/simple-weather
```

Once the Maven Archetype plugin creates the project, go into the *simple-weather* directory and take a look at the *pom.xml* file. You should see the XML document that's shown in Example 4-1.

Example 4-1. Initial POM for the simple-weather project

```
<project xmlns="http://maven.apache.org/POM/4.0.0"
         xmlns:xsi="http://www.w3.org/2001/XMLSchema-instance"
  xsi:schemaLocation="http://maven.apache.org/POM/4.0.0
                      http://maven.apache.org/maven-v4_0_0.xsd">
  <modelVersion>4.0.0</modelVersion>
  <groupId>org.sonatype.mavenbook.ch04</groupId>
  <artifactId>simple-weather</artifactId>
  <packaging>jar</packaging>
  <version>1.0</version>
  <name>simple-weather2</name>
  <url>http://maven.apache.org</url>
  <dependencies>
    <dependency>
      <groupId>junit</groupId>
      <artifactId>junit</artifactId>
      <version>3.8.1</version>
      <scope>test</scope>
    </dependency>
  </dependencies>
  <build>
    <plugins>
      <plugin>
        <artifactId>maven-compiler-plugin</artifactId>
        <configuration>
          <source>1.5</source>
          <target>1.5</target>
        </configuration>
      </plugin>
    </plugins>
  </build>
</project>
```

Notice that we passed in the `version` parameter to the `archetype:create` goal. This overrides the default value of `1.0-SNAPSHOT`. In this project, we're developing the `1.0` version of the `simple-weather` project, as you can see in the *pom.xml* `version` element.

Customize Project Information

Before we start writing code, let's customize the project information a bit. We want to add some information about the project's license, the organization, and a few of the developers associated with the project. This is all standard information you would expect to see in most projects. Example 4-2 shows the XML that supplies the organizational information, the licensing information, and the developer information.

Example 4-2. Adding organizational, legal, and developer information to the pom.xml

```
<project xmlns="http://maven.apache.org/POM/4.0.0"
         xmlns:xsi="http://www.w3.org/2001/XMLSchema-instance"
  xsi:schemaLocation="http://maven.apache.org/POM/4.0.0
                      http://maven.apache.org/maven-v4_0_0.xsd">
...

  <name>simple-weather</name>
  <url>http://www.sonatype.com</url>

  <licenses>
    <license>
      <name>Apache 2</name>
      <url>http://www.apache.org/licenses/LICENSE-2.0.txt</url>
      <distribution>repo</distribution>
      <comments>A business-friendly OSS license</comments>
    </license>
  </licenses>

  <organization>
    <name>Sonatype</name>
    <url>http://www.sonatype.com</url>
  </organization>

  <developers>
    <developer>
      <id>jason</id>
      <name>Jason Van Zyl</name>
      <email>jason@maven.org</email>
      <url>http://www.sonatype.com</url>
      <organization>Sonatype</organization>
      <organizationUrl>http://www.sonatype.com</organizationUrl>
      <roles>
        <role>developer</role>
      </roles>
      <timezone>-6</timezone>
    </developer>
  </developers>
...
</project>
```

The ellipses in this example are shorthand for an abbreviated listing. Whenever you see a *pom.xml* with "..." directly after the project element's start tag and directly before the end tag, it indicates that we are not showing the entire *pom.xml* file. In this case, the licenses, organization, and developers elements are all added before the dependencies element.

Add New Dependencies

The simple weather application will need to complete the following three tasks: retrieve XML data from Yahoo! Weather, parse the XML from Yahoo, and then print formatted output to standard output. To accomplish these tasks, we have to introduce some new dependencies to our project's *pom.xml*. To parse the XML response from Yahoo!, we'll use Dom4J and Jaxen; to format the output of this command-line program, we'll use Velocity; and we also need to add a dependency for Log4J, which we will be using for logging. After we add these dependencies, our `dependencies` element will look like Example 4-3.

Example 4-3. Adding Dom4J, Jaxen, Velocity, and Log4J as dependencies

```
<project>
  [...]
  <dependencies>
    <dependency>
      <groupId>log4j</groupId>
      <artifactId>log4j</artifactId>
      <version>1.2.14</version>
    </dependency>
    <dependency>
      <groupId>dom4j</groupId>
      <artifactId>dom4j</artifactId>
      <version>1.6.1</version>
    </dependency>
    <dependency>
      <groupId>jaxen</groupId>
      <artifactId>jaxen</artifactId>
      <version>1.1.1</version>
    </dependency>
    <dependency>
      <groupId>velocity</groupId>
      <artifactId>velocity</artifactId>
      <version>1.5</version>
    </dependency>
    <dependency>
      <groupId>junit</groupId>
      <artifactId>junit</artifactId>
      <version>3.8.1</version>
      <scope>test</scope>
    </dependency>
  </dependencies>
  [...]
</project>
```

As you can see, we've added four more dependency elements in addition to the existing element that was referencing the `test`-scoped dependency on JUnit. If you add these dependencies to the project's *pom.xml* file and then run *mvn install*, you will see Maven downloading all of these dependencies and other transitive dependencies to your local Maven repository.

How did we find these dependencies? Did we just "know" the appropriate `groupId` and `artifactId` values? Some of the dependencies are so common (such as Log4J) that you'll just remember what the `groupId` and `artifactId` are every time you need to use them. As for Velocity, Dom4J, and Jaxen, we located them using the very helpful web site *http://www.mvnrepository.com*. This site provides a search interface for the Maven repository that you can use to search for dependencies. To test this yourself, visit *http://www.mvnrepository.com* and search for some commonly used libraries such as Hibernate or the Spring Framework. When you search for an artifact on this site, it will show you an `artifactId` and all of the versions known to the central Maven repository. Clicking on the details for a specific version will load a page that contains the dependency element you'll need to copy and paste into your own project's *pom.xml*. If you need to find a dependency, you'll want to check out *http://www.mvnrepository.com*, because you'll often find that certain libraries have more than one `groupId`. With this tool, you can make sense of the Maven repository.

Simple Weather Source Code

The simple weather command-line application consists of the following five Java classes:

`org.sonatype.mavenbook.weather.Main`

> The `Main` class contains a static `main()` function, and is the entry point for this system.

`org.sonatype.mavenbook.weather.Weather`

> The `Weather` class is a straightforward Java bean that holds the location of our weather report and some key facts, such as the temperature and humidity.

`org.sonatype.mavenbook.weather.YahooRetriever`

> The `YahooRetriever` class connects to Yahoo! Weather and returns an `InputStream` of the data from the feed.

`org.sonatype.mavenbook.weather.YahooParser`

> The `YahooParser` class parses the XML from Yahoo! Weather, and returns a `Weather` object.

`org.sonatype.mavenbook.weather.WeatherFormatter`

> The `WeatherFormatter` class takes a `Weather` object, creates a `VelocityContext`, and evaluates a Velocity template.

Although we won't dwell on the code here, we will provide all the necessary code for you to get the example working. We assume that most readers have downloaded the examples that accompany this book, but we're also mindful of those who may wish to follow the example in this chapter step-by-step. The sections that follow list classes in the `simple-weather` project. Each of these classes should be placed in the same package: `org.sonatype.mavenbook.weather`.

Let's remove the `App` and the `AppTest` classes created by `archetype:create` and add our new package. In a Maven project, all of a project's source code is stored in *src/main/java*. From the base directory of the new project, execute the following commands:

```
$ cd src/test/java/org/sonatype/mavenbook
$ rm AppTest.java
```

```
$ cd ../../../../../..
$ cd src/main/java/org/sonatype/mavenbook
$ rm App.java
$ mkdir weather
$ cd weather
```

This creates a new package named `org.sonatype.mavenbook.weather`. Now we need to put some classes in this directory. Using your favorite text editor, create a new file named *Weather.java* with the contents shown in Example 4-4.

Example 4-4. simple-weather's Weather model object

```java
package org.sonatype.mavenbook.weather;

public class Weather {
  private String city;
  private String region;
  private String country;
  private String condition;
  private String temp;
  private String chill;
  private String humidity;

  public Weather() {}

  public String getCity() { return city; }
  public void setCity(String city) { this.city = city; }

  public String getRegion() { return region; }
  public void setRegion(String region) { this.region = region; }

  public String getCountry() { return country; }
  public void setCountry(String country) { this.country = country; }

  public String getCondition() { return condition; }
  public void setCondition(String condition) { this.condition = condition; }

  public String getTemp() { return temp; }
  public void setTemp(String temp) { this.temp = temp; }

  public String getChill() { return chill; }
  public void setChill(String chill) { this.chill = chill; }

  public String getHumidity() { return humidity; }
  public void setHumidity(String humidity) { this.humidity = humidity; }
}
```

The `Weather` class defines a simple bean that is used to hold the weather information parsed from the Yahoo! Weather feed. This feed provides a wealth of information, from the sunrise and sunset times to the speed and direction of the wind. To keep this example as simple as possible, the `Weather` model object keeps track of only the temperature, chill, humidity, and a textual description of current conditions.

Now, in the same directory, create a file named *Main.java*. This `Main` class will hold the static `main()` function—the entry point for this example. See Example 4-5.

Example 4-5. simple-weather's Main class

```
package org.sonatype.mavenbook.weather;

import java.io.InputStream;

import org.apache.log4j.PropertyConfigurator;


public class Main {

  public static void main(String[] args) throws Exception {
    // Configure Log4J
    PropertyConfigurator.configure(Main.class.getClassLoader()
                              .getResource("log4j.properties"));

    // Read the Zip Code from the Command-line (if none supplied, use 60202)
    String zipcode = "60202";
    try {
      zipcode = args[0]);
    } catch( Exception e ) {}

    // Start the program
    new Main(zipcode).start();
  }

  private String zip;

  public Main(String zip) {
    this.zip = zip;
  }

  public void start() throws Exception {
    // Retrieve Data
    InputStream dataIn = new YahooRetriever().retrieve( zip );

    // Parse Data
    Weather weather = new YahooParser().parse( dataIn );

    // Format (Print) Data
    System.out.print( new WeatherFormatter().format( weather ) );
  }
}
```

The `main()` function shown in this example configures Log4J by retrieving a resource from the classpath. It then tries to read a zip code from the command line. If an exception is thrown while it is trying to read the zip code, the program will default to a zip code of 60202. Once it has a zip code, it instantiates an instance of `Main` and calls the `start()` method on an instance of `Main`. The `start()` method calls out to the `YahooRetriever` to retrieve the weather XML. The `YahooRetriever` returns an

InputStream, which is then passed to the `YahooParser`. The `YahooParser` parses the Yahoo! Weather XML and returns a `Weather` object. Finally, the `WeatherFormatter` takes a `Weather` object and spits out a formatted `String`, which is printed to standard output.

Create a file named *YahooRetriever.java* in the same directory with the contents shown in Example 4-6.

Example 4-6. simple-weather's YahooRetriever class

```
package org.sonatype.mavenbook.weather;

import java.io.InputStream;
import java.net.URL;
import java.net.URLConnection;

import org.apache.log4j.Logger;

public class YahooRetriever {

  private static Logger log = Logger.getLogger(YahooRetriever.class);

  public InputStream retrieve(int zipcode) throws Exception {
    log.info( "Retrieving Weather Data" );
    String url = "http://weather.yahooapis.com/forecastrss?p=" + zipcode;
    URLConnection conn = new URL(url).openConnection();
    return conn.getInputStream();
  }
}
```

This simple class opens a `URLConnection` to the Yahoo! Weather API and returns an `InputStream`. To create something to parse this feed, we'll need to create the *YahooParser.java* file in the same directory. See Example 4-7.

Example 4-7. simple-weather's YahooParser class

```
package org.sonatype.mavenbook.weather;

import java.io.InputStream;
import java.util.HashMap;
import java.util.Map;

import org.apache.log4j.Logger;
import org.dom4j.Document;
import org.dom4j.DocumentFactory;
import org.dom4j.io.SAXReader;

public class YahooParser {

  private static Logger log = Logger.getLogger(YahooParser.class);

  public Weather parse(InputStream inputStream) throws Exception {
    Weather weather = new Weather();

    log.info( "Creating XML Reader" );
```

```
    SAXReader xmlReader = createXmlReader();
    Document doc = xmlReader.read( inputStream );

    log.info( "Parsing XML Response" );
    weather.setCity( doc.valueOf("/rss/channel/y:location/@city") );
    weather.setRegion( doc.valueOf("/rss/channel/y:location/@region") );
    weather.setCountry( doc.valueOf("/rss/channel/y:location/@country") );
    weather.setCondition( doc.valueOf("/rss/channel/item/y:condition/@text") );
    weather.setTemp( doc.valueOf("/rss/channel/item/y:condition/@temp") );
    weather.setChill( doc.valueOf("/rss/channel/y:wind/@chill") );
    weather.setHumidity( doc.valueOf("/rss/channel/y:atmosphere/@humidity") );

    return weather;
  }

  private SAXReader createXmlReader() {
    Map<String,String> uris = new HashMap<String,String>();
        uris.put( "y", "http://xml.weather.yahoo.com/ns/rss/1.0" );

    DocumentFactory factory = new DocumentFactory();
    factory.setXPathNamespaceURIs( uris );

    SAXReader xmlReader = new SAXReader();
    xmlReader.setDocumentFactory( factory );
    return xmlReader;
  }
}
```

The YahooParser is the most complex class in this example. We're not going to dive into the details of Dom4J or Jaxen here, but the class deserves some explanation. YahooParser's parse() method takes an InputStream and returns a Weather object. To do this, it needs to parse an XML document with Dom4J. Since we're interested in elements under the Yahoo! Weather XML namespace, we need to create a namespace-aware SAXReader in the createXmlReader() method. Once we create this reader and parse the document, we get an org.dom4j.Document object back. Instead of iterating through child elements, we simply address each piece of information we need using an XPath expression. Dom4J provides the XML parsing in this example, and Jaxen provides the XPath capabilities.

Once we've created a Weather object, we need to format our output for human consumption. Create a file named *WeatherFormatter.java* in the same directory as the other classes. See Example 4-8.

Example 4-8. simple-weather's WeatherFormatter class

```
package org.sonatype.mavenbook.weather;

import java.io.InputStreamReader;
import java.io.Reader;
import java.io.StringWriter;

import org.apache.log4j.Logger;
import org.apache.velocity.VelocityContext;
```

```
import org.apache.velocity.app.Velocity;

public class WeatherFormatter {

  private static Logger log = Logger.getLogger(WeatherFormatter.class);

  public String format( Weather weather ) throws Exception {
    log.info( "Formatting Weather Data" );
    Reader reader =
      new InputStreamReader( getClass().getClassLoader()
                                  .getResourceAsStream("output.vm"));
    VelocityContext context = new VelocityContext();
    context.put("weather", weather );
    StringWriter writer = new StringWriter();
    Velocity.evaluate(context, writer, "", reader);
    return writer.toString();
  }
}
```

The WeatherFormatter uses Velocity to render a template. The format() method takes a Weather bean and spits out a formatted String. The first thing the format() method does is load a Velocity template from the classpath named *output.vm*. We then create a VelocityContext, which is populated with a single Weather object named weather. A StringWriter is created to hold the results of the template merge. The template is then evaluated with a call to Velocity.evaluate(), and the results are returned as a String.

Before we can run this example, we'll need to add some resources to our classpath.

Add Resources

This project depends on two classpath resources: the Main class that configures Log4J with a classpath resource named *log4j.properties*, and the WeatherFormatter that references a Velocity template from the classpath named *output.vm*. Both of these resources need to be in the default package (or the root of the classpath).

To add these resources, we'll need to create a new directory from the base directory of the project: *src/main/resources*. Since this directory was not created by the archetype:create task, we need to create it by executing the following commands from the project's base directory:

```
$ cd src/main
$ mkdir resources
$ cd rcsources
```

Once the resources directory is created, we can add the two resources. First, add the *log4j.properties* file in the *resources* directory, as shown in Example 4-9.

Example 4-9. simple-weather's Log4J configuration file

```
# Set root category priority to INFO and its only appender to CONSOLE.
log4j.rootCategory=INFO, CONSOLE
```

```
# CONSOLE is set to be a ConsoleAppender using a PatternLayout.
log4j.appender.CONSOLE=org.apache.log4j.ConsoleAppender
log4j.appender.CONSOLE.Threshold=INFO
log4j.appender.CONSOLE.layout=org.apache.log4j.PatternLayout
log4j.appender.CONSOLE.layout.ConversionPattern=%-4r %-5p %c{1} %x - %m%n
```

This *log4j.properties* file simply configures Log4J to print all log messages to standard output using a `PatternLayout`. Lastly, we need to create the *output.vm*, which is the Velocity template used to render the output of this command-line program. Create *output.vm* in the *resources/* directory. See Example 4-10.

Example 4-10. simple-weather's output Velocity template

```
********************************
 Current Weather Conditions for:
  ${weather.city}, ${weather.region}, ${weather.country}

 Temperature: ${weather.temp}
   Condition: ${weather.condition}
    Humidity: ${weather.humidity}
  Wind Chill: ${weather.chill}
********************************
```

This template contains a number of references to a variable named `weather`, which is the `Weather` bean that was passed to the `WeatherFormatter`. The `${weather.temp}` syntax is shorthand for retrieving and displaying the value of the `temp` bean property. Now that we have all of our project's code in the right place, we can use Maven to run the example.

Running the Simple Weather Program

Using the Exec plugin from the Codehaus Mojo project (*http://mojo.codehaus.org*), we can execute this program. To execute the `Main` class, run the following command from the project's base directory:

```
$ mvn install
$ mvn exec:java -Dexec.mainClass=org.sonatype.mavenbook.weather.Main
...
[INFO] [exec:java]
0    INFO  YahooRetriever   - Retrieving Weather Data
134  INFO  YahooParser      - Creating XML Reader
333  INFO  YahooParser      - Parsing XML Response
420  INFO  WeatherFormatter - Formatting Weather Data
********************************
 Current Weather Conditions for:
  Evanston, IL, US

 Temperature: 45
   Condition: Cloudy
    Humidity: 76
  Wind Chill: 38
********************************

...
```

We didn't supply a command-line argument to the `Main` class, so we ended up with the default zip code, 60202. To supply a zip code, we would use the `-Dexec.args` argument and pass in a zip code:

```
$ mvn exec:java -Dexec.mainClass=org.sonatype.mavenbook.weather.Main \
    -Dexec.args="70112"
...
[INFO] [exec:java]
0    INFO YahooRetriever  - Retrieving Weather Data
134  INFO YahooParser    - Creating XML Reader
333  INFO YahooParser    - Parsing XML Response
420  INFO WeatherFormatter  - Formatting Weather Data
********************************
 Current Weather Conditions for:
 New Orleans, LA, US

 Temperature: 82
   Condition: Fair
    Humidity: 71
 Wind Chill: 82
********************************
[INFO] Finished at: Sun Aug 31 09:33:34 CDT 2008
...
```

As you can see, we've successfully executed the simple weather command-line tool, retrieved some data from Yahoo! Weather, parsed the result, and formatted the resulting data with Velocity. We achieved all of this without doing much more than writing our project's source code and adding some minimal configuration to the *pom.xml*. Notice that no "build process" was involved. We didn't need to define how or where the Java compiler compiles our source to bytecode, and we didn't need to instruct the build system how to locate the bytecode when we executed the example application. All we needed to do to include a few dependencies was locate the appropriate Maven coordinates.

The Maven Exec Plugin

The Exec plugin allows you to execute Java classes and other scripts. It is not a core Maven plugin, but it is available from the Mojo (*http://mojo.codehaus.org*) project hosted by Codehaus. For a full description of the Exec plugin, run:

```
$ mvn help:describe -Dplugin=exec -Dfull
```

This will list all of the goals that are available in the Maven Exec plugin. The Help plugin will also list all of the valid parameters for the Exec plugin. If you would like to customize the behavior of the Exec plugin to pass in command-line arguments, you should use the documentation provided by `help:describe` as a guide. Although the Exec plugin is useful, you shouldn't rely on it as a way to execute your application outside of running tests during development. For a more robust solution, use the Maven Assembly plugin that is demonstrated in the section "Building a Packaged Command-Line Application," later in this chapter.

Exploring Your Project Dependencies

The Exec plugin makes it possible for us to run the simplest weather program without having to load the appropriate dependencies into the classpath. In any other build system, we would have to copy all of the program dependencies into some sort of *lib/* directory containing a collection of JAR files. Then, we would have to write a simple script that includes our program's bytecode and all of our dependencies in a classpath. Only then could we run *java org.sonatype.mavenbook.weather.Main*. The Exec plugin leverages the fact that Maven already knows how to create and manage your classpath and dependencies.

This is convenient, but it's also nice to know exactly what is being included in your project's classpath. Although the project depends on a few libraries such as Dom4J, Log4J, Jaxen, and Velocity, it also relies on a few transitive dependencies. If you need to find out what is on the classpath, you can use the Maven Dependency plugin to print out a list of resolved dependencies. To print out this list for the simple weather project, execute the dependency:resolve goal:

```
$ mvn dependency:resolve
...
[INFO] [dependency:resolve]
[INFO]
[INFO] The following files have been resolved:
[INFO]    com.ibm.icu:icu4j:jar:2.6.1 (scope = compile)
[INFO]    commons-collections:commons-collections:jar:3.1 (scope = compile)
[INFO]    commons-lang:commons-lang:jar:2.1 (scope = compile)
[INFO]    dom4j:dom4j:jar:1.6.1 (scope = compile)
[INFO]    jaxen:jaxen:jar:1.1.1 (scope = compile)
[INFO]    jdom:jdom:jar:1.0 (scope = compile)
[INFO]    junit:junit:jar:3.8.1 (scope = test)
[INFO]    log4j:log4j:jar:1.2.14 (scope = compile)
[INFO]    oro:oro:jar:2.0.8 (scope = compile)
[INFO]    velocity:velocity:jar:1.5 (scope = compile)
[INFO]    xalan:xalan:jar:2.6.0 (scope = compile)
[INFO]    xerces:xercesImpl:jar:2.6.2 (scope = compile)
[INFO]    xerces:xmlParserAPIs:jar:2.6.2 (scope = compile)
[INFO]    xml-apis:xml-apis:jar:1.0.b2 (scope = compile)
[INFO]    xom:xom:jar:1.0 (scope = compile)
```

As you can see, our project has a very large set of dependencies. Although we included direct dependencies on only 4 libraries, we appear to be depending on 15 dependencies in total. Dom4J depends on Xerces and the XML Parser APIs, whereas Jaxen depends on Xalan being available in the classpath. The Dependency plugin will print out the final combination of dependencies under which your project is being compiled. If you would like to know about the entire dependency tree of your project, you can run the dependency:tree goal.

```
$ mvn dependency:tree
...
[INFO] [dependency:tree]
[INFO] org.sonatype.mavenbook.ch04:simple-weather:jar:1.0
```

```
[INFO] +- log4j:log4j:jar:1.2.14:compile
[INFO] +- dom4j:dom4j:jar:1.6.1:compile
[INFO] |  \- xml-apis:xml-apis:jar:1.0.b2:compile
[INFO] +- jaxen:jaxen:jar:1.1.1:compile
[INFO] |  +- jdom:jdom:jar:1.0:compile
[INFO] |  +- xerces:xercesImpl:jar:2.6.2:compile
[INFO] |  \- xom:xom:jar:1.0:compile
[INFO] |     +- xerces:xmlParserAPIs:jar:2.6.2:compile
[INFO] |     +- xalan:xalan:jar:2.6.0:compile
[INFO] |     \- com.ibm.icu:icu4j:jar:2.6.1:compile
[INFO] +- velocity:velocity:jar:1.5:compile
[INFO] |  +- commons-collections:commons-collections:jar:3.1:compile
[INFO] |  +- commons-lang:commons-lang:jar:2.1:compile
[INFO] |  \- oro:oro:jar:2.0.8:compile
[INFO] +- org.apache.commons:commons-io:jar:1.3.2:test
[INFO] \- junit:junit:jar:3.8.1:test
...
```

If you're truly adventurous or want to see the full dependency trail, including artifacts that were rejected due to conflicts and other reasons, run Maven with the debug flag:

```
$ mvn install -X
...
[DEBUG] org.sonatype.mavenbook.ch04:simple-weather:jar:1.0 (selected for null)
[DEBUG]    log4j:log4j:jar:1.2.14:compile (selected for compile)
[DEBUG]    dom4j:dom4j:jar:1.6.1:compile (selected for compile)
[DEBUG]      xml-apis:xml-apis:jar:1.0.b2:compile (selected for compile)
[DEBUG]    jaxen:jaxen:jar:1.1.1:compile (selected for compile)
[DEBUG]      jaxen:jaxen:jar:1.1-beta-6:compile (removed - causes a cycle
   in the graph)
[DEBUG]      jaxen:jaxen:jar:1.0-FCS:compile (removed - causes a cycle in
   the graph)
[DEBUG]      jdom:jdom:jar:1.0:compile (selected for compile)
[DEBUG]      xml-apis:xml-apis:jar:1.3.02:compile (removed - nearer found:
   1.0.b2)
[DEBUG]      xerces:xercesImpl:jar:2.6.2:compile (selected for compile)
[DEBUG]      xom:xom:jar:1.0:compile (selected for compile)
[DEBUG]        xerces:xmlParserAPIs:jar:2.6.2:compile (selected for compile)
[DEBUG]        xalan:xalan:jar:2.6.0:compile (selected for compile)
[DEBUG]        xml-apis:xml-apis:1.0.b2.
[DEBUG]        com.ibm.icu:icu4j:jar:2.6.1:compile (selected for compile)
[DEBUG]    velocity:velocity:jar:1.5:compile (selected for compile)
[DEBUG]      commons-collections:commons-collections:jar:3.1:compile
   (selected for compile)
[DEBUG]      commons-lang:commons-lang:jar:2.1:compile (selected for compile)
[DEBUG]      oro:oro:jar:2.0.8:compile (selected for compile)
[DEBUG]    junit:junit:jar:3.8.1:test (selected for test)
...
```

In the debug output, we see some of the guts of the dependency management system at work. What you see here is the tree of dependencies for this project. Maven is printing out the full Maven coordinates for all of your project's dependencies and the dependencies of your dependencies (and the dependencies of your dependencies' dependencies). You can see that simple-weather depends on jaxen, which depends on xom, which in turn depends on `icu4j`. You can also see that Maven is creating a graph of dependencies, eliminating duplicates, and resolving any conflicts between different versions. If you are having problems with dependencies, it is often helpful to dig a little deeper than the list generated by `dependency:resolve`. Turning on the debug output allows you to see Maven's dependency mechanism at work.

Writing Unit Tests

Maven has built-in support for unit tests, and testing is a part of the default Maven lifecycle. Let's add some unit tests to our simple weather project. First, let's create the `org.sonatype.mavenbook.weather` package under *src/test/java*:

```
$ cd src/test/java
$ cd org/sonatype/mavenbook
$ mkdir weather
$ cd weather
```

At this point, we will create two unit tests. The first will test the `YahooParser`, and the second will test the `WeatherFormatter`. In the `weather` package, create a file named *YahooParserTest.java* with the contents shown in Example 4-11.

Example 4-11. simple-weather's YahooParserTest unit test

```
package org.sonatype.mavenbook.weather.yahoo;

import java.io.InputStream;

import junit.framework.TestCase;

import org.sonatype.mavenbook.weather.Weather;
import org.sonatype.mavenbook.weather.YahooParser;

public class YahooParserTest extends TestCase {

  public YahooParserTest(String name) {
    super(name);
  }

  public void testParser() throws Exception {
    InputStream nyData =
      getClass().getClassLoader().getResourceAsStream("ny-weather.xml");
    Weather weather = new YahooParser().parse( nyData );
    assertEquals( "New York", weather.getCity() );
    assertEquals( "NY", weather.getRegion() );
    assertEquals( "US", weather.getCountry() );
    assertEquals( "39", weather.getTemp() );
    assertEquals( "Fair", weather.getCondition() );
    assertEquals( "39", weather.getChill() );
    assertEquals( "67", weather.getHumidity() );
  }
}
```

This YahooParserTest extends the TestCase class defined by JUnit. It follows the usual pattern for a JUnit test: a constructor that takes a single String argument that calls the constructor of the superclass, and a series of public methods that begin with "test" that are invoked as unit tests. We define a single test method, testParser, which tests the YahooParser by parsing an XML document with known values. The test XML document is named *ny-weather.xml* and is loaded from the classpath. We'll add test resources in "Adding Unit Test Resources." In our Maven project's directory layout, the *ny-weather.xml* file is found in the directory that contains test resources—*${basedir}/src/test/resources* under *org/sonatype/mavenbook/weather/yahoo/ny-weather.xml*. The file is read as an InputStream and passed to the parse() method on YahooParser. The parse() method returns a Weather object, which is then tested with a series of calls to assetEquals(), a method defined by TestCase.

In the same directory, create a file named *WeatherFormatterTest.java*. See Example 4-12.

Example 4-12. simple-weather's WeatherFormatterTest unit test

```
package org.sonatype.mavenbook.weather.yahoo;

import java.io.InputStream;

import org.apache.commons.io.IOUtils;

import org.sonatype.mavenbook.weather.Weather;
import org.sonatype.mavenbook.weather.WeatherFormatter;
import org.sonatype.mavenbook.weather.YahooParser;

import junit.framework.TestCase;

public class WeatherFormatterTest extends TestCase {

  public WeatherFormatterTest(String name) {
    super(name);
  }

  public void testFormat() throws Exception {
    InputStream nyData =
      getClass().getClassLoader().getResourceAsStream("ny-weather.xml");
    Weather weather = new YahooParser().parse( nyData );
    String formattedResult = new WeatherFormatter().format( weather );
    InputStream expected =
      getClass().getClassLoader().getResourceAsStream("format-expected.dat");
    assertEquals( IOUtils.toString( expected ).trim(),
                  formattedResult.trim() );
  }
}
```

The second unit test in this simple project tests the WeatherFormatter. Like the YahooParserTest, the WeatherFormatterTest also extends JUnit's TestCase class. The single test function reads the same test resource from *${basedir}/src/test/resources* under the *org/sonatype/mavenbook/weather/yahoo* directory via this unit test's classpath. We'll add test resources in the section "Adding Unit Test Resources," later in this chapter. WeatherFormatterTest runs this sample input file through the YahooParser, which spits out a Weather object, and this object is then formatted with the WeatherFor matter. Since the WeatherFormatter prints out a String, we need to test it against some expected input. Our expected input has been captured in a text file named *format-expected.dat*, which is in the same directory as *ny-weather.xml*. To compare the test's output to the expected output, we read this expected output in as an InputStream and use Apache Commons IO's IOUtils class to convert this file to a String. This String is then compared to the test output using assertEquals().

Adding Test-Scoped Dependencies

In WeatherFormatterTest, we used a utility from Apache Commons IO—the IOUtils class. IOUtils provides a number of helpful static functions that take most of the work out of input/output operations. In this particular unit test, we used IOUtils.toString() to copy the *format-expected.dat* classpath resource to a String. We could have done this without using Commons IO, but it would have required an extra six or seven lines of code to deal with the various InputStreamReader and StringWriter objects. The main reason we used Commons IO was to give us an excuse to add a test-scoped dependency on Commons IO.

A test-scoped dependency is a dependency that is available on the classpath only during test compilation and test execution. If your project has war or ear packaging, a test-scoped dependency would not be included in the project's output archive. To add a test-scoped dependency, add the dependency element to your project's dependencies section, as shown in Example 4-13.

Example 4-13. Adding a test-scoped dependency

```
<project>
  ...
  <dependencies>
    ...
    <dependency>
      <groupId>org.apache.commons</groupId>
      <artifactId>commons-io</artifactId>
      <version>1.3.2</version>
      <scope>test</scope>
    </dependency>
    ...
  </dependencies>
</project>
```

After you add this dependency to the *pom.xml*, run *mvn dependency:resolve* and you should see that commons-io is now listed as a dependency with scope test. We need to do one more thing before we are ready to run this project's unit tests: create the classpath resources these unit tests depend on. Dependency scopes are explained in detail in "Dependency Scope" in Chapter 8.

Adding Unit Test Resources

A unit test has access to a set of resources that are specific to tests. Often, you'll store files containing expected results and files containing dummy input in the test classpath. In this project, we're storing a test XML document for YahooParserTest named *ny-weather.xml* and a file containing expected output from the WeatherFormatter in *format-expected.dat*.

To add test resources, you'll need to create the *src/test/resources* directory. This is the default directory in which Maven looks for unit test resources. To create this directory, execute the following commands from your project's base directory:

```
$ cd src/test
$ mkdir resources
$ cd resources
```

Once you've created the *resources/* directory, create a file named *format-expected.dat* there. See Example 4-14.

Example 4-14. simple-weather's WeatherFormatterTest expected output

```
********************************
Current Weather Conditions for:
  New York, NY, US

Temperature: 39
  Condition: Fair
   Humidity: 67
 Wind Chill: 39
********************************
```

This file should look familiar. It is the same output that was generated previously when you ran the simple weather project with the Maven Exec plugin. The second file you'll need to add to the resources directory is *ny-weather.xml*. See Example 4-15.

Example 4-15. simple-weather's YahooParserTest XML input

```
<?xml version="1.0" encoding="UTF-8" standalone="yes" ?>
<rss version="2.0" xmlns:yweather="http://xml.weather.yahoo.com/ns/rss/1.0"
     xmlns:geo="http://www.w3.org/2003/01/geo/wgs84_pos#">
 <channel>
 <title>Yahoo! Weather - New York, NY</title>
 <link>http://us.rd.yahoo.com/dailynews/rss/weather/New_York__NY/</link>
 <description>Yahoo! Weather for New York, NY</description>
 <language>en-us</language>
 <lastBuildDate>Sat, 10 Nov 2007 8:51 pm EDT</lastBuildDate>

 <ttl>60</ttl>
 <yweather:location city="New York" region="NY" country="US" />
```

```
<yweather:units temperature="F" distance="mi" pressure="in" speed="mph" />
<yweather:wind chill="39" direction="0" speed="0" />
<yweather:atmosphere humidity="67" visibility="1609" pressure="30.18"
                rising="1" />
 <yweather:astronomy sunrise="6:36 am" sunset="4:43 pm" />
 <image>
<title>Yahoo! Weather</title>

<width>142</width>
<height>18</height>
<link>http://weather.yahoo.com/</link>
<url>http://l.yimg.com/us.yimg.com/i/us/nws/th/main_142b.gif</url>
</image>
<item>
<title>Conditions for New York, NY at 8:51 pm EDT</title>

 <geo:lat>40.67</geo:lat>
<geo:long>-73.94</geo:long>
 <link>http://us.rd.yahoo.com/dailynews/rss/weather/New_York__NY/\</link>
<pubDate>Sat, 10 Nov 2007 8:51 pm EDT</pubDate>
<yweather:condition text="Fair" code="33" temp="39"
                date="Sat, 10 Nov 2007 8:51 pm EDT" />
<description><![CDATA[
<img src="http://l.yimg.com/us.yimg.com/i/us/we/52/33.gif" /><br />
<b>Current Conditions:</b><br />
Fair, 39 F<BR /><BR />
<b>Forecast:</b><BR />
 Sat - Partly Cloudy. High: 45 Low: 32<br />
 Sun - Sunny. High: 50 Low: 38<br />
<br />
]]></description>
<yweather:forecast day="Sat" date="10 Nov 2007" low="32" high="45"
                text="Partly Cloudy" code="29" />

<yweather:forecast day="Sun" date="11 Nov 2007" low="38" high="50"
                text="Sunny" code="32" />
 <guid isPermaLink="false">10002_2007_11_10_20_51_EDT</guid>
</item>
</channel>
</rss>
```

This file contains a test XML document for the `YahooParserTest`. We store this file so that we can test the `YahooParser` without having to retrieve an XML response from Yahoo! Weather.

Executing Unit Tests

Now that your project has unit tests, let's run them. You don't have to do anything special to run a unit test; the `test` phase is a normal part of the Maven lifecycle. You run Maven tests whenever you run *mvn package* or *mvn install*. If you would like to run all the lifecycle phases up to and including the `test` phase, run *mvn test*:

```
$ mvn test
...
[INFO] [surefire:test]
[INFO] Surefire report directory: ~/examples/simple-weather/target/\
                                   surefire-reports


-------------------------------------------------------
 T E S T S
-------------------------------------------------------
Running org.sonatype.mavenbook.weather.yahoo.WeatherFormatterTest
0    INFO  YahooParser     - Creating XML Reader
177  INFO  YahooParser     - Parsing XML Response
239  INFO  WeatherFormatter  - Formatting Weather Data
Tests run: 1, Failures: 0, Errors: 0, Skipped: 0, Time elapsed: 0.547 sec
Running org.sonatype.mavenbook.weather.yahoo.YahooParserTest
475  INFO  YahooParser     - Creating XML Reader
483  INFO  YahooParser     - Parsing XML Response
Tests run: 1, Failures: 0, Errors: 0, Skipped: 0, Time elapsed: 0.018 sec

Results :

Tests run: 2, Failures: 0, Errors: 0, Skipped: 0
```

Executing *mvn test* from the command line causes Maven to execute all lifecycle phases up to the test phase. The Maven Surefire plugin has a `test` goal that is bound to the test phase. This `test` goal executes all of the unit tests that this project can find under *src/test/java*. In the case of this project, you can see that the Surefire plugin's `test` goal executes `WeatherFormatterTest` and `YahooParserTest`. When the Surefire plugin runs the JUnit tests, it also generates XML and text reports in the *${basedir}/target/surefire-reports* directory. If your tests are failing, you should look in this directory for details such as stack traces and error messages generated by your unit tests.

Ignoring Test Failures

You will often find yourself developing on a system that has failing unit tests. If you are practicing Test-Driven Development (TDD), you might use test failure as a measure of how close your project is to completeness. If you have failing unit tests, and you would still like to produce build output, you are going to have to tell Maven to ignore build failures. When Maven encounters a build failure, its default behavior is to stop the current build. To continue building a project even when the Surefire plugin encounters failed test cases, you'll need to set the `testFailureIgnore` configuration property of the Surefire plugin to `true`. See Example 4-16.

Example 4-16. Ignoring unit test failures

```
<project>
  [...]
  <build>
    <plugins>
      <plugin>
        <groupId>org.apache.maven.plugins</groupId>
```

```
      <artifactId>maven-surefire-plugin</artifactId>
      <configuration>
        <testFailureIgnore>true</testFailureIgnore>
      </configuration>
    </plugin>
  </plugins>
  </build>
  [...]
</project>
```

The plugin documents (*http://maven.apache.org/plugins/maven-surefire-plugin/test
-mojo.html*) show that this parameter declares an expression, as shown in Example 4-17.

Example 4-17. Plugin parameter expressions

```
testFailureIgnore  Set this to true to ignore a failure during \
                   testing. Its use is NOT RECOMMENDED, but quite \
                   convenient on occasion.

* Type: boolean
* Required: No
* Expression: ${maven.test.failure.ignore}
```

This expression can be set from the command line using the -D parameter:

```
$ mvn test -Dmaven.test.failure.ignore=true
```

Skipping Unit Tests

You may want to configure Maven to skip unit tests altogether. Maybe you have a very
large system where the unit tests take minutes to complete and you don't want to wait
for them before producing output. Or maybe you are working with a legacy system that
has a series of failing unit tests, and instead of fixing them, you just want to produce a
JAR. Maven allows you to skip unit tests using the skip parameter of the Surefire plugin.
To skip tests from the command line, simply add the maven.test.skip property to any
goal:

```
$ mvn install -Dmaven.test.skip=true
...
[INFO] [compiler:testCompile]
[INFO] Not compiling test sources
[INFO] [surefire:test]
[INFO] Tests are skipped.
...
```

When the Surefire plugin reaches the test goal, it will skip the unit tests if the
maven.test.skip properties is set to true. Another way to configure Maven to skip unit
tests is to add the configuration shown in Example 4-18 to your project's *pom.xml*. To
do this, you would add a plugin element to your build configuration.

Example 4-18. Skipping unit tests

```
<project>
  [...]
  <build>
    <plugins>
      <plugin>
        <groupId>org.apache.maven.plugins</groupId>
        <artifactId>maven-surefire-plugin</artifactId>
        <configuration>
          <skip>true</skip>
        </configuration>
      </plugin>
    </plugins>
  </build>
  [...]
</project>
```

Building a Packaged Command-Line Application

In the "Running the Simple Weather Program" section, earlier in this chapter, we executed our application using the Maven Exec plugin. Although that plugin executed the program and produced some output, you shouldn't look to Maven as an execution container for your applications. If you are distributing this command-line application to others, you will probably want to distribute a JAR or an archive as a ZIP or TAR'd GZIP file. This section outlines a process for using a predefined assembly descriptor in the Maven Assembly plugin to produce a distributable JAR file, which contains the project's bytecode and all of the dependencies.

You can use the Maven Assembly plugin to create arbitrary distributions for your applications. Use it to assemble the output of your project in any format you desire by defining a custom assembly descriptor. In a later chapter, we will show you how to create a custom assembly descriptor that produces a more complex archive for the simple weather application. In this chapter, we're going to use the predefined `jar-with-dependencies` format. To configure the Assembly Plugin, we need to add the `plugin` configuration shown in Example 4-19 to our existing build configuration in the *pom.xml*.

Example 4-19. Configuring the Maven Assembly descriptor

```
<project>
  [...]
  <build>
    <plugins>
      <plugin>
        <artifactId>maven-assembly-plugin</artifactId>
        <configuration>
          <descriptorRefs>
            <descriptorRef>jar-with-dependencies</descriptorRef>
          </descriptorRefs>
        </configuration>
```

```
          </plugin>
        </plugins>
      </build>
      [...]
    </project>
```

Once you've added this configuration, you can build the assembly by running *mvn assembly:assembly*, like so:

```
$ mvn install assembly:assembly
...
[INFO] [jar:jar]
[INFO] Building jar: ~/examples/simple-weather/target/simple-weather-1.0.jar
[INFO] [assembly:assembly]
[INFO] Processing DependencySet (output=)
[INFO] Expanding: \
        .m2/repository/dom4j/dom4j/1.6.1/dom4j-1.6.1.jar into \
        /tmp/archived-file-set.1437961776.tmp
[INFO] Expanding: .m2/repository/commons-lang/commons-lang/2.1/\
                     commons-lang-2.1.jar
        into /tmp/archived-file-set.305257225.tmp
... (Maven Expands all dependencies into a temporary directory) ...
[INFO] Building jar: \
        ~/examples/simple-weather/target/\
          simple-weather-1.0-jar-with-dependencies.jar
```

Once the assembly is assembled in *target/simple-weather-1.0-jar-with-dependen cies.jar*, you can run the Main class again from the command line. To run the simple weather app's Main class, execute the following from your project's base directory:

```
$ cd target
$ java -cp simple-weather-1.0-jar-with-dependencies.jar \
                  org.sonatype.mavenbook.weather.Main 10002
  0   INFO  YahooRetriever  - Retrieving Weather Data
221   INFO  YahooParser     - Creating XML Reader
399   INFO  YahooParser     - Parsing XML Response
474   INFO  WeatherFormatter - Formatting Weather Data
********************************
  Current Weather Conditions for:
  New York, NY, US

  Temperature: 44
    Condition: Fair
     Humidity: 40
   Wind Chill: 40
********************************
```

The jar-with-dependencies format creates a single JAR file that includes all of the bytecode from the simple-weather project as well as the unpacked bytecode from all of the dependencies. This somewhat unconventional format produces a 9 MiB JAR file containing approximately 5,290 classes, but it does provide for an easy distribution format for applications you've developed with Maven. Later in this book, we'll show you how to create a custom assembly descriptor to produce a more standard distribution.

## CHAPTER 5

A Simple Web Application

Introduction

In this chapter, we create a simple web application with the Maven Archetype plugin. We'll run this web application in a Servlet container named Jetty, add some dependencies, write a simple Servlet, and generate a WAR file. At the end of this chapter, you will be able to start using Maven to accelerate the development of web applications.

Downloading This Chapter's Example

The example in this chapter is generated with the Maven Archetype plugin. While you should be able to follow the development of this chapter without the example source code, we recommend downloading a copy of the example code to use as a reference. This chapter's example project may be downloaded with the book's example code at *http://www.sonatype.com/book/mvn-examples-1.0.zip* or *http://www.sonatype.com/book/mvn-examples-1.0.tar.gz*. Unzip this archive in any directory, and then go to the *ch05/* directory. In the *ch05/* directory you will see a directory named *simple-webapp/* that contains the Maven project developed in this chapter. If you wish to follow along with the example code in a web browser, go to *http://www.sonatype.com/book/examples -1.0* and click on the *ch05/* directory.

Defining the Simple Web Application

We've purposefully kept this chapter focused on Plain-Old Web Applications (POWA)—a servlet and a JavaServer Pages (JSP) page. We're not going to tell you how to develop your Struts 2, Tapestry, Wicket, Java Server Faces (JSF), or Waffle application in the next 20-odd pages, and we're not going to get into integrating an Inversion of Control (IoC) container such as Plexus, Guice, or the Spring Framework. The goal of this chapter is to show you the basic facilities that Maven provides for developing web applications—no more, no less. Later in this book, we're going to take a look at developing two web applications: one that uses Hibernate, Velocity, and the Spring Framework; and the other that uses Plexus.

Creating the Simple Web Project

To create your web application project, run *mvn archetype:create* with an artifactId and a groupId. Specify the archetypeArtifactId as maven-archetype-webapp. Running this will create the appropriate directory structure and Maven POM:

```
~/examples$ mvn archetype:create -DgroupId=org.sonatype.mavenbook.ch05 \
                                  -DartifactId=simple-webapp \
                                  -DpackageName=org.sonatype.mavenbook \
                                  -DarchetypeArtifactId=maven-archetype-webapp
[INFO] [archetype:create]
[INFO] ----------------------------------------------------------
[INFO] Using following parameters for creating Archetype:
          maven-archetype-webapp:RELEASE
[INFO] ----------------------------------------------------------
[INFO] Parameter: groupId, Value: org.sonatype.mavenbook.ch05
[INFO] Parameter: packageName, Value: org.sonatype.mavenbook
[INFO] Parameter: basedir, Value: ~/examples
[INFO] Parameter: package, Value: org.sonatype.mavenbook
[INFO] Parameter: version, Value: 1.0-SNAPSHOT
[INFO] Parameter: artifactId, Value: simple-webapp
[INFO] ******************** End of debug info from resources from
          generated POM *******
[INFO] Archetype created in dir: ~/examples/simple-webapp
```

Once the Maven Archetype plugin creates the project, change directories into the *simple-web* directory and take a look at the *pom.xml*. You should see the XML document shown in Example 5-1.

Example 5-1. Initial POM for the simple-web project

```
<project xmlns="http://maven.apache.org/POM/4.0.0"
         xmlns:xsi="http://www.w3.org/2001/XMLSchema-instance"
  xsi:schemaLocation="http://maven.apache.org/POM/4.0.0
         http://maven.apache.org/maven-v4_0_0.xsd">
  <modelVersion>4.0.0</modelVersion>
  <groupId>org.sonatype.mavenbook.ch05</groupId>
  <artifactId>simple-webapp</artifactId>
  <packaging>war</packaging>
  <version>1.0-SNAPSHOT</version>
  <name>simple-webapp Maven Webapp</name>
  <url>http://maven.apache.org</url>
  <dependencies>
    <dependency>
      <groupId>junit</groupId>
      <artifactId>junit</artifactId>
      <version>3.8.1</version>
      <scope>test</scope>
    </dependency>
  </dependencies>
</project>
```

```
<build>
  <finalName>simple-webapp</finalName>
  <plugins>
    <plugin>
      <artifactId>maven-compiler-plugin</artifactId>
      <configuration>
        <source>1.5</source>
        <target>1.5</target>
      </configuration>
    </plugin>
  </plugins>
</build>
</project>
```

Notice the `packaging` element contains the value `war`. This packaging type is what configures Maven to produce a web application archive in a WAR file. A project with `war` packaging is going to create a WAR file in the *target/* directory. The default name of this file is *${artifactId}-${version}.war*. In this project, the default WAR would be generated in *target/simple-webapp-1.0-SNAPSHOT.war*. In the `simple-webapp` project, we've customized the name of the generated WAR file by adding a `finalName` element inside of this project's build configuration. With a `finalName` of `simple-webapp`, the `package` phase produces a WAR file in *target/simple-webapp.war*.

Configuring the Jetty Plugin

Once you've compiled, tested, and packaged your web application, you'll likely want to deploy it to a servlet container and test the *index.jsp* that was created by the Maven Archetype plugin. Normally, this would involve downloading something like Jetty or Apache Tomcat, unpacking a distribution, copying your application's WAR file to a *webapps/* directory, and then starting your container. Although you can still do such a thing, there is no need. Instead, you can use the Maven Jetty plugin to run your web application within Maven. To do this, we'll need to configure the Maven Jetty plugin in our project's *pom.xml*. Add the `plugin` element shown in Example 5-2 to your project's build configuration.

Example 5-2. Configuring the Jetty plugin

```
<project>
  [...]
  <build>
    <finalName>simple-webapp</finalName>
    <plugins>
      <plugin>
        <groupId>org.mortbay.jetty</groupId>
        <artifactId>maven-jetty-plugin</artifactId>
      </plugins>
    </plugins>
  </build>
  [...]
</project>
```

Once you've configured the Maven Jetty plugin in your project's *pom.xml*, you can then invoke the run goal of the Jetty plugin to start your web application in the Jetty Servlet container. Run *mvn jetty:run* as follows:

```
~/examples$ mvn jetty:run
...
[INFO] [jetty:run]
[INFO] Configuring Jetty for project: simple-webapp Maven Webapp
[INFO] Webapp source directory = \
        /Users/tobrien/svnw/sonatype/examples/simple-webapp/src/
        main/webapp
[INFO] web.xml file = \
        /Users/tobrien/svnw/sonatype/examples/simple-webapp/src/
        main/webapp/WEB-INF/web.xml
[INFO] Classes = /Users/tobrien/svnw/sonatype/examples/simple-webapp/
        target/classes
2007-11-17 22:11:50.532::INFO:  Logging to STDERR via
        org.mortbay.log.StdErrLog
[INFO] Context path = /simple-webapp
[INFO] Tmp directory =  determined at runtime
[INFO] Web defaults = org/mortbay/jetty/webapp/webdefault.xml
[INFO] Web overrides =  none
[INFO] Webapp directory = \
        /Users/tobrien/svnw/sonatype/examples/simple-webapp/src/
        main/webapp
[INFO] Starting jetty 6.1.6rc1 ...
2007-11-17 22:11:50.673::INFO:  jetty-6.1.6rc1
2007-11-17 22:11:50.846::INFO:  No Transaction manager found - if\
        your webapp requires one, please configure one.
2007-11-17 22:11:51.057::INFO:  Started SelectChannelConnector@0.0.0.0:8080
[INFO] Started Jetty Server
```

After Maven starts the Jetty Servlet container, load the URL *http://localhost:8080/simple -webapp/* in a web browser. The simple *index.jsp* generated by the Archetype is trivial; it contains a second-level heading with the text "Hello World!". Maven expects the document root of the web application to be stored in *src/main/webapp*. This is the directory where you will find the *index.jsp* file shown in Example 5-3.

Example 5-3. Contents of src/main/webapp/index.jsp

```
<html>
  <body>
    <h2>Hello World!</h2>
  </body>
</html>
```

In *src/main/webapp/WEB-INF*, we will find the smallest possible web application descriptor in *web.xml*, shown in Example 5-4.

Example 5-4. Contents of src/main/webapp/WEB-INF/web.xml

```
<!DOCTYPE web-app PUBLIC
 "-//Sun Microsystems, Inc.//DTD Web Application 2.3//EN"
 "http://java.sun.com/dtd/web-app_2_3.dtd" >
```

```
<web-app>
  <display-name>Archetype Created Web Application</display-name>
</web-app>
```

Adding a Simple Servlet

A web application with a single JSP page and no configured servlets is next to useless. Let's add a simple servlet to this application and make some changes to the *pom.xml* and *web.xml* to support this change. First, we'll need to create a new package under *src/main/java* named `org.sonatype.mavenbook.web`:

```
$ mkdir -p src/main/java/org/sonatype/mavenbook/web
$ cd src/main/java/org/sonatype/mavenbook/web
```

Once you've created this package, change to the *src/main/java/org/sonatype/maven book/web* directory and create a class named `SimpleServlet` in *SimpleServlet.java*, which contains the code shown in Example 5-5.

Example 5-5. SimpleServlet class

```java
package org.sonatype.mavenbook.web;

import java.io.*;
import javax.servlet.*;
import javax.servlet.http.*;

public class SimpleServlet extends HttpServlet {
    public void doGet(HttpServletRequest request,
                      HttpServletResponse response)
        throws ServletException, IOException {

        PrintWriter out = response.getWriter();
        out.println( "SimpleServlet Executed" );
        out.flush();
        out.close();
    }
}
```

Our `SimpleServlet` class is just that: a servlet that prints a simple message to the response's `Writer`. To add this servlet to your web application and map it to a request path, add the `servlet` and `servlet-mapping` elements shown in Example 5-6 to your project's *web.xml* file. The *web.xml* file can be found in *src/main/webapp/WEB-INF*.

Example 5-6. Mapping the simple servlet

```
<!DOCTYPE web-app PUBLIC
 "-//Sun Microsystems, Inc.//DTD Web Application 2.3//EN"
 "http://java.sun.com/dtd/web-app_2_3.dtd" >

<web-app>
  <display-name>Archetype Created Web Application</display-name>
  <servlet>
```

```
    <servlet-name>simple</servlet-name>
    <servlet-class>org.sonatype.mavenbook.web.SimpleServlet</servlet-class>
  </servlet>
  <servlet-mapping>
    <servlet-name>simple</servlet-name>
    <url-pattern>/simple</url-pattern>
  </servlet-mapping>
</web-app>
```

Everything is in place to test this servlet; the class is in *src/main/java* and the *web.xml* has been updated. Before we launch the Jetty plugin, compile your project by running *mvn compile*:

```
~/examples$ mvn compile
...
[INFO] [compiler:compile]
[INFO] Compiling 1 source file to ~/examples/ch05/simple-webapp/target/classes
[INFO] -----------------------------------------------------------------------
[ERROR] BUILD FAILURE
[INFO] -----------------------------------------------------------------------
[INFO] Compilation failure

/src/main/java/org/sonatype/mavenbook/web/SimpleServlet.java:[4,0] \
   package javax.servlet does not exist

/src/main/java/org/sonatype/mavenbook/web/SimpleServlet.java:[5,0] \
   package javax.servlet.http does not exist

/src/main/java/org/sonatype/mavenbook/web/SimpleServlet.java:[7,35] \
   cannot find symbol
   symbol: class HttpServlet
   public class SimpleServlet extends HttpServlet {

/src/main/java/org/sonatype/mavenbook/web/SimpleServlet.java:[8,22] \
   cannot find symbol
   symbol  : class HttpServletRequest
   location: class org.sonatype.mavenbook.web.SimpleServlet

/src/main/java/org/sonatype/mavenbook/web/SimpleServlet.java:[9,22] \
   cannot find symbol
   symbol  : class HttpServletResponse
   location: class org.sonatype.mavenbook.web.SimpleServlet

/src/main/java/org/sonatype/mavenbook/web/SimpleServlet.java:[10,15] \
   cannot find symbol
   symbol  : class ServletException
   location: class org.sonatype.mavenbook.web.SimpleServlet
```

The compilation fails because your Maven project doesn't have a dependency on the Servlet API. In the next section, we'll add the Servlet API to this project's POM.

Adding J2EE Dependencies

To write a servlet, we'll need to add the Servlet API as a project dependency. The Servlet specification is a JAR file that can be downloaded from Sun Microsystems at *http://java .sun.com/products/servlet/download.html*. Once the JAR file is downloaded, you'll need to install the resulting JAR in your local Maven repository located at *~/.m2/repository*. The same process will have to be repeated for all of the Java Platform Enterprise Edition (J2EE) APIs maintained by Sun Microsystems—Java Naming and Directory Interface (JNDI), Java Database Connectivity (JDBC), Servlet, JSP, Java Transaction API (JTA), and others. If this strikes you as somewhat tedious, you are not alone. Lucky for you, there is a simpler alternative to downloading all of these libraries and installing them manually—Apache Geronimo's independent open source implementations.

For years, the only way to get the Servlet specification JAR was to download it directly from Sun Microsystems. You had to go to the Sun web site, agree to a click-through licensing agreement, and only then could you access the Servlet JAR. This was all necessary because the Sun specification JARs were not made available under a license that allowed for redistribution. Manually downloading Sun artifacts was something you just had to do to write a Servlet or to use JDBC from a Maven project for a few years. It was tedious and annoying until the Apache Geronimo project was able to create a Sun-certified implementation of a number of enterprise specifications releasing these specification JARs under the Apache Software License version 2.0, a license that allows for free redistribution of source and binary. Now, for the purposes of your programming, there is little to no difference between the Servlet API JAR downloaded from Sun Microsystems and the Servlet API JAR implemented by the Apache Geronimo project. Both have passed a rigorous Test Compatibility Kit (TCK) from Sun Microsystems.

Adding a dependency on something like the JSP API or the Servlet API is now very straightforward, and it does not require you to manually download a JAR file from a web site and install it in your local repository. The catch is that you have to know where to look: what `groupId`, `artifactId`, and `version` to use to reference the appropriate Apache Geronimo implementation. To add the Servlet specification API as a dependency to your project's POM, add the dependency element shown in Example 5-7 to *pom.xml*.

Example 5-7. Add the Servlet 2.4 specification as a dependency

```
<project>
  [...]
  <dependencies>
    [...]
    <dependency>
      <groupId>org.apache.geronimo.specs</groupId>
      <artifactId>geronimo-servlet_2.4_spec</artifactId>
      <version>1.1.1</version>
      <scope>provided</scope>
    </dependency>
  </dependencies>
```

```
  [...]
</project>
```

The `groupId` for all of the Apache Geronimo specification implementations is `org.apache.geronimo.specs`. The `artifactId` contains the version of the specification that you are most familiar with; for example, if you were going to include the Servlet 2.3 specification, you would have an `artifactId` of `geronimo-servlet_2.3_spec`, and if you were targeting the Servlet 2.4 specification, your `artifactId` would be `geronimo-servlet_2.4_spec`. As for the version, you'll have to take a look at the public Maven repository to figure out which version you should use. For versions, your best bet is going to be the latest version for a particular specification implementation. If you are looking for a specific alternative to a Sun specification from the Apache Geronimo project, we've assembled a list of available specifications in Appendix B.

It is also worth pointing out that we have used the `provided` scope for this dependency. This tells Maven that the JAR is "provided" by the container and thus should not be included in the WAR.

If you were interested in writing a custom JSP tag for this simple web application, you would need to add a dependency on the JSP 2.0 spec. Use the configuration shown in Example 5-8 to add this dependency.

Example 5-8. Adding the JSP 2.0 specification as a dependency

```
<project>
  [...]
  <dependencies>
    [...]
    <dependency>
      <groupId>org.apache.geronimo.specs</groupId>
      <artifactId>geronimo-jsp_2.0_spec</artifactId>
      <version>1.1</version>
      <scope>provided</scope>
    </dependency>
  </dependencies>
  [...]
</project>
```

Once you've add the Servlet specification as a dependency, run *mvn clean install* followed by *mvn jetty:run*.

```
[tobrien@t1 simple-webapp]$ mvn clean install
...
[tobrien@t1 simple-webapp]$ mvn jetty:run
[INFO] [jetty:run]
...
2007-12-14 16:18:31.305::INFO:  jetty-6.1.6rc1
2007-12-14 16:18:31.453::INFO:  No Transaction manager found - if your webapp\
          requires one, please configure one.
2007-12-14 16:18:32.745::INFO:  Started SelectChannelConnector@0.0.0.0:8080
[INFO] Started Jetty Server
```

At this point, you should be able to retrieve the output of the `SimpleServlet`. From the command line, you can use *curl* to print the output of this servlet to standard output:

```
~/examples$ curl http://localhost:8080/simple-webapp/simple
SimpleServlet Executed
```

Conclusion

After reading this chapter, you should be able to bootstrap a simple web application. This chapter didn't dwell on the million different ways to create a complete web application. Other chapters provide a more comprehensive overview of projects that involve some of the more popular web frameworks and technologies.

A Multimodule Project

Introduction

In this chapter, we create a multimodule project that combines the examples from the two previous chapters. The `simple-weather` code developed in Chapter 4 will be combined with the `simple-webapp` project defined in Chapter 5 to create a web application that retrieves and displays weather forecast information on a web page. At the end of this chapter, you will be able to use Maven to develop complex, multimodule projects.

Downloading This Chapter's Example

The multimodule project developed in this example consists of modified versions of the projects developed in Chapters 4 and 5, and we are not using the Maven Archetype plugin to generate this multimodule project. We strongly recommend downloading a copy of the example code to use as a supplemental reference while reading the content in this chapter. This chapter's example project may be downloaded with the book's example code at *http://www.sonatype.com/book/mvn-examples-1.0.zip* or *http://www.sonatype.com/book/mvn-examples-1.0.tar.gz*. Unzip this archive in any directory, and then go to the *ch06/* directory. There you will see a directory named *simple-parent/*, which contains the multimodule Maven project developed in this chapter. In this directory, you will see a *pom.xml* and the two submodule directories, *simple-weather/* and *simple-webapp/*. If you wish to follow along with the example code in a web browser, go to *http://www.sonatype.com/book/examples-1.0* and click on the *ch06/* directory.

The Simple Parent Project

A multimodule project is defined by a parent POM referencing one or more submodules. In the *simple-parent/* directory, you will find the parent POM (also called the top-level POM) in *simple-parent/pom.xml*. See Example 6-1.

Example 6-1. simple-parent project POM

```xml
<project xmlns="http://maven.apache.org/POM/4.0.0"
  xmlns:xsi="http://www.w3.org/2001/XMLSchema-instance"
  xsi:schemaLocation="http://maven.apache.org/POM/4.0.0
                      http://maven.apache.org/maven-v4_0_0.xsd">
  <modelVersion>4.0.0</modelVersion>

  <groupId>org.sonatype.mavenbook.ch06</groupId>
  <artifactId>simple-parent</artifactId>
  <packaging>pom</packaging>
  <version>1.0</version>
  <name>Chapter 6 Simple Parent Project</name>

  <modules>
    <module>simple-weather</module>
    <module>simple-webapp</module>
  </modules>

  <build>
    <pluginManagement>
      <plugins>
        <plugin>
          <groupId>org.apache.maven.plugins</groupId>
          <artifactId>maven-compiler-plugin</artifactId>
          <configuration>
            <source>1.5</source>
            <target>1.5</target>
          </configuration>
        </plugin>
      </plugins>
    </pluginManagement>
  </build>

  <dependencies>
    <dependency>
      <groupId>junit</groupId>
      <artifactId>junit</artifactId>
      <version>3.8.1</version>
      <scope>test</scope>
    </dependency>
  </dependencies>
</project>
```

Notice that the parent defines a set of Maven coordinates: the `groupId` is `com.sona type.maven`, the `artifactId` is `simple-parent`, and the `version` is `1.0`. The parent project doesn't create a JAR or a WAR like our previous projects; instead, it is simply a POM that refers to other Maven projects. The appropriate packaging for a project like `simple-parent` that simply provides a Project Object Model is `pom`. The next section in the *pom.xml* lists the project's submodules. These modules are defined in the `modules` element, and each `module` element corresponds to a subdirectory of the *simple-parent/*

directory. Maven knows to look in these directories for *pom.xml* files, and it will add submodules to the list of Maven projects included in a build.

Lastly, we define some settings that will be inherited by all submodules. The `simple-parent` build configuration configures the target for all Java compilation to be the Java 5 JVM. Since the Compiler plugin is bound to the lifecycle by default, we can use the `pluginManagement` section do to this. We will discuss `pluginManagement` in more detail in later chapters, but the separation between providing configuration to default plugins and actually binding plugins is much easier to see when they are separated this way. The `dependencies` element adds JUnit 3.8.1 as a global dependency. Both the build configuration and the dependencies are inherited by all submodules. Using POM inheritance allows you to add common dependencies for universal dependencies such as JUnit or Log4J.

The Simple Weather Module

The first submodule we're going to look at is the `simple-weather` submodule. This submodule contains all of the classes that take care of interacting with and parsing the Yahoo! Weather feeds. See Example 6-2.

Example 6-2. simple-weather module POM

```
<project xmlns="http://maven.apache.org/POM/4.0.0"
  xmlns:xsi="http://www.w3.org/2001/XMLSchema-instance"
  xsi:schemaLocation="http://maven.apache.org/POM/4.0.0
                      http://maven.apache.org/maven-v4_0_0.xsd">
  <modelVersion>4.0.0</modelVersion>
  <parent>
    <groupId>org.sonatype.mavenbook.ch06</groupId>
    <artifactId>simple-parent</artifactId>
    <version>1.0</version>
  </parent>
  <artifactId>simple-weather</artifactId>
  <packaging>jar</packaging>

  <name>Chapter 6 Simple Weather API</name>

  <build>
    <pluginManagement>
      <plugins>
        <plugin>
          <groupId>org.apache.maven.plugins</groupId>
          <artifactId>maven-surefire-plugin</artifactId>
          <configuration>
            <testFailureIgnore>true</testFailureIgnore>
          </configuration>
        </plugin>
      </plugins>
    </pluginManagement>
  </build>
```

```
    <dependencies>
      <dependency>
        <groupId>log4j</groupId>
        <artifactId>log4j</artifactId>
        <version>1.2.14</version>
      </dependency>
      <dependency>
        <groupId>dom4j</groupId>
        <artifactId>dom4j</artifactId>
        <version>1.6.1</version>
      </dependency>
      <dependency>
        <groupId>jaxen</groupId>
        <artifactId>jaxen</artifactId>
        <version>1.1.1</version>
      </dependency>
      <dependency>
        <groupId>velocity</groupId>
        <artifactId>velocity</artifactId>
        <version>1.5</version>
      </dependency>
      <dependency>
        <groupId>org.apache.commons</groupId>
        <artifactId>commons-io</artifactId>
        <version>1.3.2</version>
        <scope>test</scope>
      </dependency>
    </dependencies>
</project>
```

In simple-weather's *pom.xml* file, we see this module referencing a parent POM using a set of Maven coordinates. The parent POM for simple-weather is identified by a groupId of org.sonatype.mavenbook, an artifactId of simple-parent, and a version of 1.0. See Example 6-3.

Example 6-3. The WeatherService class

```
package org.sonatype.mavenbook.weather;

import java.io.InputStream;

public class WeatherService {

    public WeatherService() {}

    public String retrieveForecast( String zip ) throws Exception {
        // Retrieve Data
        InputStream dataIn = new YahooRetriever().retrieve( zip );

        // Parse Data
        Weather weather = new YahooParser().parse( dataIn );

        // Format (Print) Data
        return new WeatherFormatter().format( weather );
```

```
      }
}
```

The `WeatherService` class is defined in *src/main/java/org/sonatype/mavenbook/*
weather, and it simply calls out to the three objects defined in Chapter 4. In this chapter's example, we're creating a separate project that contains service objects that are
referenced in the web application project. This is a common model in enterprise Java
development; often a complex application consists of more than just a single, simple
web application. You might have an enterprise application that consists of multiple
web applications and some command-line applications. Often, you'll want to refactor
common logic to a service class that can be reused across a number of projects. This is
the justification for creating a `WeatherService` class; by doing so, you can see how the
`simple-webapp` project references a service object defined in `simple-weather`.

The `retrieveForecast()` method takes a `String` containing a zip code. This zip code
parameter is then passed to the `YahooRetriever`'s `retrieve()` method, which gets the
XML from Yahoo! Weather. The XML returned from `YahooRetriever` is then passed to
the `parse()` method on `YahooParser` which returns a `Weather` object. This `Weather` object
is then formatted into a presentable `String` by the `WeatherFormatter`.

The Simple Web Application Module

The `simple-webapp` module is the second submodule referenced in the `simple-parent`
project. This web application project depends on the `simple-weather` module, and it
contains some simple servlets that present the results of the Yahoo! Weather service
query. See Example 6-4.

Example 6-4. simple-webapp module POM

```xml
<project xmlns="http://maven.apache.org/POM/4.0.0"
         xmlns:xsi="http://www.w3.org/2001/XMLSchema-instance"
   xsi:schemaLocation="http://maven.apache.org/POM/4.0.0
                       http://maven.apache.org/maven-v4_0_0.xsd">
  <modelVersion>4.0.0</modelVersion>
  <parent>
    <groupId>org.sonatype.mavenbook.ch06</groupId>
    <artifactId>simple-parent</artifactId>
    <version>1.0</version>
  </parent>

  <artifactId>simple-webapp</artifactId>
  <packaging>war</packaging>
  <name>simple-webapp Maven Webapp</name>
  <dependencies>
    <dependency>
      <groupId>org.apache.geronimo.specs</groupId>
      <artifactId>geronimo-servlet_2.4_spec</artifactId>
      <version>1.1.1</version>
    </dependency>
    <dependency>
```

```
        <groupId>org.sonatype.mavenbook.ch06</groupId>
        <artifactId>simple-weather</artifactId>
        <version>1.0</version>
      </dependency>
    </dependencies>
    <build>
      <finalName>simple-webapp</finalName>
      <plugins>
        <plugin>
          <groupId>org.mortbay.jetty</groupId>
          <artifactId>maven-jetty-plugin</artifactId>
        </plugin>
      </plugins>
    </build>
</project>
```

This **simple-weather** module defines a very simple servlet that reads a zip code from an HTTP request, calls the **WeatherService** shown in Example 6-3, and prints the results to the response's **Writer**. See Example 6-5.

Example 6-5. simple-webapp WeatherServlet

```
package org.sonatype.mavenbook.web;

import org.sonatype.mavenbook.weather.WeatherService;
import java.io.*;
import javax.servlet.*;
import javax.servlet.http.*;

public class WeatherServlet extends HttpServlet {
    public void doGet(HttpServletRequest request,
                      HttpServletResponse response)
        throws ServletException, IOException {
        String zip = request.getParameter("zip" );
        WeatherService weatherService = new WeatherService();
        PrintWriter out = response.getWriter();
        try {
            out.println( weatherService.retrieveForecast( zip ) );
        } catch( Exception e ) {
            out.println( "Error Retrieving Forecast: " + e.getMessage() );
        }
        out.flush();
        out.close();
    }
}
```

In **WeatherServlet**, we instantiate an instance of the **WeatherService** class defined in **simple-weather**. The zip code supplied in the request parameter is passed to the **retrieveForecast()** method, and the resulting test is printed to the response's **Writer**.

Finally, to tie all of this together is the *web.xml* for **simple-webapp** in *src/main/webapp/WEB-INF*. The **servlet** and **servlet-mapping** elements in the *web.xml* shown in Example 6-6 map the request path */weather* to the **WeatherServlet**.

Example 6-6. simple-webapp web.xml

```
<!DOCTYPE web-app PUBLIC
 "-//Sun Microsystems, Inc.//DTD Web Application 2.3//EN"
 "http://java.sun.com/dtd/web-app_2_3.dtd" >

<web-app>
  <display-name>Archetype Created Web Application</display-name>
  <servlet>
    <servlet-name>simple</servlet-name>
    <servlet-class>org.sonatype.mavenbook.web.SimpleServlet</servlet-class>
  </servlet>
  <servlet>
    <servlet-name>weather</servlet-name>
    <servlet-class>org.sonatype.mavenbook.web.WeatherServlet</servlet-class>
  </servlet>
  <servlet-mapping>
    <servlet-name>simple</servlet-name>
    <url-pattern>/simple</url-pattern>
  </servlet-mapping>
  <servlet-mapping>
    <servlet-name>weather</servlet-name>
    <url-pattern>/weather</url-pattern>
  </servlet-mapping>
</web-app>
```

Building the Multimodule Project

With the simple-weather project containing all the general code for interacting with the Yahoo! Weather service and the simple-webapp project containing a simple servlet, it is time to compile and package the application into a WAR file. To do this, you will want to compile and install both projects in the appropriate order; since simple-webapp depends on simple-weather, the simple-weather JAR needs to be created before the simple-webapp project can compile. To do this, you will run *mvn clean install* from the simple-parent project:

```
~/examples/ch06/simple-parent$ mvn clean install
[INFO] Scanning for projects...
[INFO] Reactor build order:
[INFO]   Simple Parent Project
[INFO]   simple-weather
[INFO]   simple-webapp Maven Webapp
[INFO] ------------------------------------------------------------------------
[INFO] Building simple-weather
[INFO]    task-segment: [clean, install]
[INFO] ------------------------------------------------------------------------
[...]
[INFO] [install:install]
[INFO] Installing simple-weather-1.0.jar to simple-weather-1.0.jar
[INFO] ------------------------------------------------------------------------
[INFO] Building simple-webapp Maven Webapp
[INFO]    task-segment: [clean, install]
[INFO] ------------------------------------------------------------------------
```

```
[...]
[INFO] [install:install]
[INFO] Installing simple-webapp.war to simple-webapp-1.0.war
[INFO]
[INFO] ------------------------------------------------------------------------
[INFO] Reactor Summary:
[INFO] ------------------------------------------------------------------------
[INFO] Simple Parent Project .............................. SUCCESS [3.041s]
[INFO] simple-weather ..................................... SUCCESS [4.802s]
[INFO] simple-webapp Maven Webapp ......................... SUCCESS [3.065s]
[INFO] ------------------------------------------------------------------------
```

When Maven is executed against a project with submodules, Maven first loads the parent POM and locates all of the submodule POMs. Maven then puts all of these project POMs into something called the Maven Reactor, which analyzes the dependencies between modules. The Reactor takes care of ordering components to ensure that interdependent modules are compiled and installed in the proper order.

The Reactor preserves the order of modules as defined in the POM unless changes need to be made. A helpful mental model for this is to picture that modules with dependencies on sibling projects are "pushed down" the list until the dependency ordering is satisfied. On rare occasions, it may be handy to rearrange the module order of your build—for example, if you want a frequently unstable module toward the beginning of the build.

Once the Reactor figures out the order in which projects must be built, Maven executes the specified goals for every module in a multimodule build. In this example, you can see that Maven builds `simple-weather` before `simple-webapp`, effectively executing *mvn clean install* for each submodule.

When you run Maven from the command line, you'll frequently want to specify the `clean` lifecycle phase before any other lifecycle stages. When you specify `clean`, you make sure that Maven is going to remove old output before it compiles and packages an application. Running `clean` isn't necessary, but it is a useful precaution to make sure that you are performing a "clean build."

Running the Web Application

Once the multimodule project has been installed with *mvn clean install* from the parent project, simple-project, you can then change directories into the simple-webapp project and run the run goal of the Jetty plugin:

```
~/examples/ch06/simple-parent/simple-webapp $ mvn jetty:run
[INFO] ------------------------------------------------------------------
[INFO] Building simple-webapp Maven Webapp
[INFO]    task-segment: [jetty:run]
[INFO] ------------------------------------------------------------------
[...]
[INFO] [jetty:run]
[INFO] Configuring Jetty for project: simple-webapp Maven Webapp
[...]
[INFO] Webapp directory = ~/examples/ch06/simple-parent/simple-webapp/src/
        main/webapp
[INFO] Starting jetty 6.1.6rc1 ...
2007-11-18 1:58:26.980::INFO:  jetty-6.1.6rc1
2007-11-18 1:58:26.125::INFO:  No Transaction manager found - if your webapp\
          requires one, please configure one.
2007-11-18 1:58:27.633::INFO:  Started SelectChannelConnector@0.0.0.0:8080
[INFO] Started Jetty Server
```

Once Jetty has started, load *http://localhost:8080/simple-webapp/weather?zip=01201* in a browser and you should see the formatted weather output.

Multimodule Enterprise Project

Introduction

In this chapter, we create a multimodule project that evolves the examples from Chapters 5 and 6 into a project that uses the Spring Framework and Hibernate to create both a simple web application and a command-line utility to read data from the Yahoo! Weather feed. The `simple-weather` code developed in Chapter 4 will be combined with the `simple-webapp` project defined in Chapter 5. In the process of creating this multimodule project, we'll explore Maven and discuss the different ways it can be used to create modular projects that encourage reuse.

Downloading This Chapter's Example

The multimodule project developed in this example consists of modified versions of the projects developed in Chapters 4 and 5, and we are not using the Maven Archetype plugin to generate this multimodule project. We strongly recommend downloading a copy of the example code to use as a supplemental reference while reading the content in this chapter. Without the examples, you won't be able to recreate this chapter's example code. This chapter's example project may be downloaded with the book's example code at *http://www.sonatype.com/book/mvn-examples-1.0.zip* or *http://www.sonatype.com/book/mvn-examples-1.0.tar.gz*. Unzip this archive in any directory, and then go to the *ch07/* directory. In the *ch07/* directory, you will see a directory named *simple-parent/* that contains the multimodule Maven project developed in this chapter. In the *simple-parent/* project directory you will see a *pom.xml* and the five submodule directories *simple-model/*, *simple-persist/*, *simple-command/*, *simple-weather/*, and *simple-webapp/*. If you wish to follow along with the example code in a web browser, go to *http://www.sonatype.com/book/examples-1.0* and click on the *ch07/* directory.

Multimodule Enterprise Project

Presenting the complexity of a massive enterprise-level project far exceeds the scope of this book. Such projects are characterized by multiple databases, integration with

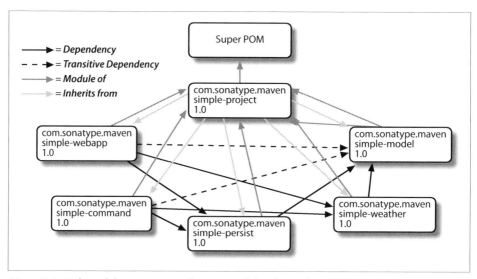

Figure 7-1. Multimodule enterprise application module relationships

external systems, and subprojects that may be divided by departments. These projects usually span thousands of lines of code and involve the effort of tens or hundreds of software developers. Although such a complete example is outside the scope of this book, we can provide you with a sample project that suggests the complexity of a larger Enterprise application. In the conclusion, we suggest some possibilities for modularity beyond that presented in this chapter.

In this chapter, we're going to look at a multimodule Maven project that will produce two applications: a command-line query tool for the Yahoo! Weather feed, and a web application that queries the Yahoo! Weather feed. Both of these applications will store the results of queries in an embedded database. Each will allow the user to retrieve historical weather data from this embedded database. Both applications will reuse application logic and share a persistence library. This chapter's example builds upon the Yahoo! Weather parsing code introduced in Chapter 4. This project is divided into five submodules as shown in Figure 7-1.

In Figure 7-1, you can see that there are five submodules of `simple-parent`. They are:

`simple-model`

> This module defines a simple object model that models the data returned from the Yahoo! Weather feed. This object model contains the `Weather`, `Condition`, `Atmosphere`, `Location`, and `Wind` objects. When our application parses the Yahoo! Weather feed, the parsers defined in `simple-weather` will parse the XML and create `Weather` objects, which are then used by the application. This project contains model objects annotated with Hibernate 3 Annotations, which are used by the logic in `simple-persist` to map each model object to a corresponding table in a relational database.

simple-weather

This module contains all of the logic required to retrieve data from the Yahoo! Weather feed and parse the resulting XML. The XML returned from this feed is converted into the model objects defined in `simple-model`. `simple-weather` has a dependency on `simple-model`. `simple-weather` defines a `WeatherService` object that is referenced by both the `simple-command` and `simple-webapp` projects.

simple-persist

This module contains some Data Access Objects (DAO) that are configured to store `Weather` objects in an embedded database. Both of the applications defined in this multimodule project will use the DAOs defined in `simple-persist` to store data in an embedded database. The DAOs defined in this project understand and return the model objects defined in `simple-model`. `simple-persist` has a direct dependency on `simple-model`, and it depends on the Hibernate Annotations present on the model objects.

simple-webapp

The web application project contains two Spring MVC Controller implementations that use the `WeatherService` defined in `simple-weather` and the DAOs defined in `simple-persist`. `simple-webapp` has a direct dependency on `simple-weather` and `simple-persist`; it has a transitive dependency on `simple-model`.

simple-command

This module contains a simple command-line tool that can be used to query the Yahoo! Weather feed. This project contains a class with a static `main()` function and interacts with the `WeatherService` defined in `simple-weather` and the DAOs defined in `simple-persist`. `simple-command` has a direct dependency on `simple-weather` and `simple-persist`; it has a transitive dependency on `simple-model`.

This chapter contains a contrived example simple enough to introduce in a book, yet complex enough to justify a set of five submodules. Our contrived example has a model project with five classes, a persistence library with two service classes, and a weather parsing library with five or six classes, but a real-world system might have a model project with a hundred objects, several persistence libraries, and service libraries spanning multiple departments. Although we've tried to make sure that the code contained in this example is straightforward enough to comprehend in a single sitting, we've also gone out of our way to build a modular project. You might be tempted to look at the examples in this chapter and walk away with the idea that Maven encourages too much complexity given that our model project has only five classes. Although using Maven does suggest a certain level of modularity, do realize that we've gone out of our way to complicate our simple example projects for the purpose of demonstrating Maven's multimodule features.

Technology Used in This Example

This chapter's example involves some technology that, while popular, is not directly related to Maven. These technologies are the Spring Framework and Hibernate. The Spring Framework is an Inversion of Control (IoC) container and a set of frameworks that aim to simplify interaction with various J2EE libraries. Using the Spring Framework as a foundational framework for application development gives you access to a number of helpful abstractions that can take much of the meddlesome busywork out of dealing with persistence frameworks such as Hibernate or iBATIS or enterprise APIs such as JDBC, JNDI, and Java Message Service (JMS). The Spring Framework has grown in popularity over the past few years as a replacement for the heavyweight enterprise standards coming out of Sun Microsystems. Hibernate is a widely used Object-Relational Mapping framework that allows you to interact with a relational database as if it were a collection of Java objects. This example focuses on building a simple web application and a command-line application that uses the Spring Framework to expose a set of reusable components to applications and that also uses Hibernate to persist weather data in an embedded database.

We've decided to include references to these frameworks to demonstrate how one would construct projects using these technologies when using Maven. Although we make brief efforts to introduce these technologies throughout this chapter, we will not go out of our way to fully explain these technologies. For more information about the Spring Framework, please see the project's web site at *http://www.springframework .org/*. For more information about Hibernate and Hibernate Annotations, please see the project's web site at *http://www.hibernate.org*. This chapter uses Hyper-threaded Structured Query Language Database (HSQLDB) as an embedded database; for more information about this database, see the project's web site at *http://hsqldb.org/*.

The Simple Parent Project

This `simple-parent` project has a *pom.xml* that references five submodules: `simple-command`, `simple-model`, `simple-weather`, `simple-persist`, and `simple-webapp`. The top-level *pom.xml* is shown in Example 7-1.

Example 7-1. simple-parent project POM

```
<project xmlns="http://maven.apache.org/POM/4.0.0"
  xmlns:xsi="http://www.w3.org/2001/XMLSchema-instance"
  xsi:schemaLocation="http://maven.apache.org/POM/4.0.0
                    http://maven.apache.org/maven-v4_0_0.xsd">
  <modelVersion>4.0.0</modelVersion>

  <groupId>org.sonatype.mavenbook.ch07</groupId>
  <artifactId>simple-parent</artifactId>
  <packaging>pom</packaging>
  <version>1.0</version>
  <name>Chapter 7 Simple Parent Project</name>
```

```
<modules>
  <module>simple-command</module>
  <module>simple-model</module>
  <module>simple-weather</module>
  <module>simple-persist</module>
  <module>simple-webapp</module>
</modules>

<build>
  <pluginManagement>
    <plugins>
      <plugin>
        <groupId>org.apache.maven.plugins</groupId>
        <artifactId>maven-compiler-plugin</artifactId>
        <configuration>
          <source>1.5</source>
          <target>1.5</target>
        </configuration>
      </plugin>
    </plugins>
  </pluginManagement>
</build>

<dependencies>
  <dependency>
    <groupId>junit</groupId>
    <artifactId>junit</artifactId>
    <version>3.8.1</version>
    <scope>test</scope>
  </dependency>
</dependencies>
</project>
```

Note the similarities between this parent POM and the parent POM defined in Example 6-1. The only real difference between these two POMs is the list of submodules. Where the earlier example listed only two submodules, this parent POM lists five submodules. The next few sections explore each of these five submodules in some detail. Because our example uses Java annotations, we've configured the compiler to target the Java 5 JVM.

The Simple Model Module

The first thing most enterprise projects need is an object model. An object model captures the core set of domain objects in any system. A banking system might have an object model that consists of Account, Customer, and Transaction objects, or a system to capture and communicate sports scores might have Team and Game objects. Whatever it is, there's a good chance that you've modeled the concepts in your system in an object model. It is a common practice in Maven projects to separate this project into a separate project that is widely referenced. In this example system, we are capturing each query

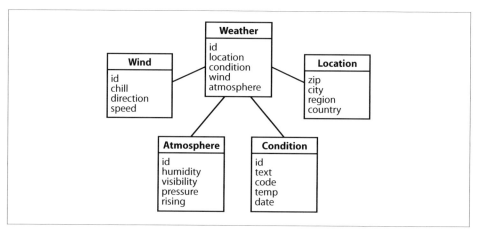

Figure 7-2. Simple object model for weather data

to the Yahoo! Weather feed with a `Weather` object that references four other objects. Wind direction, chill, and speed are stored in a `Wind` object. Location data including the zip code, city, region, and country are stored in a `Location` class. Atmospheric conditions such as the humidity, maximum visibility, barometric pressure, and whether the pressure is rising or falling is stored in an `Atmosphere` class. A textual description of conditions, the temperature, and the data of the observation is stored in a `Condition` class. See Figure 7-2.

The *pom.xml* file for this simple model object contains one dependency that bears some explanation. Our object model is annotated with Hibernate Annotations. We use these annotations to map the model objects in this model to tables in a relational database. The dependency is `org.hibernate:hibernate-annotations:3.3.0.ga`. Take a look at the *pom.xml* shown in Example 7-2, and then look at the next few examples for some illustrations of these annotations.

Example 7-2. simple-model pom.xml

```
<project xmlns="http://maven.apache.org/POM/4.0.0"
        xmlns:xsi="http://www.w3.org/2001/XMLSchema-instance"
  xsi:schemaLocation="http://maven.apache.org/POM/4.0.0
                      http://maven.apache.org/maven-v4_0_0.xsd">
  <modelVersion>4.0.0</modelVersion>
  <parent>
    <groupId>org.sonatype.mavenbook.ch07</groupId>
    <artifactId>simple-parent</artifactId>
    <version>1.0</version>
  </parent>
  <artifactId>simple-model</artifactId>
  <packaging>jar</packaging>

  <name>Simple Object Model</name>

  <dependencies>
    <dependency>
```

```
      <groupId>org.hibernate</groupId>
      <artifactId>hibernate-annotations</artifactId>
      <version>3.3.0.ga</version>
    </dependency>
    <dependency>
      <groupId>org.hibernate</groupId>
      <artifactId>hibernate-commons-annotations</artifactId>
      <version>3.3.0.ga</version>
    </dependency>
  </dependencies>
</project>
```

In *src/main/java/org/sonatype/mavenbook/weather/model*, we have *Weather.java*, which contains the annotated `Weather` model object. The `Weather` object is a simple Java bean. This means that we have private member variables like `id`, `location`, `condition`, `wind`, `atmosphere`, and `date` exposed with public getter and setter methods that adhere to the following pattern: if a property is named `name`, there will be a public no-arg getter method named `getName()`, and there will be a one-argument *setter* named `setName(String name)`. Although we show the getter and setter method for the `id` property, we've omitted most of the getters and setters for most of the other properties to save a few trees. See Example 7-3.

Example 7-3. Annotated Weather model object

```
package org.sonatype.mavenbook.weather.model;

import javax.persistence.*;

import java.util.Date;

@Entity
@NamedQueries({
  @NamedQuery(name="Weather.byLocation",
              query="from Weather w where w.location = :location")
})
public class Weather {

    @Id
    @GeneratedValue(strategy=GenerationType.IDENTITY)
    private Integer id;

    @ManyToOne(cascade=CascadeType.ALL)
    private Location location;

    @OneToOne(mappedBy="weather",cascade=CascadeType.ALL)
    private Condition condition;

    @OneToOne(mappedBy="weather",cascade=CascadeType.ALL)
    private Wind wind;

    @OneToOne(mappedBy="weather",cascade=CascadeType.ALL)
    private Atmosphere atmosphere;

    private Date date;
```

```
    public Weather() {}

    public Integer getId() { return id; }
    public void setId(Integer id) { this.id = id; }

    // All getter and setter methods omitted...
}
```

In the `Weather` class, we are using Hibernate annotations to provide guidance to the `simple-persist` project. These annotations are used by Hibernate to map an object to a table in a relational database. Although a full explanation of Hibernate annotations is beyond the scope of this chapter, here is a brief explanation for the curious. The `@Entity` annotation marks this class as a persistent entity. We've omitted the `@Table` annotation on this class, so Hibernate is going to use the name of the class as the name of the table to map `Weather` to. The `@NamedQueries` annotation defines a query that is used by the `WeatherDAO` in `simple-persist`. The query language in the `@NamedQuery` annotation is written in something called Hibernate Query Language (HQL). Each member variable is annotated with annotations that define the type of column and any relationships implied by that column:

Id

> The `id` property is annotated with `@Id`. This marks the `id` property as the property that contains the primary key in a database table. The `@GeneratedValue` controls how new primary key values are generated. In the case of `id`, we're using the `IDENTITY GenerationType`, which will use the underlying database's identity generation facilities.

Location

> Each `Weather` object instance corresponds to a `Location` object. A `Location` object represents a zip code, and the `@ManyToOne` makes sure that `Weather` objects that point to the same `Location` object reference the same instance. The `cascade` attribute of the `@ManyToOne` makes sure that we persist a `Location` object every time we persist a `Weather` object.

Condition, Wind, Atmosphere

> Each of these objects is mapped as a `@OneToOne` with the `CascadeType` of `ALL`. This means that every time we save a `Weather` object, we'll be inserting a row into the `Weather` table, the `Condition` table, the `Wind` table, and the `Atmosphere` table.

Date

> `Date` is not annotated. This means that Hibernate is going to use all of the column defaults to define this mapping. The column name is going to be `date`, and the column type is going to be the appropriate time to match the `Date` object.

If you have a property you wish to omit from a table mapping, you would annotate that property with @Transient.

Next, take a look at one of the secondary model objects, Condition, shown in Example 7-4. This class also resides in *src/main/java/org/sonatype/mavenbook/weather/model*.

Example 7-4. simple-model's Condition model object

```
package org.sonatype.mavenbook.weather.model;

import javax.persistence.*;

@Entity
public class Condition {

    @Id
    @GeneratedValue(strategy=GenerationType.IDENTITY)
    private Integer id;

    private String text;
    private String code;
    private String temp;
    private String date;

    @OneToOne(cascade=CascadeType.ALL)
    @JoinColumn(name="weather_id", nullable=false)
    private Weather weather;

    public Condition() {}

    public Integer getId() { return id; }
    public void setId(Integer id) { this.id = id; }

    // All getter and setter methods omitted...
}
```

The Condition class resembles the Weather class. It is annotated as an @Entity, and it has similar annotations on the id property. The text, code, temp, and date properties are all left with the default column settings, and the weather property is annotated with a @OneToOne annotation and another annotation that references the associated Weather object with a foreign key column named weather_id.

The Simple Weather Module

The next module we're going to examine could be considered something of a "service." The Simple Weather module is the module that contains all of the logic necessary to retrieve and parse the data from the Yahoo! Weather RSS feed. Although Simple

Weather contains three Java classes and one JUnit test, it is going to present a single component, `WeatherService`, to both the Simple Web Application and the Simple Command-line Utility. Very often an enterprise project will contain several API modules that contain critical business logic or logic that interacts with external systems. A banking system might have a module that retrieves and parses data from a third-party data provider, and a system to display sports scores might interact with an XML feed that presents real-time scores for basketball or soccer. In Example 7-5, this module encapsulates all of the network activity and XML parsing that is involved in the interaction with Yahoo! Weather. Other modules can depend on this module and simply call out to the `retrieveForecast()` method on `WeatherService`, which takes a zip code as an argument and which returns a `Weather` object.

Example 7-5. simple-weather module POM

```
<project xmlns="http://maven.apache.org/POM/4.0.0"
        xmlns:xsi="http://www.w3.org/2001/XMLSchema-instance"
  xsi:schemaLocation="http://maven.apache.org/POM/4.0.0
                      http://maven.apache.org/maven-v4_0_0.xsd">
  <modelVersion>4.0.0</modelVersion>
  <parent>
    <groupId>org.sonatype.mavenbook.ch07</groupId>
    <artifactId>simple-parent</artifactId>
    <version>1.0</version>
  </parent>
  <artifactId>simple-weather</artifactId>
  <packaging>jar</packaging>

  <name>Simple Weather API</name>

  <dependencies>
    <dependency>
      <groupId>org.sonatype.mavenbook.ch07</groupId>
      <artifactId>simple-model</artifactId>
      <version>1.0</version>
    </dependency>
    <dependency>
      <groupId>log4j</groupId>
      <artifactId>log4j</artifactId>
      <version>1.2.14</version>
    </dependency>
    <dependency>
      <groupId>dom4j</groupId>
      <artifactId>dom4j</artifactId>
      <version>1.6.1</version>
    </dependency>
    <dependency>
      <groupId>jaxen</groupId>
      <artifactId>jaxen</artifactId>
      <version>1.1.1</version>
    </dependency>
    <dependency>
      <groupId>org.apache.commons</groupId>
      <artifactId>commons-io</artifactId>
```

```
      <version>1.3.2</version>
      <scope>test</scope>
    </dependency>
  </dependencies>
</project>
```

The simple-weather POM extends the simple-parent POM, sets the packaging to jar, and then adds the following dependencies:

org.sonatype.mavenbook.ch07:simple-model:1.0

simple-weather parses the Yahoo! Weather RSS feed into a Weather object. It has a direct dependency on simple-model.

log4j:log4j:1.2.14

simple-weather uses the Log4J library to print log messages.

dom4j:dom4j:1.6.1 and jaxen:jaxen:1.1.1

Both of these dependencies are used to parse the XML returned from Yahoo! Weather.

org.apache.commons:commons-io:1.3.2 (scope=test)

This test-scoped dependency is used by the YahooParserTest.

Next is the WeatherService class, shown in Example 7-6. This class is going to look very similar to the WeatherService class from Example 6-3. Although the WeatherService is the same, there are some subtle differences in this chapter's example. This version's retrieveForecast() method returns a Weather object, and the formatting is going to be left to the applications that call WeatherService. The other major change is that the YahooRetriever and YahooParser are both bean properties of the WeatherService bean.

Example 7-6. The WeatherService class

```
package org.sonatype.mavenbook.weather;

import java.io.InputStream;

import org.sonatype.mavenbook.weather.model.Weather;

public class WeatherService {

  private YahooRetriever yahooRetriever;
  private YahooParser yahooParser;

  public WeatherService() {}

  public Weather retrieveForecast(String zip) throws Exception {
    // Retrieve Data
    InputStream dataIn = yahooRetriever.retrieve(zip);

    // Parse DataS
    Weather weather = yahooParser.parse(zip, dataIn);

    return weather;
```

```
    }

    public YahooRetriever getYahooRetriever() {
      return yahooRetriever;
    }

    public void setYahooRetriever(YahooRetriever yahooRetriever) {
      this.yahooRetriever = yahooRetriever;
    }

    public YahooParser getYahooParser() {
      return yahooParser;
    }

    public void setYahooParser(YahooParser yahooParser) {
      this.yahooParser = yahooParser;
    }
}
```

Finally, in this project we have an XML file that is used by the Spring Framework to create something called an `ApplicationContext`. First, some explanation: both of our applications, the web application and the command-line utility, need to interact with the `WeatherService` class, and they both do so by retrieving an instance of this class from a Spring `ApplicationContext` using the name `weatherService`. Our web application uses a Spring MVC controller that is associated with an instance of `WeatherService`, and our command-line utility loads the `WeatherService` from an `ApplicationContext` in a static `main()` function. To encourage reuse, we've included an *applicationContext-weather.xml* file in *src/main/resources*, which is available on the classpath. Modules that depend on the `simple-weather` module can load this application context using the `ClasspathXmlApplicationContext` in the Spring Framework. They can then reference a named instance of the `WeatherService` named `weatherService`. See Example 7-7.

Example 7-7. Spring ApplicationContext for the simple-weather module

```
<?xml version="1.0" encoding="UTF-8"?>

<beans xmlns="http://www.springframework.org/schema/beans"
    xmlns:xsi="http://www.w3.org/2001/XMLSchema-instance"
    xsi:schemaLocation="http://www.springframework.org/schema/beans
            http://www.springframework.org/schema/beans/spring-beans-2.0.xsd
    default-lazy-init="true">

    <bean id="weatherService"
            class="org.sonatype.mavenbook.weather.WeatherService">
      <property name="yahooRetriever" ref="yahooRetriever"/>
      <property name="yahooParser" ref="yahooParser"/>
    </bean>

    <bean id="yahooRetriever"
            class="org.sonatype.mavenbook.weather.YahooRetriever"/>

    <bean id="yahooParser"
```

```
            class="org.sonatype.mavenbook.weather.YahooParser"/>
</beans>
```

This document defines three beans: yahooParser, yahooRetriever, and weatherService. The weatherService bean is an instance of WeatherService, and this XML document populates the yahooParser and yahooRetriever properties with references to the named instances of the corresponding classes. Think of this *application Context-weather.xml* file as defining the architecture of a subsystem in this multimodule project. Projects like simple-webapp and simple-command can reference this context and retrieve an instance of WeatherService that already has relationships to instances of YahooRetriever and YahooParser.

The Simple Persist Module

This module defines two very simple Data Access Objects (DAOs). A DAO is an object that provides an interface for persistence operations. In an application that makes use of an Object-Relational Mapping (ORM) framework such as Hibernate, DAOs are usually defined around objects. In this project, we are defining two DAO objects: WeatherDAO and LocationDAO. The WeatherDAO class allows us to save a Weather object to a database and retrieve a Weather object by id, and to retrieve Weather objects that match a specific Location. The LocationDAO has a method that allows us to retrieve a Location object by zip code. First, let's take a look at the simple-persist POM in Example 7-8.

Example 7-8. simple-persist POM

```xml
<project xmlns="http://maven.apache.org/POM/4.0.0"
         xmlns:xsi="http://www.w3.org/2001/XMLSchema-instance"
  xsi:schemaLocation="http://maven.apache.org/POM/4.0.0
                      http://maven.apache.org/maven-v4_0_0.xsd">
  <modelVersion>4.0.0</modelVersion>
  <parent>
    <groupId>org.sonatype.mavenbook.ch07</groupId>
    <artifactId>simple-parent</artifactId>
    <version>1.0</version>
  </parent>
  <artifactId>simple-persist</artifactId>
  <packaging>jar</packaging>

  <name>Simple Persistence API</name>

  <dependencies>
    <dependency>
      <groupId>org.sonatype.mavenbook.ch07</groupId>
      <artifactId>simple-model</artifactId>
      <version>1.0</version>
    </dependency>
    <dependency>
      <groupId>org.hibernate</groupId>
      <artifactId>hibernate</artifactId>
```

```
      <version>3.2.5.ga</version>
      <exclusions>
        <exclusion>
          <groupId>javax.transaction</groupId>
          <artifactId>jta</artifactId>
        </exclusion>
      </exclusions>
    </dependency>
    <dependency>
      <groupId>org.hibernate</groupId>
      <artifactId>hibernate-annotations</artifactId>
      <version>3.3.0.ga</version>
    </dependency>
    <dependency>
      <groupId>org.hibernate</groupId>
      <artifactId>hibernate-commons-annotations</artifactId>
      <version>3.3.0.ga</version>
    </dependency>
    <dependency>
      <groupId>org.apache.geronimo.specs</groupId>
      <artifactId>geronimo-jta_1.1_spec</artifactId>
      <version>1.1</version>
    </dependency>
    <dependency>
      <groupId>org.springframework</groupId>
      <artifactId>spring</artifactId>
      <version>2.0.7</version>
    </dependency>
  </dependencies>
</project>
```

This POM file references simple-parent as a parent POM, and it defines a few dependencies. The dependencies listed in simple-persist's POM are:

org.sonatype.mavenbook.ch07:simple-model:1.0

> Just like the simple-weather module, this persistence module references the core model objects defined in simple-model.

org.hibernate:hibernate:3.2.5.ga

> We define a dependency on Hibernate version 3.2.5.ga, but notice that we're excluding a dependency of Hibernate. We're doing this because the javax.transaction:javax dependency is not available in the public Maven repository. This dependency happens to be one of those Sun dependencies that has not yet made it into the free central Maven repository. To avoid an annoying message telling us to go download these nonfree dependencies, we simple exclude this dependency from Hibernate and add a dependency on...

org.apache.geronimo.specs:geronimo-jta_1.1_spec:1.1

> Just like the Servlet and JSP APIs, the Apache Geronimo project was nice enough to release a certified version of many of the enterprise APIs under an Apache License. This means that whenever a component tells you that it depends on the

JDBC, JNDI, and JTA APIs (among others), you can look for a corresponding library under the `org.apache.geronimo.specs` groupId.

`org.springframework:spring:2.0.7`

This includes the entire Spring Framework as a dependency.

 It is generally a good practice to depend on only the components of Spring you happen to be using. The Spring Framework project has been nice enough to create focused artifacts such as `spring-hibernate3`.

Why depend on Spring? When it comes to Hibernate integration, Spring allows us to leverage helper classes such as `HibernateDaoSupport`. For an example of what is possible with the help of `HibernateDaoSupport`, take a look at the code for the `WeatherDAO` in Example 7-9.

Example 7-9. simple-persist's WeatherDAO class

```
package org.sonatype.mavenbook.weather.persist;

import java.util.ArrayList;
import java.util.List;

import org.hibernate.Query;
import org.hibernate.Session;
import org.springframework.orm.hibernate3.HibernateCallback;
import org.springframework.orm.hibernate3.support.HibernateDaoSupport;

import org.sonatype.mavenbook.weather.model.Location;
import org.sonatype.mavenbook.weather.model.Weather;

public class WeatherDAO extends HibernateDaoSupport❶ {

    public WeatherDAO() {}

    public void save(Weather weather) {❷
      getHibernateTemplate().save( weather );
    }

    public Weather load(Integer id) {❸
      return (Weather) getHibernateTemplate().load( Weather.class, id);
    }

    @SuppressWarnings("unchecked")
    public List<Weather> recentForLocation( final Location location ) {
      return (List<Weather>) getHibernateTemplate().execute(
        new HibernateCallback() {❹
        public Object doInHibernate(Session session) {
          Query query = getSession().getNamedQuery("Weather.byLocation");
          query.setParameter("location", location);
          return new ArrayList<Weather>( query.list() );
        }
```

```
        });
    }
}
```

That's it. No, really, you are done writing a class that can insert new rows, select by primary key, and find all rows in `Weather` that join to an `id` in the `Location` table. Clearly, we can't stop this book and insert the 500 pages it would take to get you up to speed on the intricacies of Hibernate, but we can do some very quick explanation:

❶ This class extends `HibernateDaoSupport`. What this means is that the class is going to be associated with a Hibernate `SessionFactory`, which it is going to use to create Hibernate `Session` objects. In Hibernate, every operation goes through a `Session` object. A `Session` mediates access to the underlying database and takes care of managing the connection to the JDBC `DataSource`. Extending `HibernateDaoSupport` also means that we can access the `HibernateTemplate` using `getHibernateTemplate()`.

❷ The `save()` method takes an instance of `Weather` and calls the `save()` method on a `HibernateTemplate`. The `HibernateTemplate` simplifies calls to common Hibernate operations and converts any database-specific exceptions to runtime exceptions. Here we call out to `save()`, which inserts a new record into the `Weather` table. Alternatives to `save()` are `update()`, which updates an existing row, or `saveOrUpdate()`, which would either save or update depending on the presence of a nonnull `id` property in Weather.

❸ The `load()` method, once again, is a one-liner that just calls a method on an instance of `HibernateTemplate`. `load()` on `HibernateTemplate` takes a `Class` object and a `Serializable` object. In this case, the `Serializable` corresponds to the `id` value of the `Weather` object to load.

❹ This last method, `recentForLocation()`, calls out to a `NamedQuery` defined in the `Weather` model object. If you can think back that far, the `Weather` model object defined a named query `Weather.byLocation` with a query of `"from Weather w where w.location = :location"`. We're loading this `NamedQuery` using a reference to a Hibernate `Session` object inside a `HibernateCallback` that is executed by the `exe cute()` method on `HibernateTemplate`. You can see in this method that we're populating the named parameter `location` with the parameter passed into the `recentForLocation()` method.

Now is a good time for some clarification. `HibernateDaoSupport` and `HibernateTem plate` are classes from the Spring Framework. They were created by the Spring Framework to make writing Hibernate DAO objects painless. To support this DAO, we'll need to do some configuration in the `simple-persist` Spring `ApplicationContext` definition. The XML document shown in Example 7-10 is stored in *src/main/resources* in a file named *applicationContext-persist.xml*.

Example 7-10. Spring ApplicationContext for simple-persist

```xml
<beans xmlns="http://www.springframework.org/schema/beans"
    xmlns:xsi="http://www.w3.org/2001/XMLSchema-instance"
    xsi:schemaLocation="http://www.springframework.org/schema/beans
            http://www.springframework.org/schema/beans/spring-beans-2.0.xsd"
    default-lazy-init="true">

    <bean id="sessionFactory"
class="org.springframework.orm.hibernate3.annotation.AnnotationSessionFactoryBean">
        <property name="annotatedClasses">
            <list>
                <value>org.sonatype.mavenbook.weather.model.Atmosphere</value>
                <value>org.sonatype.mavenbook.weather.model.Condition</value>
                <value>org.sonatype.mavenbook.weather.model.Location</value>
                <value>org.sonatype.mavenbook.weather.model.Weather</value>
                <value>org.sonatype.mavenbook.weather.model.Wind</value>
            </list>
        </property>
        <property name="hibernateProperties">
            <props>
                <prop key="hibernate.show_sql">false</prop>
                <prop key="hibernate.format_sql">true</prop>
                <prop key="hibernate.transaction.factory_class">
                  org.hibernate.transaction.JDBCTransactionFactory
                </prop>
                <prop key="hibernate.dialect">
                  org.hibernate.dialect.HSQLDialect
                </prop>
                <prop key="hibernate.connection.pool_size">0</prop>
                <prop key="hibernate.connection.driver_class">
                  org.hsqldb.jdbcDriver
                </prop>
                <prop key="hibernate.connection.url">
                  jdbc:hsqldb:data/weather;shutdown=true
                </prop>
                <prop key="hibernate.connection.username">sa</prop>
                <prop key="hibernate.connection.password"></prop>
                <prop key="hibernate.connection.autocommit">true</prop>
                <prop key="hibernate.jdbc.batch_size">0</prop>
            </props>
        </property>
    </bean>

    <bean id="locationDAO"
            class="org.sonatype.mavenbook.weather.persist.LocationDAO">
        <property name="sessionFactory" ref="sessionFactory"/>
    </bean>

    <bean id="weatherDAO"
            class="org.sonatype.mavenbook.weather.persist.WeatherDAO">
        <property name="sessionFactory" ref="sessionFactory"/>
    </bean>
</beans>
```

In this application context, we're accomplishing a few things. The `sessionFactory` bean is the bean from which the DAOs retrieve Hibernate `Session` objects. This bean is an instance of `AnnotationSessionFactoryBean` and is supplied with a list of `annotatedClasses`. Note that the list of annotated classes is the list of classes defined in our `simple-model` module. Next, the `sessionFactory` is configured with a set of Hibernate configuration properties (`hibernateProperties`). In this example, our Hibernate properties define a number of settings:

`hibernate.dialect`

> This setting controls how SQL is to be generated for our database. Since we are using the HSQLDB database, our database dialect is set to `org.hibernate.dialect.HSQLDialect`. Hibernate has dialects for all major databases such as Oracle, MySQL, Postgres, and SQL Server.

`hibernate.connection.*`

> In this example, we're configuring the JDBC connection properties from the Spring configuration. Our applications are configured to run against a HSQLDB in the *./data/weather* directory. In a real enterprise application, it is more likely you would use something like JNDI to externalize database configuration from your application's code.

Lastly, in this bean definition file, both of the `simple-persist` DAO objects are created and given a reference to the `sessionFactory` bean just defined. Just like the Spring application context in `simple-weather`, this *applicationContext-persist.xml* file defines the architecture of a submodule in a larger enterprise design. If you were working with a larger collection of persistence classes, you might find it useful to capture them in an application context that is separate from your application.

There's one last piece of the puzzle in `simple-persist`. Later in this chapter, we're going to see how we can use the Maven Hibernate3 plugin to generate our database schema from the annotated model objects. For this to work properly, the Maven Hibernate3 plugin needs to read the JDBC connection configuration parameters, the list of annotated classes, and other Hibernate configuration from a file named *hibernate.cfg.xml* in *src/main/resources*. The purpose of this file (which duplicates some of the configuration in *applicationContext-persist.xml*) is to allow us to leverage the Maven Hibernate3 plugin to generate Data Definition Language (DDL) from nothing more than our annotations. See Example 7-11.

Example 7-11. simple-persist hibernate.cfg.xml

```
<!DOCTYPE hibernate-configuration PUBLIC
        "-//Hibernate/Hibernate Configuration DTD 3.0//EN"
        "http://hibernate.sourceforge.net/hibernate-configuration-3.0.dtd">

<hibernate-configuration>
  <session-factory>

    <!-- SQL dialect -->
```

```
<property name="dialect">org.hibernate.dialect.HSQLDialect</property>

<!-- Database connection settings -->
<property name="connection.driver_class">org.hsqldb.jdbcDriver</property>
<property name="connection.url">jdbc:hsqldb:data/weather</property>
<property name="connection.username">sa</property>
<property name="connection.password"></property>
<property name="connection.shutdown">true</property>

<!-- JDBC connection pool (use the built-in one) -->
<property name="connection.pool_size">1</property>

<!-- Enable Hibernate's automatic session context management -->
<property name="current_session_context_class">thread</property>

<!-- Disable the second-level cache  -->
<property name="cache.provider_class">org.hibernate.cache.NoCacheProvider</property>

<!-- Echo all executed SQL to stdout -->
<property name="show_sql">true</property>

<!-- disable batching so HSQLDB will propagate errors correctly. -->
<property name="jdbc.batch_size">0</property>

<!-- List all the mapping documents we're using -->
<mapping class="org.sonatype.mavenbook.weather.model.Atmosphere"/>
<mapping class="org.sonatype.mavenbook.weather.model.Condition"/>
<mapping class="org.sonatype.mavenbook.weather.model.Location"/>
<mapping class="org.sonatype.mavenbook.weather.model.Weather"/>
<mapping class="org.sonatype.mavenbook.weather.model.Wind"/>

    </session-factory>
</hibernate-configuration>
```

The contents of Examples 7-10 and 7-11 are redundant. While the Spring Application Context XML is going to be used by the web application and the command-line application, the *hibernate.cfg.xml* exists only to support the Maven Hibernate3 plugin. Later in this chapter, we'll see how to use this *hibernate.cfg.xml* and the Maven Hibernate3 plugin to generate a database schema based on the annotated object model defined in simple-model. This *hibernate.cfg.xml* file is the file that will configure the JDBC connection properties and enumerate the list of annotated model classes for the Maven Hibernate3 plugin.

The Simple Web Application Module

The web application is defined in a simple-webapp project. This simple web application project is going to define two Spring MVC Controllers: WeatherController and HistoryController. Both of these controllers are going to reference components defined in simple-weather and simple-persist. The Spring container is configured in this application's *web.xml*, which references the *applicationContext-weather.xml* file in

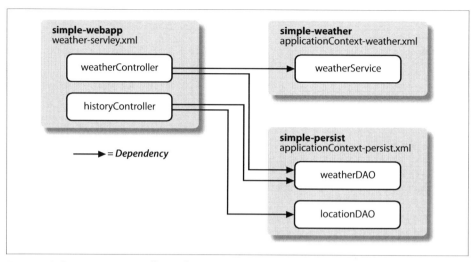

Figure 7-3. Spring MVC controllers referencing components in simple-weather and simple-persist

simple-weather and the *applicationContext-persist.xml* file in simple-persist. The component architecture of this simple web application is shown in Figure 7-3.

The POM for simple-webapp is shown in Example 7-12.

Example 7-12. POM for simple-webapp

```
<project xmlns="http://maven.apache.org/POM/4.0.0"
        xmlns:xsi="http://www.w3.org/2001/XMLSchema-instance"
  xsi:schemaLocation="http://maven.apache.org/POM/4.0.0
                    http://maven.apache.org/maven-v4_0_0.xsd">
  <modelVersion>4.0.0</modelVersion>
  <parent>
    <groupId>org.sonatype.mavenbook.ch07</groupId>
    <artifactId>simple-parent</artifactId>
    <version>1.0</version>
  </parent>

  <artifactId>simple-webapp</artifactId>
  <packaging>war</packaging>
  <name>Simple Web Application</name>
  <dependencies>
    <dependency> ❶
      <groupId>org.apache.geronimo.specs</groupId>
      <artifactId>geronimo-servlet_2.4_spec</artifactId>
      <version>1.1.1</version>
    </dependency>
    <dependency>
      <groupId>org.sonatype.mavenbook.ch07</groupId>
      <artifactId>simple-weather</artifactId>
      <version>1.0</version>
    </dependency>
    <dependency>
      <groupId>org.sonatype.mavenbook.ch07</groupId>
```

```
      <artifactId>simple-persist</artifactId>
      <version>1.0</version>
    </dependency>
    <dependency>
      <groupId>org.springframework</groupId>
      <artifactId>spring</artifactId>
      <version>2.0.7</version>
    </dependency>
    <dependency>
      <groupId>org.apache.velocity</groupId>
      <artifactId>velocity</artifactId>
      <version>1.5</version>
    </dependency>
  </dependencies>
  <build>
    <finalName>simple-webapp</finalName>
    <plugins>
      <plugin> ❷
        <groupId>org.mortbay.jetty</groupId>
        <artifactId>maven-jetty-plugin</artifactId>
        <dependencies> ❸
          <dependency>
            <groupId>hsqldb</groupId>
            <artifactId>hsqldb</artifactId>
            <version>1.8.0.7</version>
          </dependency> ❹
        </dependencies>
      </plugin>
      <plugin>
        <groupId>org.codehaus.mojo</groupId> ❺
        <artifactId>hibernate3-maven-plugin</artifactId>
        <version>2.0</version>
        <configuration>
          <components>
            <component>
              <name>hbm2ddl</name>
              <implementation>annotationconfiguration</implementation> ❻
            </component>
          </components>
        </configuration>
        <dependencies>
          <dependency>
            <groupId>hsqldb</groupId>
            <artifactId>hsqldb</artifactId>
            <version>1.8.0.7</version>
          </dependency>
        </dependencies>
      </plugin>
    </plugins>
  </build>
</project>
```

As this book progresses and the examples become more and more substantial, you'll notice that the *pom.xml* begins to take on some weight. In this POM, we're configuring four dependencies and two plugins. Let's go through this POM in detail and dwell on some of the important configuration points:

❶ This `simple-webapp` project defines four dependencies: the Servlet 2.4 specification implementation from Apache Geronimo, the simple-weather service library, the simple-persist persistence library, and the entire Spring Framework 2.0.7.

❷ In our build configuration, we're going to be configuring the Maven Hibernate3 plugin to hit an embedded HSQLDB instance. For the Maven Hibernate 3 plugin to successfully connect to this database using JDBC, the plugin will need to reference the HSQLDB JDBC driver on the classpath. To make a dependency available for a plugin, we add a reference to the dependency as an extension. You can think about extensions as providing you with the ability to add something to the classpath for plugin execution. In this case, we're referencing `hsqldb:hsqldb:1.8.0.7`.

❸ The Maven Jetty plugin couldn't be easier to add to this project; we simply add a `plugin` element that references the appropriate `groupId` and `artifactId`. The fact that this plugin is so trivial to configure means that the plugin developers did a good job of providing adequate defaults that don't need to be overridden in most cases. If you did need to override the configuration of the Jetty plugin, you would do so by providing a `configuration` element.

❹ In our build configuration, we're going to be configuring the Maven Hibernate3 plugin to hit an embedded HSQLDB instance. For the Maven Hibernate3 plugin to successfully connect to this database using JDBC, the plugin will need reference the HSQLDB JDBC driver on the classpath. To make a dependency available for a plugin, we add a `dependency` declaration right inside a `plugin` declaration. In this case, we're referencing `hsqldb:hsqldb:1.8.0.7`. The Hibernate plugin also needs the JDBC driver to create the database, so we have also added this dependency to its configuration.

❺ The Maven Hibernate plugin is when this POM starts to get interesting. In the next section, we're going to run the `hbm2ddl` goal to generate a HSQLDB database. In this *pom.xml*, we're including a reference to version 2.0 of the `hibernate3-maven-plugin` hosted by the Codehaus Mojo plugin.

❻ The Maven Hibernate3 plugin has different ways to obtain Hibernate mapping information that are appropriate for different usage scenarios of the Hibernate3 plugin. If you were using Hibernate Mapping XML (*.hbm.xml*) files, and you wanted to generate model classes using the `hbm2java` goal, you would set your implementation to configuration. If you were using the Hibernate3 plugin to reverse engineer a database to produce *.hbm.xml* files and model classes from an existing database, you would use an implementation of `jdbcconfiguration`. In this case, we're simply using an existing annotated object model to generate a database. In other words, we have our Hibernate mapping, but we don't yet have a database. In this usage scenario, the appropriate implementation value is `annotationconfiguration`. The Maven

Hibernate3 plugin is discussed in more detail in the later section "Running the Web Application."

 A common mistake is to use the extensions configuration to add dependencies required by a plugin. This is strongly discouraged, as the extensions can cause classpath pollution across your project, among other nasty side effects. Additionally, the extensions behavior is being reworked in 2.1, so you'll eventually need to change it anyway. The only normal use for extensions is to define new wagon implementations.

Next, we turn our attention to the two Spring MVC controllers that will handle all of the requests. Both of these controllers reference the beans defined in simple-weather and simple-persist. See Example 7-13.

Example 7-13. simple-webapp WeatherController

```
package org.sonatype.mavenbook.web;

import org.sonatype.mavenbook.weather.model.Weather;
import org.sonatype.mavenbook.weather.persist.WeatherDAO;
import org.sonatype.mavenbook.weather.WeatherService;
import javax.servlet.http.*;
import org.springframework.web.servlet.ModelAndView;
import org.springframework.web.servlet.mvc.Controller;

public class WeatherController implements Controller {

  private WeatherService weatherService;
  private WeatherDAO weatherDAO;

  public ModelAndView handleRequest(HttpServletRequest request,
      HttpServletResponse response) throws Exception {

    String zip = request.getParameter("zip");
    Weather weather = weatherService.retrieveForecast(zip);
    weatherDAO.save(weather);
    return new ModelAndView("weather", "weather", weather);
  }

  public WeatherService getWeatherService() {
    return weatherService;
  }

  public void setWeatherService(WeatherService weatherService) {
    this.weatherService = weatherService;
  }

  public WeatherDAO getWeatherDAO() {
    return weatherDAO;
  }

  public void setWeatherDAO(WeatherDAO weatherDAO) {
```

```
    this.weatherDAO = weatherDAO;
  }
}
```

`WeatherController` implements the Spring MVC Controller interface that mandates the presence of a `handleRequest()` method with the signature shown in the example. If you look at the meat of this method, you'll see that it invokes the `retrieveForecast()` method on the `weatherService` instance variable. Unlike the previous chapter, which had a Servlet that instantiated the `WeatherService` class, the `WeatherController` is a bean with a `weatherService` property. The Spring IoC container is responsible for wiring the controller to the `weatherService` component. Also notice that we're not using the `WeatherFormatter` in this Spring controller implementation; instead, we're passing the `Weather` object returned by `retrieveForecast()` to the constructor of `ModelAndView`. This `ModelAndView` class is going to be used to render a Velocity template, and this template will have references to a `${weather}` variable. The *weather.vm* template is stored in *src/main/webapp/WEB-INF/vm* and is shown in Example 7-14.

In the `WeatherController`, before we render the output of the forecast, we pass the `Weather` object returned by the `WeatherService` to the `save()` method on `WeatherDAO`. Here we are saving this `Weather` object—using Hibernate—to an HSQLDB database. Later, in `HistoryController`, we will see how we can retrieve a history of weather forecasts that were saved by the `WeatherController`.

Example 7-14. weather.vm template rendered by WeatherController

```
<b>Current Weather Conditions for:
  ${weather.location.city}, ${weather.location.region},
  ${weather.location.country}</b><br/>

<ul>
  <li>Temperature: ${weather.condition.temp}</li>
  <li>Condition: ${weather.condition.text}</li>
  <li>Humidity: ${weather.atmosphere.humidity}</li>
  <li>Wind Chill: ${weather.wind.chill}</li>
  <li>Date: ${weather.date}</li>
</ul>
```

The syntax for this Velocity template is straightforward; variables are referenced using `${}` notation. The expression between the curly braces references a property, or a property of a property on the `weather` variable that was passed to this template by the `WeatherController`.

The `HistoryController` is used to retrieve recent forecasts that have been requested by the `WeatherController`. Whenever we retrieve a forecast from the `WeatherController`, that controller saves the `Weather` object to the database via the `WeatherDAO`. `WeatherDAO` then uses Hibernate to dissect the `Weather` object into a series of rows in a set of related database tables. The `HistoryController` is shown in Example 7-15.

Example 7-15. simple-web HistoryController

```java
package org.sonatype.mavenbook.web;

import java.util.*;
import javax.servlet.http.*;
import org.springframework.web.servlet.ModelAndView;
import org.springframework.web.servlet.mvc.Controller;
import org.sonatype.mavenbook.weather.model.*;
import org.sonatype.mavenbook.weather.persist.*;

public class HistoryController implements Controller {

  private LocationDAO locationDAO;
  private WeatherDAO weatherDAO;

  public ModelAndView handleRequest(HttpServletRequest request,
      HttpServletResponse response) throws Exception {
    String zip = request.getParameter("zip");
    Location location = locationDAO.findByZip(zip);
    List<Weather> weathers = weatherDAO.recentForLocation( location );

    Map<String,Object> model = new HashMap<String,Object>();
    model.put( "location", location );
    model.put( "weathers", weathers );

    return new ModelAndView("history", model);
  }

  public WeatherDAO getWeatherDAO() {
    return weatherDAO;
  }

  public void setWeatherDAO(WeatherDAO weatherDAO) {
    this.weatherDAO = weatherDAO;
  }

  public LocationDAO getLocationDAO() {
    return locationDAO;
  }

  public void setLocationDAO(LocationDAO locationDAO) {
    this.locationDAO = locationDAO;
  }
}
```

The HistoryController is wired to two DAO objects defined in simple-persist. The DAOs are bean properties of the HistoryController: WeatherDAO and LocationDAO. The goal of the HistoryController is to retrieve a List of Weather objects that correspond to the zip parameter. When the WeatherDAO saves the Weather object to the database, it doesn't just store the zip code; it stores a Location object that is related to the Weather object in the simple-model. To retrieve a List of Weather objects, the

HistoryController first retrieves the Location object that corresponds to the zip parameter. It does this by invoking the findByZip() method on LocationDAO.

Once the Location object has been retrieved, the HistoryController will then attempt to retrieve recent Weather objects that match the given Location. Once the List<Weather> has been retrieved, a HashMap is created to hold two variables for the *history.vm* Velocity template shown in Example 7-16.

Example 7-16. history.vm rendered by the HistoryController

```
<b>
Weather History for: ${location.city}, ${location.region}, ${location.country}
</b>
<br/>

#foreach( $weather in $weathers )
  <ul>
    <li>Temperature: $weather.condition.temp</li>
    <li>Condition: $weather.condition.text</li>
    <li>Humidity: $weather.atmosphere.humidity</li>
    <li>Wind Chill: $weather.wind.chill</li>
    <li>Date: $weather.date</li>
  </ul>
#end
```

The *history.vm* template in *src/main/webapp/WEB-INF/vm* references the location variable to print out information about the location of the forecasts retrieved from the WeatherDAO. This template then uses a Velocity control structure, #foreach, to loop through each element in the weathers variable. Each element in weathers is assigned to a variable named weather, and the template between #foreach and #end is rendered for each forecast.

You've seen these Controller implementations, and you've seen that they reference other beans defined in simple-weather and simple-persist. They respond to HTTP requests, and they yield control to some mysterious templating system that knows how to render Velocity templates. All of this magic is configured in a Spring application context in *src/main/webapp/WEB-INF/weather-servlet.xml*. This XML configures the controllers and references other Spring-managed beans; it is loaded by a ServletContextListener, which is also configured to load the *applicationContext-weather.xml* and *applicationContext-persist.xml* from the classpath. Let's take a closer look at the *weather-servlet.xml* shown in Example 7-17.

Example 7-17. Spring controller configuration weather-servlet.xml

```
<beans>
    <bean id="weatherController" ❶
        class="org.sonatype.mavenbook.web.WeatherController">
      <property name="weatherService" ref="weatherService"/>
      <property name="weatherDAO" ref="weatherDAO"/>
    </bean>
```

```
    <bean id="historyController"
          class="org.sonatype.mavenbook.web.HistoryController">
      <property name="weatherDAO" ref="weatherDAO"/>
      <property name="locationDAO" ref="locationDAO"/>
    </bean>

    <!-- you can have more than one handler defined -->
    <bean id="urlMapping"
          class="org.springframework.web.servlet.handler.SimpleUrlHandlerMapping">
      <property name="urlMap">
          <map>
              <entry key="/weather.x"> ❷
                      <ref bean="weatherController" />
              </entry>
              <entry key="/history.x">
                      <ref bean="historyController" />
              </entry>
          </map>
      </property>
    </bean>


    <bean id="velocityConfig" ❸
          class="org.springframework.web.servlet.view.velocity.VelocityConfigurer">
      <property name="resourceLoaderPath" value="/WEB-INF/vm/"/>
    </bean>

    <bean id="viewResolver" ❹
          class="org.springframework.web.servlet.view.velocity.VelocityViewResolver">
      <property name="cache" value="true"/>
      <property name="prefix" value=""/>
      <property name="suffix" value=".vm"/>
      <property name="exposeSpringMacroHelpers" value="true"/>
    </bean>
</beans>
```

❶ The *weather-servlet.xml* defines the two controllers as Spring-managed beans.
weatherController has two properties that are references to weatherService and
weatherDAO. historyController references the beans weatherDAO and locationDAO.
When this ApplicationContext is created, it is created in an environment that has
access to the ApplicationContexts defined in both simple-persist and simple-
weather. In Example 7-18, you will see how Spring is configured to merge components from multiple Spring configuration files.

❷ The urlMapping bean defines the URL patterns that invoke the WeatherController
and the HistoryController. In this example, we are using the
SimpleUrlHandlerMapping and mapping */weather.x* to WeatherController
and */history.x* to HistoryController.

❸ Since we are using the Velocity templating engine, we will need to pass in some
configuration options. In the velocityConfig bean, we are telling Velocity to look
for all templates in the */WEB-INF/vm* directory.

❹ Last, the `viewResolver` is configured with the class `VelocityViewResolver`. There are a number of `ViewResolver` implementations in Spring from a standard `View Resolver` to render JSP or JSTL (JavaServer Pages Standard Tag Library) pages to a resolver that can render FreeMarker templates. In this example, we're configuring the Velocity templating engine and setting the default prefix and suffix that will be automatically appended to the names of the template passed to `ModelAndView`.

Finally, the `simple-webapp` project was a *web.xml* that provides the basic configuration for the web application. The *web.xml* file is shown in Example 7-18.

Example 7-18. web.xml for simple-webapp

```
<web-app id="simple-webapp" version="2.4"
    xmlns="http://java.sun.com/xml/ns/j2ee"
    xmlns:xsi="http://www.w3.org/2001/XMLSchema-instance"
    xsi:schemaLocation="http://java.sun.com/xml/ns/j2ee
                        http://java.sun.com/xml/ns/j2ee/web-app_2_4.xsd">
  <display-name>Simple Web Application</display-name>

  <context-param> ❶
    <param-name>contextConfigLocation</param-name>
    <param-value>
      classpath:applicationContext-weather.xml
      classpath:applicationContext-persist.xml
    </param-value>
  </context-param>

  <context-param> ❷
    <param-name>log4jConfigLocation</param-name>
    <param-value>/WEB-INF/log4j.properties</param-value>
  </context-param>

  <listener> ❸
    <listener-class>
      org.springframework.web.util.Log4jConfigListener
    </listener-class>
  </listener>

  <listener>
    <listener-class> ❹
      org.springframework.web.context.ContextLoaderListener
    </listener-class>
  </listener>

  <servlet> ❺
    <servlet-name>weather</servlet-name>
    <servlet-class>
      org.springframework.web.servlet.DispatcherServlet
    </servlet-class>
    <load-on-startup>1</load-on-startup>
  </servlet>
```

```
  <servlet-mapping> ❻
    <servlet-name>weather</servlet-name>
    <url-pattern>*.x</url-pattern>
  </servlet-mapping>
</web-app>
```

❶ Here's a bit of magic that allows us to reuse *applicationContext-weather.xml* and *applicationContext-persist.xml* in this project. The `contextConfigLocation` is used by the `ContextLoaderListener` to create an `ApplicationContext`. When the weather servlet is created, the *weather-servlet.xml* from Example 7-17 is going to be evaluated with the `ApplicationContext` created from this `contextConfigLocation`. In this way, you can define a set of beans in another project and you can reference these beans via the classpath. Since the `simple-persist` and `simple-weather` JARs are going to be in *WEB-INF/lib*, all we do is use the `classpath:` prefix to reference these files. (Another option would have been to copy these files to */WEB-INF* and reference them with something like */WEB-INF/applicationContext-persist.xml*.)

❷ The `log4jConfigLocation` is used to tell the `Log4JConfigListener` where to look for Log4J logging configuration. In this example, we tell Log4J to look in */WEB-INF/ log4j.properties*.

❸ This makes sure that the Log4J system is configured when the web application starts. It is important to put this `Log4JConfigListener` before the `ContextLoaderListener`; otherwise, you may miss important logging messages that point to a problem preventing application startup. If you have a particularly large set of beans managed by Spring and one of them happens to blow up on application startup, your application will fail. If you have logging initialized before Spring starts, you might have a chance to catch a warning or an error. If you don't have logging initialized before Spring starts up, you'll have no idea why your application refuses to start.

❹ The `ContextLoaderListener` is essentially the Spring container. When the application starts, this listener will build an `ApplicationContext` from the `contextConfigLocation` parameter.

❺ We define a Spring MVC `DispatcherServlet` with a name of `weather`. This will cause Spring to look for a Spring configuration file in */WEB-INF/weather-servlet.xml*. You can have as many `DispatcherServlet`s as you need. A `DispatcherServlet` can contain one or more Spring MVC `Controller` implementations.

❻ All requests ending in *.x* will be routed to the `weather` servlet. Note that the *.x* extension has no particular meaning; it is an arbitrary choice and you can use whatever URL pattern you like.

Running the Web Application

To run the web application, you'll first need to build the database using the Hibernate3 plugin. To do this, run the following from the `simple-webapp` project directory:

```
$ mvn hibernate3:hbm2ddl
[INFO] Scanning for projects...
[INFO] Searching repository for plugin with prefix: 'hibernate3'.
[INFO] org.codehaus.mojo: checking for updates from central
[INFO] ------------------------------------------------------------
[INFO] Building Chapter 7 Simple Web Application
[INFO]    task-segment: [hibernate3:hbm2ddl]
[INFO] ------------------------------------------------------------
[INFO] Preparing hibernate3:hbm2ddl

...

10:24:56,151  INFO org.hibernate.tool.hbm2ddl.SchemaExport - schema\
          export complete
[INFO] ------------------------------------------------------------
[INFO] BUILD SUCCESSFUL
[INFO] ------------------------------------------------------------
```

Once you've done this, there should be a *${basedir}/data* directory that will contain the HSQLDB database. You can then start the web application with:

```
$ mvn jetty:run
[INFO] Scanning for projects...
[INFO] Searching repository for plugin with prefix: 'jetty'.
[INFO] ------------------------------------------------------------
[INFO] Building Chapter 7 Simple Web Application
[INFO]    task-segment: [jetty:run]
[INFO] ------------------------------------------------------------
[INFO] Preparing jetty:run

...

[INFO] [jetty:run]
[INFO] Configuring Jetty for project: Chapter 7 Simple Web Application
...
[INFO] Context path = /simple-webapp
[INFO] Tmp directory =  determined at runtime
[INFO] Web defaults = org/mortbay/jetty/webapp/webdefault.xml
[INFO] Web overrides =  none
[INFO] Starting jetty 6.1.7 ...
2008-03-25 10:28:03.639::INFO:  jetty-6.1.7
...
2147 INFO  DispatcherServlet  - FrameworkServlet 'weather':
          initialization completed in 1654 ms
2008-03-25 10:28:06.341::INFO:
          Started SelectChannelConnector@0.0.0.0:8080
[INFO] Started Jetty Server
```

Once Jetty is started, you can load *http://localhost:8080/simple-webapp/weather.x?zip =60202*, and you should see the weather for Evanston, Illinois, in your web browser. Change the zip code and you should be able to get your own weather report:

```
Current Weather Conditions for: Evanston, IL, US
```

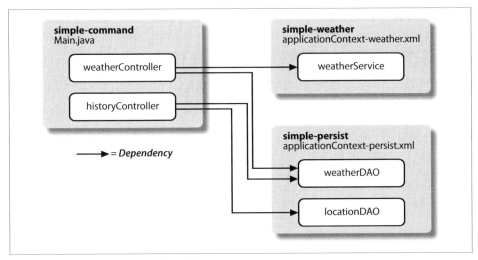

Figure 7-4. The simple-command module

```
* Temperature: 42
* Condition: Partly Cloudy
* Humidity: 55
* Wind Chill: 34
* Date: Tue Mar 25 10:29:45 CDT 2008
```

The simple-command Module

The `simple-command` project is a command-line version of the `simple-webapp`. It is a utility that relies on the same dependencies: `simple-persist` and `simple-weather`. Instead of interacting with this application via a web browser, you would run the `simple-command` utility from the command line. See Figure 7-4 and Example 7-19.

Example 7-19. POM for simple-command

```
<project xmlns="http://maven.apache.org/POM/4.0.0"
        xmlns:xsi="http://www.w3.org/2001/XMLSchema-instance"
  xsi:schemaLocation="http://maven.apache.org/POM/4.0.0
                    http://maven.apache.org/maven-v4_0_0.xsd">
  <modelVersion>4.0.0</modelVersion>
  <parent>
    <groupId>org.sonatype.mavenbook.ch07</groupId>
    <artifactId>simple-parent</artifactId>
    <version>1.0</version>
  </parent>

  <artifactId>simple-command</artifactId>
  <packaging>jar</packaging>
  <name>Simple Command Line Tool</name>

  <build>
```

```xml
      <finalName>${project.artifactId}</finalName>
      <plugins>
        <plugin>
          <groupId>org.apache.maven.plugins</groupId>
          <artifactId>maven-compiler-plugin</artifactId>
          <configuration>
            <source>1.5</source>
            <target>1.5</target>
          </configuration>
        </plugin>
        <plugin>
          <groupId>org.apache.maven.plugins</groupId>
          <artifactId>maven-surefire-plugin</artifactId>
          <configuration>
            <testFailureIgnore>true</testFailureIgnore>
          </configuration>
        </plugin>
        <plugin>
          <artifactId>maven-assembly-plugin</artifactId>
          <configuration>
            <descriptorRefs>
              <descriptorRef>jar-with-dependencies</descriptorRef>
            </descriptorRefs>
          </configuration>
        </plugin>
        <plugin>
          <groupId>org.codehaus.mojo</groupId>
          <artifactId>hibernate3-maven-plugin</artifactId>
          <version>2.1</version>
          <configuration>
            <components>
              <component>
                <name>hbm2ddl</name>
                <implementation>annotationconfiguration</implementation>
              </component>
            </components>
          </configuration>
          <dependencies>
            <dependency>
              <groupId>hsqldb</groupId>
              <artifactId>hsqldb</artifactId>
              <version>1.8.0.7</version>
            </dependency>
          </dependencies>
        </plugin>
      </plugins>
  </build>

  <dependencies>
    <dependency>
      <groupId>org.sonatype.mavenbook.ch07</groupId>
      <artifactId>simple-weather</artifactId>
      <version>1.0</version>
    </dependency>
    <dependency>
```

```
      <groupId>org.sonatype.mavenbook.ch07</groupId>
      <artifactId>simple-persist</artifactId>
      <version>1.0</version>
    </dependency>
    <dependency>
      <groupId>org.springframework</groupId>
      <artifactId>spring</artifactId>
      <version>2.0.7</version>
    </dependency>
    <dependency>
      <groupId>hsqldb</groupId>
      <artifactId>hsqldb</artifactId>
      <version>1.8.0.7</version>
    </dependency>
  </dependencies>
</project>
```

This POM creates a JAR file that will contain the org.sonatype.maven
book.weather.Main class shown in Example 7-20. In this POM, we configure the Maven
Assembly plugin to use a built-in assembly descriptor named jar-with-dependencies,
which creates a single JAR file containing all the bytecode a project needs to execute,
including the bytecode from the project you are building and all the dependency
bytecode.

Example 7-20. The Main class for simple-command

```java
package org.sonatype.mavenbook.weather;

import java.util.List;

import org.apache.log4j.PropertyConfigurator;
import org.springframework.context.ApplicationContext;
import org.springframework.context.support.ClassPathXmlApplicationContext;

import org.sonatype.mavenbook.weather.model.Location;
import org.sonatype.mavenbook.weather.model.Weather;
import org.sonatype.mavenbook.weather.persist.LocationDAO;
import org.sonatype.mavenbook.weather.persist.WeatherDAO;

public class Main {

  private WeatherService weatherService;
  private WeatherDAO weatherDAO;
  private LocationDAO locationDAO;

  public static void main(String[] args) throws Exception {
    // Configure Log4J
    PropertyConfigurator.configure(Main.class.getClassLoader().getResource(
        "log4j.properties"));

    // Read the Zip Code from the Command-line (if none supplied, use 60202)
    String zipcode = "60202";
    try {
      zipcode = args[0];
```

```
    } catch (Exception e) {
    }

    // Read the Operation from the Command-line (if none supplied use weather)
    String operation = "weather";
    try {
      operation = args[1];
    } catch (Exception e) {
    }

    // Start the program
    Main main = new Main(zipcode);

    ApplicationContext context =
      new ClassPathXmlApplicationContext(
        new String[] { "classpath:applicationContext-weather.xml",
                       "classpath:applicationContext-persist.xml" });
    main.weatherService = (WeatherService) context.getBean("weatherService");
    main.locationDAO = (LocationDAO) context.getBean("locationDAO");
    main.weatherDAO = (WeatherDAO) context.getBean("weatherDAO");
    if( operation.equals("weather")) {
      main.getWeather();
    } else {
      main.getHistory();
    }
  }

  private String zip;

  public Main(String zip) {
    this.zip = zip;
  }

  public void getWeather() throws Exception {
    Weather weather = weatherService.retrieveForecast(zip);
    weatherDAO.save( weather );
    System.out.print(new WeatherFormatter().formatWeather(weather));
  }

  public void getHistory() throws Exception {
    Location location = locationDAO.findByZip(zip);
    List<Weather> weathers = weatherDAO.recentForLocation(location);
    System.out.print(new WeatherFormatter().formatHistory(location, weathers));
  }
}
```

The Main class has a reference to WeatherDAO, LocationDAO, and WeatherService. The static main() method in this class:

- Reads the zip code from the first command-line argument.

- Reads the operation from the second command-line argument. If the operation is "weather", the latest weather will be retrieved from the web service. If the operation is "history", the program will fetch historical weather records from the local database.

- Loads a Spring `ApplicationContext` using two XML files loaded from `simple-persist` and `simple-weather`.

- Creates an instance of `Main`.

- Populates the `weatherService`, `weatherDAO`, and `locationDAO` with beans from the Spring `ApplicationContext`.

- Runs the appropriate method `getWeather()` or `getHistory()`, depending on the specified operation.

In the web application, we use Spring `VelocityViewResolver` to render a Velocity template. In the standalone implementation, we need to write a simple class that renders our weather data with a Velocity template. Example 7-21 is a listing of the `WeatherFormatter`, a class with two methods that render the weather report and the weather history.

Example 7-21. WeatherFormatter renders weather data using a Velocity template

```
package org.sonatype.mavenbook.weather;

import java.io.InputStreamReader;
import java.io.Reader;
import java.io.StringWriter;
import java.util.List;

import org.apache.log4j.Logger;
import org.apache.velocity.VelocityContext;
import org.apache.velocity.app.Velocity;

import org.sonatype.mavenbook.weather.model.Location;
import org.sonatype.mavenbook.weather.model.Weather;

public class WeatherFormatter {

  private static Logger log = Logger.getLogger(WeatherFormatter.class);

  public String formatWeather( Weather weather ) throws Exception {
    log.info( "Formatting Weather Data" );
    Reader reader =
      new InputStreamReader( getClass().getClassLoader().
                             getResourceAsStream("weather.vm"));
    VelocityContext context = new VelocityContext();
    context.put("weather", weather );
    StringWriter writer = new StringWriter();
    Velocity.evaluate(context, writer, "", reader);
    return writer.toString();
  }

  public String formatHistory( Location location, List<Weather> weathers )
        throws Exception {
    log.info( "Formatting History Data" );
    Reader reader =
      new InputStreamReader( getClass().getClassLoader().
                             getResourceAsStream("history.vm"));
```

```
    VelocityContext context = new VelocityContext();
    context.put("location", location );
    context.put("weathers", weathers );
    StringWriter writer = new StringWriter();
    Velocity.evaluate(context, writer, "", reader);
    return writer.toString();
  }
}
```

The *weather.vm* template simply prints the zip code's city, country, and region as well as the current temperature, as shown in Example 7-22. The *history.vm* template prints the location and then iterates through the weather forecast records stored in the local database, as shown in Example 7-23. Both of these templates are in *${basedir}/src/main/resources*.

Example 7-22. The weather.vm Velocity template

```
****************************************
Current Weather Conditions for:
  ${weather.location.city},
  ${weather.location.region},
  ${weather.location.country}
****************************************

 * Temperature: ${weather.condition.temp}
 * Condition: ${weather.condition.text}
 * Humidity: ${weather.atmosphere.humidity}
 * Wind Chill: ${weather.wind.chill}
 * Date: ${weather.date}
```

Example 7-23. The history.vm Velocity template

```
Weather History for:
${location.city},
${location.region},
${location.country}


#foreach( $weather in $weathers )
****************************************
 * Temperature: $weather.condition.temp
 * Condition: $weather.condition.text
 * Humidity: $weather.atmosphere.humidity
 * Wind Chill: $weather.wind.chill
 * Date: $weather.date
#end
```

Running simple-command

The `simple-command` project is configured to create a single JAR containing the bytecode of the project and all of the bytecode from the dependencies. To create this assembly, run the `assembly` goal of the Maven Assembly plugin from the `simple-command` project directory:

```
$ mvn assembly:assembly
[INFO] ------------------------------------------------------------------------
[INFO] Building Chapter 7 Simple Command Line Tool
[INFO]    task-segment: [assembly:assembly] (aggregator-style)
[INFO] ------------------------------------------------------------------------
[INFO] [resources:resources]
[INFO] Using default encoding to copy filtered resources.
[INFO] [compiler:compile]
[INFO] Nothing to compile - all classes are up to date
[INFO] [resources:testResources]
[INFO] Using default encoding to copy filtered resources.
[INFO] [compiler:testCompile]
[INFO] Nothing to compile - all classes are up to date
[INFO] [surefire:test]
...
[INFO] [jar:jar]
[INFO] Building jar: .../simple-parent/simple-command/target/simple-command.jar
[INFO] [assembly:assembly]
[INFO] Processing DependencySet (output=)
[INFO] Expanding: .../.m2/repository/.../simple-weather-1-SNAPSHOT.jar into \
                                      /tmp/archived-file-set.93251505.tmp
[INFO] Expanding: .../.m2/repository/.../simple-model-1-SNAPSHOT.jar into \
                                      /tmp/archived-file-set.2012480870.tmp
[INFO] Expanding: .../.m2/repository/../hibernate-3.2.5.ga.jar into \
                                      /tmp/archived-file-set.1296516202.tmp
... skipping 25 lines of dependency unpacking ...
[INFO] Expanding: .../.m2/repository/.../velocity-1.5.jar into \
                                      /tmp/archived-file-set.379482226.tmp
[INFO] Expanding: .../.m2/repository/.../commons-lang-2.1.jar into \
                                      /tmp/archived-file-set.1329200163.tmp
[INFO] Expanding: .../.m2/repository/.../oro-2.0.8.jar into \
                                      /tmp/archived-file-set.1993155327.tmp
[INFO] Building jar: .../simple-parent/simple-command/target/\
                                      simple-command-jar-with-dependencies.jar
```

The build progresses through the lifecycle compiling bytecode, running tests, and finally building a JAR for the project. Then the `assembly:assembly` goal creates a JAR with dependencies by unpacking all of the dependencies to temporary directories and then collecting all of the bytecode into a single JAR in *target/* that is named *simple-command-jar-with-dependencies.jar*. This "uber" JAR weighs in at 15 MB.

Before you run the command-line tool, you will need to invoke the `hbm2ddl` goal of the Hibernate3 plugin to create the HSQLDB database. Do this by running the following command from the *simple-command* directory:

```
$ mvn hibernate3:hbm2ddl
[INFO] Scanning for projects...
[INFO] Searching repository for plugin with prefix: 'hibernate3'.
[INFO] org.codehaus.mojo: checking for updates from central
[INFO] ------------------------------------------------------------------------
[INFO] Building Chapter 7 Simple Command Line Tool
```

```
[INFO]    task-segment: [hibernate3:hbm2ddl]
[INFO] ------------------------------------------------------------------------
[INFO] Preparing hibernate3:hbm2ddl
...
10:24:56,151  INFO org.hibernate.tool.hbm2ddl.SchemaExport - export complete
[INFO] ------------------------------------------------------------------------
[INFO] BUILD SUCCESSFUL
[INFO] ------------------------------------------------------------------------
```

Once you run this, you should see a *data/* directory under *simple-command*. This *data/* directory holds the HSQLDB database. To run the command-line weather forecaster, run the following from the *simple-command* project directory:

```
$ java -cp target/simple-command-jar-with-dependencies.jar \
        org.sonatype.mavenbook.weather.Main 60202
2321 INFO  YahooRetriever   - Retrieving Weather Data
2489 INFO  YahooParser      - Creating XML Reader
2581 INFO  YahooParser      - Parsing XML Response
2875 INFO  WeatherFormatter - Formatting Weather Data
**************************************
Current Weather Conditions for:
  Evanston,
  IL,
  US
**************************************

 * Temperature: 75
 * Condition: Partly Cloudy
 * Humidity: 64
 * Wind Chill: 75
 * Date: Wed Aug 06 09:35:30 CDT 2008
```

To run a history query, execute the following command:

```
$ java -cp target/simple-command-jar-with-dependencies.jar \
        org.sonatype.mavenbook.weather.Main 60202 history
2470 INFO  WeatherFormatter - Formatting History Data
Weather History for:
Evanston, IL, US

**************************************
 * Temperature: 39
 * Condition: Heavy Rain
 * Humidity: 93
 * Wind Chill: 36
 * Date: 2007-12-02 13:45:27.187
**************************************
 * Temperature: 75
 * Condition: Partly Cloudy
 * Humidity: 64
 * Wind Chill: 75
 * Date: 2008-08-06 09:24:11.725
**************************************
 * Temperature: 75
 * Condition: Partly Cloudy
 * Humidity: 64
```

```
* Wind Chill: 75
* Date: 2008-08-06 09:27:28.475
```

Conclusion

We've spent a great deal of time on topics not directly related Maven to get this far. We've done this to present a complete and meaningful example project that you can use to implement real-world systems. We didn't take any short cuts to produce slick, canned results quickly, and we're not going to dazzle you with some Ruby on Rails-esque wizardry and lead you to believe that you can create a finished Java Enterprise application in "10 easy minutes!" There's too much of this in the market; there are too many people trying to sell you the easiest framework that requires zero investment of time or attention. What we've tried to do in this chapter is present the entire picture, the entire ecosystem of a multimodule build. We've presented Maven in the context of an application that resembles something you might see in the wild—not a fast-food, 10-minute screencast that slings mud at Apache Ant and tries to convince you to adopt Apache Maven.

If you walk away from this chapter wondering what it has to do with Maven, we've succeeded. We presented a complex set of projects, using popular frameworks, and we tied them together using declarative builds. The fact that more than 60% of this chapter was spent explaining Spring and Hibernate should tell you that Maven, for the most part, stepped out of the way. It worked. It allowed us to focus on the application itself, not on the build process. Instead of spending time discussing Maven, and the work you would have to do to "build a build" that integrated with Spring and Hibernate, we talked almost exclusively about the technologies used in this contrived project. If you start to use Maven, and you take the time to learn it, you really do start to benefit from the fact that you don't have to spend time coding up some procedural build script. You don't have to spend your time worrying about mundane aspects of your build.

You can use the skeleton project introduced in this chapter as the foundation for your own, and chances are that if you do, you'll find yourself creating more and more modules as you need them. For example, the project on which this chapter was based has two distinct model projects, two persistence projects that persist to dramatically different databases, several web applications, and a Java mobile application. In total, the real-world system it's based on contains at least 15 interrelated modules. The point is that you've seen the most complex multimodule example we're going to include in this book, but you should also know that this example just scratches the surface of what is possible with Maven.

Programming to Interface Projects

This chapter explored a multimodule project that was more complex than the simple example presented in Chapter 6, yet it was still a simplification of a real-world project. In a larger project, you might find yourself building a system resembling Figure 7-5.

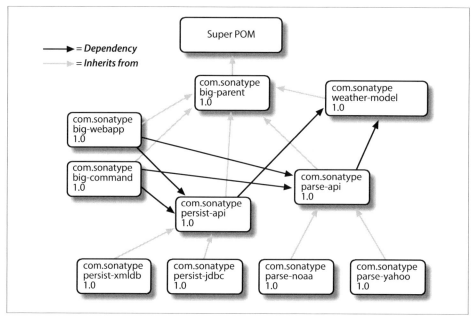

Figure 7-5. An example of a large, complicated system

## PART III

Maven Reference

Maven needs more than a series of helpful guided introductions. This section provides comprehensive reference material.

Optimizing and Refactoring POMs

Introduction

In Chapter 7, we showed how many pieces of Maven come together to produce a fully functional multimodule build. Although the example from that chapter suggests a real application—one that interacts with a database, a web service, and that itself presents two interfaces: one in a web application, and one on the command line—that example project is still contrived. To present the complexity of a real project would require a book far larger than the one you are now reading. Real-life applications evolve over years and are often maintained by large, diverse groups of developers, each with a different focus. In a real-world project, you are often evaluating decisions and designs made and created by others. In this chapter, we take a step back from the examples you've seen in Part II, and we ask ourselves if there are any optimizations that might make more sense given what we now know about Maven. Maven is a very capable tool that can be as simple or as complex as you need it to be. Because of this, there are often a million ways to accomplish the same task, and there is often no one "right" way to configure your Maven project.

Don't misinterpret that last sentence as a license to go off and ask Maven to do something it wasn't designed for. Although Maven allows for a diversity of approach, there is certainly "A Maven Way," and you'll be more productive using Maven as it was designed to be used. All this chapter is trying to do is communicate some of the optimizations you can perform on an existing Maven project. Why didn't we just introduce an optimized POM in the first place? Designing POMs for pedagogy is a very different requirement from designing POMs for efficiency. Although it is of course much easier to define a certain setting in your *~/.m2/settings.xml* than to declare a profile in a *pom.xml*, writing a book is mostly about pacing and making sure we're not introducing concepts before you are ready. In Part II, we've made an effort not to overwhelm you with too much information, and, in doing so, we've skipped some core concepts such as the `dependencyManagement` element introduced later in this chapter.

There are many instances in Part II when the authors of this book took a shortcut or glossed over an important detail to shuffle you along to the main point of a specific chapter. You learned how to create a Maven project, and you compiled and installed it without having to wade through hundreds of pages introducing every last switch and dial available to you. We've done this because we believe it is important to deliver the new Maven user to a result faster rather than meandering our way through a very long, seemingly interminable story. Once you've started to use Maven, you should know how to analyze your own projects and POMs. In this chapter, we take a step back and look at what we are left with after the example from Chapter 7.

POM Cleanup

Optimizing a multimodule project's POM is best done in several passes, as there are many areas to focus on. In general, we are looking for repetition within a POM and across the sibling POMs. When you are starting out, or when a project is still evolving rapidly, it is acceptable to duplicate some dependencies and plugin configurations here and there, but as the project matures and as the number of modules increases, you will want to take some time to refactor common dependencies and configuration points. Making your POMs more efficient will go a long way to helping you manage complexity as your project grows. Whenever there is duplication of some piece of information, there is usually a better way.

Optimizing Dependencies

If you look through the various POMs created in Chapter 7, note several patterns of replication. The first pattern we can see is that some dependencies such as spring and hibernate-annotations are declared in several modules. The hibernate dependency also has the exclusion on javax.transaction replicated in each definition. The second pattern of duplication to note is that sometimes several dependencies are related and share the same version. This is often the case when a project's release consists of several closely coupled components. For example, look at the dependencies on hibernate-annotations and hibernate-commons-annotations. Both are listed as version 3.3.0.ga, and we can expect the versions of both these dependencies to change together going forward. Both the hibernate-annotations and hibernate-commons-annotations are components of the same project released by JBoss, and so when there is a new project release, both of these dependencies will change. The third and last pattern of duplication is the duplication of sibling module dependencies and sibling module versions. Maven provides simple mechanisms that let you factor all of this duplication into a parent POM.

Just as in your project's source code, any time you have duplication in your POMs, you open the door a bit for trouble down the road. Duplicated dependency declarations make it difficult to ensure consistent versions across a large project. When you only have two or three modules, this might not be a primary issue, but when your organization is using a large, multimodule Maven build to manage hundreds of components across multiple departments, one single mismatch between dependencies can cause chaos and confusion. A simple version mismatch in a project's dependency on a byte-code manipulation package called ASM three levels deep in the project hierarchy could throw a wrench into a web application maintained by a completely different group of developers who depend on that particular module. Unit tests could pass because they are being run with one version of a dependency, but they could fail disastrously in production where the bundle (WAR, in this case) was packaged up with a different version. If you have tens of projects using something like Hibernate Annotations, each repeating and duplicating the dependencies and exclusions, the mean time between someone screwing up a build is going to be very short. As your Maven projects become more complex, your dependency lists are going to grow, and you are going to want to consolidate versions and dependency declarations in parent POMs.

The duplication of the sibling module versions can introduce a particularly nasty problem that is not directly caused by Maven and is learned only after you've been bitten by this bug a few times. If you use the Maven Release plugin to perform your releases, all these sibling dependency versions will be updated automatically for you, so maintaining them is not the concern. If `simple-web` version `1.3-SNAPSHOT` depends on `simple-persist` version `1.3-SNAPSHOT`, and if you are performing a release of the 1.3 version of both projects, the Maven Release plugin is smart enough to change the versions throughout your multimodule project's POMs automatically. Running the release with the Release plugin will automatically increment all of the versions in your build to `1.4-SNAPSHOT`, and the release plugin will commit the code change to the repository. Releasing a huge multimodule project couldn't be easier, until...

Problems occur when developers merge changes to the POM and interfere with a release that is in progress. Often a developer merges and occasionally mishandles the conflict on the sibling dependency, inadvertently reverting that version to a previous release. Since the consecutive versions of the dependency are often compatible, it does not show up when the developer builds, and won't show up in any continuous integration build system as a failed build. Imagine a very complex build where the trunk is full of components at `1.4-SNAPSHOT`, and now imagine that Developer A has updated Component A deep within the project's hierarchy to depend on version `1.3-SNAPSHOT` of Component B. Even though most developers have `1.4-SNAPSHOT`, the build succeeds if version `1.3-SNAPSHOT` and `1.4-SNAPSHOT` of Component B are compatible. Maven continues to build the project using the `1.3-SNAPSHOT` version of Component B from the developer's local repositories. Everything seems to be going quite smoothly—the project builds, the continuous integration build works fine, and so on. Someone might have a mystifying bug related to Component B, but she chalks it up to malevolent gremlins and moves on. Meanwhile, a pump in the reactor room is steadily building up pressure, until something blows....

Someone, let's call him Mr. Inadvertent, has a merge conflict in Component A and mistakenly pegs Component A's dependency on Component B to `1.3-SNAPSHOT`, while the rest of the project marches on. A bunch of developers have been trying to fix a bug in Component B all this time, and they've been mystified as to why they can't seem to fix the bug in production. Eventually, someone looks at Component A and realizes that the dependency is pointing to the wrong version. Hopefully, the bug isn't large enough to cost money or lives, but Mr. Inadvertent feels stupid and people tend to trust him a little less than they did before the whole sibling dependency screwup. (Ideally, Mr. Inadvertent realizes that this was user error and not Maven's fault, but more likely he starts an awful blog and complains about Maven endlessly to make himself feel better.)

Fortunately, dependency duplication and sibling dependency mismatch are easily preventable if you make some small changes. The first thing we're going to do is find all the dependencies used in more than one project and move them up to the parent POM's `dependencyManagement` section. We'll leave out the sibling dependencies for now. The `simple-parent` pom now contains the following:

```
<project>
  ...
  <dependencyManagement>
    <dependencies>
      <dependency>
        <groupId>org.springframework</groupId>
        <artifactId>spring</artifactId>
        <version>2.0.7</version>
      </dependency>
      <dependency>
        <groupId>org.apache.velocity</groupId>
        <artifactId>velocity</artifactId>
        <version>1.5</version>
      </dependency>
      <dependency>
        <groupId>org.hibernate</groupId>
        <artifactId>hibernate-annotations</artifactId>
        <version>3.3.0.ga</version>
      </dependency>
      <dependency>
        <groupId>org.hibernate</groupId>
        <artifactId>hibernate-commons-annotations</artifactId>
        <version>3.3.0.ga</version>
      </dependency>
      <dependency>
        <groupId>org.hibernate</groupId>
        <artifactId>hibernate</artifactId>
        <version>3.2.5.ga</version>
        <exclusions>
          <exclusion>
            <groupId>javax.transaction</groupId>
            <artifactId>jta</artifactId>
          </exclusion>
        </exclusions>
      </dependency>
    </dependencies>
  </dependencyManagement>
  ...
</project>
```

Once these are moved up, we need to remove the versions for these dependencies from each of the POMs; otherwise, they will override the dependencyManagement defined in the parent project. Let's look at only simple-model for brevity's sake:

```
<project>
  ...
  <dependencies>
    <dependency>
      <groupId>org.hibernate</groupId>
      <artifactId>hibernate-annotations</artifactId>
    </dependency>
    <dependency>
      <groupId>org.hibernate</groupId>
      <artifactId>hibernate</artifactId>
    </dependency>
  </dependencies>
  ...
</project>
```

The next thing we should do is fix the replication of the hibernate-annotations and hibernate-commons-annotations version, because these should match. We'll do this by creating a property called hibernate-annotations-version. The resulting simple-parent section looks like this:

```
<project>
  ...
  <properties>
    <hibernate.annotations.version>3.3.0.ga</hibernate.annotations.version>
  </properties>

  <dependencyManagement>
    ...
    <dependency>
      <groupId>org.hibernate</groupId>
      <artifactId>hibernate-annotations</artifactId>
      <version>${hibernate.annotations.version}</version>
    </dependency>
    <dependency>
      <groupId>org.hibernate</groupId>
      <artifactId>hibernate-commons-annotations</artifactId>
      <version>${hibernate.annotations.version}</version>
    </dependency>
    ...
  </dependencyManagement>
  ...
</project
```

The last issue we have to resolve is with the sibling dependencies. One technique we could use is to move these up to the dependencyManagement section, just like all the others, and define the versions of sibling projects in the top-level parent project. This is certainly a valid approach, but we can also solve the version problem just by using two built-in properties—${project.groupId} and ${project.version}. Since they are sibling dependencies, there is not much value to be gained by enumerating them in the parent, so we'll rely on the built-in `${project.version}` property. Because they all share the same group, we can further future-proof these declarations by referring to the current POM's group using the built-in `${project.groupId}` property. The `simple-command` dependency section now looks like this:

```
<project>
  ...
  <dependencies>
    ...
    <dependency>
      <groupId>${project.groupId}</groupId>
      <artifactId>simple-weather</artifactId>
      <version>${project.version}</version>
    </dependency>
    <dependency>
      <groupId>${project.groupId}</groupId>
      <artifactId>simple-persist</artifactId>
      <version>${project.version}</version>
    </dependency>
    ...
  </dependencies>
  ...
</project>
```

Here's a summary of the two optimizations we completed that reduce duplication of dependencies:

Pull-up common dependencies to `dependencyManagement`

If more than one project depends on a specific dependency, you can list the dependency in `dependencyManagement`. The parent POM can contain a version and a set of exclusions; all the child POM needs to do to reference this dependency is use the `groupId` and `artifactId`. Child projects can omit the version and exclusions if the dependency is listed in `dependencyManagement`.

Use built-in project `version` and `groupId` for sibling projects

Use `${project.version}` and `${project.groupId}` when referring to a sibling project. Sibling projects almost always share the same `groupId`, and they almost always share the same release version. Using `${project.version}` will help you avoid the sibling version mismatch problem discussed previously.

Optimizing Plugins

If we take a look at the various plugin configurations, we can see the HSQLDB dependencies duplicated in several places. Unfortunately, `dependencyManagement` doesn't apply to plugin dependencies, but we can still use a property to consolidate the versions. Most complex Maven multimodule projects tend to define all versions in the top-level POM. This top-level POM then becomes a focal point for changes that affect the entire project. Think of version numbers as string literals in a Java class; if you are constantly repeating a literal, you'll likely want to make it a variable so that when it needs to be changed, you have to change it in only one place. Rolling up the version of HSQLDB into a property in the top-level POM yields the following `properties` element:

```
<project>
  ...
  <properties>
    <hibernate.annotations.version>3.3.0.ga</hibernate.annotations.version>
    <hsqldb.version>1.8.0.7</hsqldb.version>
  </properties>
  ...
</project>
```

The next thing we notice is that the `hibernate3-maven-plugin` configuration is duplicated in the `simple-webapp` and `simple-command` modules. We can manage the plugin configuration in the top-level POM just as we managed the dependencies in the top-level POM with the `dependencyManagement` section. To do this, we use the `pluginManagement` element in the top-level POM's build element:

```
<project>
  ...
  <build>
    <pluginManagement>
      <plugins>
        <plugin>
          <groupId>org.apache.maven.plugins</groupId>
          <artifactId>maven-compiler-plugin</artifactId>
          <configuration>
            <source>1.5</source>
            <target>1.5</target>
          </configuration>
        </plugin>
        <plugin>
          <groupId>org.codehaus.mojo</groupId>
          <artifactId>hibernate3-maven-plugin</artifactId>
          <version>2.1</version>
          <configuration>
            <components>
              <component>
                <name>hbm2ddl</name>
                <implementation>annotationconfiguration</implementation>
              </component>
            </components>
          </configuration>
          <dependencies>
            <dependency>
              <groupId>hsqldb</groupId>
              <artifactId>hsqldb</artifactId>
              <version>${hsqldb.version}</version>
            </dependency>
          </dependencies>
        </plugin>
      </plugins>
    </pluginManagement>
  </build>
```

```
...
</project>
```

Optimizing with the Maven Dependency Plugin

On larger projects, additional dependencies often tend to creep into a POM as the
number of dependencies grow. As dependencies change, you are often left with dependencies that are not being used, and just as often, you may forget to declare explicit
dependencies for libraries you require. Because Maven 2.x includes transitive dependencies in the compile scope, your project may compile properly but fail to run in production. Consider a case where a project uses classes from a widely used project such
as Jakarta Commons BeanUtils. Instead of declaring an explicit dependency on
BeanUtils, your project simply relies on a project such as Hibernate that references
BeanUtils as a transitive dependency. Your project may compile successfully and run
just fine, but if you upgrade to a new version of Hibernate that doesn't depend on
BeanUtils, you'll start to get compile and runtime errors, and it won't be immediately
obvious why your project stopped compiling. Also, because you haven't explicitly listed
a dependency version, Maven cannot resolve any version conflicts that may arise.

A good rule of thumb in Maven is to always declare explicit dependencies for classes
referenced in your code. If you are going to be importing Commons BeanUtils classes,
you should also be declaring a direct dependency on Commons BeanUtils. Fortunately,
via bytecode analysis, the Maven Dependency plugin is able to assist you in uncovering
direct references to dependencies. Using the updated POMs we previously optimized,
let's look to see if any errors pop up:

```
$ mvn dependency:analyze
[INFO] Scanning for projects...
[INFO] Reactor build order:
[INFO]    Chapter 8 Simple Parent Project
[INFO]    Chapter 8 Simple Object Model
[INFO]    Chapter 8 Simple Weather API
[INFO]    Chapter 8 Simple Persistence API
[INFO]    Chapter 8 Simple Command Line Tool
[INFO]    Chapter 8 Simple Web Application
[INFO]    Chapter 8 Parent Project
[INFO] Searching repository for plugin with prefix: 'dependency'.

...

[INFO] ------------------------------------------------------------------------
[INFO] Building Chapter 8 Simple Object Model
[INFO]    task-segment: [dependency:analyze]
[INFO] ------------------------------------------------------------------------
[INFO] Preparing dependency:analyze
[INFO] [resources:resources]
[INFO] Using default encoding to copy filtered resources.
[INFO] [compiler:compile]
[INFO] Nothing to compile - all classes are up to date
[INFO] [resources:testResources]
```

```
[INFO] Using default encoding to copy filtered resources.
[INFO] [compiler:testCompile]
[INFO] Nothing to compile - all classes are up to date
[INFO] [dependency:analyze]
[WARNING] Used undeclared dependencies found:
[WARNING]    javax.persistence:persistence-api:jar:1.0:compile
[WARNING] Unused declared dependencies found:
[WARNING]    org.hibernate:hibernate-annotations:jar:3.3.0.ga:compile
[WARNING]    org.hibernate:hibernate:jar:3.2.5.ga:compile
[WARNING]    junit:junit:jar:3.8.1:test

...

[INFO] ------------------------------------------------------------------------
[INFO] Building Chapter 8 Simple Web Application
[INFO]    task-segment: [dependency:analyze]
[INFO] ------------------------------------------------------------------------
[INFO] Preparing dependency:analyze
[INFO] [resources:resources]
[INFO] Using default encoding to copy filtered resources.
[INFO] [compiler:compile]
[INFO] Nothing to compile - all classes are up to date
[INFO] [resources:testResources]
[INFO] Using default encoding to copy filtered resources.
[INFO] [compiler:testCompile]
[INFO] No sources to compile
[INFO] [dependency:analyze]
[WARNING] Used undeclared dependencies found:
[WARNING]    org.sonatype.mavenbook.ch08:simple-model:jar:1.0:compile
[WARNING] Unused declared dependencies found:
[WARNING]    org.apache.velocity:velocity:jar:1.5:compile
[WARNING]    javax.servlet:jstl:jar:1.1.2:compile
[WARNING]    taglibs:standard:jar:1.1.2:compile
[WARNING]    junit:junit:jar:3.8.1:test
```

In the truncated output just shown, you can see the output of the depend
ency:analyze goal. This goal analyzes the project to see whether there are any indirect
dependencies, or dependencies that are being referenced but are not directly declared.
In the simple-model project, the Dependency plugin indicates a "used undeclared dependency" on javax.persistence:persistence-api. To investigate further, go to the
simple-model directory and run the dependency:tree goal, which will list all of the
project's direct and transitive dependencies:

```
$ mvn dependency:tree
[INFO] Scanning for projects...
[INFO] Searching repository for plugin with prefix: 'dependency'.
[INFO] ------------------------------------------------------------------------
[INFO] Building Chapter 8 Simple Object Model
[INFO]    task-segment: [dependency:tree]
[INFO] ------------------------------------------------------------------------
[INFO] [dependency:tree]
[INFO] org.sonatype.mavenbook.ch08:simple-model:jar:1.0
[INFO] +- org.hibernate:hibernate-annotations:jar:3.3.0.ga:compile
[INFO] |  \- javax.persistence:persistence-api:jar:1.0:compile
```

```
[INFO] +- org.hibernate:hibernate:jar:3.2.5.ga:compile
[INFO] |  +- net.sf.ehcache:ehcache:jar:1.2.3:compile
[INFO] |  +- commons-logging:commons-logging:jar:1.0.4:compile
[INFO] |  +- asm:asm-attrs:jar:1.5.3:compile
[INFO] |  +- dom4j:dom4j:jar:1.6.1:compile
[INFO] |  +- antlr:antlr:jar:2.7.6:compile
[INFO] |  +- cglib:cglib:jar:2.1_3:compile
[INFO] |  +- asm:asm:jar:1.5.3:compile
[INFO] |  \- commons-collections:commons-collections:jar:2.1.1:compile
[INFO] \- junit:junit:jar:3.8.1:test
[INFO] ------------------------------------------------------------------------
[INFO] BUILD SUCCESSFUL
[INFO] ------------------------------------------------------------------------
```

From this output, we can see that the `persistence-api` dependency is coming from
`hibernate`. A cursory scan of the source in this module will reveal many `javax.persis`
`tence` import statements confirming that we are, indeed, directly referencing this dependency. The simple fix is to add a direct reference to the dependency. In this example,
we put the dependency version in `simple-parent`'s `dependencyManagement` section because the dependency is linked to Hibernate, and the Hibernate version is declared
here. Eventually you are going to want to upgrade your project's version of Hibernate.
Listing the `persistence-api` dependency version near the Hibernate dependency version will make it more obvious later when your team modifies the parent POM to
upgrade the Hibernate version.

If you look at the `dependency:analyze` output from the `simple-web` module, you will see
that we also need to add a direct reference to the `simple-model` dependency. The code
in `simple-webapp` directly references the model objects in `simple-model`, and the `simple-`
`model` is exposed to `simple-webapp` as a transitive dependency via `simple-persist`. Since
this is a sibling dependency that shares both the `version` and `groupId`, the dependency
can be defined in `simple-webapp`'s *pom.xml* using the `${project.groupId}` and
`${project.version}`.

How did the Maven Dependency plugin uncover these issues? How does
`dependency:analyze` know which classes and dependencies are directly referenced by
your project's bytecode? The Dependency plugin uses the ObjectWeb ASM (*http://asm*
.objectweb.org/) toolkit to analyze the raw bytecode. The Dependency plugin uses ASM
to walk through all the classes in the current project, and it builds a list of every other
class referenced. It then walks through all the dependencies, direct and transitive, and
marks off the classes discovered in the direct dependencies. Any classes not located in
the direct dependencies are discovered in the transitive dependencies, and the list of
"used, undeclared dependencies" is produced.

In contrast, the list of unused, declared dependencies is a little trickier to validate, and
less useful than the "used, undeclared dependencies." For one, some dependencies are
used only at runtime or for tests, and they won't be found in the bytecode. These are
pretty obvious when you see them in the output; for example, JUnit appears in this list,
but this is expected because it is used only for unit tests. You'll also notice that the

Velocity and Servlet API dependencies are listed in this list for the `simple-web` module. This is also expected because, although the project doesn't have any direct references to the classes of these artifacts, they are still essential during runtime.

Be careful when removing any unused, declared dependencies unless you have very good test coverage, or you might introduce a runtime error. A more sinister issue pops up with bytecode optimization. For example, it is legal for a compiler to substitute the value of a constant and optimize away the reference. Removing this dependency will cause the compile to fail, yet the tool shows it as unused. Future versions of the Maven Dependency plugin will provide better techniques for detecting and/or ignoring these types of issues.

You should use the `dependency:analyze` tool periodically to detect these common errors in your projects. It can be configured to fail the build if certain conditions are found, and it is also available as a report.

Final POMs

As an overview, the final POM files are listed as a reference for this chapter. Example 8-1 shows the top-level POM for `simple-parent`.

Example 8-1. Final POM for simple-parent

```
<project xmlns="http://maven.apache.org/POM/4.0.0"
        xmlns:xsi="http://www.w3.org/2001/XMLSchema-instance"
        xsi:schemaLocation="http://maven.apache.org/POM/4.0.0
                            http://maven.apache.org/maven-v4_0_0.xsd">
  <modelVersion>4.0.0</modelVersion>

  <groupId>org.sonatype.mavenbook.ch08</groupId>
  <artifactId>simple-parent</artifactId>
  <packaging>pom</packaging>
  <version>1.0</version>
  <name>Chapter 8 Simple Parent Project</name>

  <modules>
    <module>simple-command</module>
    <module>simple-model</module>
    <module>simple-weather</module>
    <module>simple-persist</module>
    <module>simple-webapp</module>
  </modules>

  <build>
    <pluginManagement>
      <plugins>
        <plugin>
          <groupId>org.apache.maven.plugins</groupId>
          <artifactId>maven-compiler-plugin</artifactId>
          <configuration>
            <source>1.5</source>
```

```
        <target>1.5</target>
      </configuration>
    </plugin>
    <plugin>
      <groupId>org.codehaus.mojo</groupId>
      <artifactId>hibernate3-maven-plugin</artifactId>
      <version>2.1</version>
      <configuration>
        <components>
          <component>
            <name>hbm2ddl</name>
            <implementation>annotationconfiguration</implementation>
          </component>
        </components>
      </configuration>
      <dependencies>
        <dependency>
          <groupId>hsqldb</groupId>
          <artifactId>hsqldb</artifactId>
          <version>${hsqldb.version}</version>
        </dependency>
      </dependencies>
    </plugin>
  </plugins>
 </pluginManagement>
</build>

<properties>
  <hibernate.annotations.version>3.3.0.ga</hibernate.annotations.version>
  <hsqldb.version>1.8.0.7</hsqldb.version>
</properties>
<dependencyManagement>
  <dependencies>
    <dependency>
      <groupId>org.springframework</groupId>
      <artifactId>spring</artifactId>
      <version>2.0.7</version>
    </dependency>
    <dependency>
      <groupId>org.apache.velocity</groupId>
      <artifactId>velocity</artifactId>
      <version>1.5</version>
    </dependency>
    <dependency>
      <groupId>javax.persistence</groupId>
      <artifactId>persistence-api</artifactId>
      <version>1.0</version>
    </dependency>
    <dependency>
      <groupId>org.hibernate</groupId>
      <artifactId>hibernate-annotations</artifactId>
      <version>${hibernate.annotations.version}</version>
    </dependency>
    <dependency>
      <groupId>org.hibernate</groupId>
```

```
          <artifactId>hibernate-commons-annotations</artifactId>
          <version>${hibernate.annotations.version}</version>
        </dependency>
        <dependency>
          <groupId>org.hibernate</groupId>
          <artifactId>hibernate</artifactId>
          <version>3.2.5.ga</version>
          <exclusions>
            <exclusion>
              <groupId>javax.transaction</groupId>
              <artifactId>jta</artifactId>
            </exclusion>
          </exclusions>
        </dependency>
      </dependencies>
    </dependencyManagement>

    <dependencies>
      <dependency>
        <groupId>junit</groupId>
        <artifactId>junit</artifactId>
        <version>3.8.1</version>
        <scope>test</scope>
      </dependency>
    </dependencies>
</project>
```

The POM shown in Example 8-2 captures the POM for simple-command, the command-line version of the tool.

Example 8-2. Final POM for simple-command

```
<project xmlns="http://maven.apache.org/POM/4.0.0"
         xmlns:xsi="http://www.w3.org/2001/XMLSchema-instance"
         xsi:schemaLocation="http://maven.apache.org/POM/4.0.0
                             http://maven.apache.org/maven-v4_0_0.xsd">
  <modelVersion>4.0.0</modelVersion>
  <parent>
    <groupId>org.sonatype.mavenbook.ch08</groupId>
    <artifactId>simple-parent</artifactId>
    <version>1.0</version>
  </parent>

  <artifactId>simple-command</artifactId>
  <packaging>jar</packaging>
  <name>Chapter 8 Simple Command Line Tool</name>

  <build>
    <pluginManagement>
      <plugins>
        <plugin>
          <groupId>org.apache.maven.plugins</groupId>
          <artifactId>maven-jar-plugin</artifactId>
          <configuration>
            <archive>
```

```
            <manifest>
              <mainClass>org.sonatype.mavenbook.weather.Main</mainClass>
              <addClasspath>true</addClasspath>
            </manifest>
          </archive>
        </configuration>
      </plugin>
      <plugin>
        <groupId>org.apache.maven.plugins</groupId>
        <artifactId>maven-surefire-plugin</artifactId>
        <configuration>
          <testFailureIgnore>true</testFailureIgnore>
        </configuration>
      </plugin>
      <plugin>
       <artifactId>maven-assembly-plugin</artifactId>
        <configuration>
          <descriptorRefs>
            <descriptorRef>jar-with-dependencies</descriptorRef>
          </descriptorRefs>
        </configuration>
      </plugin>
    </plugins>
  </pluginManagement>
</build>

<dependencies>
  <dependency>
    <groupId>${project.groupId}</groupId>
    <artifactId>simple-weather</artifactId>
    <version>${project.version}</version>
  </dependency>
  <dependency>
    <groupId>${project.groupId}</groupId>
    <artifactId>simple-persist</artifactId>
    <version>${project.version}</version>
  </dependency>
  <dependency>
    <groupId>org.springframework</groupId>
    <artifactId>spring</artifactId>
  </dependency>
  <dependency>
    <groupId>org.apache.velocity</groupId>
    <artifactId>velocity</artifactId>
  </dependency>
</dependencies>
</project>
```

The POM shown in Example 8-3 is the simple-model project's POM. The simple-model project contains all of the model objects used throughout the application.

Example 8-3. Final POM for simple-model

```
<project xmlns="http://maven.apache.org/POM/4.0.0"
         xmlns:xsi="http://www.w3.org/2001/XMLSchema-instance"
         xsi:schemaLocation="http://maven.apache.org/POM/4.0.0
                             http://maven.apache.org/maven-v4_0_0.xsd">
  <modelVersion>4.0.0</modelVersion>
  <parent>
    <groupId>org.sonatype.mavenbook.ch08</groupId>
    <artifactId>simple-parent</artifactId>
    <version>1.0</version>
  </parent>
  <artifactId>simple-model</artifactId>
  <packaging>jar</packaging>

  <name>Chapter 8 Simple Object Model</name>

  <dependencies>
    <dependency>
      <groupId>org.hibernate</groupId>
      <artifactId>hibernate-annotations</artifactId>
    </dependency>
    <dependency>
      <groupId>org.hibernate</groupId>
      <artifactId>hibernate</artifactId>
    </dependency>
    <dependency>
      <groupId>javax.persistence</groupId>
      <artifactId>persistence-api</artifactId>
    </dependency>
  </dependencies>
</project>
```

The POM shown in Example 8-4 is the `simple-persist` project's POM. The `simple-persist` project contains all of the persistence logic that is implemented using Hibernate.

Example 8-4. Final POM for simple-persist

```
<project xmlns="http://maven.apache.org/POM/4.0.0"
         xmlns:xsi="http://www.w3.org/2001/XMLSchema-instance"
         xsi:schemaLocation="http://maven.apache.org/POM/4.0.0
                             http://maven.apache.org/maven-v4_0_0.xsd">
  <modelVersion>4.0.0</modelVersion>
  <parent>
    <groupId>org.sonatype.mavenbook.ch08</groupId>
    <artifactId>simple-parent</artifactId>
    <version>1.0</version>
  </parent>
  <artifactId>simple-persist</artifactId>
  <packaging>jar</packaging>

  <name>Chapter 8 Simple Persistence API</name>

  <dependencies>
```

```
    <dependency>
      <groupId>${project.groupId}</groupId>
      <artifactId>simple-model</artifactId>
      <version>${project.version}</version>
    </dependency>
    <dependency>
      <groupId>org.hibernate</groupId>
      <artifactId>hibernate</artifactId>
    </dependency>
    <dependency>
      <groupId>org.hibernate</groupId>
      <artifactId>hibernate-annotations</artifactId>
    </dependency>
    <dependency>
      <groupId>org.hibernate</groupId>
      <artifactId>hibernate-commons-annotations</artifactId>
    </dependency>
    <dependency>
      <groupId>org.apache.geronimo.specs</groupId>
      <artifactId>geronimo-jta_1.1_spec</artifactId>
      <version>1.1</version>
    </dependency>
    <dependency>
      <groupId>org.springframework</groupId>
      <artifactId>spring</artifactId>
    </dependency>
  </dependencies>
</project>
```

The POM shown in Example 8-5 is the simple-weather project's POM. The simple-weather project is the project that contains all of the logic to parse the Yahoo! Weather RSS feed. This project depends on the simple-model project.

Example 8-5. Final POM for simple-weather

```
<project xmlns="http://maven.apache.org/POM/4.0.0"
         xmlns:xsi="http://www.w3.org/2001/XMLSchema-instance"
         xsi:schemaLocation="http://maven.apache.org/POM/4.0.0
                             http://maven.apache.org/maven-v4_0_0.xsd">
  <modelVersion>4.0.0</modelVersion>
  <parent>
    <groupId>org.sonatype.mavenbook.ch08</groupId>
    <artifactId>simple-parent</artifactId>
    <version>1.0</version>
  </parent>
  <artifactId>simple-weather</artifactId>
  <packaging>jar</packaging>

  <name>Chapter 8 Simple Weather API</name>

  <dependencies>
    <dependency>
      <groupId>${project.groupId}</groupId>
      <artifactId>simple-model</artifactId>
      <version>${project.version}</version>
```

```
      </dependency>
      <dependency>
        <groupId>log4j</groupId>
        <artifactId>log4j</artifactId>
        <version>1.2.14</version>
      </dependency>
      <dependency>
        <groupId>dom4j</groupId>
        <artifactId>dom4j</artifactId>
        <version>1.6.1</version>
      </dependency>
      <dependency>
        <groupId>jaxen</groupId>
        <artifactId>jaxen</artifactId>
        <version>1.1.1</version>
      </dependency>
      <dependency>
        <groupId>org.apache.commons</groupId>
        <artifactId>commons-io</artifactId>
        <version>1.3.2</version>
        <scope>test</scope>
      </dependency>
    </dependencies>
</project>
```

Finally, the POM shown in Example 8-6 is the `simple-webapp` project's POM. The
`simple-webapp` project contains a web application that stores retrieved weather forecasts
in an HSQLDB database and that also interacts with the libraries generated by the
`simple-weather` project.

Example 8-6. Final POM for simple-webapp

```
<project xmlns="http://maven.apache.org/POM/4.0.0"
  xmlns:xsi="http://www.w3.org/2001/XMLSchema-instance"
  xsi:schemaLocation="http://maven.apache.org/POM/4.0.0
                      http://maven.apache.org/maven-v4_0_0.xsd">
  <modelVersion>4.0.0</modelVersion>
  <parent>
    <groupId>org.sonatype.mavenbook.ch08</groupId>
    <artifactId>simple-parent</artifactId>
    <version>1.0</version>
  </parent>

  <artifactId>simple-webapp</artifactId>
  <packaging>war</packaging>
  <name>Chapter 8 Simple Web Application</name>
  <dependencies>
    <dependency>
      <groupId>org.apache.geronimo.specs</groupId>
      <artifactId>geronimo-servlet_2.4_spec</artifactId>
      <version>1.1.1</version>
    </dependency>
    <dependency>
      <groupId>${project.groupId}</groupId>
      <artifactId>simple-model</artifactId>
```

```xml
          <version>${project.version}</version>
      </dependency>
      <dependency>
        <groupId>${project.groupId}</groupId>
        <artifactId>simple-weather</artifactId>
        <version>${project.version}</version>
      </dependency>
      <dependency>
        <groupId>${project.groupId}</groupId>
        <artifactId>simple-persist</artifactId>
        <version>${project.version}</version>
      </dependency>
      <dependency>
        <groupId>org.springframework</groupId>
        <artifactId>spring</artifactId>
      </dependency>
      <dependency>
        <groupId>javax.servlet</groupId>
        <artifactId>jstl</artifactId>
        <version>1.1.2</version>
      </dependency>
      <dependency>
        <groupId>taglibs</groupId>
        <artifactId>standard</artifactId>
        <version>1.1.2</version>
      </dependency>
      <dependency>
        <groupId>org.apache.velocity</groupId>
        <artifactId>velocity</artifactId>
      </dependency>
    </dependencies>
    <build>
      <finalName>simple-webapp</finalName>
      <plugins>
        <plugin>
          <groupId>org.mortbay.jetty</groupId>
          <artifactId>maven-jetty-plugin</artifactId>
          <version>6.1.9</version>
          <dependencies>
            <dependency>
              <groupId>hsqldb</groupId>
              <artifactId>hsqldb</artifactId>
              <version>${hsqldb.version}</version>
            </dependency>
          </dependencies>
        </plugin>
      </plugins>
    </build>
</project>
```

Conclusion

This chapter has shown you several techniques for improving the control of your dependencies and plugins to ease future maintenance of your builds. We recommend periodically reviewing your builds in this way to ensure that duplication and thus potential trouble spots are minimized. As a project matures, new dependencies are inevitably introduced, and you may find that a dependency previously used in 1 place is now used in 10 and should be moved up. The used and unused dependencies list changes over time and can easily be cleaned up with the Maven Dependency plugin.

## CHAPTER 9

The Project Object Model

Introduction

This chapter covers the central concept of Maven—the Project Object Model (POM). The POM is where a project's identity and structure are declared, builds are configured, and projects are related to one another. The presence of a *pom.xml* file defines a Maven project.

The POM

Maven projects, dependencies, builds, artifacts: all of these are objects to be modeled and described. These objects are described by an XML file called a Project Object Model. The POM tells Maven what sort of project it is dealing with and how to modify default behavior to generate output from source. In the same way a Java web application has a *web.xml* that describes, configures, and customizes the application, a Maven project is defined by the presence of a *pom.xml*. It is a descriptive declaration of a project for Maven; it is the figurative "map" that Maven needs to understand what it is looking at when it builds your project.

You could also think of the *pom.xml* as analogous to a *Makefile* or an Ant *build.xml*. When you are using GNU *make* to build something like MySQL, you'll usually have a file named *Makefile* that contains explicit instructions for building a binary from source. When you are using Apache Ant, you likely have a file named *build.xml* that contains explicit instructions for cleaning, compiling, packaging, and deploying an application. *make*, Ant, and Maven are similar in that they rely on the presence of a commonly named file such as *Makefile*, *build.xml*, or *pom.xml*, but that is where the similarities end. If you look at a Maven *pom.xml*, the majority of the POM is going to deal with descriptions: Where is the source code? Where are the resources? What is the packaging? If you look at an Ant *build.xml* file, you'll see something entirely different. You'll see explicit instructions for tasks such as compiling a set of Java classes. The Maven POM is declarative, and although you can certainly choose to include some procedural customizations via the Maven Ant plugin, for the most part you will not need to get into the gritty procedural details of your project's build.

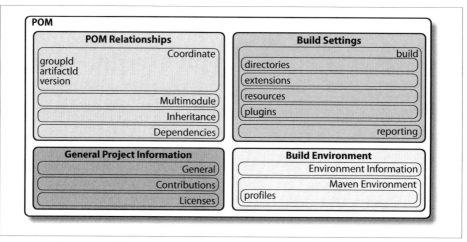

Figure 9-1. The Project Object Model

The POM is also not specific to building Java projects. Though most of the examples in this book are geared toward Java applications, there is nothing Java-specific in the definition of a Maven Project Object Model. Maven's default plugins are targeted to building JAR artifacts from a set of source, tests, and resources, but nothing is preventing you from defining a POM for a project that contains C# sources and produces some proprietary Microsoft binary using Microsoft tools. Similarly, nothing is stopping you from defining a POM for a technical book. In fact, the source for this book and this book's examples is captured in a multimodule Maven project that uses one of the many Maven DocBook plugins to apply the standard DocBook XSL to a series of chapter XML files. Others have created Maven plugins to build Adobe Flex code into Shockwave Components (SWCs) and Shockwave Flash files (SWFs), and yet others have used Maven to build projects written in C.

We've established that the POM describes and declares; it is unlike Ant or *make* in that it doesn't provide explicit instructions, and we've noted that POM concepts are not specific to Java. Diving into more specifics, take a look at Figure 9-1 for a survey of the contents of a POM.

The POM contains four categories of description and configuration:

General project information
> This includes a project's name, the URL for a project, the sponsoring organization, and a list of developers and contributors along with the license for a project.

Build settings
> In this section, we customize the behavior of the default Maven build. We can change the location of source and tests, we can add new plugins, we can attach plugin goals to the lifecycle, and we can customize the site generation parameters.

Build environment

> The build environment consists of profiles that can be activated for use in different environments. For example, during development you may want to deploy to a development server, whereas in production you want to deploy to a production server. The build environment customizes the build settings for specific environments and is often supplemented by a custom *settings.xml* in *~/.m2*. This settings file is discussed in Chapter 11 and in the section "Quick Overview" in Appendix A.

POM relationships

> A project rarely stands alone; it depends on other projects, inherits POM settings from parent projects, defines its own coordinates, and may include submodules.

The Super POM

Before we dive into some examples of POMs, let's take a quick look at the Super POM. All Maven project POMs extend the Super POM, which defines a set of defaults shared by all projects. This Super POM is a part of the Maven installation and can be found in the *maven-2.0.9-uber.jar* file in *${M2_HOME}/lib*. If you look in this JAR file, you will find a file named *pom-4.0.0.xml* under the `org.apache.maven.project` package. The Super POM for Maven is shown in Example 9-1.

Example 9-1. The Super POM

```
<project>
  <modelVersion>4.0.0</modelVersion>
  <name>Maven Default Project</name>

  <repositories>
    <repository>
      <id>central</id> ❶
      <name>Maven Repository Switchboard</name>
      <layout>default</layout>
      <url>http://repo1.maven.org/maven2</url>
      <snapshots>
        <enabled>false</enabled>
      </snapshots>
    </repository>
  </repositories>

  <pluginRepositories>
    <pluginRepository>
      <id>central</id> ❷
      <name>Maven Plugin Repository</name>
      <url>http://repo1.maven.org/maven2</url>
      <layout>default</layout>
      <snapshots>
        <enabled>false</enabled>
      </snapshots>
      <releases>
        <updatePolicy>never</updatePolicy>
      </releases>
```

```
      </pluginRepository>
  </pluginRepositories>

  <build> ❸
    <directory>target</directory>
    <outputDirectory>target/classes</outputDirectory>
    <finalName>${pom.artifactId}-${pom.version}</finalName>
    <testOutputDirectory>target/test-classes</testOutputDirectory>
    <sourceDirectory>src/main/java</sourceDirectory>
    <scriptSourceDirectory>src/main/scripts</scriptSourceDirectory>
    <testSourceDirectory>src/test/java</testSourceDirectory>
    <resources>
      <resource>
        <directory>src/main/resources</directory>
      </resource>
    </resources>
    <testResources>
      <testResource>
        <directory>src/test/resources</directory>
      </testResource>
    </testResources>
  </build>

    <pluginManagement> ❹
     <plugins>
       <plugin>
         <artifactId>maven-antrun-plugin</artifactId>
         <version>1.1</version>
       </plugin>
       <plugin>
         <artifactId>maven-assembly-plugin</artifactId>
         <version>2.2-beta-1</version>
       </plugin>
       <plugin>
         <artifactId>maven-clean-plugin</artifactId>
         <version>2.2</version>
       </plugin>
       <plugin>
         <artifactId>maven-compiler-plugin</artifactId>
         <version>2.0.2</version>
       </plugin>
       <plugin>
         <artifactId>maven-dependency-plugin</artifactId>
         <version>2.0</version>
       </plugin>
       <plugin>
         <artifactId>maven-deploy-plugin</artifactId>
         <version>2.3</version>
       </plugin>
       <plugin>
         <artifactId>maven-ear-plugin</artifactId>
         <version>2.3.1</version>
       </plugin>
       <plugin>
         <artifactId>maven-ejb-plugin</artifactId>
```

```
          <version>2.1</version>
        </plugin>
        <plugin>
          <artifactId>maven-install-plugin</artifactId>
          <version>2.2</version>
        </plugin>
        <plugin>
          <artifactId>maven-jar-plugin</artifactId>
          <version>2.2</version>
        </plugin>
        <plugin>
          <artifactId>maven-javadoc-plugin</artifactId>
          <version>2.4</version>
        </plugin>
        <plugin>
          <artifactId>maven-plugin-plugin</artifactId>
          <version>2.3</version>
        </plugin>
        <plugin>
          <artifactId>maven-rar-plugin</artifactId>
          <version>2.2</version>
        </plugin>
        <plugin>
          <artifactId>maven-release-plugin</artifactId>
          <version>2.0-beta-7</version>
        </plugin>
        <plugin>
          <artifactId>maven-resources-plugin</artifactId>
          <version>2.2</version>
        </plugin>
        <plugin>
          <artifactId>maven-site-plugin</artifactId>
          <version>2.0-beta-6</version>
        </plugin>
        <plugin>
          <artifactId>maven-source-plugin</artifactId>
          <version>2.0.4</version>
        </plugin>
        <plugin>
           <artifactId>maven-surefire-plugin</artifactId>
           <version>2.4.2</version>
        </plugin>
        <plugin>
          <artifactId>maven-war-plugin</artifactId>
          <version>2.1-alpha-1</version>
        </plugin>
      </plugins>
    </pluginManagement>

  <reporting>
    <outputDirectory>target/site</outputDirectory>
  </reporting>
</project>
```

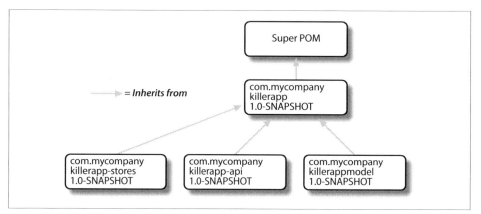

Figure 9-2. The Super POM is always the base parent

The Super POM defines some standard configuration variables that are inherited by all projects. Those values are captured in the annotated sections (see also Figure 9-2):

❶ The default Super POM defines a single remote Maven repository with an ID of central. This is the central Maven repository that all Maven clients are configured to read from by default. This setting can be overridden by a custom *settings.xml* file. Note that the default Super POM has disabled snapshot artifacts on the central Maven repository. If you need to use a snapshot repository, you will need to customize repository settings in your *pom.xml* or in your *settings.xml*. Settings and profiles are covered in Chapter 11 and in the section "Quick Overview" in Appendix A.

❷ The central Maven repository also contains Maven plugins. The default plugin repository is the central Maven repository. Snapshots are disabled, and the update policy is set to "never," which means that Maven will never automatically update a plugin if a new version is released.

❸ The build element sets the default values for directories in the Maven Standard Directory layout.

❹ Starting in Maven 2.0.9, default versions of core plugins have been provided in the Super POM. This was done to provide some stability for users who are not specifying versions in their POMs.

The Simplest POM

All Maven POMs inherit defaults from the Super POM (introduced earlier in the section "The Super POM"). If you are just writing a simple project that produces a JAR from some source in *src/main/java*, want to run your JUnit tests in *src/test/java*, and want to build a project site using *mvn site*, you don't have to customize anything. All you would need, in this case, is the simplest possible POM shown in Example 9-2. This POM defines a `groupId`, `artifactId`, and `version`: the three required coordinates for every project.

Example 9-2. The simplest POM

```
<project>
  <modelVersion>4.0.0</modelVersion>
  <groupId>org.sonatype.mavenbook.ch08</groupId>
  <artifactId>simplest-project</artifactId>
  <version>1</version>
</project>
```

Such a simple POM would be more than adequate for a simple project—e.g., a Java library that produces a JAR file. It isn't related to any other projects, it has no dependencies, and it lacks basic information such as a name and a URL. If you were to create this file and then create the subdirectory *src/main/java* with some source code, running *mvn package* would produce a JAR in *target/simple-project-1.jar*.

The Effective POM

This simplest POM brings us to the concept of the "effective POM." Since POMs can inherit configuration from other POMs, you must always think of a Maven POM in terms of the combination of the Super POM, plus any parent POMs, and finally the current project's POM. Maven starts with the Super POM and then overrides default configuration with one or more parent POMs. Then it overrides the resulting configuration with the current project's POM. You end up with an effective POM that is a mixture of various POMs. If you want to see a project's effective POM, you'll need to run the `effective-pom` goal in the Maven Help plugin, which was introduced earlier in the section "Using the Maven Help Plugin." To run the `effective-pom` goal, execute the following in a directory with a *pom.xml* file:

```
$ mvn help:effective-pom
```

Executing the `effective-pom` goal should print out an XML document capturing the merge between the Super POM and the POM from Example 9-2.

Real POMs

Instead of typing up a contrived set of POMs to walk you through step-by-step, you should take a look at the examples in Part II. Maven is something of a chameleon; you can pick and choose the features you want to take advantage of. Some open source projects may value the ability to list developers and contributors, generate clean project documentation, and manage releases automatically using the Maven Release plugin. On the other hand, someone working in a corporate environment on a small team might not be interested in the distribution management capabilities of Maven nor the ability to list developers. The remainder of this chapter is going to discuss features of the POM in isolation. Instead of bombarding you with a 10-page listing of a set of related

POMs, we're going to focus on creating a good reference for specific sections of the POM. In this chapter, we discuss relationships between POMs, but we don't illustrate such a project here. If you are looking for such an illustration, refer to Chapter 7.

POM Syntax

The POM is always in a file named *pom.xml* in the base directory of a Maven project. This XML document can start with the XML declaration, or you can choose to omit it. All values in a POM are captured as XML elements.

Project Versions

A Maven project's `version` encodes a release version number that is used to group and order releases. Maven versions contain the following parts: major version, minor version, incremental version, and qualifier. In a version, these parts correspond to the following format:

```
<major version>.<minor version>.<incremental version>-<qualifier>
```

For example, the version "1.3.5" has a major version of 1, a minor version of 3, and an incremental version of 5. The version "5" has a major version of 5 and no minor or incremental version. The qualifier exists to capture milestone builds such as alpha and beta releases, and the qualifier is separated from the major, minor, and incremental versions by a hyphen. For example, the version "1.3-beta-01" has a major version of 1, a minor version of 3, and a qualifier of beta-01.

Keeping your version numbers aligned with this standard will become very important when you start using version ranges in your POMs. Version ranges (introduced in the section "Dependency Version Ranges," later in this chapter) allow you to specify a dependency on a range of versions, and they are supported only because Maven has the ability to sort versions based on the version release number format introduced in this section.

If your version release number matches the format `<major>.<minor>.<incremental>-<qualifier>`, your versions will be compared properly; "1.2.3" will be evaluated as a more recent build than "1.0.2," and the comparison will be made using the numeric values of the major, minor, and incremental versions. If your version release number does not fit the standard introduced in this section, your versions will be compared as strings; "1.0.1b" will be compared to "1.2.0b" using a String comparison.

Version build numbers

One gotcha for release version numbers is the ordering of the qualifiers. Take the version release numbers "1.2.3-alpha-2" and "1.2.3-alpha-10," where the "alpha-2" build corresponds to the 2nd alpha build, and the "alpha-10" build corresponds to the 10th alpha build. Even though "alpha-10" should be considered more recent than "alpha-2,"

Maven is going to sort "alpha-10" before "alpha-2" due to a known issue in the way Maven handles version numbers.

Maven is supposed to treat the number after the qualifier as a build number. In other words, the qualifier should be "alpha," and the build number should be "2." Even though Maven has been designed to separate the build number from the qualifier, this parsing is currently broken. As a result, "alpha-2" and "alpha-10" are compared using a String comparison, and "alpha-10" comes before "alpha-2" alphabetically. To get around this limitation, you will need to left-pad your qualified build numbers. If you use "alpha-02" and "alpha-10," this problem will go away, and it will continue to work once Maven properly parses the version build number.

SNAPSHOT versions

Maven versions can contain a string literal to signify that a project is currently under active development. If a version contains the string "SNAPSHOT," then Maven will expand this token to a date and time value converted to UTC (Coordinated Universal Time) when you install or release this component. For example, if your project has a version of "1.0-SNAPSHOT" and you deploy this project's artifacts to a Maven repository, Maven would expand this version to "1.0-20080207-230803-1" if you were to deploy a release at 11:08 PM on February 7th, 2008 UTC. In other words, when you deploy a snapshot, you are not making a release of a software component; you are releasing a snapshot of a component at a specific time.

Why would you use this? Snapshot versions are used for projects under active development. If your project depends on a software component that is under active development, you can depend on a snapshot release, and Maven will periodically attempt to download the latest snapshot from a repository when you run a build. Similarly, if the next release of your system is going to have a version "1.4," your project would have a "1.4-SNAPSHOT" version until it was formally released.

As a default setting, Maven will not check for snapshot releases on remote repositories; to depend on snapshot releases, users must explicitly enable the ability to download snapshots using a `repository` or `pluginRepository` element in the POM.

When releasing a project, you should resolve all dependencies on snapshot versions to dependencies on released versions. If a project depends on a snapshot, it is not stable, as the dependencies may change over time. Artifacts published to nonsnapshot Maven repositories such as *http://repo1.maven.org/maven2* cannot depend on snapshot versions, since Maven's Super POM has disabled snapshots from the central repository. Snapshot versions are for development only.

Property References

A POM can include references to properties preceded by a dollar sign and surrounded by two curly braces. For example, consider the following POM:

```
<project>
  <modelVersion>4.0.0</modelVersion>
  <groupId>org.sonatype.mavenbook</groupId>
  <artifactId>project-a</artifactId>
  <version>1.0-SNAPSHOT</version>
  <packaging>jar</packaging>
  <build>
    <finalName>${project.groupId}-${project.artifactId}</finalName>
  </build>
</project>
```

If you put this XML in a *pom.xml* and run *mvn help:effective-pom*, you will see that the output contains the line:

```
...
<finalName>org.sonatype.mavenbook-project-a</finalName>
...
```

When Maven reads a POM, it replaces references to properties when it loads the POM XML. Maven properties occur frequently in advanced Maven usage, and they are similar to properties in other systems, such as Ant or Velocity. They are simply variables delimited by ${...}. Maven provides three implicit variables that can be used to access environment variables, POM information, and Maven settings:

env

> The env variable exposes environment variables exposed by your operating system or shell. For example, a reference to ${env.PATH} in a Maven POM would be replaced by the ${PATH} environment variable (or %PATH% in Windows).

project

> The project variable exposes the POM. You can use a dot-notated (.) path to reference the value of a POM element. For example, in this section we used the groupId and artifactId to set the finalName element in the build configuration. The syntax for this property reference was: ${project.groupId}-${project.artifactId}.

settings

> The settings variable exposes Maven settings information. You can use a dot-notated (.) path to reference the value of an element in a *settings.xml* file. For example, ${settings.offline} would reference the value of the offline element in *~/.m2/settings.xml*.

 You may see older builds that use ${pom.xxx} or just ${xxx} to reference POM properties. These methods have been deprecated, and only ${project.xxx} should be used.

In addition to the three implicit variables, you can reference system properties and any custom properties set in the Maven POM or in a build profile:

Java system properties

All properties accessible via `getProperties()` on `java.lang.System` are exposed as POM properties. Some examples of system properties are: `${user.name}`, `${user.home}`, `${java.home}`, and `${os.name}`. A full list of system properties can be found in the Javadoc for the `java.lang.System` class.

x

Arbitrary properties can be set with a **properties** element in a *pom.xml* or *settings.xml*, or properties can be loaded from external files. If you set a property named `fooBar` in your *pom.xml*, that same property is referenced with `${fooBar}`. Custom properties come in handy when you are building a system that filters resources and targets different deployment platforms. Here is the syntax for setting `${foo}=bar` in a POM:

```
<properties>
  <foo>bar</foo>
</properties>
```

For a more comprehensive list of available properties, see Chapter 13.

Project Dependencies

Maven can manage both internal and external dependencies. An external dependency for a Java project might be a library such as Plexus, the Spring Framework, or Log4J. An internal dependency is illustrated by a web application project depending on another project that contains service classes, model objects, or persistence logic. Example 9-3 shows some examples of project dependencies.

Example 9-3. Project dependencies

```
<project>
  ...
  <dependencies>
    <dependency>
      <groupId>org.codehaus.xfire</groupId>
      <artifactId>xfire-java5</artifactId>
      <version>1.2.5</version>
    </dependency>
    <dependency>
      <groupId>junit</groupId>
      <artifactId>junit</artifactId>
      <version>3.8.1</version>
      <scope>test</scope>
    </dependency>
    <dependency>
      <groupId>org.apache.geronimo.specs</groupId>
      <artifactId>geronimo-servlet_2.4_spec</artifactId>
      <version>1.0</version>
      <scope>provided</scope>
    </dependency>
  </dependencies>
```

```
    ...
</project>
```

The first dependency is a compile dependency on the XFire SOAP library from Code-haus. You would use this type of dependency if your project depended on this library for compilation, testing, and during execution. The second dependency is a `test`-scoped dependency on JUnit. You would use a `test`-scoped dependency when you need to reference this library only during testing. The last dependency in Example 9-3 is a dependency on the Servlet 2.4 API as implemented by the Apache Geronimo project. The last dependency is scoped as a provided dependency. You would use a provided scope when the application you are developing needs a library for compilation and testing, but this library is supplied by a container at runtime.

Dependency Scope

Example 9-3 briefly introduced three of the five dependency scopes: `compile`, `test`, and `provided`. Scope controls which dependencies are available in which classpath, and which dependencies are included with an application. Let's explore each scope in detail:

`compile`

> `compile` is the default scope; all dependencies are `compile`-scoped if a scope is not supplied. `compile` dependencies are available in all classpaths, and they are packaged.

`provided`

> `provided` dependencies are used when you expect the JDK or a container to provide them. For example, if you were developing a web application, you would need the Servlet API available on the compile classpath to compile a servlet, but you wouldn't want to include the Servlet API in the packaged WAR; the Servlet API JAR is supplied by your application server or servlet container. `provided` dependencies are available on the compilation classpath (not runtime). They are not transitive, nor are they packaged.

`runtime`

> `runtime` dependencies are required to execute and test the system, but they are not required for compilation. For example, you may need a JDBC API JAR at compile time and the JDBC driver implementation only at runtime.

`test`

> `test`-scoped dependencies are not required during the normal operation of an application, and they are available only during test compilation and execution phases. The `test` scope was previously introduced in "Adding Test-Scoped Dependencies" in Chapter 4.

`system`

> The `system` scope is similar to `provided` except that you have to provide an explicit path to the JAR on the local file system. This is intended to allow compilation against native objects that may be part of the system libraries. The artifact is as-

sumed to always be available and is not looked up in a repository. If you declare the scope to be `system`, you must also provide the `systemPath` element. Note that this scope is not recommended (you should always try to reference dependencies in a public or custom Maven repository).

Optional Dependencies

Assume that you are working on a library that provides caching behavior. Instead of writing a caching system from scratch, you want to use some of the existing libraries that provide caching on the file system and distributed caches. Also assume that you want to give the end user an option to cache on the file system or to use an in-memory distributed cache. To cache on the file system, you'll want to use a freely available library called EHCache (*http://ehcache.sourceforge.net/*), and to cache in a distributed in-memory cache, you want to use another freely available caching library named SwarmCache (*http://swarmcache.sourceforge.net/*). You'll code an interface and create a library that can be configured to use either EHCache or SwarmCache, but you want to avoid adding a dependency on both caching libraries to any project that depends on your library.

In other words, you need both libraries to compile this library project, but you don't want both libraries to show up as transitive runtime dependencies for the project that uses your library. You can accomplish this by using optional dependencies as shown in Example 9-4.

Example 9-4. Declaring optional dependencies

```
<project>
  <modelVersion>4.0.0</modelVersion>
  <groupId>org.sonatype.mavenbook</groupId>
  <artifactId>my-project</artifactId>
  <version>1.0.0</version>
  <dependencies>
    <dependency>
      <groupId>net.sf.ehcache</groupId>
      <artifactId>ehcache</artifactId>
      <version>1.4.1</version>
      <optional>true</optional>
    </dependency>
    <dependency>
      <groupId>swarmcache</groupId>
      <artifactId>swarmcache</artifactId>
      <version>1.0RC2</version>
      <optional>true</optional>
    </dependency>
    <dependency>
      <groupId>log4j</groupId>
      <artifactId>log4j</artifactId>
      <version>1.2.13</version>
    </dependency>
```

```
    </dependencies>
</project>
```

Once you've declared these dependencies as optional, you are required to include them explicitly in the project that depends on my-project. For example, if you were writing an application that depended on my-project and wanted to use the EHCache implementation, you would need to add the following **dependency** element to your project:

```
<project>
  <modelVersion>4.0.0</modelVersion>
  <groupId>org.sonatype.mavenbook</groupId>
  <artifactId>my-application</artifactId>
  <version>1.0.0</version>
  <dependencies>
    <dependency>
      <groupId>org.sonatype.mavenbook</groupId>
      <artifactId>my-project</artifactId>
      <version>1.0.0</version>
    </dependency>
    <dependency>
      <groupId>net.sf.ehcache</groupId>
      <artifactId>swarmcache</artifactId>
      <version>1.4.1</version>
    </dependency>
  </dependencies>
</project>
```

In an ideal world, you wouldn't have to use optional dependencies. Instead of having one large project with a series of optional dependencies, you would separate the EHCache-specific code to a my-project-ehcache submodule and the SwarmCache-specific code to a my-project-swarmcache submodule. This way, instead of requiring projects that reference my-project to specifically add a dependency, projects can just reference a particular implementation project and benefit from the transitive dependency.

Dependency Version Ranges

You don't just have to depend on a specific version of a dependency; you can specify a range of versions that would satisfy a given dependency. For example, you can specify that your project depends on version 3.8 or greater of JUnit, or anything between versions 1.2.10 and 1.2.14 of JUnit. You do this by surrounding one or more version numbers with the following characters:

(,)
   Exclusive quantifiers

[,]
   Inclusive quantifiers

For example, if you wished to access any JUnit version greater than or equal to 3.8 but less than 4.0, your dependency would be as shown in Example 9-5.

Example 9-5. Specifying a dependency range: JUnit 3.8–JUnit 4.0

```
<dependency>
  <groupId>junit</groupId>
  <artifactId>junit</artifactId>
  <version>[3.8,4.0)</version>
  <scope>test</scope>
</dependency>
```

If you want to depend on any version of JUnit no higher than 3.8.1, you would specify only an upper inclusive boundary, as shown in Example 9-6.

Example 9-6. Specifying a dependency range: JUnit <= 3.8.1

```
<dependency>
  <groupId>junit</groupId>
  <artifactId>junit</artifactId>
  <version>[,3.8.1]</version>
  <scope>test</scope>
</dependency>
```

A version before or after the comma means +/– infinity, and is not required. For example, "[4.0,)" means any version greater than or equal to 4.0. "(,2.0)" is any version less than 2.0. "[1.2]" means only version 1.2, and nothing else.

 When declaring a "normal" version such as 3.8.2 for JUnit, internally this is represented as "allow anything, but prefer 3.8.2." This means that when a conflict is detected, Maven is allowed to use the conflict algorithms to choose the best version. If you specify [3.8.2], only 3.8.2 will be used and nothing else. If somewhere else there is a dependency that specifies [3.8.1], you would get a build failure telling you of the conflict. We point this out to make you aware of the option, but use it sparingly and only when really needed. The preferred way to resolve this is via `dependencyManagement`.

Transitive Dependencies

A transitive dependency is a dependency of a dependency. If `project-a` depends on `project-b`, which in turn depends on `project-c`, then `project-c` is considered a transitive dependency of `project-a`. If `project-c` depended on `project-d`, then `project-d` would also be considered a transitive dependency of `project-a`. Part of Maven's appeal is that it can manage transitive dependencies and shield the developer from having to keep track of all of the dependencies required to compile and run an application. You can just depend on something like the Spring Framework and not have to worry about tracking down every last dependency of the Spring Framework.

Maven accomplishes this by building a graph of dependencies and dealing with any conflicts and overlaps that might occur. For example, if Maven sees that two projects depend on the same `groupId` and `artifactId`, it will sort out which dependency to use automatically, always favoring the more recent version of a dependency. Although this sounds convenient, there are some edge cases where transitive dependencies can cause some configuration issues. For these scenarios, you can use a dependency exclusion.

Transitive dependencies and scope

Each of the scopes outlined earlier in the section "Dependency Scope" affects not just the scope of the dependency in the declaring project, but also how it acts as a transitive dependency. The easiest way to convey this information is through a table, as in Table 9-1. Scopes in the top row represent the scope of a transitive dependency. Scopes in the leftmost column represent the scope of a direct dependency. The intersection of the row and column is the scope that is assigned to a transitive dependency. A blank cell in this table means that the transitive dependency will be omitted.

Table 9-1. How scope affects transitive dependencies

-	compile	provided	runtime	test
compile	compile	-	runtime	-
provided	provided	provided	provided	-
runtime	runtime	-	runtime	-
test	test	-	test	-

To illustrate the relationship of transitive dependency scope to direct dependency scope, consider the following example. If project-a contains a test-scoped dependency on project-b, which contains a compile-scoped dependency on project-c, then project-c would be a test-scoped transitive dependency of project-a.

You can think of this as a transitive boundary that acts as a filter on dependency scope. Transitive dependencies that are provided- and test-scoped usually do not affect a project. The exception to this rule is that a provided-scoped transitive dependency to a provided-scope direct dependency is still a provided dependency of a project. Transitive dependencies that are compile- and runtime-scoped usually affect a project regardless of the scope of a direct dependency. Transitive dependencies that are compile-scoped will have the same scope regardless of the scope of the direct dependency. Transitive dependencies that are runtime-scoped will generally have the same scope of the direct dependency except when the direct dependency has a scope of compile. When a transitive dependency is runtime-scoped and a direct is compile-scoped, the direct dependency and the transitive dependency will have an effective scope of runtime.

Conflict Resolution

There will be times when you need to exclude a transitive dependency, such as when you are depending on a project that depends on another project, but you would like to either exclude the dependency altogether or replace the transitive dependency with another dependency that provides the same functionality. Example 9-7 shows an example of a dependency element that adds a dependency on `project-a`, but excludes the transitive dependency `project-b`.

Example 9-7. Excluding a transitive dependency

```
<dependency>
  <groupId>org.sonatype.mavenbook</groupId>
  <artifactId>project-a</artifactId>
  <version>1.0</version>
  <exclusions>
    <exclusion>
      <groupId>org.sonatype.mavenbook</groupId>
      <artifactId>project-b</artifactId>
    </exclusion>
  </exclusions>
</dependency>
```

Often, you will want to replace a transitive dependency with another implementation. For example, if you are depending on a library that depends on the Sun JTA API, you may want to replace the declared transitive dependency. Hibernate is one example. Hibernate depends on the Sun JTA API JAR, which is not available in the central Maven repository because it cannot be freely redistributed. Fortunately, the Apache Geronimo project has created an independent implementation of this library that can be freely redistributed. To replace a transitive dependency with another dependency, you would exclude the transitive dependency and declare a dependency on the project you wanted instead. Example 9-8 shows an example of a such replacement.

Example 9-8. Excluding and replacing a transitive dependency

```
<dependencies>
  <dependency>
    <groupId>org.hibernate</groupId>
    <artifactId>hibernate</artifactId>
    <version>3.2.5.ga</version>
    <exclusions>
      <exclusion>
        <groupId>javax.transaction</groupId>
        <artifactId>jta</artifactId>
      </exclusion>
    </exclusions>
  </dependency>
  <dependency>
    <groupId>org.apache.geronimo.specs</groupId>
    <artifactId>geronimo-jta_1.1_spec</artifactId>
    <version>1.1</version>
  </dependency>
</dependencies>
```

In this example, nothing is marking the dependency on `geronimo-jta_1.1_spec` as a replacement; it just happens to be a library that provides the same API as the original JTA dependency. Here are some other reasons you might want to exclude or replace transitive dependencies:

- The `groupId` or `artifactId` of the artifact has changed, where the current project requires an alternately named version from a dependency's version, resulting in two copies of the same project in the classpath. Normally, Maven would capture this conflict and use a single version of the project, but when `groupId` or `artifactId` are different, Maven will consider this to be two different libraries.

- An artifact is not used in your project, and the transitive dependency has not been marked as an optional dependency. In this case, you might want to exclude a dependency because it isn't something your system needs, and you are trying to cut down on the number of libraries distributed with an application.

- An artifact that is provided by your runtime container, and thus should not be included with your build. An example of this is if a dependency depends on something like the Servlet API and you want to make sure that the dependency is not included in a web application's *WEB-INF/lib* directory.

- You want to exclude a dependency that might be an API with multiple implementations. This is the situation illustrated by Example 9-8; a Sun API requires click-wrap licensing and a time-consuming manual install into a custom repository (Sun's JTA JAR) versus a freely distributed version of the same API available in the central Maven repository (Geronimo's JTA implementation).

Dependency Management

Once you've adopted Maven at your super-complex enterprise and you have 220 interrelated Maven projects, you are going to start wondering if there is a better way to get a handle on dependency versions. If every single project that uses a dependency like the MySQL Java connector needs to independently list the version number of the dependency, you are going to run into problems when you need to upgrade to a new version. Because the version numbers are distributed throughout your project tree, you are going to have to manually edit each of the *pom.xml* files that reference a dependency to make sure that you are changing the version number everywhere. Even with *find*, *xargs*, and *awk*, you are still running the risk of missing a single POM.

Luckily, Maven provides a way for you to consolidate dependency version numbers in the `dependencyManagement` element. You'll usually see the `dependencyManagement` element in a top-level parent POM for an organization or project. Using the `dependencyManagement` element in a *pom.xml* allows you to reference a dependency in a child project without having to explicitly list the version. Maven will walk up the parent-child hierarchy until it finds a project with a `dependencyManagement` element; it will then use the version specified in this `dependencyManagement` element.

For example, if you have a large set of projects that make use of the MySQL Java connector version 5.1.2, you could define the `dependencyManagement` element shown in Example 9-9 in your multimodule project's top-level POM.

Example 9-9. Defining dependency versions in a top-level POM

```
<project>
  <modelVersion>4.0.0</modelVersion>
  <groupId>org.sonatype.mavenbook</groupId>
  <artifactId>a-parent</artifactId>
  <version>1.0.0</version>
  ...
  <dependencyManagement>
    <dependencies>
      <dependency>
        <groupId>mysql</groupId>
        <artifactId>mysql-connector-java</artifactId>
        <version>5.1.2</version>
      </dependency>
      ...
    <dependencies>
  </dependencyManagement>
```

Then, in a child project, you can add a dependency to the MySQL Java connector using the following dependency XML:

```
<project>
  <modelVersion>4.0.0</modelVersion>
  <parent>
    <groupId>org.sonatype.mavenbook</groupId>
    <artifactId>a-parent</artifactId>
    <version>1.0.0</version>
  </parent>
  <artifactId>project-a</artifactId>
  ...
  <dependencies>
    <dependency>
      <groupId>mysql</groupId>
      <artifactId>mysql-connector-java</artifactId>
    </dependency>
  </dependencies>
</project>
```

You should notice that the child project did not have to explicitly list the version of the `mysql-connector-java` dependency. Because this dependency was defined in the top-level POM's `dependencyManagement` element, the version number is going to propagate to the child project's dependency on `mysql-connector-java`. Note that if this child project did define a version, it would override the version listed in the top-level POM's `dependencyManagement` section. That is, the `dependencyManagement` version is used only when the child does not declare a version directly.

Dependency management in a top-level POM is different from just defining a dependency on a widely shared parent POM. For starters, all dependencies are inherited. If `mysql-connector-java` were listed as a dependency of the top-level parent project, every single project in the hierarchy would have a reference to this dependency. Instead of adding in unnecessary dependencies, using `dependencyManagement` allows you to consolidate and centralize the management of dependency versions without adding dependencies that are inherited by all children. In other words, the dependencyManagement element is equivalent to an environment variable that allows you to declare a dependency anywhere below a project without specifying a version number.

Project Relationships

One of the compelling reasons to use Maven is that it makes the process of tracking down dependencies (and dependencies of dependencies) very easy. When a project depends on an artifact of another project, we can say that this artifact is a dependency. In the case of a Java project, this can be as simple as a project depending on an external dependency such as Log4J or JUnit. Although dependencies can model external dependencies, they can also manage the dependencies between a set of related projects; if project-a depends on project-b, Maven is smart enough to know that project-b must be built before project-a.

Relationships are not only about dependencies and figuring out what one project needs to be able to build an artifact. Maven can model the relationship of a project to a parent, and the relationship of a project to submodules. This section gives an overview of the various relationships between projects and how such relationships are configured.

More on Coordinates

Coordinates define a unique location for a project. They were first introduced in Chapter 3. Projects are related to one another using Maven coordinates. project-a doesn't just depend on project-b; a project with a groupId, artifactId, and version depends on another project with a groupId, artifactId, and version. To review, a Maven coordinate is made up of three components:

groupId

> A groupId groups a set of related artifacts. Group identifiers generally resemble a Java package name. For example, the groupId org.apache.maven is the base groupId for all artifacts produced by the Apache Maven project. Group identifiers are translated into paths in the Maven repository; for example, the org.apache.maven groupId can be found in */maven2/org/apache/maven* on *http://repo1.maven.org/maven2/org/apache/maven*.

artifactId

> The artifactId is the project's main identifier. When you generate an artifact, this artifact is going to be named with the artifactId. When you refer to a project, you are going to refer to it using the artifactId. The artifactId, groupId combination must be unique. In other words, you can't have two separate projects with the same artifactId and groupId; artifactIds are unique within a particular groupId.

Although dots (.) are commonly used in groupIds, you should try to avoid using them in artifactIds. They can cause issues when trying to parse a fully qualified name down into the subcomponents.

version

When an artifact is released, it is released with a version number. This version number is a numeric identifier such as "1.0," "1.1.1," or "1.1.2-alpha-01." You can also use what is known as a snapshot version. A snapshot version is a version for a component that is under development. Snapshot version numbers always end in SNAPSHOT; for example, "1.0-SNAPSHOT," "1.1.1-SNAPSHOT," and "1-SNAPSHOT." The section "Project Versions," earlier in this chapter, introduced versions and version ranges.

There is a fourth, less-used qualifier:

classifier

You would use a classifier if you were releasing the same code, but needed to produce two separate artifacts for technical reasons. For example, if you wanted to build two separate artifacts of a JAR, one compiled with the Java 1.4 compiler and another compiled with the Java 6 compiler, you might use the classifier to produce two separate JAR artifacts under the same *groupId:artifactId:version* combination. If your project uses native extensions, you might use the classifier to produce an artifact for each target platform. Classifiers are commonly used to package up an artifact's sources, Javadocs, or binary assemblies.

When we talk of dependencies in this book, we often use the following shorthand notation to describe a dependency: *groupId:artifactId:version*. To refer to the 2.5 release of the Spring Framework, we would refer to it as `org.springframework:spring:2.5`. When you ask Maven to print out a list of dependencies with the Maven Dependency plugin, you will also see that Maven tends to print out log messages with this shorthand dependency notation.

Multimodule Projects

Multimodule projects are projects that contain a list of modules to build. A multimodule project always has a packaging of pom and rarely produces an artifact. A multimodule project exists only to group projects together in a build. Figure 9-3 shows a project hierarchy that includes two parent projects with packaging of pom, and three projects with packaging of jar.

The directory structure on the file system would also mirror the module relationships. A set of projects illustrated by Figure 9-3 would have the following directory structure:

```
top-group/pom.xml
top-group/sub-group/pom.xml
```

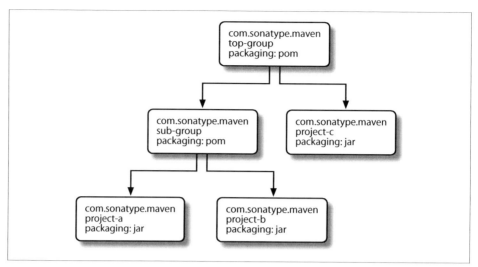

Figure 9-3. Multimodule project relationships

```
top-group/sub-group/project-a/pom.xml
top-group/sub-group/project-b/pom.xml
top-group/project-c/pom.xml
```

The projects are related to one another because top-group and sub-group are referencing sub-modules in a POM. For example, the org.sonatype.mavenbook:top-group project is a multimodule project with packaging of type pom. top-group's *pom.xml* would include the modules element shown in Example 9-10.

Example 9-10. top-group modules element

```
<project>
  <groupId>org.sonatype.mavenbook</groupId>
  <artifactId>top-group</artifactId>
  ...
  <modules>
    <module>sub-group</module>
    <module>project-c</module>
  </modules>
  ...
</project>
```

When Maven is reading the top-group POM, it will look at the modules element and see that top-group references the projects sub-group and project-c. Maven will then look for a *pom.xml* in each of these subdirectories. Maven repeats this process for each of the submodules: it will read the *sub-group/pom.xml* and see that the sub-group project references two projects with the modules element shown in Example 9-11.

Example 9-11. sub-group modules element

```
<project>
  ...
```

```
  <modules>
    <module>project-a</module>
    <module>project-b</module>
  </modules>
  ...
</project>
```

Note that we call the projects under the multimodule projects "modules" and not "children" or "child projects." This is purposeful, so as not to confuse projects grouped by multimodule projects with projects that inherit POM information from each other.

Project Inheritance

There are going to be times when you want a project to inherit values from a parent POM. You might be building a large system, and you don't want to have to repeat the same dependency elements over and over again. You can avoid repeating yourself if your projects make use of inheritance via the parent element. When a project specifies a parent, it inherits the information in the parent project's POM. It can then override and add to the values specified in this parent POM.

All Maven POMs inherit values from a parent POM. If a POM does not specify a direct parent using the parent element, that POM will inherit values from the Super POM. Example 9-12 shows the parent element of project-a, which inherits the POM defined by the a-parent project.

Example 9-12. Project inheritance

```
<project>
  <parent>
    <groupId>com.training.killerapp</groupId>
    <artifactId>a-parent</artifactId>
    <version>1.0-SNAPSHOT</version>
  </parent>
  <artifactId>project-a</artifactId>
  ...
</project>
```

Running *mvn help:effective-pom* in project-a would show a POM that is the result of merging the Super POM with the POM defined by a-parent and the POM defined in project-a. The implicit and explicit inheritance relationships for project-a are shown in Figure 9-4.When a project specifies a parent project, Maven uses that parent POM as a starting point before it reads the current project's POM. It inherits everything, including the groupId and version number. You'll notice that project-a does not specify either; both groupId and version are inherited from a-parent. With a parent element, all a POM really needs to define is an artifactId. This isn't mandatory; project-a could have a different groupId and version, but by not providing values, Maven will use the values specified in the parent POM. If you start using Maven to manage and build large multimodule projects, you will often be creating many projects that share a common groupId and version.

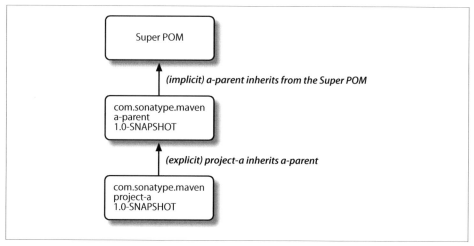

Figure 9-4. Project inheritance for a-parent and project-a

When you inherit a POM, you can choose to live with the inherited POM information or to selectively override it. The following is a list of items a Maven POM inherits from its parent POM:

- Identifiers (at least one of `groupId` or `artifactId` must be overridden)
- Dependencies
- Developers and contributors
- Plugin lists
- Reports lists
- Plugin executions (executions with matching IDs are merged)
- Plugin configuration

When Maven inherits dependencies, it will add dependencies of child projects to the dependencies defined in parent projects. You can use this feature of Maven to specify widely used dependencies across all projects that inherit from a top-level POM. For example, if your system makes universal use of the Log4J logging framework, you can list this dependency in your top-level POM. Any projects that inherit POM information from this project will automatically have Log4J as a dependency. Similarly, if you need to make sure that every project is using the same version of a Maven plugin, you can list that version explicitly in a top-level parent POM's `pluginManagement` section.

Maven assumes that the parent POM is available from the local repository, or available in the parent directory (*../pom.xml*) of the current project. If neither location is valid, this default behavior may be overridden via the `relativePath` element. For example, some organizations prefer a flat project structure where a parent project's *pom.xml* isn't in the parent directory of a child project. It might be in a sibling directory to the project. If your child project were in a directory named *./project-a* and the parent project were in a directory named *./a-parent*, you could specify the relative location of parent-a's POM with the following configuration:

```
<project>
  <parent>
    <groupId>org.sonatype.mavenbook</groupId>
    <artifactId>a-parent</artifactId>
    <version>1.0-SNAPSHOT</version>
    <relativePath>../a-parent/pom.xml</relativePath>
  </parent>
  <artifactId>project-a</artifactId>
</project>
```

POM Best Practices

Maven can be used to manage everything from simple, single-project systems to builds that involve hundreds of interrelated submodules. Part of the learning process with Maven isn't just figuring out the syntax for configuring Maven; it is learning the "Maven Way"—that is, the current set of best practices for organizing and building projects using Maven. This section attempts to distill some of this knowledge to help you adopt best practices from the start without having to wade through years of discussions on the Maven mailing lists.

Grouping Dependencies

If you have a set of dependencies that are logically grouped together, you can create a project with pom packaging that groups dependencies together. For example, let's assume that your application uses Hibernate, a popular Object-Relational Mapping framework. Every project that uses Hibernate might also have a dependency on the Spring Framework and a MySQL JDBC driver. Instead of having to include these dependencies in every project that uses Hibernate, Spring, and MySQL, you could create a special POM that does nothing more than declare a set of common dependencies. You could create a project called persistence-deps (short for "persistence dependencies") and have every project that needs to do persistence depend on this convenience project. See Example 9-13.

Example 9-13. Consolidating dependencies in a single POM project

```
<project>
  <groupId>org.sonatype.mavenbook</groupId>
  <artifactId>persistence-deps</artifactId>
  <version>1.0</version>
  <packaging>pom</packaging>
  <dependencies>
    <dependency>
      <groupId>org.hibernate</groupId>
      <artifactId>hibernate</artifactId>
      <version>${hibernateVersion}</version>
    </dependency>
```

```
      <dependency>
        <groupId>org.hibernate</groupId>
        <artifactId>hibernate-annotations</artifactId>
        <version>${hibernateAnnotationsVersion}</version>
      </dependency>
      <dependency>
        <groupId>org.springframework</groupId>
        <artifactId>spring-hibernate3</artifactId>
        <version>${springVersion}</version>
      </dependency>
      <dependency>
        <groupId>mysql</groupId>
        <artifactId>mysql-connector-java</artifactId>
        <version>${mysqlVersion}</version>
      </dependency>
    </dependencies>
    <properties>
      <mysqlVersion>(5.1,)</mysqlVersion>
      <springVersion>(2.0.6,)</springVersion>
      <hibernateVersion>3.2.5.ga</hibernateVersion>
      <hibernateAnnotationsVersion>3.3.0.ga</hibernateAnnotationsVersion>
    </properties>
</project>
```

If you create this project in a directory named persistence-deps, all you need to do is
create this *pom.xml* and run *mvn install*. Since the packaging type is pom, this POM is
installed in your local repository. You can now add this project as a dependency, and
all of its dependencies will be added to your project. When you declare a dependency
on this persistence-deps project, as shown in Example 9-14, don't forget to specify the
dependency type as pom.

Example 9-14. Declaring a dependency on a POM

```
<project>
  <description>This is a project requiring JDBC</description>
  ...
  <dependencies>
    ...
    <dependency>
      <groupId>org.sonatype.mavenbook</groupId>
      <artifactId>persistence-deps</artifactId>
      <version>1.0</version>
      <type>pom</type>
    </dependency>
  </dependencies>
</project>
```

If you later decide to switch to a different JDBC driver (for example, JTDS), just replace
the dependencies in the persistence-deps project to use net.sourceforge.jtds:jtds
instead of mysql:mysql-java-connector and update the version number. All projects
depending on persistence-deps will use JTDS if they decide to update to the newer
version. Consolidating related dependencies is a good way to cut down on the length

of *pom.xml* files that start having to depend on a large number of dependencies. If you need to share a large number of dependencies between projects, you could also just establish parent-child relationships between projects and refactor all common dependencies to the parent project, but the disadvantage of the parent-child approach is that a project can have only one parent. Sometimes it makes more sense to group similar dependencies together and reference a pom dependency. This way, your project can reference as many of these consolidated dependency POMs as it needs.

 Maven uses the depth of a dependency in the tree when resolving conflicts using a nearest-wins approach. Using the dependency grouping technique pushes those dependencies one level down in the tree. Keep this in mind when choosing between grouping in a POM or using dependencyManagement in a parent POM.

Multimodule Versus Inheritance

There is a difference between inheriting from a parent project and being managed by a multimodule project. A parent project is one that passes its values to its children. A multimodule project simply manages a group of other subprojects or modules. The multimodule relationship is defined from the topmost level downwards. When setting up a multimodule project, you are simply telling a project that its build should include the specified modules. Multimodule builds are to be used to group modules together in a single build. The parent-child relationship is defined from the leaf node upward. The parent-child relationship deals more with the definition of a particular project. When you associate a child with its parent, you are telling Maven that a project's POM is derived from another.

To illustrate the decision process that goes into choosing a design that uses inheritance versus multimodule, or both approaches, consider the following two examples: the Maven project used to generate this book, and a hypothetical project that contains a number of logically grouped modules.

Simple project

First, let's take a look at the Maven book project. The inheritance and multimodule relationships are shown in Figure 9-5.

When we built this Maven book you are reading, we ran *mvn package* in a multimodule project named maven-book. This multimodule project includes two submodules: book-examples and book-chapters. Neither of these projects share the same parent; they are related only in that they are modules in the maven-book project. book-examples builds the ZIP and TGZ archives you downloaded to get this book's example. When we ran the book-examples build from *book-examples/* directory with *mvn package*, it had no knowledge that it was a part of the larger maven-book project. book-examples doesn't really care about maven-book; all it knows in life is that its parent is the topmost sonatype

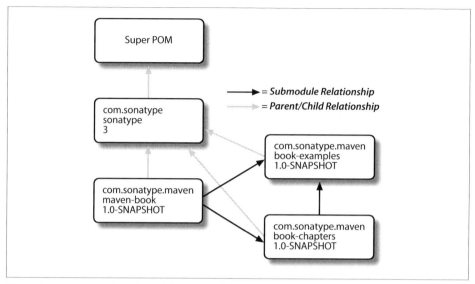

Figure 9-5. maven-book multimodule versus inheritance

POM and that it creates an archive of examples. In this case, the `maven-book` project exists only as a convenience and as an aggregator of modules.

The book projects do all define a parent. Each of the three projects—`maven-book`, `book-examples`, and `book-chapters`—all list a shared "corporate" parent: `sonatype`. This is a common practice in organizations that have adopted Maven. Instead of having every project extend the Super POM by default, some organizations define a top-level corporate POM that serves as the default parent when a project doesn't have any good reason to depend on another. In this book example, there is no compelling reason to have `book-examples` and `book-chapters` share the same parent POM; they are entirely different projects that have a different set of dependencies, have a different build configuration, and use drastically different plugins to create the content you are now reading. The `sonatype` POM gives the organization a chance to customize the default behavior of Maven and supply some organization-specific information to configure deployment settings and build profiles.

Multimodule enterprise project

Let's take a look at an example that provides a more accurate picture of a real-world project where inheritance and multimodule relationships exist side by side. Figure 9-6 shows a collection of projects that resemble a typical set of projects in an enterprise application. There is a top-level POM for the corporation with an `artifactId` of `sonatype`. There is also a multimodule project named `big-system` that references submodules `server-side` and `client-side`.

What's going on in this figure? Let's try to deconstruct the confusing set of arrows. First, take a look at `big-system`. The `big-system` might be the project on which you

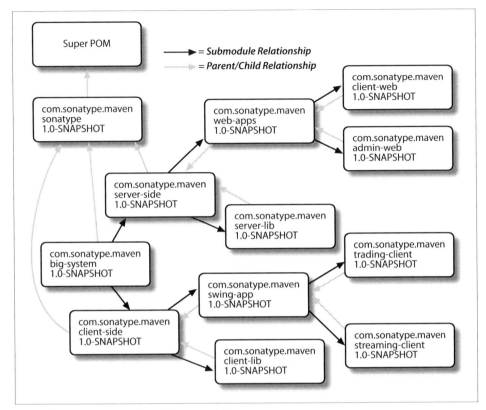

Figure 9-6. Enterprise multimodule versus inheritance

would run *mvn package* to build and test the entire system. big-system references sub-modules client-side and server-side. Each of these projects effectively rolls up all of the code that runs on either the server or on the client. Let's focus on the server-side project. Under the server-side project, we have a project called server-lib and a multimodule project named web-apps. Under web-apps, we have two Java web applications: client-web and admin-web.

Let's start with the parent-child relationships from client-web and admin-web to web-apps. Since both of the web applications are implemented in the same web application framework (let's say Wicket), both projects would share the same set of core dependencies. The dependencies on the Servlet API, the JSP API, and Wicket would all be captured in the web-apps project. Both client-web and admin-web also need to depend on server-lib. This dependency would be defined as a dependency between web-apps and server-lib. Because client-web and admin-web share so much configuration by inheriting from web-apps, both client-web and admin-web will have very small POMs containing little more than identifiers, a parent declaration, and a final build name.

Next, we focus on the parent-child relationship from `web-apps` and `server-lib` to `server-side`. In this case, let's just assume that there is a separate working group of developers who work on the server-side code and another group of developers who work on the client-side code. The list of developers would be configured in the `server-side` POM and inherited by all of the child projects underneath it: `web-apps`, `server-lib`, `client-web`, and `admin-web`. We could also imagine that the `server-side` project might have different build and deployment settings that are unique to the development for the server side. The `server-side` project might define a build profile that only makes sense for all of the `server-side` projects. This build profile might contain the database host and credentials, or the `server-side` project's POM might configure a specific version of the Maven Jetty plugin, which should be universal across all projects that inherit the `server-side` POM.

In this example, the main reason to use parent-child relationships is shared dependencies and common configuration for a group of projects that are logically related. All of the projects below `big-system` are related to one another as submodules, but not all submodules are configured to point back to a parent project that is included as a submodule. Everything is a submodule for reasons of convenience: to build the entire system, just go to the `big-system` project directory and run *mvn package*. Look more closely at the figure and you'll see that there is no parent-child relationship between `server-side` and `big-system`. Why is this? POM inheritance is very powerful, but it can be overused. When it makes sense to share dependencies and build configurations, a parent-child relationship should be used. When it doesn't make sense is when there are distinct differences between two projects. Take, for example, the `server-side` and `client-side` projects. It is possible to create a system where `client-side` and `server-side` inherited a common POM from `big-system`, but as soon as a significant divergence between the two child projects develops, you have to figure out creative ways to factor out common build configuration to `big-system` without affecting all of the children. Even though `client-side` and `server-side` might both depend on Log4J, they also might have distinct plugin configurations.

You may reach a certain point, defined more by style and experience, where you decide that minimal duplication of configuration is a small price to pay for allowing projects such as `client-side` and `server-side` to remain completely independent. Designing a huge set of 30-plus projects that all inherit five levels of POM configuration isn't always the best idea. In such a setup, you might not have to duplicate your Log4J dependency more than once, but you'll also end up having to wade through five levels of POM just to figure out how Maven calculated your effective POM—all of this complexity to avoid duplicating five lines of dependency declaration. In Maven, there is a "Maven Way," but there are also many ways to accomplish the same thing. It all boils down to preference and style. For the most part, you won't go wrong if all of your submodules turn out to define back-references to the same project as a parent, but your use of Maven may evolve over time.

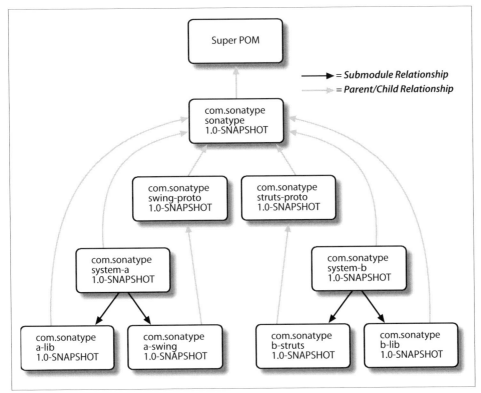

Figure 9-7. Using parent projects as "prototypes" for specialized projects

Prototype parent projects

Take the example shown in Figure 9-7 as another hypothetical and creative way to use inheritance and multimodule builds to reuse dependencies.This figure represents yet another way to think about inheritance and multimodule projects. In this example, you have two distinct systems: system-a and system-b. Each define independent applications. system-a defines two modules, a-lib and a-swing. system-a and a-lib both define the top-level sonatype POM as a parent project, but the a-swing project defines swing-proto as a parent project. In this system, swing-proto supplies a foundational POM for Swing applications, and the struts-proto project provides a foundational POM for Struts 2 web applications. While the sonatype POM provides high-level information such as the groupId, organization information, and build profiles, struts-proto defines all of the dependencies that you need to create a Struts application. This approach would work well if your development is characterized by many independent applications that each have to follow the same set of rules. If you are creating a lot of Struts applications but they are not really related to one another, you might just define everything you need in struts-proto. The downside to this approach is that you won't be able to use parent-child relationships within the system-a and system-b project hierarchies to share information like developers and other build configurations. A project can have only one parent.

The other downside of this approach is that as soon as you have one project that "breaks the mold," you'll either have to override the prototype parent POM or find a way to factor customizations into the shared parent, without those customizations affecting all the children. In general, using POMs as prototypes for specialized project "types" isn't a recommended practice.

## CHAPTER 10

The Build Lifecycle

Introduction

Maven models projects as nouns that are described by a POM. The POM captures the identity of a project: What does a project contain? What type of packaging does a project need? Does the project have a parent? What are the dependencies? We've explored the idea of describing a project in the previous chapters, but we haven't introduced the mechanism that allows Maven to act upon these objects. In Maven, the "verbs" are goals packaged in Maven plugins that are tied to phases in a build lifecycle. A Maven lifecycle consists of a sequence of named phases: `prepare-resources`, `compile`, `package`, and `install`, among others. There is a phase that captures compilation and a phase that captures packaging. There are pre- and postphases that can be used to register goals that must run prior to compilation, or tasks that must be run after a particular phase. When you tell Maven to build a project, you are telling Maven to step through a defined sequence of phases and to execute any goals that may have been registered with each phase.

A build lifecycle is an organized sequence of phases that exist to give order to a set of goals. Those goals are chosen and bound by the packaging type of the project being acted upon. There are three standard lifecycles in Maven: `clean`, `default` (sometimes called `build`), and `site`. In this chapter, you will learn how Maven ties goals to lifecycle phases and how the lifecycle can be customized. You will also learn about the default lifecycle phases.

Clean Lifecycle (clean)

The first lifecycle you'll be interested in is the simplest lifecycle in Maven. Running *mvn clean* invokes the clean lifecycle that consists of three lifecycle phases:

- `pre-clean`
- `clean`
- `post-clean`

The interesting phase in the clean lifecycle is the clean phase. The Clean plugin's clean goal (clean:clean) is bound to the clean phase in the clean lifecycle. The clean:clean goal deletes the output of a build by deleting the build directory. If you haven't customized the location of the build directory, it will be the *${basedir}/target* directory as defined by the Super POM. When you execute the clean:clean goal, you do not do so by executing the goal directly with *mvn clean:clean*; you do so by executing the clean phase of the clean lifecycle. Executing the clean phase gives Maven an opportunity to execute any other goals that may be bound to the pre-clean phase.

For example, suppose you wanted to trigger an antrun:run goal task to echo a notification on pre-clean, or to make an archive of a project's build directory before it is deleted. Simply running the clean:clean goal will not execute the lifecycle at all, but specifying the clean phase will use the clean lifecycle and advance through the three lifecycle phases until it reaches the clean phase. Example 10-1 shows a build configuration that binds the antrun:run goal to the pre-clean phase to echo an alert that the project artifact is about to be deleted. In this example, the antrun:run goal is being used to execute some arbitrary Ant commands to check for an existing project artifact. If the project's artifact is about to be deleted, it will print this to the screen.

Example 10-1. Triggering a goal on pre-clean

```
<project>
  ...
  <build>
    <plugins>... <plugin>
    <artifactId>maven-antrun-plugin</artifactId>
    <executions>
      <execution>
        <id>file-exists</id>
        <phase>pre-clean</phase>
        <goals>
          <goal>run</goal>
        </goals>
        <configuration>
          <tasks>
            <!-- adds the ant-contrib tasks (if/then/else used below) -->
            <taskdef resource="net/sf/antcontrib/antcontrib.properties" />
            <available file="${project.build.directory}/${project.build.finalName}.jar"
                       property="file.exists" value="true" />

            <if>
              <not>
                <isset property="file.exists" />
              </not>
              <then>
                <echo>No
                  ${project.build.finalName}.${project.packaging} to
                  delete</echo>
              </then>
              <else>
                <echo>Deleting
```

```
                    ${project.build.finalName}.${project.packaging}</echo>
              </else>
            </if>
          </tasks>
        </configuration>
      </execution>
    </executions>
    <dependencies>
      <dependency>
        <groupId>ant-contrib</groupId>
        <artifactId>ant-contrib</artifactId>
        <version>1.0b2</version>
      </dependency>
    </dependencies>
  </plugin>
  </plugins>
  </build>
</project>
```

Running *mvn clean* on a project with this build configuration will produce output similar to the following:

```
[INFO] Scanning for projects...
[INFO] ------------------------------------------------------------------------
[INFO] Building Your Project
[INFO]    task-segment: [clean]
[INFO] ------------------------------------------------------------------------
[INFO] [antrun:run {execution: file-exists}]
[INFO] Executing tasks
      [echo] Deleting your-project-1.0-SNAPSHOT.jar
[INFO] Executed tasks
[INFO] [clean:clean]
[INFO] Deleting directory ~/corp/your-project/target
[INFO] Deleting directory ~/corp/your-project/target/classes
[INFO] Deleting directory ~/corp/your-project/target/test-classes
[INFO] ------------------------------------------------------------------------
[INFO] BUILD SUCCESSFUL
[INFO] ------------------------------------------------------------------------
[INFO] Total time: 1 second
[INFO] Finished at: Wed Nov 08 11:46:26 CST 2006
[INFO] Final Memory: 2M/5M
[INFO] ------------------------------------------------------------------------
```

In addition to configuring Maven to run a goal during the pre-clean phase, you can also customize the Clean plugin to delete files to the build output directory. You can configure the plugin to remove specific files in a fileSet. Example 10-2 configures clean to remove all *.class* files in a directory named *target-other/* using standard Ant file wildcards: * and **.

Example 10-2. Customizing the behavior of the Clean plugin

```
<project>
  <modelVersion>4.0.0</modelVersion>
  ...
  <build>
```

```
  <plugins>
    <plugin>
      <artifactId>maven-clean-plugin</artifactId>
      <configuration>
        <filesets>
          <fileset>
            <directory>target-other</directory>
            <includes>
              <include>*.class</include>
            </includes>
          </fileset>
        </filesets>
      </configuration>
    </plugin>
  </plugins>
</build>
</project>
```

Default Lifecycle (default)

Most Maven users will be familiar with the default lifecycle. It is a general model of a build process for a software application. The first phase is validate, and the last phase is deploy. The phases in the default Maven lifecycle are shown in Table 10-1.

Table 10-1. Maven lifecycle phases

Lifecycle phase	Description
validate	Validate that the project is correct and all necessary information is available to complete a build.
generate-sources	Generate any source code for inclusion in compilation.
process-sources	Process the source code; for example, to filter any values.
generate-resources	Generate resources for inclusion in the package.
process-resources	Copy and process the resources into the destination directory, ready for packaging.
compile	Compile the source code of the project.
process-classes	Post-process the generated files from compilation; for example, to do bytecode enhancement on Java classes.
generate-test-sources	Generate any test source code for inclusion in compilation.
process-test-sources	Process the test source code; for example, to filter any values.
generate-test-resources	Create resources for testing.
process-test-resources	Copy and process the resources into the test destination directory.
test-compile	Compile the test source code into the test destination directory.
test	Run tests using a suitable unit testing framework. These tests should not require the code be packaged or deployed.
prepare-package	Perform any operations necessary to prepare a package before the actual packaging. This often results in an unpacked, processed version of the package (coming in Maven 2.1+).

Lifecycle phase	Description
package	Take the compiled code and package it in its distributable format, such as a JAR, WAR, or EAR.
pre-integration-test	Perform actions required before integration tests are executed. This may involve things such as setting up the required environment.
integration-test	Process and deploy the package if necessary into an environment where integration tests can be run.
post-integration-test	Perform actions required after integration tests have been executed. This may include cleaning up the environment.
verify	Run any checks to verify the package is valid and meets quality criteria.
install	Install the package into the local repository, for use as a dependency in other projects locally.
deploy	Copies the final package to the remote repository for sharing with other developers and projects (usually relevant only during a formal release).

Site Lifecycle (site)

Maven does more than build software artifacts from project; it can also generate project documentation and reports about the project, or about a collection of projects. Project documentation and site generation have a dedicated lifecycle that contains four phases:

1. pre-site
2. site
3. post-site
4. site-deploy

The default goals bound to the site lifecycle are:

- site (site:site)
- site-deploy (site:deploy)

The packaging type does not usually alter this lifecycle, since packaging types are concerned primarily with artifact creation, not with the type of site generated. The Site plugin kicks off the execution of Doxia (*http://maven.apache.org/doxia/*) document generation and other report generation plugins. You can generate a site from a Maven project by running the following command:

    $ mvn site

For more information about Maven site generation, see Chapter 15.

Package-Specific Lifecycles

The specific goals bound to each phase default to a set of goals specific to a project's packaging. A project with jar packaging has a different set of default goals from a project with a packaging of `war`. The `packaging` element affects the steps required to build a project. For an example of how the packaging affects the build, consider two projects: one with `pom` packaging and the other with `jar` packaging. The project with `pom` packaging will run the `site:attach-descriptor` goal during the `package` phase, and the project with `jar` packaging will run the `jar:jar` goal instead.

The following sections describe the lifecycle for all built-in packaging types in Maven. Use these sections to find out which default goals are mapped to default lifecycle phases.

JAR

JAR is the default packaging type—the most common and thus the most commonly encountered lifecycle configuration. The default goals for the JAR lifecycle are shown in Table 10-2.

Table 10-2. Default goals for JAR packaging

Lifecycle phase	Goal
process-resources	resources:resources
compile	compiler:compile
process-test-resources	resources:testResources
test-compile	compiler:testCompile
test	surefire:test
package	jar:jar
install	install:install
deploy	deploy:deploy

POM

POM is the simplest packaging type. The artifact that it generates is itself only, rather than a JAR, SAR, or EAR. There is no code to test or compile, and there are no resources to process. The default goals for projects with POM packaging are shown in Table 10-3.

Table 10-3. Default goals for POM packaging

Lifecycle phase	Goal
package	site:attach-descriptor
install	install:install
deploy	deploy:deploy

Maven Plugin

This packaging type is similar to the `jar` packaging type with three additions: `plugin:descriptor`, `plugin:addPluginArtifactMetadata`, and `plugin:updateRegistry`.

These goals generate a descriptor file and perform some modifications to the repository data. The default goals for projects with plugin packaging are shown in Table 10-4.

Table 10-4. Default goals for plugin packaging

Lifecycle phase	Goal
generate-resources	plugin:descriptor
process-resources	resources:resources
compile	compiler:compile
process-test-resources	resources:testResources
test-compile	compiler:testCompile
test	surefire:test
package	jar:jar,plugin:addPluginArtifactMetadata
install	install:install,plugin:updateRegistry
deploy	deploy:deploy

EJB

EJBs, or Enterprise JavaBeans, are a common data access mechanism for model-driven development in Enterprise Java. Maven provides support for EJB 2 and 3. You must configure the EJB plugin to specifically package for EJB 3; otherwise, the plugin defaults to 2.1 and looks for the presence of certain EJB configuration files. The default goals for projects with EJB packaging are shown in Table 10-5.

Table 10-5. Default goals for EJB packaging

Lifecycle phase	Goal
process-resources	resources:resources
compile	compiler:compile
process-test-resources	resources:testResources
test-compile	compiler:testCompile
test	surefire:test
package	ejb:ejb
install	install:install
deploy	deploy:deploy

WAR

The WAR packaging type is similar to the JAR and EJB types. The exception being the package goal of war:war. Note that the war:war plugin requires a *web.xml* configuration in your *src/main/webapp/WEB-INF* directory. The default goals for projects with WAR packaging are shown in Table 10-6.

Table 10-6. Default goals for WAR packaging

Lifecycle phase	Goal
process-resources	resources:resources
compile	compiler:compile
process-test-resources	resources:testResources
test-compile	compiler:testCompile
test	surefire:test
package	war:war
install	install:install
deploy	deploy:deploy

EAR

EARs are probably the simplest Java Enterprise Edition (EE) constructs, consisting primarily of the deployment descriptor *application.xml* file, some resources, and some modules. The EAR plugin has a goal named `generate-application-xml` that generates the *application.xml* based on the configuration in the EAR project's POM. The default goals for projects with EAR packaging are shown in Table 10-7.

Table 10-7. Default goals for EAR packaging

Lifecycle phase	Goal
generate-resources	ear:generate-application-xml
process-resources	resources:resources
package	ear:ear
install	install:install
deploy	deploy:deploy

Other Packaging Types

This is not an exhaustive list of every packaging type available for Maven. There are a number of packaging formats available through external projects and plugins: the NAR (native archive) packaging type, the SWF and SWC packaging types for projects that produce Adobe Flash and Flex content, and many others. You can also define a custom packaging type and customize the default lifecycle goals to suit your own project packaging requirements.

To use one of these custom packaging types, you need two things: a plugin that defines the lifecycle for a custom packaging type and a repository that contains this plugin. Some custom packaging types are defined in plugins available from the central Maven repository. Example 10-3 shows an example of a project that references the Israfil Flex plugin and uses a custom packaging type of SWF to produce output from Adobe Flex source.

Example 10-3. Custom packaging type for Adobe Flex (SWF)

```
<project>
  ...
  <packaging>swf</packaging>
  ...
  <build>
    <plugins>
      <plugin>
        <groupId>net.israfil.mojo</groupId>
        <artifactId>maven-flex2-plugin</artifactId>
        <version>1.4-SNAPSHOT</version>
        <extensions>true</extensions>
        <configuration>
          <debug>true</debug>
          <flexHome>${flex.home}</flexHome>
          <useNetwork>true</useNetwork>
          <main>org/sonatype/mavenbook/Main.mxml</main>
        </configuration>
      </plugin>
    </plugins>
  </build>
  ...
</project>
```

We will show you how to create your own packaging type later in this chapter, but this example should give you an idea of what you'll need to do to reference a custom packaging type. All you need to do is reference the plugin that supplies the custom packaging type. The Israfil Flex plugin is a third-party Maven plugin hosted at Google Code. For more information about this plugin and to learn how to use Maven to compile Adobe Flex, go to *http://code.google.com/p/israfil-mojo*. This plugin supplies the lifecycle shown in Table 10-8 for the SWF packaging type.

Table 10-8. Default lifecycle for SWF packaging

Lifecycle phase	Goal
compile	flex2:compile-swc
install	install
deploy	deploy

Common Lifecycle Goals

Many of the packaging lifecycles have similar goals. If you look at the goals bound to the WAR and JAR lifecycles, you'll see that they differ only in the package phase. The package phase of the WAR lifecycle calls war:war and the package phase of the JAR lifecycle calls jar:jar. Most of the lifecycles you will come into contact with share some common lifecycle goals for managing resources, running tests, and compiling source code. In this section, we'll explore some of these common lifecycle goals in detail.

Process Resources

Most lifecycles bind the `resources:resources` goal to the `process-resources` phase. The `process-resources` phase "processes" resources and copies them to the output directory. If you haven't customized the default directory locations defined in the Super POM, this means that Maven will copy the files from *${basedir}/src/main/resources* to *${basedir}/target/classes* or the directory defined in *${project.build.outputDirectory}*. In addition to copying the resources to the output directory, Maven can also apply a filter to the resources that allows you to replace tokens within resource file. Just as variables are referenced in a POM using ${...} notation, you can reference variables in your project's resources using the same syntax. Coupled with build profiles, such a facility can be used to produce build artifacts that target different deployment platforms. This is something that is common in environments that need to produce output for development, testing, staging, and production platforms from the same project. For more information about build profiles, see Chapter 11.

To illustrate resource filtering, assume that you have a project with an XML file in *src/main/resources/META-INF/service.xml*. You want to externalize some configuration variables to a properties file. In other words, you might want to reference a JDBC URL, username, and password for your database, and you don't want to put these values directly into the *service.xml* file. Instead, you would like to use a properties file to capture all of the configuration points for your program. Doing this will allow you to consolidate all configuration into a single properties file and make it easier to change configuration values when you need to target a new deployment environment. First, take a look at the contents of *service.xml* in *src/main/resources/META-INF*, shown in Example 10-4.

Example 10-4. Using properties in project resources

```
<service>
  <!-- This URL was set by project version ${project.version} -->
  <url>${jdbc.url}</url>
  <user>${jdbc.username}</user>
  <password>${jdbc.password}</password>
</service>
```

This XML file uses the same property reference syntax you can use in the POM. In fact, the first variable referenced is the `project` variable that is also an implicit variable made available in the POM. The `project` variable provides access to POM information. The next three variable references are `jdbc.url`, `jdbc.username`, and `jdbc.password`. These custom variables are defined in a properties file, *src/main/filters/default.properties*, shown in Example 10-5.

Example 10-5. default.properties in src/main/filters

```
jdbc.url=jdbc:hsqldb:mem:mydb
jdbc.username=sa
jdbc.password=
```

To configure resource filtering with this *default.properties* file, we need to specify two things in a project's POM: a list of properties files in the `filters` element of the build configuration, and a flag telling Maven that the resources directory is to be filtered. The default Maven behavior is to skip filtering and just copy the resources to the output directory; you'll need to explicitly configure the resource filter, or Maven will skip the step altogether. This default ensures that Maven's resource-filtering feature doesn't surprise you out of nowhere, clobbering any `${...}` references you didn't want it to replace. See Example 10-6.

Example 10-6. Filter resources (replacing properties)

```
<build>
  <filters>
    <filter>src/main/filters/default.properties</filter>
  </filters>
  <resources>
    <resource>
      <directory>src/main/resources</directory>
      <filtering>true</filtering>
    </resource>
  </resources>
</build>
```

As with all directories in Maven, the resources directory does not need to be in *src/main/resources*. This is just the default value defined in the Super POM. You should also note that you don't need to consolidate all of your resources into a single directory. You can always separate resources into separate directories under *src/main*. Assume that you have a project that contains hundreds of XML documents and hundreds of images. Instead of mixing the resources in the *src/main/resources* directory, you might want to create two directories—*src/main/xml* and *src/main/images*—to hold this content. To add directories to the list of resource directories, you would add the `resource` elements shown in Example 10-7 to your build configuration.

Example 10-7. Configuring additional resource directories

```
<build>
  ...
  <resources>
    <resource>
      <directory>src/main/resources</directory>
    </resource>
    <resource>
      <directory>src/main/xml</directory>
    </resource>
    <resource>
      <directory>src/main/images</directory>
```

```
    </resource>
  </resources>
  ...
</build>
```

When you are building a project that produces a console application or a command-line tool, you'll often find yourself writing simple shell scripts that need to reference the JAR produced by a build. When you are using the assembly plugin to produce a distribution for an application as a ZIP or TAR, you might place all of your scripts in a directory such as *src/main/command*. In the POM resource configuration shown in Example 10-8, you'll see how we can use resource filtering and a reference to the project variable to capture the final output name of the JAR. For more information about the Maven Assembly plugin, see Chapter 12.

Example 10-8. Filtering script resources

```
<build>
  <groupId>org.sonatype.mavenbook</groupId>
  <artifactId>simple-cmd</artifactId>
  <version>2.3.1</version>
  ...
  <resources>
    <resource>
      <filtering>true</filtering>
      <directory>${basedir}/src/main/command</directory>
      <includes>
        <include>run.bat</include>
        <include>run.sh</include>
      </includes>
      <targetPath>${basedir}</targetPath>
    </resource>
    <resource>
      <directory>${basedir}/src/main/resources</directory>
    </resource>
  </resources>
  ...
</build>
```

If you run *mvn process-resources* in this project, you will end up with two files, *run.sh* and *run.bat*, in ${basedir}. We've singled out these two files in a resource element, configuring filtering, and set the targetPath to be ${basedir}. In a second resource element, we've configured the default resources path to be copied to the default output directory without any filtering. Example 10-8 shows you how to declare two resource directories and supply them with different filtering and target directory preferences. The project from Example 10-8 would contain a *run.bat* file in *src/main/command* with the following content:

```
@echo off
java -jar ${project.build.finalName}.jar %*
```

After running *mvn process-resources*, a file named *run.bat* would appear in
${basedir} with the following content:

```
@echo off
java -jar simple-cmd-2.3.1.jar %*
```

The ability to customize filtering for specific subsets of resources is another reason why
complex projects with many different kinds of resources often find it advantageous to
separate resources into multiple directories. The alternative to storing different kinds
of resources with different filtering requirements in different directories is to use a more
complex set of include and exclude patterns to match all resource files that match a
certain pattern.

Compile

Most lifecycles bind the Compiler plugin's `compile` goal to the `compile` phase. This phase
calls out to `compile:compile`, which is configured to compile all of the source code and
copy the bytecode to the build output directory. If you haven't customized the values
defined in the Super POM, `compile:compile` is going to compile everything from *src/
main/java* to *target/classes*. The Compiler plugin calls out to *javac* and uses default
source and target settings of 1.3 and 1.1. In other words, the Compiler plugin assumes
that your Java source conforms to Java 1.3 and that you are targeting a Java 1.1 JVM.
If you would like to change these settings, you'll need to supply the target and source
configuration to the Compiler plugin in your project's POM, as shown in Example 10-9.

Example 10-9. Setting the source and target versions for the Compiler plugin

```
<project>
  ...
  <build>
    ...
    <plugins>
      <plugin>
        <artifactId>maven-compiler-plugin</artifactId>
        <configuration>
          <source>1.5</source>
          <target>1.5</target>
        </configuration>
      </plugin>
    </plugins>
    ...
  </build>
  ...
</project>
```

Notice we are configuring the Compiler plugin, and not the specific `compile:compile`
goal. If we were going to configure the source and target for just the `compile:compile`
goal, we would place the `configuration` element below an `execution` element for the
`compile:compile` goal. We've configured the target and source for the plugin because
`compile:compile` isn't the only goal we're interested in configuring. The Compiler

plugin is reused when Maven compiles tests using the `compile:testCompile` goal, and configuring target and source at the plugin level allows us to define it once for all goals in a plugin.

If you need to customize the location of the source code, you can do so by changing the build configuration. If you wanted to store your project's source code in *src/java* instead of *src/main/java*, and if you wanted build output to go to *classes* instead of *target/classes*, you could always override the default `sourceDirectory` defined by the Super POM, as shown in Example 10-10.

Example 10-10. Overriding the default source directory

```
<build>
  ...
  <sourceDirectory>src/java</sourceDirectory>
  <outputDirectory>classes</outputDirectory>
  ...
</build>
```

 Although you may think it's necessary to bend Maven to your own ideas of project directory structure, we can't emphasize enough that you should sacrifice these ideas in favor of the Maven defaults. This isn't because we're trying to brainwash you into accepting the Maven Way; it's because your project will be easier for people to understand if it adheres to the most basic conventions. So forget about designing your own project directory structure. Don't do it.

Process Test Resources

The `process-test-resources` phase is almost indistinguishable from the `process-resources` phase. There are some trivial differences in the POM, but most everything else is the same. You can filter test resources just as you filter regular resources. The default location for test resources is defined in the Super POM as *src/test/resources*, and the default output directory for test resources is *target/test-classes* defined in `${project.build.testOutputDirectory}`.

Test Compile

The `test-compile` phase is almost identical to the `compile` phase. The only difference is that `test-compile` is going to invoke `compile:testCompile` to compile source from the test source directory to the test build output directory. If you haven't customized the default directories from the Super POM, `compile:testCompile` is going to compile the source in *src/test/java* to the *target/test-classes* directory.

As with the source code directory, if you want to customize the location of the test source code and the output of test compilation, you can do so by overriding the `testSourceDirectory` and the `testOutputDirectory`. If you wanted to store test source in *src-test/* instead of *src/test/java*, and you wanted to save test bytecode to *classes-test/* instead of *target/test-classes*, you would use the configuration shown in Example 10-11.

Example 10-11. Overriding the location of test source and output

```
<build>
  ...
  <testSourceDirectory>src-test</testSourceDirectory>
  <testOutputDirectory>classes-test</testOutputDirectory>
  ...
</build>
```

Test

Most lifecycles bind the test goal of the Surefire plugin to the test phase. The Surefire plugin is Maven's unit testing plugin. The default behavior of Surefire is to look for all classes ending in *Test in the test source directory and to run them as JUnit (*http://www .junit.org*) tests. The Surefire plugin can also be configured to run TestNG (*http://www .testng.org*) unit tests.

After running *mvn test*, you should also notice that the Surefire plugin produces a number of reports in *target/surefire-reports*. This report's directory will have two files for each test executed by the Surefire plugin: an XML document containing execution information for the test, and a text file containing the output of the unit test. If there is a problem during the test phase and a unit test has failed, you can use the output of Maven and the contents of this directory to track down the cause of a test failure. This *surefire-reports/* directory is also used during site generation to create an easy-to-read summary of all the unit tests in a project.

If you are working on a project that has some failing unit tests, but you want the project to produce output, you'll need to configure the Surefire plugin to continue a build even if it encounters a failure. The default behavior is to stop a build whenever a unit test failure is encountered. To override this behavior, you'll need to set the `testFailureIgnore` configuration property on the Surefire plugin to `true`, as shown in Example 10-12.

Example 10-12. Configuring Surefire to ignore test failures

```
<build>
  <plugins>
    <plugin>
      <groupId>org.apache.maven.plugins</groupId>
      <artifactId>maven-surefire-plugin</artifactId>
    <configuration>
      <testFailureIgnore>true</testFailureIgnore>
    </configuration>
    </plugin>
    ...
  </plugins>
</build>
```

If you would like to skip tests altogether, you can do so by executing the following command:

```
$ mvn install -Dmaven.test.skip=true
```

The `maven.test.skip` variable controls both the Compiler and the Surefire plugin. If you pass in `maven.test.skip`, you've told Maven to ignore tests altogether.

Install

The `install` goal of the Install plugin is almost always bound to the `install` lifecycle phase. This `install:install` goal simply installs a project's main artifact to the local repository. If you have a project with a `groupId` of `org.sonatype.mavenbook`, an `artifactId` of `simple-test`, and a `version` of 1.0.2, the `install:install` goal is going to copy the JAR file from *target/simple-test-1.0.2.jar* to *~/.m2/repository/org/sonatype/ma venbook/simple-test/1.0.2/simple-test-1.0.2.jar*. If the project has POM packaging, this goal will copy the POM to the local repository.

Deploy

The `deploy` goal of the Deploy plugin is usually bound to the `deploy` lifecycle phase. This phase is used to deploy an artifact to a remote Maven repository, which is usually required to update a remote repository when you are performing a release. The deployment procedure can be as simple as copying a file to another directory or as complex as transferring a file over SCP using a public key. Deployment settings usually involve transporting credentials to a remote repository, and as such, deployment settings are usually not stored in a *pom.xml*. Instead, deployment settings are more frequently found in an individual user's *~/.m2/settings.xml*. For now, all you need to know is that the `deploy:deploy` goal is bound to the `deploy` phase and that it takes care of transporting an artifact to a published repository and updating any repository information that might be affected by such a deployment.

## CHAPTER 11

Build Profiles

What Are They For?

Profiles allow for the ability to customize a particular build for a particular environment; profiles enable portability between different build environments.

What do we mean by different build environments? Two example build environments are production and development. When you are working in a development environment, your system might be configured to read from a development database instance running on your local machine, whereas in production your system is configured to read from the production database. Maven allows you to define any number of build environments (build profiles) that can override any of the settings in the *pom.xml*. You can configure your application to read from your local, development instance of a database in your "development" profile, and you can configure it to read from the production database in the "production" profile. Profiles can also be activated by the environment and platform; you can customize a build to run differently depending on the operating system or the installed JDK version. Before we talk about using and configuring Maven profiles, we need to define the concept of "build portability."

What Is Build Portability?

A build's "portability" is a measure of how easy it is to take a particular project and build it in different environments. A build that works without any custom configuration or customization of properties files is more portable than a build that requires a great deal of work to build from scratch. The most portable projects tend to be widely used open source projects such as Apache Commons or Apache Velocity, which ship with Maven builds that require little or no customization. Put simply, the most portable project builds tend to just work out of the box, and the least portable builds require you to jump through hoops and configure platform specific paths to locate build tools. Before we show you how to achieve build portability, let's survey the different kinds of portability we are talking about.

Nonportable builds

The lack of portability is exactly what all build tools are made to prevent; however, any tool can be configured to be nonportable (even Maven). A nonportable project is buildable only under a specific set of circumstances and criteria (e.g., your local machine). Unless you are working by yourself and you have no plans to ever deploy your application to another machine, it is best to avoid nonportability entirely. A nonportable build runs only on a single machine; it is a "one-off." Maven is designed to discourage nonportable builds by offering the ability to customize builds using profiles.

When a new developer gets the source for a nonportable project, he will not be able to build the project without rewriting large portions of a build script.

Environment portability

A build exhibits environment portability if it has a mechanism for customizing behavior and configuration when targeting different environments. For example, a project that contains a reference to a test database in a test environment and a production database in a production environment is environmentally portable. It is likely that this build has a different set of properties for each environment. When you move to a different environment, one that is not defined and has no profile created for it, the project will not work. Hence, it is only portable between defined environments.

When a new developer gets the source for an environmentally portable project, she will have to run the build within a defined environment, or she will have to create a custom environment to successfully build the project.

Organizational (in-house) portability

The center of this level of portability is a project's requirement that only a select few may access internal resources such as source control or an internally maintained Maven repository. A project at a large corporation may depend on a database available only to in-house developers, or an open source project might require a specific level of credentials to publish a web site and deploy the products of a build to a public repository.

If you attempt to build an in-house project from scratch outside of the in-house network (for example, outside of a corporate firewall), the build will fail. It may fail because certain required custom plugins are unavailable, or project dependencies cannot be found because you don't have the appropriate credentials to retrieve dependencies from a custom remote repository. Such a project is only portable across environments in a single organization.

Wide (universal) portability

Anyone may download a widely portable project's source and compile and install it without customizing a build for a specific environment. This is the highest level of portability; anything less requires extra work for those who wish to build your project.

This level of portability is especially important for open source projects, which depend on the ability for would-be contributors to easily download and build from source.

Any developer could download the source for a widely portable project.

Selecting an Appropriate Level of Portability

Clearly, you'll want to avoid creating the worst-case scenario: the nonportable build. You may have had the misfortune to work or study at an organization that has critical applications with nonportable builds. In such organizations, you cannot deploy an application without the help of a specific individual on a specific machine. In such an organization, it is also very difficult to introduce new project dependencies or changes without coordinating the change with the single person who maintains such a nonportable build. Nonportable builds tend to grow in highly political environments when one individual or group needs to exert control over how and when a project is built and deployed. "How do we build the system? Oh, we've got to call Jack and ask him to build it for us; no one else deploys to production." This is a dangerous situation that is more common that you would think. If you work for this organization, Maven and Maven profiles provide a way out of this mess.

On the opposite end of the portability spectrum are widely portable builds. Widely portable builds are generally the most difficult build systems to attain. These builds restrict your dependencies to those projects and tools that may be freely distributed and are publicly available. Many commercial software packages might be excluded from the most portable builds because they cannot be downloaded before you have accepted a certain license. Wide portability also restricts dependencies to those pieces of software that may be distributed as Maven artifacts. For example, if you depend on Oracle JDBC drivers, your users will have to download and install them manually; this is not widely portable, as you will have to distribute a set of environment setup instructions for people interested in building your application. On the other hand, you could use a JDBC driver that is available from the public Maven repositories such as MySQL or HSQLDB.

As stated previously, open source projects benefit from having the most widely portable builds possible. Widely portable builds reduce the inefficiencies associated with contributing to a project. In an open source project (such as Maven), there are two distinct groups: end users and developers. When an end user uses a project like Maven and decides to contribute a patch to the project, he has to make the transition from using the output of a build to running a build. He first has to become a developer, and if it is difficult to learn how to build a project, this end user has a disincentive to take the time to contribute to a project. In a widely portable project, an end user doesn't have to follow a set of arcane build instructions to start becoming a developer; she can download the source, modify the source, build, and submit a contribution without asking someone to help her set up a build environment. When the cost of contributing source back to an open source project is lower, you'll see an increase in source code contributions, especially casual contributions, which can make the difference between a project's success and a project's failure. One side effect of Maven's adoption across a wide group of open source projects is that it has made it easier for developers to contribute code to various open source projects.

Portability Through Maven Profiles

A profile in Maven is an alternative set of configuration values that set or override default values. Using a profile, you can customize a build for different environments. Profiles are configured in the *pom.xml* and are given an identifier. Then you can run Maven with a command-line flag that tells Maven to execute goals in a specific profile. The *pom.xml* shown in Example 11-1 uses a `production` profile to override the default settings of the Compiler plugin.

Example 11-1. Using a Maven profile to override production compiler settings

```
<project xmlns="http://maven.apache.org/POM/4.0.0"
        xmlns:xsi="http://www.w3.org/2001/XMLSchema-instance"
  xsi:schemaLocation="http://maven.apache.org/POM/4.0.0
        http://maven.apache.org/maven-v4_0_0.xsd">
  <modelVersion>4.0.0</modelVersion>
  <groupId>org.sonatype.mavenbook</groupId>
  <artifactId>simple</artifactId>
  <packaging>jar</packaging>
  <version>1.0-SNAPSHOT</version>
  <name>simple</name>
  <url>http://maven.apache.org</url>
  <dependencies>
    <dependency>
      <groupId>junit</groupId>
      <artifactId>junit</artifactId>
      <version>3.8.1</version>
      <scope>test</scope>
    </dependency>
  </dependencies>
  <profiles>❶
    <profile>
      <id>production</id>❷
      <build>❸
        <plugins>
          <plugin>
            <groupId>org.apache.maven.plugins</groupId>
            <artifactId>maven-compiler-plugin</artifactId>
            <configuration>
              <debug>false</debug>❹
              <optimize>true</optimize>
            </configuration>
          </plugin>
        </plugins>
      </build>
    </profile>
```

```
    </profiles>
</project>
```

In this example, we've added a profile named `production` that overrides the default configuration of the Maven Compiler plugin. Let's examine the syntax of this profile in detail:

❶ The `profiles` element is in the *pom.xml*. It contains one or more `profile` elements. Since profiles override the default settings in a *pom.xml*, the `profiles` element is usually listed as the last element in a *pom.xml*.

❷ Each profile has to have an `id` element. This `id` element contains the name that is used to invoke this profile from the command line. A profile is invoked by passing the *-Pprofile_id* command-line argument to Maven.

❸ A `profile` element can contain many of the elements that can appear under the `project` element of a POM XML document. In this example, we're overriding the behavior of the Compiler plugin, and we have to override the plugin configuration that is normally enclosed in a `build` and a `plugins` element.

❹ We're overriding the configuration of the Maven Compiler plugin. We're making sure that the bytecode produced by the production profile doesn't contain debug information and that the bytecode has gone through the compiler's optimization routines.

To execute *mvn install* under the `production` profile, you need to pass the *-Pproduction* argument on the command line. To verify that the `production` profile overrides the default Compiler plugin configuration, execute Maven with debug output enabled (*-X*) as follows:

```
~/examples/profile $ mvn clean install -Pproduction -X
... (omitting debugging output) ...
[DEBUG] Configuring mojo
      'org.apache.maven.plugins:maven-compiler-plugin:2.0.2:testCompile' -->
[DEBUG]    (f) basedir = ~\examples\profile
[DEBUG]    (f) buildDirectory = ~\examples\profile\target
...
[DEBUG]    (f) compilerId = javac
[DEBUG]    (f) debug = false
[DEBUG]    (f) failOnError = true
[DEBUG]    (f) fork = false
[DEBUG]    (f) optimize = true
[DEBUG]    (f) outputDirectory =
        c:\Users\tobrien\svnw\sonatype\examples\profile\target\test-classes
[DEBUG]    (f) outputFileName = simple-1.0-SNAPSHOT
[DEBUG]    (f) showDeprecation = false
[DEBUG]    (f) showWarnings = false
[DEBUG]    (f) staleMillis = 0
[DEBUG]    (f) verbose = false
[DEBUG] -- end configuration --
... (omitting debugging output) ...
```

This excerpt from the debug output of Maven shows the configuration of the Compiler plugin under the production profile. As shown in the output, debug is set to false and optimize is set to true.

Overriding a Project Object Model

Although the previous example showed you how to override the default configuration properties of a single Maven plugin, you still don't know exactly what a Maven profile is allowed to override. The short answer to that question is that a Maven profile can override almost everything you would have in a *pom.xml*. The Maven POM contains an element under project called profiles containing a project's alternate configurations, and under this element are profile elements that define each profile. Each profile must have an id, and other than that, it can contain almost any of the elements one would expect to see under project. The XML document in Example 11-2 shows all of the elements, a profile is allowed to override.

Example 11-2. Elements allowed in a profile

```
<project>
  <profiles>
    <profile>
      <build>
        <defaultGoal>...</defaultGoal>
        <finalName>...</finalName>
        <resources>...</resources>
        <testResources>...</testResources>
        <plugins>...</plugins>
      </build>
      <reporting>...</reporting>
      <modules>...</modules>
      <dependencies>...</dependencies>
      <dependencyManagement>...</dependencyManagement>
      <distributionManagement>...</distributionManagement>
      <repositories>...</repositories>
      <pluginRepositories>...</pluginRepositories>
      <properties>...</properties>
    </profile>
  </profiles>
</project>
```

A profile can override an element shown with ellipses. A profile can override the final name of a project's artifact in a profile, the dependencies, and the behavior of a project's build via plugin configuration. A profile can also override the configuration of distribution settings depending on the profile. For example, if you needed to publish an artifact to a staging server in a staging profile, you would create a staging profile that overrides the distributionManagement element in a profile.

Profile Activation

In the previous section, we showed you how to create a profile that overrides default behavior for a specific target environment. In the previous build, the default build was designed for development, and the production profile exists to provide configuration for a production environment. What happens when you need to provide customizations based on variables such as operating systems or JDK version? Maven provides a way to "activate" a profile for different environmental parameters. This is called profile activation.

Take the following example. Assume we have a Java library that has a specific feature available only in the Java 6 release—the Scripting Engine as defined in JSR-223 (see *http://jcp.org/en/jsr/detail?id=223*). You've separated the portion of the library that deals with the scripting library into a separate Maven project, and you want people running Java 5 to be able to build the project without attempting to build the Java 6 specific library extension. You can do this by using a Maven profile that adds the script extension module to the build only when the build is running within a Java 6 JDK. First, let's take a look at our project's directory layout and how we want developers to build the system.

When someone runs *mvn install* with a Java 6 JDK, you want the build to include the simple-script project's build; when they are running in Java 5, you would like to skip the simple-script project build. If you failed to skip the simple-script project build in Java 5, your build would fail because Java 5 does not have ScriptEngine on the classpath. Let's take a look at the library project's *pom.xml* shown in Example 11-3.

Example 11-3. Dynamic inclusion of submodules using profile activation

```
<project xmlns="http://maven.apache.org/POM/4.0.0"
         xmlns:xsi="http://www.w3.org/2001/XMLSchema-instance"
         xsi:schemaLocation="http://maven.apache.org/POM/4.0.0
                             http://maven.apache.org/maven-v4_0_0.xsd">
  <modelVersion>4.0.0</modelVersion>
  <groupId>org.sonatype.mavenbook</groupId>
  <artifactId>simple</artifactId>
  <packaging>jar</packaging>
  <version>1.0-SNAPSHOT</version>
  <name>simple</name>
  <url>http://maven.apache.org</url>
  <dependencies>
    <dependency>
      <groupId>junit</groupId>
      <artifactId>junit</artifactId>
      <version>3.8.1</version>
      <scope>test</scope>
    </dependency>
  </dependencies>
  <profiles>
    <profile>
      <id>jdk16</id>
```

```
      <activation>❶
        <jdk>1.6</jdk>
      </activation>
      <modules>❷
        <module>simple-script</module>
      </modules>
    </profile>
  </profiles>
</project>
```

If you run *mvn install* under Java 1.6, you will see Maven descending into the *simple-script* subdirectory to build the `simple-script` project. If you are running *mvn install* in Java 1.5, the build will not try to build the `simple-script` submodule. Let's explore this activation configuration in more detail:

❶ The `activation` element lists the conditions for profile activation. In this example, we've specified that this profile will be activated by Java versions that begin with "1.6." This would include "1.6.0_03," "1.6.0_02," or any other string that begins with "1.6." Activation parameters are not limited to Java version; for a full list of activation parameters, see the next section, "Activation Configuration."

❷ In this profile, we are adding the module `simple-script`. Adding this module will cause Maven to look in the *simple-script/* subdirectory for a *pom.xml*.

Activation Configuration

Activations can contain one or more selectors, including JDK versions, operating system parameters, files, and properties. A profile is activated when all activation criteria has been satisfied. For example, a profile could list an operating system family of Windows and a JDK version of 1.4; this profile will be activated only when the build is executed on a Windows machine running Java 1.4. If the profile is active, then all elements override the corresponding project-level elements as if the profile were included with the *-P* command-line argument. Example 11-4 lists a profile that is activated by a very specific combination of operating system parameters, properties, and a JDK version.

Example 11-4. Profile activation parameters: JDK version, OS parameters, and properties

```
<project>
  ...
  <profiles>
    <profile>
      <id>dev</id>
      <activation>
        <activeByDefault>false</activeByDefault>❶
        <jdk>1.5</jdk>❷
        <os>
          <name>Windows XP</name>❸
          <family>Windows</family>
          <arch>x86</arch>
```

```
          <version>5.1.2600</version>
        </os>
        <property>
          <name>mavenVersion</name>❹
          <value>2.0.5</value>
        </property>
        <file>
          <exists>file2.properties</exists>❺
          <missing>file1.properties</missing>
        </file>
      </activation>
      ...
    </profile>
  </profiles>
</project>
```

This example defines a very narrow set of activation parameters. Let's examine each activation criterion in detail:

❶ The `activeByDefault` element controls whether this profile is considered active by default.

❷ This profile will be active only for JDK versions that begin with "1.5." This includes "1.5.0_01" and "1.5.1."

❸ This profile targets a very specific version of Windows XP: version 5.1.2600 on a 32-bit platform. If your project uses the native plugin to build a C program, you might find yourself writing projects for specific platforms.

❹ The `property` element tells Maven to activate this profile if the property `mavenVersion` is set to the value `2.0.5`. `mavenVersion` is an implicit property that is available to all Maven builds.

❺ The `file` element allows us to activate a profile based on the presence (or absence) of files. The `dev` profile will be activated if a file named *file2.properties* exists in the base directory of the project. The `dev` profile will be activated only if there is no file named *file1.properties* file in the base directory of the project.

Activation by the Absence of a Property

You can activate a profile based on the value of a property such as `environment.type`. You can activate a `development` profile if `environment.type` equals `dev`, or a `production` profile if `environment.type` equals `prod`. You can also activate a profile in the absence of a property. The configuration shown in Example 11-5 activates a profile if the property `environment.type` is not present during Maven execution.

Example 11-5. Activating profiles in the absence of a property

```
<project>
  ...
  <profiles>
```

```
      <profile>
        <id>development</id>
        <activation>
          <property>
            <name>!environment.type</name>
          </property>
        </activation>
      </profile>
    </profiles>
  </project>
```

Note the exclamation point prefixing the property name. The exclamation point is often referred to as the "bang" character and signifies "not." This profile is activated when no ${environment.type} property is set.

External Profiles

If you start making extensive use of Maven profiles, you may want to separate your profiles from your POM in a separate file named *profiles.xml*. You can mix and match profiles defined in the *pom.xml* with profiles defined in the external *profiles.xml* file. Just place the profiles element into *profiles.xml* in ${basedir} and run Maven as you normally would. This *profiles.xml* file would look something like Example 11-6.

Example 11-6. Placing profiles in a profiles.xml file

```
<profiles>
    <profile>
      <id>development</id>
      <build>
        <plugins>
          <plugin>
            <groupId>org.apache.maven.plugins</groupId>
            <artifactId>maven-compiler-plugin</artifactId>
            <configuration>
              <debug>true</debug>
              <optimize>false</optimize>
            </configuration>
          </plugin>
        </plugins>
      </build>
    </profile>
    <profile>
      <id>production</id>
      <build>
        <plugins>
          <plugin>
            <groupId>org.apache.maven.plugins</groupId>
            <artifactId>maven-compiler-plugin</artifactId>
            <configuration>
              <debug>false</debug>
              <optimize>true</optimize>
            </configuration>
```

```
        </plugin>
      </plugins>
    </build>
  </profile>
</profiles>
```

You might find that your profiles have grown so large that you are having trouble managing the *pom.xml*, or you might just find separating the *pom.xml* from the *profiles.xml* file is a cleaner approach to putting everything into a single file. You can invoke profiles stored in *profiles.xml* the same way you would invoke them if they were defined in the *pom.xml*.

Settings Profiles

Project profiles are useful when a specific project needs to customize a build setting for a specific environment, but why would you want to override a build setting for every project in Maven? How do you do something like add an internal repository that is consulted on every Maven build? You can do this with a settings profile. Where project profiles are concerned with overriding the configuration of a specific project, settings profiles can be applied to any and all projects you build with Maven. You can place settings profiles in two locations: a user-specific settings profile defined in *~/.m2/settings.xml* or a global settings profile defined in *${M2_HOME}/conf/set tings.xml*. Here is an example of a settings profile defined in *~/.m2/settings.xml* that might set some user-specific configuration properties for all builds. The *settings.xml* file shown in Example 11-7 is defined for user `tobrien`.

Example 11-7. Defining user-specific settings profiles (~/.m2/settings.xml)

```
<settings>
  <profiles>
    <profile>
      <id>dev</id>
      <plugin>
        <groupId>org.apache.maven.plugins</groupId>
        <artifactId>maven-jar-plugin</artifactId>
        <executions>
          <execution>
            <goals>
              <goal>sign</goal>
            </goals>
          </execution>
        </executions>
        <configuration>
          <keystore>/home/tobrien/java/keystore</keystore>
          <alias>tobrien</alias>
          <storepass>s3cr3tp@ssw0rd</storepass>
          <signedjar>${project.build.directory}/signed/
              ${project.build.finalName}.jar</signedjar>
          <verify>true</verify>
        </configuration>
```

```
        </plugin>
      </profile>
    </profiles>
  </settings>
```

The previous example is a plausible use of a user-specific settings profile. This example sets user-specific settings like the password and alias to use when signing a JAR file during a release. These are configuration parameters you wouldn't want to store in a project's shared *pom.xml* or a *profiles.xml* file because they involve some secrets that should not be public.

The downside of settings profiles is that they tend to interfere with project portability. If the previous example were an open source project, a new developer would not be able to sign a JAR until he had manually configured a settings profile and talked to one of the existing developers. In this case, the security requirements of signing a JAR are in conflict with the larger goal of achieving a universally portable project build. On most open source projects, there are tasks that require security credentials, such as publishing an artifact to a remote repository, publishing a project's web site, or signing a JAR file. For these tasks, the highest level of portability we can hope for is organizational portability. These higher-security tasks usually require some manual setup and configuration of a profile.

Instead of explicitly specifying the name of the profile with the *-P* command-line argument, you can define a list of active profiles that are activated for every project you run. For example, if you wanted to activate the **dev** profile defined in *settings.xml* for every project you run, you would add the section shown in Example 11-8 to your *~/.m2/ settings.xml* file.

Example 11-8. Defining active settings profiles

```
<settings>
  ...
  <activeProfiles>
    <activeProfile>dev</activeProfile>
  </activeProfiles>
</settings>
```

This will activate settings profiles only, not project profiles with matching **id** elements. For example, if you have a project with a profile defined in its *pom.xml* with an **id** of **dev**, it will not be affected by the **activeProfile** set in your *settings.xml*. This **activeProfile** setting affects only profiles defined in your *settings.xml* file.

Global Settings Profiles

Just like settings profiles, you can also define a set of global profiles in *${M2_HOME}/ conf/settings.xml*. Profiles defined in this configuration file are available across all users using a specific installation of Maven. The ability to define a global settings profile is useful if you are creating a customized distribution of Maven for a specific organization and you want to ensure that every user of Maven has access to a set of build profiles that ensure in-house portability. If you need to add custom plugin repositories or define a custom set of plugins that are used only by your organization, you could distribute a copy of Maven to your users that has these settings "baked in." The configuration of global settings profiles is the same as the configuration of user-specific settings profiles.

Listing Active Profiles

Maven profiles can be defined in either *pom.xml*, *profiles.xml*, *~/.m2/settings.xml*, or *${M2_HOME}/conf/settings.xml*. With these four levels, there's no good way of keeping track of profiles available to a particular project without remembering which profiles are defined in these four files. To make it easier to keep track of which profiles are available and where they have been defined, the Maven Help plugin defines a goal, `active-profiles`, that lists all the active profiles and where they have been defined. You can run the `active-profiles` goal as follows:

```
$ mvn help:active-profiles
Active Profiles for Project 'My Project':

The following profiles are active:

 - my-settings-profile (source: settings.xml)
 - my-external-profile (source: profiles.xml)
 - my-internal-profile (source: pom.xml)
```

Tips and Tricks

Profiles can encourage build portability. If your build needs subtle customizations to work on different platforms, or if you need your build to produce different results for different target platforms, project profiles increase build portability. Settings profiles generally decrease build portability by adding extra-project information that must be communicated from developer to developer. The following sections provide some guidelines and some ideas for applying Maven profiles to your project.

Common Environments

One of the core motivations for Maven project profiles was to provide for environment-specific configuration settings. In a development environment, you might want to produce bytecode with debug information and configure your system to use a development database instance. In a production environment, you might want to produce a signed JAR and configure the system to use a production database. In this chapter, we defined a number of environments with identifiers such as `dev` and `prod`. A simpler way to do this would be to define profiles that are activated by environment properties and to use these common environment properties across all of your projects. For example, if every project had a `development` profile activated by a property named `environment.type` having a value of dev, and if those same projects had a `production` profile activated by a property named `environment.type` having a value of `prod`, you could create a default profile in your *settings.xml* that always set `environment.type` to dev on your development machine. That way, each project defines a dev profile activated by the same environment variable. Let's see how this is done; the *settings.xml* shown in Example 11-9 defines a profile in *~/.m2/settings.xml* that sets the `environment.type` property to dev.

Example 11-9. ~/.m2/settings.xml defines a default profile setting environment.type

```
<settings>
  <profiles>
    <profile>
      <activation>
        <activeByDefault>true</activeByDefault>
      </activation>
      <properties>
        <environment.type>dev</environment.type>
      </properties>
    </profile>
  </profiles>
</settings>
```

This means that every time you run Maven on your machine, this profile will be activated and the property `environment.type` will have the value dev. You can then use this property to activate profiles defined in a project's *pom.xml*. Let's take a look in Example 11-10 at how a project's *pom.xml* would define a profile activated by `environment.type` having the value dev.

Example 11-10. project profile activated by environment.type equal to dev

```
<project>
  ...
  <profiles>
    <profile>
      <id>development</id>
      <activation>
        <property>
          <name>environment.type</name>
          <value>dev</value>
        </property>
      </activation>
      <properties>
        <database.driverClassName>com.mysql.jdbc.Driver</database.driverClassName>
        <database.url>jdbc:mysql://localhost:3306/app_dev</database.url>
        <database.user>development_user</database.user>
        <database.password>development_password</database.password>
      </properties>
    </profile>
    <profile>
      <id>production</id>
      <activation>
        <property>
```

```
      <name>environment.type</name>
      <value>prod</value>
    </property>
  </activation>
  <properties>
    <database.driverClassName>com.mysql.jdbc.Driver</database.driverClassName>
    <database.url>jdbc:mysql://master01:3306,slave01:3306/app_prod</database.url>
    <database.user>prod_user</database.user>
  </properties>
  </profile>
  </profiles>
</project>
```

This project defines some properties such as `database.url` and `database.user`, which might be used to configure another Maven plugin configured in the *pom.xml*. There are plugins available that can manipulate the database and run SQL, and plugins such as the Maven Hibernate3 plugin can generate annotated model objects for use in persistence frameworks. A few of these plugins can be configured in a *pom.xml* using these properties. These properties can also be used to filter resources. In this example, because we've defined a profile in *~/.m2/settings.xml* that sets `environment.type` to `dev`, the development profile will always be activated when we run Maven on our development machine. Alternatively, if we wanted to override this default, we could set a property on the command line. If we need to activate the production profile, we can always run Maven with:

```
~/examples/profiles $ mvn install -Denvironment.type=prod
```

Setting a property on the command line will override the default property set in *~/.m2/settings.xml*. We could have just defined a profile with an `id` of "dev" and invoked it directly with the -*P* command-line argument, but using this `environment.type` property allows us to code other project *pom.xml* files to this standard. Every project in the codebase can have a profile that is activated by the same `environment.type` property set in every user's *~/.m2/settings.xml*. In this way, developers can share common configuration for development without defining this configuration in nonportable *settings.xml* files.

Protecting Secrets

This best practice builds on the previous section. In Example 11-10, the `production` profile does not contain the `database.password` property. We've done this on purpose to illustrate the concept of putting secrets in your user-specific *settings.xml*. If you were developing an application at a large organization that values security, it is likely that the majority of the development group will not know the password to the production database. In an organization that draws a bold line between the development group and the operations group, this will be the norm. Developers may have access to a development and a staging environment, but they might not have (or want to have) access to the production database. There are a number of reasons why this makes sense, particularly if an organization is dealing with extremely sensitive financial, intelligence, or medical information. In this scenario, the production environment build may be carried out only by a lead developer or by a member of the production operations group. When they run this build using the `prod environment.type`, they will need to define this variable in their *settings.xml*, as shown in Example 11-11.

Example 11-11. Storing secrets in a user-specific settings profile

```
<settings>
  <profiles>
    <profile>
      <activeByDefault>true</activeByDefault>
      <properties>
        <environment.type>prod</environment.type>
        <database.password>m1ss10nimp0ss1bl3</database.password>
      </properties>
    </profile>
  </profiles>
</settings>
```

This user has defined a default profile that sets the `environment.type` to `prod` and also set the production password. When the project is executed, the production profile is activated by the `environment.type` property and the `database.password` property is populated. This way, you can put all of the production-specific configuration into a project's *pom.xml* and leave out only the single secret necessary to access the production database.

> Secrets usually conflict with wide portability, but this makes sense. You wouldn't want to share your secrets openly.

Platform Classifiers

Let's assume that you have a library or a project that produces platform-specific customizations. Even though Java is platform-neutral, there are times when you might need to write some code that invokes platform-specific native code. Another possibility is that you've written some C code that is compiled by the Maven Native plugin and you want to produce a qualified artifact depending on the build platform. You can set a classifier with the Maven Assembly plugin or with the Maven Jar plugin. The *pom.xml* shown in Example 11-12 produces a qualified artifact using profiles that are activated by operating system parameters. For more information about the Maven Assembly plugin, see Chapter 12.

Example 11-12. Qualifying artifacts with platform-activated project profiles

```
<project>
  ...
  <profiles>
    <profile>
```

```
    <id>windows</id>
    <activation>
      <os>
        <family>windows</family>
      </os>
    </activation>
    <build>
      <plugins>
        <plugin
          <artifactId>maven-jar-plugin</artifactId>
          <configuration>
            <classifier>win</classifier>
          </configuration>
        </plugin>
      </plugins>
    </build>
  </profile>
  <profile>
    <id>linux</id>
    <activation>
      <os>
        <family>unix</family>
      </os>
    </activation>
    <build>
      <plugins>
        <plugin>
          <artifactId>maven-jar-plugin</artifactId>
          <configuration>
            <classifier>linux</classifier>
          </configuration>
        </plugin>
      </plugins>
    </build>
  </profile>
  </profiles>
</project>
```

If the operating system is in the Windows family, this *pom.xml* qualifies the JAR artifact with "-win". If the operating system is in the Unix family, the artifact is qualified with "-linux". This *pom.xml* successfully adds the qualifiers to the artifacts, but it is more verbose than it needs to be due to the redundant configuration of the Maven Jar plugin in both profiles. This example could be rewritten to use variable substitution to minimize redundancy, as shown in Example 11-13.

Example 11-13. Qualifying artifacts with platform-activated project profiles and variable substitution

```
<project>
  ...
  <build>
    <plugins>
      <plugin>
        <artifactId>maven-jar-plugin</artifactId>
        <configuration>
```

```
          <classifier>${envClassifier}</classifier>
        </configuration>
      </plugin>
    </plugins>
  </build>
  ...
  <profiles>
    <profile>
      <id>windows</id>
      <activation>
        <os>
          <family>windows</family>
        </os>
      </activation>
      <properties>
        <envClassifier>win</envClassifier>
      </properties>
    </profile>
    <profile>
      <id>linux</id>
      <activation>
        <os>
          <family>unix</family>
        </os>
      </activation>
      <properties>
        <envClassifier>linux</envClassifier>
      </properties>
    </profile>
  </profiles>
</project>
```

In this *pom.xml*, each profile doesn't need to include a build element to configure the
Jar plugin. Instead, each profile is activated by the operating system family and sets the
envClassifier property to either win or linux. This envClassifier is then referenced in
the default *pom.xml* build element to add a classifier to the project's JAR artifact. The
JAR artifact will be named ${*finalName*}-${envClassifier}.jar and included as a dependency using the dependency syntax shown in Example 11-14.

Example 11-14. Depending on a qualified artifact

```
<dependency>
  <groupId>com.mycompany</groupId>
  <artifactId>my-project</artifactId>
  <version>1.0</version>
  <classifier>linux</classifier>
</dependency>
```

Summary

When used judiciously, profiles can make it very easy to customize a build for different platforms. If something in your build needs to define a platform-specific path for something like an application server, you can put these configuration points in a profile that is activated by an operating system parameter. If you have a project that needs to produce different artifacts for different environments, you can customize the build behavior for different environments and platforms via profile-specific plugin behavior. Using profiles, builds can become portable. There is no need to rewrite your build logic to support a new environment; just override the configuration that needs to change and share the configuration points that can be shared.

## CHAPTER 12

Maven Assemblies

Introduction

Maven provides plugins that are used to create the most common archive types, most of which are consumable as dependencies of other projects. Some examples include the JAR, WAR, EJB, and EAR plugins. As discussed in Chapter 10, these plugins correspond to different project packaging types, each with slightly different build processes. Although Maven has plugins and customized lifecycles to support standard packaging types, there are times when you'll need to create an archive or directory with a custom layout. Such custom archives are called Maven Assemblies.

There are any number of reasons why you may want to build custom archives for your project. Perhaps the most common is the project distribution. The word "distribution" means many different things to different people (and projects), depending on how the project is meant to be used. Essentially, these are archives that provide a convenient way for users to install or otherwise make use of the project's releases. In some cases, this may mean bundling a web application with an application server like Jetty. In others, it could mean bundling API documentation alongside source and compiled binaries like JAR files. Assemblies usually come in handy when you are building the final distribution of a product. For example, products such as Nexus (introduced in Chapter 16) are the result of large, multimodule Maven projects, and the final archive you download from Sonatype was created using a Maven Assembly.

In most cases, the Assembly plugin is ideally suited to the process of building project distributions. However, assemblies don't have to be distribution archives; assemblies are intended to provide Maven users with the flexibility they need to produce customized archives of all kinds. Essentially, assemblies are intended to fill the gaps between the standard archive formats provided by project package types. Of course, you could write an entire Maven plugin simply to generate your own custom archive format, along with a new lifecycle-mapping and artifact-handling configuration to tell Maven how to deploy it. But the Assembly plugin makes this unnecessary in most cases by providing generalized support for creating your own archive recipe, so you don't have to spend so much time writing Maven code.

Assembly Basics

Before we go any further, it's best to take a minute and talk about the two main goals in the Assembly plugin: `assembly:assembly` and the `single` mojo. We list these two goals in different ways to reflect the difference in how they're used. The `assembly:assembly` goal is designed to be invoked directly from the command line and should never be bound to a build lifecycle phase. In contrast, the `single` mojo is designed to be a part of your everyday build and should be bound to a phase in your project's build lifecycle.

The main reason for this difference is that the `assembly:assembly` goal is what Maven terms an `aggregator` mojo—that is, a mojo that is designed to run at most once in a build, regardless of how many projects are being built. It draws its configuration from the root project, usually the top-level POM or the command line. When bound to a lifecycle, an `aggregator` mojo can have some nasty side effects. It can force the execution of the `package` lifecycle phase to execute ahead of time, and it can result in builds that end up executing the `package` phase twice.

Because the `assembly:assembly` goal is an `aggregator` mojo, it raises some issues in multimodule Maven builds, and it should be called only as a standalone mojo from the command line. Never bind an `assembly:assembly` execution to a lifecycle phase. `assembly:assembly` was the original goal in the Assembly plugin and was never designed to be part of the standard build process for a project. As it became clear that assembly archives were a legitimate requirement for projects to produce, the `single` mojo was developed. The single mojo assumes that it has been bound to the correct part of the build process so that it will have access to the project files and artifacts it needs to execute within the lifecycle of a large multimodule Maven project. In a multimodule environment, it will execute as many times as it is bound to the different module POMs. Unlike `assembly:assembly`, `single` will never force the execution of another lifecycle phase ahead of itself.

The Assembly plugin provides several other goals in addition to these two. However, discussion of these other Mojos is beyond the scope of this chapter, because they serve exotic or obsolete use cases, and because they are almost never needed. Whenever possible, you should definitely stick to using `assembly:assembly` for assemblies generated from the command line, and to `single` for assemblies bound to lifecycle phases.

Predefined Assembly Descriptors

Although many people opt to create their own archive recipes—called assembly descriptors—this isn't strictly necessary. The Assembly plugin provides built-in descriptors for several common archive types that you can use immediately without writing a line of configuration. The following assembly descriptors are predefined in the Maven Assembly plugin:

bin

> The bin descriptor is used to bundle project *LICENSE*, *README*, and *NOTICE* files with the project's main artifact, assuming this project builds a JAR as its main artifact. Think of this as the smallest possible binary distribution for completely self-contained projects.

jar-with-dependencies

> The jar-with-dependencies descriptor builds a JAR archive with the contents of the main project JAR, along with the unpacked contents of all the project's runtime dependencies. Coupled with an appropriate Main-Class Manifest entry (discussed in "Plugin Configuration" later in this chapter), this descriptor can produce a self-contained, executable JAR for your project, even if the project has dependencies.

project

> The project descriptor simply archives the project directory structure as it exists in your file system and, most likely, in your version control system. Of course, the target directory is omitted, as are any version-control metadata files such as the *CVS/* and *.svn/* directories we're all used to seeing. Basically, the point of this descriptor is to create a project archive that, when unpacked, can be built using Maven.

src

> The src descriptor produces an archive of your project source and *pom.xml* files, along with any *LICENSE*, *README*, and *NOTICE* files that are in the project's root directory. This precursor to the project descriptor produces an archive that can be built by Maven in most cases. However, because of its assumption that all source files and resources reside in the standard *src/* directory, it has the potential to leave out nonstandard directories and files that are nonetheless critical to some builds.

Building an Assembly

The Assembly plugin can be executed in one of two ways: you can invoke it directly from the command line, or you can configure it as part of your standard build process by binding it to a phase of your project's build lifecycle. Direct invocation has its uses, particularly for one-off assemblies that are not considered part of your project's core deliverables. In most cases, you'll probably want to generate the assemblies for your project as part of its standard build process. Doing this has the effect of including your custom assemblies whenever the project is installed or deployed into Maven's repositories, so they are always available to your users.

As an example of the direct invocation of the Assembly plugin, suppose that you want to ship off a copy of your project that people can build from source. Instead of just deploying the end product of the build, you'll want to include the source as well. You won't need to do this often, so it doesn't make sense to add the configuration to your POM. Instead, you can use the following command:

```
$ mvn -DdescriptorId=project assembly:single
...
[INFO] [assembly:single]
[INFO] Building tar : /Users/~/mvn-examples-1.0/assemblies/direct-invocation/\
                      target/direct-invocation-1.0-SNAPSHOT-project.tar.gz
[INFO] Building tar : /Users/~/mvn-examples-1.0/assemblies/direct-invocation/\
                      target/direct-invocation-1.0-SNAPSHOT-project.tar.bz2
[INFO] Building zip: /Users/~/mvn-examples-1.0/assemblies/direct-invocation/\
                      target/direct-invocation-1.0-SNAPSHOT-project.zip
...
```

Suppose you want to produce an executable JAR from your project. If your project is totally self-contained with no dependencies, you can achieve this with the main project artifact using the archive configuration of the JAR plugin. However, most projects have dependencies, and those dependencies must be incorporated in any executable JAR. In that case, you want to make sure that every time the main project JAR is installed or deployed, your executable JAR goes along with it.

Assuming the main class for the project is `org.sonatype.mavenbook.App`, the POM configuration shown in Example 12-1 will create an executable JAR.

Example 12-1. Assembly descriptor for executable JAR

```
<project xmlns="http://maven.apache.org/POM/4.0.0"
  xmlns:xsi="http://www.w3.org/2001/XMLSchema-instance"
  xsi:schemaLocation="http://maven.apache.org/POM/4.0.0
      http://maven.apache.org/maven-v4_0_0.xsd">

  <modelVersion>4.0.0</modelVersion>
  <groupId>org.sonatype.mavenbook.assemblies</groupId>
  <artifactId>executable-jar</artifactId>
  <version>1.0-SNAPSHOT</version>
  <packaging>jar</packaging>
  <name>Assemblies Executable Jar Example</name>
  <url>http://sonatype.com/book</url>
  <dependencies>
    <dependency>
      <groupId>commons-lang</groupId>
      <artifactId>commons-lang</artifactId>
      <version>2.4</version>
    </dependency>
  </dependencies>
<build>
    <plugins>
      <plugin>
        <artifactId>maven-assembly-plugin</artifactId>
        <version>2.2-beta-2</version>
        <executions>
          <execution>
            <id>create-executable-jar</id>
            <phase>package</phase>
            <goals>
              <goal>single</goal>
            </goals>
```

```
        <configuration>
          <descriptorRefs>
            <descriptorRef>
              jar-with-dependencies
            </descriptorRef>
          </descriptorRefs>
          <archive>
            <manifest>
              <mainClass>org.sonatype.mavenbook.App</mainClass>
            </manifest>
          </archive>
        </configuration>
      </execution>
    </executions>
  </plugin>
  </plugins>
</build>
</project>
```

You should notice two things about the configuration just shown. First, we're using the `descriptorRefs` configuration section instead of the `descriptorId` parameter we used previously. This allows multiple assembly types to be built from the same Assembly plugin execution, while still supporting our use case with relatively little extra configuration. Second, the archive `element` under `configuration` sets the `Main-Class` manifest attribute in the generated JAR. This section is commonly available in plugins that create JAR files, such as the JAR plugin used for the default project package type.

Now you can produce the executable JAR simply by executing *mvn package*. Afterward, we'll also get a directory listing for the target directory, just to verify that the executable JAR was generated. Finally, just to prove that we actually do have an executable JAR, we'll try executing it:

```
$ mvn package
... (output omitted) ...
[INFO] [jar:jar]
[INFO] Building jar: /Users/~/mvn-examples-1.0/assemblies/executable-jar/target/\
                    executable-jar-1.0-SNAPSHOT.jar
[INFO] [assembly:single {execution: create-executable-jar}]
[INFO] Processing DependencySet (output=)
[INFO] Building jar: /Users/~/mvn-examples-1.0/assemblies/executable-jar/target/\
                    executable-jar-1.0-SNAPSHOT-jar-with-dependencies.jar
... (output omitted) ...
$ ls -1 target
... (output omitted) ...
executable-jar-1.0-SNAPSHOT-jar-with-dependencies.jar
executable-jar-1.0-SNAPSHOT.jar
... (output omitted) ...
$ java -jar \
      target/executable-jar-1.0-SNAPSHOT-jar-with-dependencies.jar
Hello, World!
```

From this output, you can see that the normal project build now produces a new artifact in addition to the main JAR file. The new one has a classifier of `jar-with-dependencies`. Finally, we verified that the new JAR actually is executable, and that executing the JAR produced the desired output of "Hello, World!"

Assemblies as Dependencies

When you generate assemblies as part of your normal build process, those assembly archives will be attached to your main project's artifact. This means they will be installed and deployed alongside the main artifact, and are then resolvable in much the same way. Each assembly artifact is given the same basic coordinate (`groupId`, `artifactId`, and `version`) as the main project. However, these artifacts are attachments, which in Maven means they are derivative works based on some aspect of the main project build. To provide a couple of examples, `source` assemblies contain the raw inputs for the project build, and `jar-with-dependencies` assemblies contain the project's classes plus its dependencies. Attached artifacts are allowed to circumvent the Maven requirement of "one project, one artifact" precisely because of this derivative quality.

Since assemblies are (normally) attached artifacts, each must have a classifier to distinguish it from the main artifact, in addition to the normal artifact coordinate. By default, the classifier is the same as the assembly descriptor's identifier. When using the built-in assembly descriptors, as shown earlier, the assembly descriptor's identifier is generally also the same as the identifier used in the `descriptorRef` for that type of assembly.

Once you've deployed an assembly alongside your main project artifact, how can you use that assembly as a dependency in another project? The answer is fairly straightforward. Recall the discussions in the earlier sections "Maven Coordinates" in Chapter 3 and "More on Coordinates" in Chapter 9 about project dependencies in Maven. Projects depend on other projects using a combination of four basic elements, referred to as a project's coordinates: `groupId`, `artifactId`, `version`, and `packaging`. In "Platform Classifiers" in Chapter 11, we explained that multiple platform-specific variants of a project's artifact are available, and the project specifies a `classifier` element with a value of either `win` or `linux` to select the appropriate dependency artifact for the target platform. Assembly artifacts can be used as dependencies using the required coordinates of a project plus the classifier under which the assembly was installed or deployed. If the assembly is not a JAR archive, we also need to declare its type.

Assembling Assemblies via Assembly Dependencies

How's that for a confusing section title? Let's try to set up a scenario that explains the idea of assembling assemblies. Imagine you want to create an archive that itself contains some project assemblies. Assume you have a multimodule build, and you want to deploy an assembly that contains a set of related project assemblies. In this section's example, we will create a bundle of "buildable" project directories for a set of projects that are commonly used together. For simplicity, we'll reuse the two built-in assembly descriptors discussed earlier—project and jar-with-dependencies. In this particular example, it is assumed that each project creates the project assembly in addition to its main JAR artifact. Assume that every project in a multimodule build binds the single goal to the package phase and uses the project descriptorRef. Every project in a multimodule will inherit the configuration from a top-level *pom.xml*, whose pluginManagement element is shown in Example 12-2.

Example 12-2. Configuring the project assembly in top-level POM

```
<project>
  ...
  <build>
    <pluginManagement>
      <plugins>
        <plugin>
          <artifactId>maven-assembly-plugin</artifactId>
          <version>2.2-beta-2</version>
          <executions>
            <execution>
              <id>create-project-bundle</id>
              <phase>package</phase>
              <goals>
                <goal>single</goal>
              </goals>
              <configuration>
                <descriptorRefs>
                  <descriptorRef>project</descriptorRef>
                </descriptorRefs>
              </configuration>
            </execution>
          </executions>
        </plugin>
      </plugins>
    </pluginManagement>
  </build>
  ...
</project>
```

Each project POM references the managed plugin configuration from Example 12-2 using a minimal plugin declaration in its build section, as shown in Example 12-3.

Example 12-3. Activating the Assembly plugin configuration in child projects

```
<build>
  <plugins>
    <plugin>
      <artifactId>maven-assembly-plugin</artifactId>
    </plugin>
  </plugins>
</build>
```

To produce the set of project assemblies, run *mvn install* from the top-level directory. You should see Maven installing artifacts with classifiers in your local repository:

```
$ mvn install
...
[INFO] Installing ~/mvn-examples-1.0/assemblies/as-dependencies/project-parent/\
        second-project/target/second-project-1.0-SNAPSHOT-project.tar.gz to
    ~/.m2/repository/org/sonatype/mavenbook/assemblies/second-project/1.0-SNAPSHOT/\
        second-project-1.0-SNAPSHOT-project.tar.gz
...
[INFO] Installing ~/mvn-examples-1.0/assemblies/as-dependencies/project-parent/\
        second-project/target/second-project-1.0-SNAPSHOT-project.tar.bz2 to
    ~/.m2/repository/org/sonatype/mavenbook/assemblies/second-project/1.0-SNAPSHOT/\
        second-project-1.0-SNAPSHOT-project.tar.bz2
...
[INFO] Installing ~/mvn-examples-1.0/assemblies/as-dependencies/project-parent/\
        second-project/target/second-project-1.0-SNAPSHOT-project.zip to
    ~/.m2/repository/org/sonatype/mavenbook/assemblies/second-project/1.0-SNAPSHOT/\\
        second-project-1.0-SNAPSHOT-project.zip
...
```

When you run *install*, Maven will copy each project's main artifact and each assembly to your local Maven repository. All of these artifacts are now available for reference as dependencies in other projects locally. If your ultimate goal is to create a bundle that includes assemblies from multiple projects, you can do so by creating another project that will include other project's assemblies as dependencies. This bundling project (aptly named `project-bundle`) is responsible for creating the bundled assembly. The POM for the bundling project would resemble the XML document shown in Example 12-4.

Example 12-4. POM for the assembly bundling project

```xml
<project xmlns="http://maven.apache.org/POM/4.0.0"
  xmlns:xsi="http://www.w3.org/2001/XMLSchema-instance"
  xsi:schemaLocation="http://maven.apache.org/POM/4.0.0
        http://maven.apache.org/maven-v4_0_0.xsd">
  <modelVersion>4.0.0</modelVersion>
  <groupId>org.sonatype.mavenbook.assemblies</groupId>
  <artifactId>project-bundle</artifactId>
  <version>1.0-SNAPSHOT</version>
  <packaging>pom</packaging>
  <name>Assemblies-as-Dependencies Example Project Bundle</name>
  <url>http://sonatype.com/book</url>
  <dependencies>
    <dependency>
      <groupId>org.sonatype.mavenbook.assemblies</groupId>
      <artifactId>first-project</artifactId>
      <version>1.0-SNAPSHOT</version>
      <classifier>project</classifier>
      <type>zip</type>
    </dependency>
    <dependency>
      <groupId>org.sonatype.mavenbook.assemblies</groupId>
      <artifactId>second-project</artifactId>
```

```
        <version>1.0-SNAPSHOT</version>
        <classifier>project</classifier>
        <type>zip</type>
      </dependency>
    </dependencies>
    <build>
      <plugins>
        <plugin>
          <artifactId>maven-assembly-plugin</artifactId>
          <version>2.2-beta-2</version>
          <executions>
            <execution>
              <id>bundle-project-sources</id>
              <phase>package</phase>
              <goals>
                <goal>single</goal>
              </goals>
              <configuration>
                <descriptorRefs>
                  <descriptorRef>
                    jar-with-dependencies
                  </descriptorRef>
                </descriptorRefs>
              </configuration>
            </execution>
          </executions>
        </plugin>
      </plugins>
    </build>
</project>
```

This bundling project's POM references the two assemblies from `first-project` and `second-project`. Instead of referencing the main artifact of each project, the bundling project's POM specifies a classifier of `project` and a type of `zip`. This tells Maven to resolve the ZIP archive that was created by the `project` assembly. Note that the bundling project generates a `jar-with-dependencies` assembly. `jar-with-dependencies` does not create a particularly elegant bundle; it simply creates a JAR file with the unpacked contents of all of the dependencies. `jar-with-dependencies` is really just telling Maven to take all of the dependencies, unpack them, and then create a single archive that includes the output of the current project. In this project, it has the effect of creating a single JAR file that puts the two project assemblies from `first-project` and `second-project` side by side.

This example illustrates how the basic capabilities of the Maven Assembly plugin can be combined without the need for a custom assembly descriptor. It achieves the purpose of creating a single archive that contains the project directories for multiple projects side by side. This time, the `jar-with-dependencies` is just a storage format, so we don't need to specify a `Main-Class` manifest attribute. To build the bundle, we just build the `project-bundle` project normally:

```
$ mvn package
...
```

```
[INFO] [assembly:single {execution: bundle-project-sources}]
[INFO] Processing DependencySet (output=)
[INFO] Building jar: ~/downloads/mvn-examples-1.0/assemblies/as-dependencies/\
    project-bundle/target/project-bundle-1.0-SNAPSHOT-jar-with-dependencies.jar
```

To verify that the `project-bundle` assembly contains the unpacked contents of the assembly dependencies, run *jar tf*:

```
$ java tf \
    target/project-bundle-1.0-SNAPSHOT-jar-with-dependencies.jar
...
first-project-1.0-SNAPSHOT/pom.xml
first-project-1.0-SNAPSHOT/src/main/java/org/sonatype/mavenbook/App.java
first-project-1.0-SNAPSHOT/src/test/java/org/sonatype/mavenbook/AppTest.java
...
second-project-1.0-SNAPSHOT/pom.xml
second-project-1.0-SNAPSHOT/src/main/java/org/sonatype/mavenbook/App.java
second-project-1.0-SNAPSHOT/src/test/java/org/sonatype/mavenbook/AppTest.java
```

After reading this section, the title "Assembling Assemblies via Assembly Dependencies" should make more sense. You've assembled assemblies from two projects into an assembly using a bundling project that has a dependency on each of the assemblies.

Overview of the Assembly Descriptor

When the standard assembly descriptors introduced earlier in the section "Assembly Basics" are not adequate, you will need to define your own assembly descriptor. The assembly descriptor is an XML document that defines the structure and contents of an assembly. See Figure 12-1.

The assembly descriptor contains five main configuration sections, plus two additional sections: one for specifying standard assembly-descriptor fragments, called component descriptors, and another for specifying custom file processor classes to help manage the assembly-production process. These five sections are:

Base configuration

This section contains the information required by all assemblies, plus some additional configuration options related to the format of the entire archive, such as the base path to use for all archive entries. For the assembly descriptor to be valid, you must at least specify the assembly ID, at least one format, and at least one of the other sections shown in this list.

File information

The configurations in this segment of the assembly descriptor apply to specific files on the file system within the project's directory structure. This segment contains two main sections: `files` and `fileSets`. You use `files` and `fileSets` to control the permissions of files in an assembly and to include or exclude files from an assembly.

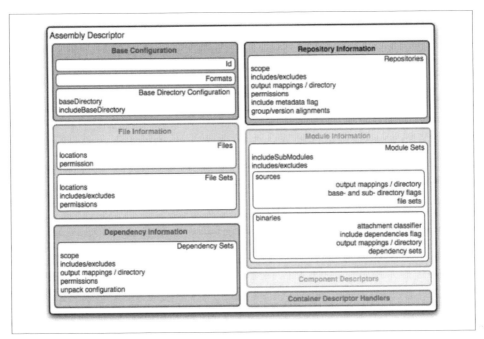

Figure 12-1. Assembly descriptor

Dependency information

Almost all projects of any size depend on other projects. When creating distribution archives, project dependencies are usually included in the end product of an assembly. This section manages the way dependencies are included in the resulting archive, and allows you to specify whether dependencies are unpacked, added directly to the *lib/* directory, or mapped to new file names. This section also allows you to control the permissions of dependencies in the assembly as well as which dependencies are included in an assembly.

Repository information

At times, it's useful to isolate the sum total of all artifacts necessary to build a project, whether they're dependency artifacts, POMs of dependency artifacts, or even a project's own POM ancestry (your parent POM, its parent, and so on). This section allows you to include one or more artifact-repository directory structures inside your assembly, with various configuration options. The Assembly plugin does not have the ability to include plugin artifacts in these repositories yet.

Module information

This section of the assembly descriptor allows you to take advantage of these parent-child relationships when assembling your custom archive, and to include source files, artifacts, and dependencies from your project's modules. This is the most complex section of the assembly descriptor, because it allows you to work with modules and submodules in two ways: as a series of `fileSets` (via the `sources` section) or as a series of `dependencySets` (via the `binaries` section).

The Assembly Descriptor

This section is a tour of the assembly descriptor, which contains some guidelines for developing a custom assembly descriptor. The Assembly plugin is one of the largest plugins in the Maven ensemble, and one of the most flexible.

Property References in Assembly Descriptors

Any property discussed in the section "Maven Properties" in Chapter 13 can be referenced in an assembly descriptor. Before any assembly descriptor is used by Maven, it is interpolated using information from the POM and the current build environment. All properties supported for interpolation within the POM itself are valid for use in assembly descriptors, including POM properties, POM element values, system properties, user-defined properties, and operating-system environment variables.

The only exceptions to this interpolation step are elements in various sections of the descriptor named `outputDirectory`, `outputDirectoryMapping`, or `outputFileNameMapping`. The reason these are held back in their raw form is to allow artifact- or module-specific information to be applied when resolving expressions in these values, on a per-item basis.

Required Assembly Information

Two essential pieces of information are required for every assembly: the `id` and the list of archive formats to produce. In practice, at least one other section of the descriptor is required, since most archive format components will choke if they don't have at least one file to include. But without at least one `format` and an `id`, there is no archive to create. The `id` is used both in the archive's file name, and as part of the archive's artifact classifier in the Maven repository. The format string also controls the archiver-component instance that will create the final assembly archive. All assembly descriptors must contain an `id` and at least one `format`. See Example 12-5.

Example 12-5. Required assembly descriptor elements

```
<assembly>
  <id>bundle</id>
  <formats>
    <format>zip</format>
  </formats>
  ...
</assembly>
```

The assembly `id` can be any string that does not contain spaces. The standard practice is to use dashes when you must separate words within the assembly `id`. If you were creating an assembly to create an interesting unique package structure, you would give your assembly an `id` of something like `interesting-unique-package`. The Maven Assembly plugin also supports multiple formats within a single assembly descriptor, allowing you to create the familiar *.zip*, *.tar.gz*, and *.tar.bz2* distribution archive set with ease. If you don't find the archive format you need, you can also create a custom format. Custom formats are discussed in the section "componentDescriptors and containerDescriptorHandlers," later in this chapter. The Assembly plugin supports several archive formats natively, including:

- `jar`
- `zip`
- `tar`
- `bzip2`
- `gzip`
- `tar.gz`
- `tar.bz2`
- `rar`
- `war`
- `ear`
- `sar`
- `dir`

The `id` and `format` are essential because they will become a part of the coordinates for the assembled archive. The example from Example 12-5 will create an assembly artifact of type `zip` with a classifier of `bundle`.

Controlling the Contents of an Assembly

In theory, `id` and `format` are the only absolute requirements for a valid assembly descriptor; however, many assembly archivers will fail if they do not have at least one file to include in the output archive. The task of defining the files to be included in the assembly is handled by the five main sections of the assembly descriptor: `files`, `fileSets`, `dependencySets`, `repositories`, and `moduleSets`. To explore these sections most effectively, we'll start by discussing the most elemental section: `files`. Then, we'll move onto the two most commonly used sections, `fileSets` and `dependencySets`. Once you understand the workings of `fileSets` and `dependencySets`, it's easier to understand `repositories` and `moduleSets`.

Files Section

The files section is the simplest part of the assembly descriptor. It is designed for files that have a definite location relative to your project's directory. Using this section, you have absolute control over the exact set of files that are included in your assembly, exactly what they are named, and where they will reside in the archive. See Example 12-6.

Example 12-6. Including a JAR file in an assembly using files

```
<assembly>
  ...
  <files>
    <file>
      <source>target/my-app-1.0.jar</source>
      <outputDirectory>lib</outputDirectory>
      <destName>my-app.jar</destName>
      <fileMode>0644</fileMode>
    </file>
  </files>
  ...
</assembly>
```

Assuming you were building a project called my-app with a version of 1.0, Example 12-6 would include your project's JAR in the assembly's *lib/* directory, trimming the version from the filename in the process so the final filename is simply *my-app.jar*. It would then make the JAR readable by everyone and writable by the user who owns it (this is what the mode 0644 means for files, using Unix four-digit octal permission notation). For more information about the format of the value in fileMode, see the Wikipedia entry on four-digit octal notation (*http://en.wikipedia.org/wiki/File_system_permissions#Octal_notation_and_additional_permissions*).

You could build a very complex assembly using file entries, if you knew the full list of files to be included. Even if you didn't know the full list before the build started, you could probably use a custom Maven plugin to discover that list and generate the assembly descriptor using references like the one just shown. Although the files section gives you fine-grained control over the permission, location, and name of each file in the assembly archive, listing a file element for every file in a large archive would be a tedious exercise. For the most part, you will be operating on groups of files and dependencies using fileSets. The remaining four file-inclusion sections are designed to help you include entire sets of files that match a particular criteria.

fileSets Section

Similar to the files section, fileSets are intended for files that have a definite location relative to your project's directory structure. However, unlike the files section, fileSets describe sets of files, defined by file and path patterns they match (or don't match), and the general directory structure in which they are located. The simplest `fileSet` just specifies the directory where the files are located:

```
<assembly>
  ...
  <fileSets>
    <fileSet>
      <directory>src/main/java</directory>
    </fileSet>
  </fileSets>
  ...
</assembly>
```

This fileset simply includes the contents of the *src/main/java* directory from our project. It takes advantage of many default settings in the section, so let's discuss those briefly.

First, you'll notice that we haven't told the file set where within the assembly matching files should be located. By default, the destination directory (specified with `outputDirectory`) is the same as the source directory (in our case, *src/main/java*). Additionally, we haven't specified any inclusion or exclusion file patterns. When these are empty, the file set assumes that all files within the source directory are included, with some important exceptions. The exceptions to this rule pertain mainly to source-control metadata files and directories, and are controlled by the `useDefaultExcludes` flag, which defaults to `true`. When active, `useDefaultExcludes` will keep directories such as *.svn/* and *CVS/* from being added to the assembly archive. The section "Default Exclusion Patterns for fileSets," later in this chapter, provides a detailed list of the default exclusion patterns.

If we want more control over this file set, we can specify it more explicitly. Example 12-7 shows a `fileSet` element with all of the default elements specified.

Example 12-7. Including files with fileSet

```
<assembly>
  ...
  <fileSets>
    <fileSet>
      <directory>src/main/java</directory>
      <outputDirectory>src/main/java</outputDirectory>
      <includes>
        <include>**</include>
      </include>
      <useDefaultExcludes>true</useDefaultExcludes>
      <fileMode>0644</fileMode>
      <directoryMode>0755</directoryMode>
    </fileSet>
  </fileSets>
  ...
</assembly>
```

The `includes` section uses a list of `include` elements, which contain path patterns. These patterns may contain wildcards, such as **, which matches one or more directories, or

*, which matches part of a filename, and ?, which matches a single character in a filename. Example 12-7 uses a `fileMode` entry to specify that files in this set should be readable by all, but only writable by the owner. Since the `fileSet` includes directories, we also have the option of specifying a `directoryMode` that works in much the same way as the `fileMode`. Since a directory's execute permission is what allows users to list its contents, we want to make sure directories are executable in addition to being readable. Like files, only the owner can write to directories in this set.

The `fileSet` entry offers some other options as well. First, it allows for an `excludes` section with a form identical to the `includes` section. These exclusion patterns allow you to exclude specific file patterns from a `fileSet`. Include patterns take precedence over exclude patterns. Additionally, you can set the `filtering` flag to `true` if you want to substitute property values for expressions within the included files. Expressions can be delimited either by `${` and `}` (standard Maven expressions such as `${project.groupId}`) or by `@` and `@` (standard Ant expressions such as `@project.groupId@`). You can adjust the line ending of your files using the `lineEnding` element. Valid values for `lineEnding` are:

keep
> Preserve line endings from original files (this is the default value)

unix
> Unix-style line endings

lf
> Only a line feed character

dos
> MS-DOS-style line endings

crlf
> Carriage return followed by a line feed

Finally, if you want to ensure that all file-matching patterns are used, you can use the `useStrictFiltering` element with a value of `true` (the default is `false`). This can be especially useful if unused patterns may signal missing files in an intermediary output directory. When `useStrictFiltering` is set to `true`, the Assembly plugin will fail if an `include` pattern is not satisfied. In other words, if you have an `include` pattern that includes a file from a build, and that file is not present, setting `useStrictFiltering` to `true` will cause a failure if Maven cannot find the file to be included.

Default Exclusion Patterns for fileSets

When you use the default exclusion patterns, the Maven Assembly plugin is going to be ignoring more than just SVN and CVS information. By default, the exclusion patterns are defined by the DirectoryScanner (*http://svn.codehaus.org/plexus/plexus-utils/ trunk/src/main/java/org/codehaus/plexus/util/DirectoryScanner.java*) class in the plexus-utils project (*http://plexus.codehaus.org/plexus-utils/*) hosted at Codehaus. The

array of exclude patterns is defined as a static, final String array named
DEFAULTEXCLUDES in DirectoryScanner. The contents of this variable are shown in Example 12-8.

Example 12-8. Definition of default exclusion patterns from plexus-utils

```
public static final String[] DEFAULTEXCLUDES = {
    // Miscellaneous typical temporary files
    "**/*~",
    "**/#*#",
    "**/.#*",
    "**/%*%",
    "**/._*",

    // CVS
    "**/CVS",
    "**/CVS/**",
    "**/.cvsignore",

    // SCCS
    "**/SCCS",
    "**/SCCS/**",

    // Visual SourceSafe
    "**/vssver.scc",

    // Subversion
    "**/.svn",
    "**/.svn/**",

    // Arch
    "**/.arch-ids",
    "**/.arch-ids/**",

    //Bazaar
    "**/.bzr",
    "**/.bzr/**",

    //SurroundSCM
    "**/.MySCMServerInfo",

    // Mac
    "**/.DS_Store"
};
```

This default array of patterns excludes temporary files from editors such as GNU Emacs (*http://www.gnu.org/software/emacs/*) and other common temporary files from Macs and a few common source control systems (although Visual SourceSafe is more of a curse than a source control system). If you need to override these default exclusion patterns, you set useDefaultExcludes to false and then define a set of exclusion patterns in your own assembly descriptor.

dependencySets Section

One of the most common requirements for assemblies is the inclusion of a project's dependencies in an assembly archive. Where `files` and `fileSets` deal with files in your project, dependency files don't have a location in your project. The artifacts your project depends on have to be resolved by Maven during the build. Dependency artifacts are abstract; they lack a definite location and are resolved using a symbolic set of Maven coordinates. Whereas `file` and `fileSet` specifications require a concrete source path, dependencies are included or excluded from an assembly using a combination of Maven coordinates and dependency scopes.

The simplest `dependencySet` is an empty element:

```
<assembly>
  ...
  <dependencySets>
    <dependencySet/>
  </dependencySets>
  ...
</assembly>
```

The `dependencySet` just shown will match all runtime dependencies of your project (`runtime` scope includes the `compile` scope implicitly), and it will add these dependencies to the root directory of your assembly archive. It will also copy the current project's main artifact into the root of the assembly archive, if it exists.

 Wait... I thought `dependencySet` was about including my project's dependencies, not my project's main archive? This counterintuitive side effect was a widely used bug in the 2.1 version of the Assembly plugin, and because Maven puts an emphasis on backward compatibility, this counterintuitive and incorrect behavior needed to be preserved between a 2.1 and 2.2 release. You can control this behavior by changing the `useProjectArtifact` flag to `false`.

Although the default dependency set can be quite useful with no configuration whatsoever, this section of the assembly descriptor also supports a wide array of configuration options, allowing you to tailor its behavior to your specific requirements. For example, the first thing you might do to the dependency set shown previously is exclude the current project artifact by setting the `useProjectArtifact` flag to `false` (again, its default value is `true` for legacy reasons). This will allow you to manage the current project's build output separately from its dependency files. Alternatively, you might choose to unpack the dependency artifacts by setting the `unpack` flag to `true` (it is `false` by default). When unpack is set to true, the Assembly plugin will combine the unpacked contents of all matching dependencies inside the archive's root directory.

From this point, there are several things you might choose to do with this dependency set. The upcoming sections discuss how to define the output location for dependency sets and how to include and exclude dependencies by scope. Finally, we'll expand on the unpacking functionality of the dependency set by exploring some advanced options for unpacking dependencies.

Customizing dependency output location

Two configuration options are used in concert to define the location for a dependency file within the assembly archive: `outputDirectory` and `outputFileNameMapping`. You may want to customize the location of dependencies in your assembly using properties of the dependency artifacts themselves. Let's say you want to put all the dependencies in directories that match the dependency artifact's `groupId`. In this case, you would use the `outputDirectory` element of the `dependencySet`, and you would supply something like this:

```
<assembly>
  ...
  <dependencySets>
    <dependencySet>
      <outputDirectory>${artifact.groupId}</outputDirectory>
    </dependencySet>
  </dependencySets>
  ...
</assembly>
```

This would have the effect of placing every single dependency in a subdirectory that matches the name of each dependency artifact's `groupId`.

If you want to perform a further customization and remove the version numbers from all dependencies, you can customize the output file name for each dependency using the `outputFileNameMapping` element as follows:

```
<assembly>
  ...
  <dependencySets>
    <dependencySet>
      <outputDirectory>${artifact.groupId}</outputDirectory>
      <outputFileNameMapping>
        ${module.groupId}-${module.artifactId}.${module.extension}
      </outputFileNameMapping>
    </dependencySet>
  </dependencySets>
  ...
</assembly>
```

In the example just shown, a dependency on `commons:commons-codec` version 1.3 would end up in the file *commons/commons-codec.jar*.

Interpolation of properties in dependency output location

As mentioned in the "Property References in Assembly Descriptors" section, earlier in this chapter, neither of these elements are interpolated with the rest of the assembly descriptor because their raw values have to be interpreted using additional, artifact-specific expression resolvers.

The artifact expressions available for these two elements vary only slightly. In both cases, all of the ${project.*}, ${pom.*}, and ${*} expressions that are available in the POM and the rest of the assembly descriptor are also available here. For the outputFileNameMapping element, the following process is applied to resolve expressions:

1. If the expression matches the pattern ${artifact.*}:

   a. Match against the dependency's Artifact instance (resolves: groupId, artifactId, version, baseVersion, scope, classifier, and file.*).

   b. Match against the dependency's ArtifactHandler instance (resolves: expression).

   c. Match against the project instance associated with the dependency's artifact (resolves: mainly POM properties).

   d. If the expression matches the patterns ${pom.*} or ${project.*}, match against the project instance (MavenProject) of the current build.

2. If the expression matches the pattern ${dashClassifier?} and the artifact instance contains a nonnull classifier, resolve to the classifier preceded by a dash (-classifier). Otherwise, resolve to an empty string.

3. Attempt to resolve the expression against the project instance of the current build.

4. Attempt to resolve the expression against the POM properties of the current build.

5. Attempt to resolve the expression against the available system properties.

6. Attempt to resolve the expression against the available operating-system environment variables.

The outputDirectory value is interpolated in much the same way, the difference being that there is no available ${artifact.*} information, only the ${project.*} instance for the particular artifact. Therefore, the expressions just shown associated with those classes (numbers 1a, 1b, and 3 in the process listing) are unavailable.

How do you know when to use outputDirectory and outputFileNameMapping? When dependencies are unpacked, only the outputDirectory is used to calculate the output location. When dependencies are managed as whole files (not unpacked), both outputDirectory and outputFileNameMapping can be used together. When used together, the result is the equivalent of:

```
<archive-root-dir>/<outputDirectory>/<outputFileNameMapping>
```

When outputDirectory is missing, it is not used. When outputFileNameMapping is missing, its default value is:

```
${artifact.artifactId}-${artifact.version}${dashClassifier?}.${artifact.extension}
```

Including and excluding dependencies by scope

In Chapter 9, we noted that all project dependencies have one scope or another. Scope determines when in the build process that dependency normally would be used. For instance, test-scoped dependencies are not included in the classpath during compilation of the main project sources, but they are included in the classpath when compiling unit test sources. This is because your project's main source code should not contain any code specific to testing, since testing is not a function of the project (it's a function of the project's build process). Similarly, provided-scoped dependencies are assumed to be present in the environment of any eventual deployment. However, if a project depends on a particular provided dependency, it is likely to require that dependency in order to compile. Therefore, provided-scoped dependencies are present in the compilation classpath, but not in the dependency set that should be bundled with the project's artifact or assembly.

Also from Chapter 9, recall that some dependency scopes imply others. For instance, the runtime dependency scope implies the compile scope, since all compile-time dependencies (except for those in the provided scope) will be required for the code to execute. A number of complex relationships exist between the various dependency scopes that control how the scope of a direct dependency affects the scope of a transitive dependency. In a Maven Assembly descriptor, we can use scopes to apply different settings to different sets of dependencies accordingly.

For instance, if we plan to bundle a web application with Jetty (*http://www.mortbay.org/jetty-6/*) to create a completely self-contained application, we'll need to include all provided-scope dependencies somewhere in the Jetty directory structure we're including. This ensures those provided dependencies actually are present in the runtime environment. Non-provided, runtime dependencies will still land in the *WEB-INF/lib* directory, so these two dependency sets must be processed separately. These dependency sets might look similar to the XML shown in Example 12-9.

Example 12-9. Defining dependency sets using scope

```
<assembly>
  ...
  <dependencySets>
    <dependencySet>
      <scope>provided</scope>
      <outputDirectory>lib/${project.artifactId}</outputDirectory>
    </dependencySet>
    <dependencySet>
      <scope>runtime</scope>
      <outputDirectory>
        webapps/${webContextName}/WEB-INF/lib
      </outputDirectory>
    </dependencySet>
  </dependencySets>
  ...
</assembly>
```

`provided`-scoped dependencies are added to the *lib/* directory in the assembly root, which is assumed to be a libraries directory that will be included in the Jetty global runtime classpath. We're using a subdirectory named for the project's `artifactId` in order to make it easier to track the origin of a particular library. `runtime` dependencies are included in the *WEB-INF/lib* path of the web application, which is located within a subdirectory of the standard Jetty *webapps/* directory that is named using a custom POM property called `webContextName`. What we've done in Example 12-9 is separate application-specific dependencies from dependencies that will be present in a Servlet that contains global classpath.

However, simply separating according to scope may not be enough, particularly in the case of a web application. It's conceivable that one or more `runtime` dependencies will actually be bundles of standardized, noncompiled resources for use in the web application. For example, consider a set of web applications that reuse a common set of JavaScript, Cascading Style Sheets (CSS), SWF, and image resources. To make these resources easy to standardize, it's common practice to bundle them up in an archive and deploy them to the Maven repository. At that point, they can be referenced as standard Maven dependencies—possibly with a dependency type of `zip`—that are normally specified with a runtime scope. Remember, these are resources, not binary dependencies of the application code itself; therefore, it's not appropriate to blindly include them in the *WEB-INF/lib* directory. Instead, these resource archives should be separated from binary runtime dependencies and unpacked into the web application document root somewhere. In order to achieve this kind of separation, we'll need to use inclusion and exclusion patterns that apply to the coordinates of a specific dependency.

In other words, say you have three or four web application that reuse the same resources, and you want to create an assembly that puts `provided` dependencies into *lib/*, puts `runtime` dependencies into *webapps/<contextName>/WEB-INF/lib*, and then unpacks a specific `runtime` dependency into your web application's document root. You can do this because the assembly allows you to define multiple `include` and `exclude` patterns for a given `dependencySet` element. Read the next section for more development of this idea.

Fine-tuning: dependency includes and excludes

A resource dependency might be as simple as a set of resources (CSS, JavaScript, and images) in a project that has an assembly that creates a ZIP archive. Depending on the particulars of our web application, we might be able to distinguish resource dependencies from binary dependencies solely according to type. Most web applications are going to depend on other dependencies of type `jar`, and it is possible that we can state with certainty that all dependencies of type `zip` are resource dependencies. Or we might have a situation where resources are stored in `jar` format, but have a classifier of something like `resources`. In either case, we can specify an inclusion pattern to target these resource dependencies and apply logic different than that used for binary dependencies.

We'll specify these tuning patterns using the `includes` and `excludes` sections of the dependencySet.

Both includes and excludes are list sections, meaning they accept the subelements `include` and `exclude` respectively. Each `include` or `exclude` element contains a string value, which can contain wildcards. Each string value can match dependencies in a few different ways. Generally speaking, three identity pattern formats are supported:

`groupId:artifactId`—version-less key

> You would use this pattern to match a dependency by only the `groupId` and the `artifactId`.

`groupId:artifactId:type[:classifier]`—conflict `id`

> The pattern allows you to specify a wider set of coordinates to create a more specific include/exclude pattern.

`groupId:artifactId:type[:classifier]:version`—full artifact identity

> If you need to get really specific, you can specify all the coordinates.

All of these pattern formats support the wildcard character *, which can match any subsection of the identity and is not limited to matching single identity parts (sections between : characters). Also, note that the classifier section is optional, because patterns matching dependencies that don't have classifiers do not need to account for the classifier section in the pattern.

In the example given earlier, where the key distinction is the artifact type `zip`, and none of the dependencies have classifiers, the following pattern would match resource dependencies, assuming that they were of type `zip`:

```
*:zip
```

This pattern makes use of the second dependency identity: the dependency's conflict `id`. Now that we have a pattern that distinguishes resource dependencies from binary dependencies, we can modify our dependency sets to handle resource archives differently, as shown in Example 12-10.

Example 12-10. Using dependency excludes and includes in dependencySets

```
<assembly>
  ...
  <dependencySets>
    <dependencySet>
      <scope>provided</scope>
      <outputDirectory>lib/${project.artifactId}</outputDirectory>
    </dependencySet>
    <dependencySet>
      <scope>runtime</scope>
      <outputDirectory>
        webapps/${webContextName}/WEB-INF/lib
      </outputDirectory>
      <excludes>
        <exclude>*:zip</exclude>
```

```
        </excludes>
      </dependencySet>
      <dependencySet>
        <scope>runtime</scope>
        <outputDirectory>
          webapps/${webContextName}/resources
        </outputDirectory>
        <includes>
          <include>*:zip</include>
        </includes>
        <unpack>true</unpack>
      </dependencySet>
    </dependencySets>
    ...
</assembly>
```

In this example, the `runtime`-scoped dependency set from our previous example has been updated to exclude resource dependencies. Only binary dependencies (non-`zip` dependencies) should be added to the *WEB-INF/lib* directory of the web application. Resource dependencies now have their own dependency set, which is configured to include these dependencies in the resources directory of the web application. The `includes` section in the last `dependencySet` reverses the exclusion from the previous `dependencySet`, so that resource dependencies are included using the same identity pattern (i.e., `*:zip`). The last `dependencySet` refers to the shared resource dependency, and it is configured to unpack the shared resource dependency in the document root of the web application.

Example 12-10 was based on the assumption that our shared resources project dependency had a type that differed from all the other dependencies. What if the shared resource dependency had the same type as all the other dependencies? How could you differentiate the dependency? In that case, if the shared resource dependency had been bundled as a JAR with the classifier `resources`, you could change to the identity pattern and match those dependencies instead:

```
*:jar:resources
```

Rather than matching on artifacts with a type of `zip` and no classifier, we're matching on artifacts with a classifier of `resources` and a type of `jar`.

Just like the `fileSets` section, `dependencySets` support the `useStrictFiltering` flag. When enabled, any specified patterns that don't match one or more dependencies will cause the assembly—and consequently, the build—to fail. This can be particularly useful as a safety valve to make sure your project dependencies and assembly descriptors are synchronized and interacting as you expect them to. By default, this flag is set to `false` for the purposes of backward compatibility.

Transitive dependencies, project attachments, and project artifacts

The `dependencySet` section supports two more general mechanisms for tuning the subset of matching artifacts: transitive selection options and options for working with project artifacts. Both of these features are a product of the need to support legacy configurations that applied a somewhat more liberal definition of the word "dependency." As a prime example, consider the project's own main artifact. Typically, this would not be considered a dependency, yet older versions of the Assembly plugin included the project artifact in calculations of dependency sets. To provide backward compatibility with this "feature," the 2.2 releases (currently at 2.2-beta-2) of the Assembly plugin support a flag in the dependencySet called useProjectArtifact, whose default value is true. By default, dependency sets will attempt to include the project artifact itself in calculations about which dependency artifacts match and which don't. If you'd rather deal with the project artifact separately, set this flag to false.

We recommend that you always set useProjectArtifact to false.

As a natural extension to the inclusion of the project artifact, the project's attached artifacts can also be managed within a dependencySet using the useProjectAttachments flag (whose default value is false). Enabling this flag allows patterns that specify classifiers and types to match on artifacts that are "attached" to the main project artifact; that is, they share the same basic groupId/artifactId/version identity, but differ in type and classifier from the main artifact. This could be useful for including Javadoc or source JARs in an assembly.

Aside from dealing with the project's own artifacts, it's also possible to fine-tune the dependency set using two transitive-resolution flags. The first, called useTransitiveDependencies (and set to true by default), simply specifies whether the dependency set should consider transitive dependencies at all when determining the matching artifact set to be included. As an example of how this could be used, consider what happens when your POM has a dependency on another assembly. That assembly (most likely) will have a classifier that separates it from the main project artifact, making it an attachment. However, one quirk of the Maven dependency-resolution process is that the transitive-dependency information for the main artifact is still used when resolving the assembly artifact. If the assembly bundles its project dependencies inside itself, using transitive dependency resolution here would effectively duplicate those dependencies. To avoid this, we simply set useTransitiveDependencies to false for the dependency set that handles that assembly dependency.

The other transitive-resolution flag is far more subtle. It's called useTransitiveFiltering and has a default value of false. To understand what this flag does, we first need to understand what information is available for any given artifact during the resolution process. When an artifact is a dependency of a dependency (that is, removed at least one level from your own POM), it has what Maven calls a "dependency trail," which is maintained as a list of strings that correspond to the full artifact identities (*groupId*:*artifactId*:*type*:[*classifier*:]*version*) of all dependencies between your POM and the artifact that owns that dependency trail. If you remember the three types of artifact identities available for pattern matching in a dependency set, you'll notice that the entries in the *dependency* trail—the full artifact identity—correspond to the third type. When `useTransitiveFiltering` is set to `true`, the entries in an artifact's dependency trail can cause the artifact to be included or excluded in the same way its own identity can.

If you're considering using transitive filtering, be careful! A given artifact can be included from multiple places in the transitive-dependency graph, but as of Maven 2.0.9, only the first inclusion's trail will be tracked for this type of matching. This can lead to subtle problems when collecting the dependencies for your project.

 Most assemblies don't really need this level of control over dependency sets; consider carefully whether yours truly does. Hint: it probably doesn't.

Advanced unpacking options

As we discussed previously, some project dependencies may need to be unpacked in order to create a working assembly archive. In the examples we have shown, the decision to unpack or not was simple. We didn't take into account what needed to be unpacked or, more importantly, what should not have been unpacked. To gain more control over the dependency unpacking process, we can configure the `unpackOptions` element of the `dependencySet`. Using this section, we have the ability to choose which file patterns to include or exclude from the assembly, and whether included files should be filtered to resolve expressions using current POM information. In fact, the options available for unpacking dependency sets are fairly similar to those available for including files from the project directory structure, using the filesets descriptor section.

To continue our web application example, suppose some of the resource dependencies have been bundled with a file that details their distribution license. In the case of our web application, we'll handle third-party license notices by way of a *NOTICES* file included in our own bundle, so we don't want to include the license file from the resource dependency. To exclude this file, we simply add it to the unpack options inside the dependency set that handles resource artifacts, as shown in Example 12-11.

Example 12-11. Excluding files from a dependency unpack

```
<asembly>
  ...
  <dependencySets>
    <dependencySet>
      <scope>runtime</scope>
      <outputDirectory>
        webapps/${webContextName}/resources
      </outputDirectory>
      <includes>
```

```
      <include>*:zip</include>
    </includes>
    <unpack>true</unpack>
    <unpackOptions>
      <excludes>
        <exclude>**/LICENSE*</exclude>
      </excludes>
    </unpackOptions>
  </dependencySet>
</dependencySets>
...
</assembly>
```

Notice that the exclude we're using looks very similar to those used in fileSet declarations. Here, we're blocking any file starting with the word *LICENSE* in any directory within our resource artifacts. You can think of the unpack options section as a lightweight fileSet applied to each dependency matched within that dependency set. In other words, it is a fileSet by way of an unpacked dependency. Just as we specified an exclusion pattern for files within resource dependencies in order to block certain files, you can also choose which restricted set of files to include using the includes section. The same code that processes inclusions and exclusions on fileSets has been reused for processing unpackOptions.

In addition to file inclusion and exclusion, the unpack options on a dependency set also provides a filtering flag, whose default value is false. Again, this should be familiar from our earlier discussion of filesets. In both cases, expressions using either the Maven syntax of ${property} or the Ant syntax of @property@ are supported. However, filtering is a particularly nice feature to have for dependency sets, since it effectively allows you to create standardized, versioned resource templates that are then customized to each assembly as they are included. Once you start mastering the use of filtered, unpacked dependencies that store shared resources, you will be able to start abstracting repeated resources into common resource projects.

Summarizing dependency sets

Finally, it's worth mentioning that dependency sets support the same fileMode and directoryMode configuration options that filesets do, though you should remember that the directoryMode setting will be used only when dependencies are unpacked.

moduleSets Sections

Multimodule builds are generally stitched together using the parent and modules sections of interrelated POMs. Typically, parent POMs specify their children in a modules section that, under normal circumstances, causes the child POMs to be included in the build process of the parent. Exactly how this relationship is constructed can have important implications for the ways in which the Assembly plugin can participate in this process, but we'll discuss that later. For now, it's enough to keep in mind this parent-module relationship as we discuss the `moduleSets` section.

Projects are stitched together into multimodule builds because they are part of a larger system. These projects are designed to be used together, and a single module in a larger build has little practical value on its own. In this way, the structure of the project's build is related to the way in which we expect the project (and its modules) to be used. If we consider the project from the user's perspective, it makes sense that the ideal end goal of that build would be a single, distributable file that the user can consume directly with minimum installation hassle. Since Maven multimodule builds typically follow a top-down structure, where dependency information, plugin configurations, and other information trickles down from parent to child, it seems natural that the task of rolling all of these modules into a single distribution file should fall to the topmost project. This is where the `moduleSet` comes into the picture.

Module sets allow the inclusion of resources that belong to each module in the project structure into the final assembly archive. Just as you can select a group of files to include in an assembly using a `fileSet` and a `dependencySet`, you can include a set of files and resources using a `moduleSet` to refer to modules in a multimodule build. They achieve this by enabling two basic types of module-specific inclusion: file-based and artifact-based. Before we get into the specifics and differences between file-based and artifact-based inclusion of module resources into an assembly, let's talk a little about selecting which modules to process.

Module selection

By now, you should be familiar with `includes` and `excludes` patterns as they are used throughout the assembly descriptor to filter files and dependencies. When you are referring to modules in an assembly descriptor, you will also use the `includes` and `excludes` patterns to define rules that apply to different sets of modules. The difference in `moduleSet` `includes` and `excludes` is that these rules do not allow for wildcard patterns. (As of the 2.2-beta-2 release, this feature has not really seen much demand, so it hasn't been implemented.) Instead, each `include` or `exclude` value is simply the `groupId` and `artifactId` for the module, separated by a colon, like this:

> `groupId:artifactId`

In addition to `includes` and `excludes`, the `moduleSet` also supports an additional selection tool: the `includeSubModules` flag (whose default value is `true`). The parent-child relationship in any multimodule build structure is not strictly limited to two tiers of projects. In fact, you can include any number of tiers, or layers, in your build. Any project that is a module of a module of the current project is considered a submodule. In some cases, you may want to deal with each individual module in the build separately (including submodules). For example, this is often simplest when dealing with artifact-based contributions from these modules. To do this, you would simply leave the `useSubModules` flag set to the default of `true`.

When you're trying to include files from each module's directory structure, you may wish to process that module's directory structure only once. If your project directory structure mirrors that of the parent-module relationships that are included in the POMs, this approach would allow file patterns such as **/src/main/java to apply not only to that direct module's project directory, but also to the directories of its own modules as well. In case you don't want to process submodules directly (they will instead be processed as subdirectories within your own project's modules), you should set the useSubModules flag to false.

Once we've determined how module selection should proceed for the module set in question, we're ready to choose what to include from each module. As mentioned earlier, this can include files or artifacts from the module project.

Sources section

Suppose you want to include the source of all modules in your project's assembly, but you would like to exclude a particular module. Maybe you have a project named secret-sauce that contains secret and sensitive code that you don't want to distribute with your project. The simplest way to accomplish this is to use a moduleSet that includes each project's directory in ${module.basedir.name} and that excludes the secret-sauce module from the assembly. See Example 12-12.

Example 12-12. Including and excluding modules with a moduleSet

```
<assembly>
  ...
  <moduleSets>
    <moduleSet>
      <includeSubModules>false</includeSubModules>
      <excludes>
        <exclude>
          com.mycompany.application:secret-sauce
        </exclude>
      </excludes>
      <sources>
        <outputDirectoryMapping>
          ${module.basedir.name}
        </outputDirectoryMapping>
        <excludeSubModuleDirectories>
          false
        </excludeSubModuleDirectories>
        <fileSets>
          <fileSet>
            <directory>/</directory>
            <excludes>
              <exclude>**/target</exclude>
            </excludes>
          </fileSet>
        </fileSets>
      </sources>
    </moduleSet>
```

```
    </moduleSets>
    ...
</assembly>
```

In this example, since we're dealing with each module's sources, it's simpler to deal only with direct modules of the current project, handling submodules using filepath wildcard patterns in the file set. We set the `includeSubModules` element to `false` so we don't have to worry about submodules showing up in the root directory of the assembly archive. The `exclude` element will take care of excluding the `secret-sauce` module. We're not going to include the project sources for the `secret-sauce` module; they're, well, secret.

Normally, module sources are included in the assembly under a subdirectory named after the module's `artifactId`. However, since Maven allows modules that are not in directories named after the module project's `artifactId`, it's often better to use the expression `${module.basedir.name}` to preserve the module directory's actual name (`${module.basedir.name}` is the same as calling `MavenProject.getBasedir().get Name()`). It is critical to remember that modules are not required to be subdirectories of the project that declares them. If your project has a particularly strange directory structure, you may need to resort to special `moduleSet` declarations that include specific projects and account for your own project's idiosyncrasies.

 Try to minimize your own project's idiosyncrasies. Although Maven is flexible, if you find yourself doing too much configuration, there is likely an easier way.

Continuing through Example 12-12, since we're not processing submodules explicitly in this module set, we need to make sure submodule directories are not excluded from the source directories we consider for each direct module. By setting the `excludeSubModuleDirectories` flag to `false`, this allows us to apply the same file pattern to directory structures within a submodule of the one we're processing. Finally in Example 12-12, we're not interested in any output of the build process for this module set. We exclude the *target/* directory from all modules.

It's also worth mentioning that the `sources` section supports `fileSet`-like elements directly within itself, in addition to supporting nested `fileSets`. These configuration elements are used to provide backward compatibility to previous versions of the Assembly plugin (versions 2.1 and under) that didn't support multiple distinct file sets for the same module without creating a separate `module` set declaration. They are deprecated and should not be used.

Interpolation of outputDirectoryMapping in moduleSets

In the section "Customizing dependency output location," earlier in this chapter, we used the element `outputDirectoryMapping` to change the name of the directory under which each module's sources would be included. The expressions contained in this element are resolved in exactly the same way as the `outputFileNameMapping`, used in dependency sets. (See the explanation of this algorithm in the section "dependencySets Section," earlier in this chapter.)

In Example 12-12, we used the expression `${module.basedir.name}`. You might notice that the root of that expression, `module`, is not listed in the mapping-resolution algorithm from the dependency sets section; this object root is specific to configurations within `moduleSets`. It works in exactly the same way as the `${artifact.*}` references available in the `outputFileNameMapping` element, except it is applied to the module's `MavenProject`, `Artifact`, and `ArtifactHandler` instances instead of those from a dependency artifact.

Binaries section

Just as the `sources` section is primarily concerned with including a module in its source form, the `binaries` section is primarily concerned with including the module's build output, or its artifacts. Though this section functions primarily as a way of specifying `dependencySets` that apply to each module in the set, a few additional features unique to module artifacts are worth exploring: `attachmentClassifier` and `includeDependencies`. In addition, the `binaries` section contains options similar to the `dependencySet` section that relate to the handling of the module artifact itself. These are: `unpack`, `outputFileNameMapping`, `outputDirectory`, `directoryMode`, and `fileMode`. Finally, module binaries can contain a `dependencySets` section to specify how each module's dependencies should be included in the assembly archive. First, let's take a look at how the options mentioned here can be used to manage the module's own artifacts.

Suppose we want to include the Javadoc JARs for each of our modules inside our assembly. In this case, we don't care about including the `module` dependencies; we just want the Javadoc JAR. However, since this particular JAR is always going to be present as an attachment to the main project artifact, we need to specify which classifier to use to retrieve it. For simplicity, we won't cover unpacking the module Javadoc JARs, since this configuration is exactly the same as what we used for dependency sets earlier in this chapter. The resulting module set might look similar to Example 12-13.

Example 12-13. Including Javadoc from modules in an assembly

```
<assembly>
  ...
  <moduleSets>
    <moduleSet>
      <binaries>
        <attachmentClassifier>javadoc</attachmentClassifier>
        <includeDependencies>false</includeDependencies>
        <outputDirectory>apidoc-jars</outputDirectory>
      </binaries>
    </moduleSet>
  </moduleSets>
  ...
</assembly>
```

In this example, we don't explicitly set the includeSubModules flag, since it's true by default. However, we definitely want to process all modules—even submodules—using this module set, since we're not using any sort of file pattern that could match on submodule directory structures within. The attachmentClassifier grabs the attached artifact with the javadoc classifier for each module processed. The includeDependencies element tells the Assembly plugin that we're not interested in any of the module's dependencies, just the javadoc attachment. Finally, the outputDirectory element tells the Assembly plugin to put all of the Javadoc JARs into a directory named *apidoc-jars/* off the assembly root directory.

Although we're not doing anything too complicated in this example, it's important to understand that the same changes to the expression-resolution algorithm discussed for the outputDirectoryMapping element of the sources section also apply here. That is, whatever was available as ${artifact.*} inside a dependencySet's outputFileNameMapping configuration is also available here as ${module.*}. The same applies for outputFileNameMapping when used directly within a binaries section.

Finally, let's examine an example where we simply want to process the module's artifact and its runtime dependencies. In this case, we want to separate the artifact set for each module into separate directory structures, according to the module's artifactId and version. The resulting module set is surprisingly simply, and it looks like the listing in Example 12-14.

Example 12-14. Including module artifacts and dependencies in an assembly

```
<assembly>
  ...
  <moduleSets>
    <moduleSet>
      <binaries>
        <outputDirectory>
          ${module.artifactId}-${module.version}
        </outputDirectory>
        <dependencySets>
          <dependencySet/>
        </dependencySets>
      </binaries>
    </moduleSet>
  </moduleSets>
  ...
</assembly>
```

In this example, we're using the empty dependencySet element, since that should include all runtime dependencies by default, with no configuration. With the outputDirectory specified at the binaries level, all dependencies should be included alongside the module's own artifact in the same directory, so we don't even need to specify that in our dependency set.

For the most part, module binaries are fairly straightforward. In both parts—the main part, concerned with handling the module artifact itself, and the dependency sets, concerned with the module's dependencies—the configuration options are very similar to those in a dependency set. Of course, the binaries section also provides options for controlling whether dependencies are included and which main-project artifact you want to use.

Like the `sources` section, the `binaries` section contains a couple of configuration options that are provided solely for backward compatibility and that should be considered deprecated. These include the `includes` and `excludes` subsections.

moduleSets, parent POMs, and the binaries section

Finally, we close the discussion about module handling with a strong warning. There are subtle interactions between Maven's internal design as it relates to parent-module relationships and the execution of a module-set's `binaries` section. When a POM declares a parent, that parent must be resolved in some way or other before the POM in question can be built. If the parent is in the Maven repository, there is no problem. However, as of Maven 2.0.9, this can cause big problems if that parent is a higher-level POM in the same build, particularly if that parent POM expects to build an assembly using its modules' binaries.

Maven 2.0.9 sorts projects in a multimodule build according to their dependencies, with a given project's dependencies being built ahead of itself. The problem is that the parent element is considered a dependency, which means the parent project's build must complete before the child project is built. If part of that parent's build process includes the creation of an assembly that uses module binaries, those binaries will not exist yet, and therefore cannot be included, causing the assembly to fail. This is a complex and subtle issue that severely limits the usefulness of the module binaries section of the assembly descriptor. In fact, it has been filed in the bug tracker for the Assembly plugin at *http://jira.codehaus.org/browse/MASSEMBLY-97*. Hopefully, future versions of Maven will find a way to restore this functionality, since the parent-first requirement may not be completely necessary.

Repositories Section

The `repositories` section represents a slightly more exotic feature in the assembly descriptor, since few applications other than Maven can take full advantage of a Maven-repository directory structure. For this reason, and because many of its features closely resemble those in the `dependencySets` section, we won't spend too much time on the `repositories` section of the assembly descriptor. In most cases, users who understand dependency sets should have no trouble constructing repositories via the Assembly plugin. We're not going to motivate you to use the `repositories` section; we're not going to go through the business of setting up a use case and walking you through the process. We're just going to bring up a few caveats for those of you who find the need to use the `repositories` section.

Having said that, two features particular to the `repositories` section deserve some mention. The first is the `includeMetadata` flag. When set to `true`, it includes metadata such as the list of real versions that correspond to `-SNAPSHOT` virtual versions, and by default it's set to `false`. At present, the only metadata included when this flag is `true` is the information downloaded from Maven's central repository.

The second feature is called `groupVersionAlignments`. Again, this section is a list of individual `groupVersionAlignment` configurations, whose purpose is to normalize all included artifacts for a particular `groupId` to use a single `version`. Each alignment entry consists of two mandatory elements—`id` and `version`—along with an optional section called `excludes` that supplies a list of `artifactId` string values that are to be excluded from this realignment. Unfortunately, this realignment doesn't seem to modify the POMs involved in the repository—neither those related to realigned artifacts nor those that depend on realigned artifacts—so it's difficult to imagine what the practical application for this sort of realignment would be.

In general, it's simplest to apply the same principles you would use in dependency sets to repositories when adding them to your assembly descriptor. Although the `repositories` section does support the extra options mentioned earlier, they are mainly provided for backward compatibility and will probably be deprecated in future releases.

Managing the Assembly's Root Directory

Now that we've made it through the main body of the assembly descriptor, we can close the discussion of content-related descriptor sections with something lighter: root-directory naming and site-directory handling.

Some may consider it a stylistic concern, but it's often important to have control over the name of the root directory for your assembly, or to decide whether the root directory is there at all. Fortunately, two configuration options in the root of the assembly descriptor make managing the archive root directory simple: `includeBaseDirectory` and `baseDirectory`. In cases such as executable JAR files, you probably don't want a root directory at all. To skip it, simply set the `includeBaseDirectory` flag to `false`. (It's `true` by default.) This will result in an archive that, when unpacked, may create more than one directory in the unpack target directory. Although this is considered bad form for archives that are meant to be unpacked before use, it's not so bad for archives that are consumable as is.

In other cases, you may want to guarantee the name of the archive root directory regardless of the POM's version or other information. By default, the `baseDirectory` element has a value equal to ${*project.artifactId*}-${*project.version*}. However, we can easily set this element to any value that consists of literal strings and expressions that can be interpolated from the current POM, such as ${*project.groupId*}-${*project.artifactId*}. This could be very good news for your documentation team! (We all have those, right?)

Another configuration available is the includeSiteDirectory flag, whose default value is false. If your project build has also constructed a web site document root using the site lifecycle or the Site plugin goals, that output can be included by setting this flag to true. However, this feature is a bit limited, since it includes only the outputDirectory from the reporting section of the current POM (by default, *target/site*) and doesn't take into consideration any site directories that may be available in module projects. Use it if you want, but a good fileSet specification or moduleSet specification with sources configured could serve equally well, if not better. This is yet another example of legacy configuration currently supported by the Assembly plugin for the purpose of backward compatibility. Your mileage may vary. If you really want to include a site that is aggregated from many modules, you'll want to consider using a fileSet or moduleSet instead of setting includeSiteDirectory to true.

componentDescriptors and containerDescriptorHandlers

To round out our exploration of the assembly descriptor, we should touch briefly on two other sections: containerDescriptorHandlers and componentDescriptors. The containerDescriptorHandlers section refers to custom components that you use to extend the capabilities of the Assembly plugin. Specifically, these custom components allow you to define and handle special files that may need to be merged from the multiple constituents used to create your assembly. A good example of this might be a custom container-descriptor handler that merged *web.xml* files from constituent WAR or WAR-fragment files included in your assembly, in order to create the single webapplication descriptor required for you to use the resulting assembly archive as a WAR file.

The componentDescriptors section allows you to reference external assembly-descriptor fragments and include them in the current descriptor. Component references can be any of the following (in this order):

1. Relative filepaths, e.g., *src/main/assembly/component.xml*
2. Artifact references, e.g., *groupId:artifactId:version[:type[:classifier]]*
3. Classpath resources, e.g., */assemblies/component.xml*
4. URLs, e.g., *http://www.sonatype.com/component.xml*

Incidentally, when resolving a component descriptor, the Assembly plugin tries those different strategies in that exact order. The first one to succeed is used.

Component descriptors can contain many of the same content-oriented sections available in the assembly descriptor itself, with the exception of moduleSets, which is considered so specific to each project that it's not a good candidate for reuse. Also included in a component descriptor is the containerDescriptorHandlers section, which we briefly discussed earlier. Component descriptors cannot contain formats, assembly IDs, or any configuration related to the base directory of the assembly archive, all of which are also considered unique to a particular assembly descriptor. Though it may make sense to allow sharing of the `formats` section, this has not been implemented as of the 2.2-beta-2 Assembly plugin release.

Best Practices

The Assembly plugin provides enough flexibility to solve many problems in a number of different ways. If your project has a unique requirement, there's a good chance that you can use the methods documented in this chapter to achieve almost any assembly structure. This section of the chapter details some common best practices that, if adhered to, will make your experiences with the Assembly plugin more productive and less painful.

Standard, Reusable Assembly Descriptors

Up till now, we've been talking mainly about one-off solutions for building a particular type of assembly. But what do you do if you have dozens of projects that all need a particular type of assembly? In short, how can we reuse the effort we've invested to get our assemblies just the way we like them across more than one project without copying and pasting our assembly descriptor?

The simplest answer is to create a standardized, versioned artifact out of the assembly descriptor, and deploy it. Once that's done, you can specify that the Assembly plugin section of your project's POM include the `assembly-descriptor` artifact as a `plugin-level` dependency, which will prompt Maven to resolve and include that artifact in the plugin's classpath. At that point, you can use the assembly descriptor via the `descriptorRefs` configuration section in the Assembly plugin declaration. To illustrate, consider this example assembly descriptor:

```
<assembly>
  <id>war-fragment</id>
  <formats>
    <format>zip</format>
  </formats>
  <includeBaseDirectory>false</includeBaseDirectory>
  <dependencySets>
    <dependencySet>
      <outputDirectory>WEB-INF/lib</outputDirectory>
    </dependencySet>
  </dependencySets>
  <fileSets>
    <fileSet>
      <directory>src/main/webapp</directory>
      <outputDirectory>/</outputDirectory>
      <excludes>
        <exclude>**/web.xml</exclude>
      </excludes>
    </fileSet>
  </fileSets>
</assembly>
```

Included in your project, this descriptor would be a useful way to bundle the project contents so that they could be unpacked directly into an existing web application, so you can add to it (an extending feature, say). However, if your team builds more than one of these `web-fragment` projects, the team will likely want to reuse this descriptor rather than duplicate it. To deploy this descriptor as its own artifact, we're going to put it in its own project, under the *src/main/resources/assemblies* directory.

The project structure for this `assembly-descriptor` artifact will look similar to the following:

```
|-- pom.xml
`-- src
    `-- main
        `-- resources
            `-- assemblies
                `-- web-fragment.xml
```

Notice the path of our `web-fragment` descriptor file. By default, Maven includes the files from the *src/main/resources* directory structure in the final JAR, which means our assembly descriptor will be included with no extra configuration on our part. Also notice the *assemblies/* path prefix: the Assembly plugin expects this path prefix on all descriptors provided in the plugin classpath. It's important that we put our descriptor in the appropriate relative location, so it will be picked up by the Assembly plugin as it executes.

Remember, this project is separate from your actual `web-fragment` project now; the assembly descriptor has become its own artifact with its own version and, possibly, its own release cycle. Once you install this new project using Maven, you'll be able to reference it in your `web-fragment` projects. For clarity, the build process should look something like this:

```
$ mvn install
(...)
[INFO] [install:install]
[INFO] Installing (...)/web-fragment-descriptor/target/\
         web-fragment-descriptor-1.0-SNAPSHOT.jar
      to /Users/~/.m2/repository/org/sonatype/mavenbook/assemblies/\
         web-fragment-descriptor/1.0-SNAPSHOT/\
         web-fragment-descriptor-1.0-SNAPSHOT.jar
[INFO] ------------------------------------------------------------
[INFO] BUILD SUCCESSFUL
[INFO] ------------------------------------------------------------
[INFO] Total time: 5 seconds
(...)
```

Since there are no sources for the `web-fragment-descriptor` project, the resulting `jar` artifact will include nothing but our `web-fragment` assembly descriptor. Now, let's use this new descriptor artifact:

```
<project>
  (...)
  <artifactId>my-web-fragment</artifactId>
```

```
(...)
<build>
  <plugins>
    <plugin>
      <artifactId>maven-assembly-plugin</artifactId>
      <version>2.2-beta-2</version>
      <dependencies>
        <dependency>
          <groupId>org.sonatype.mavenbook.assemblies</groupId>
          <artifactId>web-fragment-descriptor</artifactId>
          <version>1.0-SNAPSHOT</version>
        </dependency>
      </dependencies>
      <executions>
        <execution>
          <id>assemble</id>
          <phase>package</phase>
          <goals>
            <goal>single</goal>
          </goals>
          <configuration>
            <descriptorRefs>
              <descriptorRef>web-fragment</descriptorRef>
            </descriptorRefs>
          </configuration>
        </execution>
      </executions>
    </plugin>
    (...)
  </plugins>
</build>
(...)
</project>
```

Two things are special about this Assembly plugin configuration:

- We have to include a plugin-level dependency declaration on our new `web-fragment-descriptor` artifact in order to have access to the assembly descriptor via the plugin's classpath.

- Since we're using a classpath reference instead of a file in the local project directory structure, we must use the `descriptorRefs` section instead of the `descriptor` section. Also, notice that although the assembly descriptor is actually in the *assemblies/ web-fragment.xml* location within the plugin's classpath, we reference it without the *assemblies/* prefix. This is because the Assembly plugin assumes that built-in assembly descriptors will always reside in the classpath under this path prefix.

Now, you're free to reuse the POM configuration above in as many projects as you like, with the assurance that all of their `web-fragment` assemblies will turn out the same. As you need to make adjustments to the assembly format—maybe to include other resources, or to fine-tune the dependency and file sets—you can simply increment the version of the assembly descriptor's project and release it again. POMs referencing the `assembly-descriptor` artifact can then adopt this new version of the descriptor as they are able.

One final point about `assembly-descriptor` reuse: you may want to consider sharing the plugin configuration itself as well as publishing the descriptor as an artifact. This is a fairly easy step; you simply add the configuration listed earlier to the `pluginManagement` section of your parent POM, and then reference the managed plugin configuration from your module POM, like this:

```
(...)
  <build>
    <plugins>
      <plugin>
        <artifactId>maven-assembly-plugin</artifactId>
      </plugin>
(...)
```

If you've added the rest of the plugin's configuration—listed in the previous example—to the `pluginManagement` section of the project's parent POM, then each project inheriting from that parent POM can add a minimal entry (such as the one just shown) and take advantage of an advanced assembly format in their own builds.

Distribution (Aggregating) Assemblies

As we mentioned, the Assembly plugin provides multiple ways of creating many archive formats. Distribution archives are typically very good examples of this, since they often combine modules from a multimodule build, along with their dependencies and, possibly, other files and artifacts besides these. The distribution aims to include all these different sources into a single archive that the user can download, unpack, and run with convenience. However, we also examined some of the potential drawbacks of using the `moduleSets` section of the assembly descriptor—namely, that the parent-child relationships between POMs in a build can prevent the availability of module artifacts in some cases.

Specifically, if module POMs reference as their parent the POM that contains the Assembly plugin configuration, that parent project will be built ahead of the module projects when the multimodule build executes. The parent's assembly expects to find artifacts in place for its modules, but these module projects are waiting on the parent itself to finish building. A gridlock situation is reached, and the parent build cannot succeed (since it's unable to find artifacts for its module projects). In other words, the child project depends on the parent project, which in turn depends on the child project.

As an example, consider the following assembly descriptor, designed to be used from the top-level project of a multimodule hierarchy:

```
<assembly>
  <id>distribution</id>
  <formats>
    <format>zip</format>
```

```
        <format>tar.gz</format>
        <format>tar.bz2</format>
    </formats>

    <moduleSets>
        <moduleSet>
            <includes>
                <include>*-web</include>
            </includes>
            <binaries>
                <outputDirectory>/</outputDirectory>
                <unpack>true</unpack>
                <includeDependencies>true</includeDependencies>
                <dependencySets>
                    <dependencySet>
                        <outputDirectory>/WEB-INF/lib</outputDirectory>
                    </dependencySet>
                </dependencySets>
            </binaries>
        </moduleSet>
        <moduleSet>
            <includes>
                <include>*-addons</include>
            </includes>
            <binaries>
                <outputDirectory>/WEB-INF/lib</outputDirectory>
                <includeDependencies>true</includeDependencies>
                <dependencySets>
                    <dependencySet/>
                </dependencySets>
            </binaries>
        </moduleSet>
    </moduleSets>
</assembly>
```

Given a parent project called app-parent with three modules called app-core, app-web,
and app-addons, notice what happens when we try to execute this multimodule build:

```
$ mvn package
[INFO] Reactor build order:
[INFO]    app-parent <----- PARENT BUILDS FIRST
[INFO]    app-core
[INFO]    app-web
[INFO]    app-addons
[INFO] ------------------------------------------------------------
[INFO] Building app-parent
[INFO]    task-segment: [package]
[INFO] ------------------------------------------------------------
[INFO] [site:attach-descriptor]
[INFO] [assembly:single {execution: distro}]
[INFO] Reading assembly descriptor: src/main/assembly/distro.xml
[INFO] ------------------------------------------------------------
[ERROR] BUILD ERROR
[INFO] ------------------------------------------------------------
[INFO] Failed to create assembly: Artifact:
org.sonatype.mavenbook.assemblies:app-web:jar:1.0-SNAPSHOT (included by \
```

```
module) does not have an artifact with a file. Please ensure the \
package phase is run before the assembly is generated.
...
```

The parent project (app-parent) builds first. This is because each of the other projects lists POM as its parent, which causes it to be forced to the front of the build order. The app-web module, which is the first module to be processed in the assembly descriptor, hasn't been built yet. Therefore, it has no artifact associated with it, and the assembly cannot succeed.

One workaround for this is to remove the executions section of the Assembly plugin declaration that binds the plugin to the package lifecycle phase in the parent POM, keeping the configuration section intact. Then, execute Maven with two command-line tasks: the first, *package*, to build the multimodule project graph, and a second, *assembly:assembly*, as a direct invocation of the assembly plugin to consume the artifacts built on the previous run and create the distribution assembly. The command line for such a build might look like this:

```
$ mvn package assembly:assembly
```

However, this approach has several drawbacks. First, it makes the distribution-assembly process more of a manual task that can increase the complexity and potential for error in the overall build process significantly. Additionally, it could mean that attached artifacts—which are associated in memory as the project build executes—are not reachable on the second pass without resorting to file-system references.

Instead of using a moduleSet to collect the artifacts from your multimodule build, it often makes more sense to employ a low-tech approach: using a dedicated distribution project module and interproject dependencies. In this approach, you create a new module in your build whose sole purpose is to assemble the distribution. This module POM contains dependency references to all the other modules in the project hierarchy, and it configures the Assembly plugin to be bound the package phase of its build lifecycle. The assembly descriptor itself uses the dependencySets section instead of the moduleSets section to collect module artifacts and determine where to include them in the resulting assembly archive. This approach escapes the pitfalls associated with the parent-child relationship discussed earlier, and has the additional advantage of using a simpler configuration section within the assembly descriptor itself to do the job.

To do this, we can create a new project structure that's very similar to the one used for the module-set approach. With the addition of a new distribution project, we might end up with five POMs in total: app-parent, app-core, app-web, app-addons, and app-distribution. The new app-distribution POM looks similar to the following:

```
<project>
  <parent>
    <artifactId>app-parent</artifactId>
    <groupId>org.sonatype.mavenbook.assemblies</groupId>
    <version>1.0-SNAPSHOT</version>
  </parent>
  <modelVersion>4.0.0</modelVersion>
```

```
<artifactId>app-distribution</artifactId>
<name>app-distribution</name>

<dependencies>
  <dependency>
    <artifactId>app-web</artifactId>
    <groupId>org.sonatype.mavenbook.assemblies</groupId>
    <version>1.0-SNAPSHOT</version>
    <type>war</type>
  </dependency>
  <dependency>
    <artifactId>app-addons</artifactId>
    <groupId>org.sonatype.mavenbook.assemblies</groupId>
    <version>1.0-SNAPSHOT</version>
  </dependency>
  <!-- Not necessary since it's brought in via app-web.
  <dependency> [2]
    <artifactId>app-core</artifactId>
    <groupId>org.sonatype.mavenbook.assemblies</groupId>
    <version>1.0-SNAPSHOT</version>
  </dependency>
  -->
</dependencies>
</project>
```

Notice that we have to include dependencies for the other modules in the project structure, since we don't have a modules section to rely on in this POM. Also, notice that we're not using an explicit dependency on app-core. Since it's also a dependency of app-web, we don't need to process it (or avoid processing it) twice.

Next, when we move the *distro.xml* assembly descriptor into the app-distribution project, we must also change it to use a dependencySets section, like this:

```
<assembly>
  ...
  <dependencySets>
    <dependencySet>
      <includes>
        <include>*-web</include>
      </includes>
      <useTransitiveDependencies>false</useTransitiveDependencies>
      <outputDirectory>/</outputDirectory>
      <unpack>true</unpack>
    </dependencySet>
    <dependencySet>
      <excludes>
        <exclude>*-web</exclude>
      </excludes>
      <useProjectArtifact>false</useProjectArtifact>
      <outputDirectory>/WEB-INF/lib</outputDirectory>
    </dependencySet>
  </dependencySets>
  ...
</assembly>
```

This time, if we run the build from the top-level project directory, we get better news:

```
$ mvn package
(...)
[INFO] ------------------------------------------------------------
[INFO] Reactor Summary:
[INFO] ------------------------------------------------------------
[INFO] module-set-distro-parent ...............SUCCESS [3.070s]
[INFO] app-core ........................... SUCCESS [2.970s]
[INFO] app-web ............................ SUCCESS [1.424s]
[INFO] app-addons ......................... SUCCESS [0.543s]
[INFO] app-distribution ..................... SUCCESS [2.603s]
[INFO] ------------------------------------------------------------
[INFO] ------------------------------------------------------------
[INFO] BUILD SUCCESSFUL
[INFO] ------------------------------------------------------------
[INFO] Total time: 10 seconds
[INFO] Finished at: Thu May 01 18:00:09 EDT 2008
[INFO] Final Memory: 16M/29M
[INFO] ------------------------------------------------------------
```

As you can see, the dependency-set approach is much more stable and—at least until Maven's internal project-sorting logic catches up with the Assembly plugin's capabilities—involves fewer opportunities for things to go wrong when running a build.

Summary

As we've seen in this chapter, the Maven Assembly plugin offers quite a bit of potential for creating custom archive formats. Although the details of these assembly archives can be complex, they certainly don't have to be in all cases, as we saw with built-in assembly descriptors. Even if your aim is to include your project's dependencies and selected project files in some unique, archived directory structure, writing a custom assembly descriptor doesn't have to be an arduous task.

Assemblies are useful for a wide array of applications, but they are most commonly used as application distributions of various sorts. And, though there are many different ways to use the Assembly plugin, using standardized `assembly-descriptor` artifacts and avoiding `moduleSets` when creating distributions containing binaries are two sure ways to avoid problems.

## CHAPTER 13

Properties and Resource Filtering

Introduction

Throughout this book, you will notice references to properties that can be used in a POM file. Sibling dependencies in a multiproject build can be referenced using the ${project.groupId} and ${project.version} properties, and any part of the POM can be referenced by prefixing the variable name with "project." Environment variables and Java System properties can be referenced, as well as values from your *~/.m2/settings.xml* file. What you haven't yet seen is an enumeration of the possible property values and some discussion about how they can be used to help you create portable builds. This chapter provides such an enumeration.

If you've been using property references in your POM, you should also know that Maven has a feature called resource filtering that allows you to replace property references in any resource files stored under *src/main/resources*. By default, this feature is disabled to prevent accidental replacement of property references. This feature can be used to target builds toward a specific platform and to externalize important build variables to properties files, POMs, or profiles. This chapter introduces the resource filtering feature and provides a brief discussion of how it can be used to create portable enterprise builds.

Maven Properties

You can use Maven properties in a *pom.xml* file or in any resource that is being processed by the Maven Resource plugin's filtering features. A property is always surrounded by ${ and }. For example, to reference the project.version property, one would write:

```
${project.version}
```

Some implicit properties are available in any Maven project, namely:

`project.*`
> Maven Project Object Model. You can use the `project.*` prefix to reference values in a Maven POM.

`settings.*`
> Maven settings. You use the `settings.*` prefix to reference values from your Maven settings in *~/.m2/settings.xml*.

`env.*`
> Environment variables such as `PATH` and `M2_HOME` can be referenced using the `env.*` prefix.

System properties
> Any property that can be retrieved from the `System.getProperty()` method can be referenced as a Maven property.

In addition to these implicit properties, a Maven POM, Maven settings, or a Maven profile can define a set of arbitrary, user-defined properties. The following sections provide more detail on the various properties available in a Maven project.

Maven Project Properties

When a Maven Project Property is referenced, the property name is referencing a property of the Maven Project Object Model. Specifically, you are referencing a property of the `org.apache.maven.model.Model` class that is being exposed as the implicit variable project. When you reference a property using this implicit variable, you are using simple dot notation to reference a bean property of the `Model` object. For example, when you reference `${project.version}`, you are really invoking the `getVersion()` method on the instance of `Model` that is being exposed as project.

The POM is also represented in the *pom.xml* document present in all Maven projects. Anything in a Maven POM can be referenced with a property. A complete reference for the POM structure is available at *http://maven.apache.org/ref/2.0.9/maven-model/maven.html*. The following list shows some common property references from the Maven project:

`project.groupId` and `project.version`
> Projects in a large, multimodule build often share the same `groupId` and `version` identifiers. When you are declaring interdependencies between two modules that share the same `groupId` and `version`, it is a good idea to use a property reference for both:

```
<dependencies>
  <dependency>
    <groupId>${project.groupId}</groupId>
    <artifactId>sibling-project</artifactId>
    <version>${project.version}</version>
```

```
      </dependency>
    </dependencies>
```

`project.artifactId`

A project's `artifactId` is often used as the name of a deliverable. For example, in a project with `war` packaging, you will want to generate a WAR file without the version identifiers. To do this, you would reference the `project.artifactId` in your POM file like this:

```
<build>
  <finalName>${project.artifactId}</finalName>
</build>
```

`project.name` and `project.description`

The name and project description can often be useful properties to reference from documentation. Instead of having to worry that all of your site documents maintain the same short descriptions, you can just reference these properties.

`project.build.*`

If you are ever trying to reference output directories in Maven, you should never use a literal value such as *target/classes*. Instead, you should use property references to refer to these directories:

- `project.build.sourceDirectory`
- `project.build.scriptSourceDirectory`
- `project.build.testSourceDirectory`
- `project.build.outputDirectory`
- `project.build.testOutputDirectory`
- `project.build.directory`

`sourceDirectory`, `scriptSourceDirectory`, and `testSourceDirectory` provide access to the source directories for the project. `outputDirectory` and `testOutputDirectory` provide access to the directories where Maven is going to put bytecode or other build output. `directory` refers to the directory that contains all of these output directories.

Other project property references

There are hundreds of properties to reference in a POM. A complete reference for the POM structure is available at *http://maven.apache.org/ref/2.0.9/maven-model/ maven.html*.

For a full list of properties available on the Maven `Model` object, take a look at the Javadoc for the `maven-model` project here: *http://maven.apache.org/ref/2.0.9/maven -model/apidocs/index.html*. Once you load this Javadoc, take a look at the `Model` class. From this `Model` class Javadoc, you should be able to navigate to the POM property you wish to reference. If you need to reference the output directory of the build, you can use the Maven `Model` Javadoc to see that the output directory is referenced via `model.getBuild().getOutputDirectory()`; this method call would be translated to the Maven property reference `${project.build.outputDirectory}`.

For more information about the Maven `Model` module—the module that defines the structure of the POM—see the Maven `Model` project page at *http://maven.apache.org/ ref/2.0.9/maven-model*.

Maven Settings Properties

You can also reference any properties in the Maven Local Settings file, which is usually stored in *~/.m2/settings.xml*. This file contains user-specific configuration, such as the location of the local repository and any servers, profiles, and mirrors configured by a specific user.

A full reference for the Local Settings file and corresponding properties is available here: *http://maven.apache.org/ref/2.0.9/maven-settings/settings.html*.

Environment Variable Properties

Environment variables can be referenced with the `env.*` prefix. Some interesting environment variables are listed here:

`env.PATH`
: Contains the current `PATH` in which Maven is running. The `PATH` contains a list of directories used to locate executable scripts and programs.

`env.HOME`
: On *nix systems, this variable points to a user's home directory. Instead of referencing this, you should use the `${user.home}` property.

`env.JAVA_HOME`
: Contains the Java installation directory. This can point to either a Java Development Kit (JDK) installation or a Java Runtime Environment (JRE). Instead of using this, you should consider referencing the `${java.home}` property.

`env.M2_HOME`
: Contains the Maven 2 installation directory.

While they are available, you should always use the Java System properties if you have the choice. If you need a user's home directory, use `${user.home}` instead of `${env.HOME}`. If you do this, you'll end up with a more portable build that is more likely to adhere to the Write-One-Run-Anywhere (WORA) promise of the Java platform.

Java System Properties

Maven exposes all properties from `java.lang.System`. Anything you can retrieve from `System.getProperty()` you can reference in a Maven property. Table 13-1 lists the available properties.

Table 13-1. Java system properties

System property	Description
java.version	Java Runtime Environment version
java.vendor	Java Runtime Environment vendor
java.vendor.url	Java vendor URL
java.home	Java installation directory
java.vm.specification.version	Java Virtual Machine specification version
java.vm.specification.vendor	Java Virtual Machine specification vendor
java.vm.specification.name	Java Virtual Machine specification name
java.vm.version	Java Virtual Machine implementation version
java.vm.vendor	Java Virtual Machine implementation vendor
java.vm.name	Java Virtual Machine implementation name
java.specification.version	Java Runtime Environment specification version
java.specification.vendor	Java Runtime Environment specification vendor
java.specification.name	Java Runtime Environment specification name
java.class.version	Java class format version number
java.class.path	Java classpath
java.ext.dirs	Path of extension directory or directories
os.name	Operating system name
os.arch	Operating system architecture
os.version	Operating system version
file.separator	File separator ("/" on UNIX, "\" on Windows)
path.separator	Path separator (":" on UNIX, ";" on Windows)
line.separator	Line separator ("\n" on UNIX and Windows)
user.name	User's account name
user.home	User's home directory
user.dir	User's current working directory

User-Defined Properties

In addition to the implicit properties provided by the POM, Maven Settings, environment variables, and the Java system properties, you have the ability to define your own arbitrary properties. Properties can be defined in a POM or in a profile. The properties set in a POM or in a Maven profile can be referenced just like any other property available throughout Maven. User-defined properties can be referenced in a POM, or they can be used to filter resources via the Maven Resource plugin. Example 13-1 is an example of defining some arbitrary properties in a Maven POM.

Example 13-1. User-defined properties in a POM

```
<project>
  ...
  <properties>
    <arbitrary.property.a>This is some text</arbitrary.property.a>
    <hibernate.version>3.3.0.ga</hibernate.version>
  </properties>
  ...
  <dependencies>
    <dependency>
      <groupId>org.hibernate</groupId>
      <artifactId>hibernate</artifactId>
      <version>${hibernate.version}</version>
    </dependency>
  </dependencies>
  ...
</project>
```

This example defines two properties: `arbitrary.property.a` and `hibernate.version`. The `hibernate.version` is referenced in a dependency declaration. Using the period character (.) as a separator in property names is a standard practice throughout Maven POMs and profiles. There is nothing special about using a period as a separator; to Maven, `hibernate.version` is just a key used to retrieve the property value `3.3.0.ga`. Example 13-2 shows you how to define a property in a profile from a Maven POM.

Example 13-2. User-defined properties in a profile in a POM

```
<project>
  ...
  <profiles>
    <profile>
      <id>some-profile</id>
      <properties>
        <arbitrary.property>This is some text</arbitrary.property>
      </properties>
    </profile>
  </profiles>
  ...
</project>
```

This example demonstrates the process of defining a user-defined property in a profile from a Maven POM. For more information about user-defined properties and profiles, see Chapter 11.

Resource Filtering

You can use Maven to perform variable replacement on project resources. When resource filtering is activated, Maven will scan resources for references to Maven property references surrounded by ${ and }. When it finds these references, it will replace them with the appropriate value in much the same way that the properties defined in the previous section can be referenced from a POM. This feature is especially helpful when you need to parameterize a build with different configuration values depending on the target deployment platform.

Often a *.properties* file or an XML document in *src/main/resources* will contain a reference to an external resource, such as a database or a network location that needs to be configured differently depending on the target deployment environment. For example, a system that reads data from a database has an XML document that contains the JDBC URL along with credentials for the database. If you need to use a different database in development and a different database in production, you can use a technology such as Java Naming and Directory Interface (JNDI) to externalize the configuration from the application in an application server, or you can create a build that knows how to replace variables with different values depending on the target platform.

Using Maven resource filtering, you can reference Maven properties and then use Maven profiles to define different configuration values for different target deployment environments. To illustrate this feature, assume you have a project that uses the Spring Framework to configure a `BasicDataSource` from the Apache Commons Database Connection Pool (DBCP) project (*http://commons.apache.org/dbcp*). Your project may contain a file in *src/main/resources* named *applicationContact.xml* that contains the XML listed in Example 13-3.

Example 13-3. Referencing Maven properties from a resource

```
<beans xmlns="http://www.springframework.org/schema/beans"
     xmlns:xsi="http://www.w3.org/2001/XMLSchema-instance"
     xsi:schemaLocation="http://www.springframework.org/schema/beans
     http://www.springframework.org/schema/beans/spring-beans-2.5.xsd">

   <bean id="someDao" class="com.example.SomeDao">
      <property name="dataSource" ref="dataSource"/>
   </bean>

   <bean id="dataSource" destroy-method="close"
           class="org.apache.commons.dbcp.BasicDataSource">
      <property name="driverClassName" value="${jdbc.driverClassName}"/>
      <property name="url" value="${jdbc.url}"/>
      <property name="username" value="${jdbc.username}"/>
      <property name="password" value="${jdbc.password}"/>
   </bean>
</beans>
```

Your program would read this file at runtime, and your build would replace the references to properties such as `jdbc.url` and `jdbc.username` with the values you defined in your *pom.xml*. Resource filtering is disabled by default to prevent any unintentional resource filtering. To turn on resource filter, you need to use the `resources` child element of the `build` element in a POM. Example 13-4 shows a POM that defines the variables referenced in Example 13-3 and activates resource filtering for every resource under *src/main/resources*.

Example 13-4. Defining variables and activating resource filtering

```xml
<project>
  ...
  <properties>
    <jdbc.driverClassName>com.mysql.jdbc.Driver</jdbc.driverClassName>
    <jdbc.url>jdbc:mysql://localhost:3306/development_db</jdbc.url>
    <jdbc.username>dev_user</jdbc.username>
    <jdbc.password>s3cr3tw0rd</jdbc.password>
  </properties>
  ...
  <build>
    <resources>
      <resource>
        <directory>src/main/resources</directory>
        <filtering>true</filtering>
      </resource>
    </resources>
  </build>
  ...
  <profiles>
    <profile>
      <id>production</id>
      <properties>
        <jdbc.driverClassName>oracle.jdbc.driver.OracleDriver</jdbc.driverClassName>
        <jdbc.url>jdbc:oracle:thin:@proddb01:1521:PROD</jdbc.url>
        <jdbc.username>prod_user</jdbc.username>
        <jdbc.password>s00p3rs3cr3t</jdbc.password>
      </properties>
    </profile>
  </profiles>
</project>
```

The four variables are defined in the `properties` element, and resource filtering is activated for resources under *src/main/resources*. Resource filtering is deactivated by default, and to activate it you must explicitly set `filtering` to `true` for the resources stored in your project. Filtering is deactivated by default to prevent accidental, unintentional filtering during your build. If you build a project with the resource from Example 13-3 and the POM from Example 13-4, and if you list the contents of the resource in *target/classes*, you should see that it contains the filtered resource:

```
$ mvn install
...
$ cat target/classes/applicationContext.xml
...
    <bean id="dataSource" destroy-method="close"
          class="org.apache.commons.dbcp.BasicDataSource">
        <property name="driverClassName" value="com.mysql.jdbc.Driver"/>
        <property name="url" value="jdbc:mysql://localhost:3306/development_db"/>
        <property name="username" value="dev_user"/>
        <property name="password" value="s3cr3tw0rd"/>
    </bean>
...
```

The POM in Example 13-4 also defines a `production` profile under the `profiles/` `profile` element that overrides the default properties with values that would be appropriate for a production environment. In this particular POM, the default values for the database connection are for a local MySQL database installed on a developer's machine. When the project is built with the `production` profile activated, Maven will configure the system to connect to a production Oracle database using a different driver class, URL, username, and password. If you build a project with the resource from Example 13-3 and the POM from Example 13-4, with the `production` profile activated, and if you list the contents of the resource in *target/classes*, you should see that it contains the filtered resource with production values:

```
$ mvn -Pproduction install
...
$ cat target/classes/applicationContext.xml
...
    <bean id="dataSource" destroy-method="close"
          class="org.apache.commons.dbcp.BasicDataSource">
        <property name="driverClassName" value="oracle.jdbc.driver.OracleDriver"/>
        <property name="url" value="jdbc:oracle:thin:@proddb01:1521:PROD"/>
        <property name="username" value="prod_user"/>
        <property name="password" value="s00p3rs3cr3t"/>
    </bean>
...
```

## CHAPTER 14

Maven and Eclipse: m2eclipse

Introduction

The Eclipse Integrated Development Environment (IDE) is the most widely used IDE for Java development today. Eclipse has a huge number of plugins (see *http://www .eclipseplugincentral.com/*), and innumerable organizations are developing their own software on top of it. Quite simply, Eclipse is ubiquitous. The m2Eclipse (*http:// m2eclipse.codehaus.org/*) project provides support for Maven within the Eclipse IDE, and in this chapter, we will explore the features it provides to help you use Maven with Eclipse.

m2eclipse

The m2Eclipse plugins (see *http://m2eclipse.codehaus.org/*) provide Maven integration for Eclipse. m2Eclipse also has hooks into the features of both the Subclipse plugin (see *http://subclipse.tigris.org/*) and the Mylyn plugin (see *http://www.eclipse.org/mylyn/*). The Subclipse plugin provides the m2eclipse plugin with the ability to interact with Subversion repositories, and the Mylyn plugin provides the m2eclipse plugin with the ability to interact with a task-focused interface that can keep track of development context. Just a few of the features m2eclipse provides include:

- Creating and importing Maven projects
- Dependency management and integration with the Eclipse classpath
- Automatic dependency downloads and updates
- Artifact Javadoc and source resolution
- Creating projects with Maven archetypes
- Browsing and searching remote Maven repositories
- POM management with automatic update to dependency list
- Materializing a project from a Maven POM
- Checking out a Maven project from several SCM repositories

- Adapting nested multimodule Maven projects to the Eclipse IDE
- Integration with Web Tools Project (WTP)
- Integration with AspectJ Development Tools (AJDT)
- Integration with Subclipse
- Integration with Mylyn
- Form-based POM Editor
- Graphical display of dependency graph
- GUI presentation of Dependency Tree and resolved dependencies

m2eclipse has many more features beyond those listed here, and this chapter introduces some of the more impressive features that are currently available. Let's get started by installing the m2Eclipse plugin.

Installing the m2eclipse Plugin

To install the m2Eclipse plugin, you need to install some prerequisites. You need to be running Eclipse 3.2 or higher, JDK 1.4 or higher, and you also need to make sure that Eclipse is running on a JDK, not a JRE. Once you have Eclipse and a compatible JDK, you need to install two Eclipse plugins: Subclipse and Mylyn.

Installing Prerequisites

You can install these prerequisites when you install m2eclipse; just add a new remote update site to Eclipse for each of the prerequisite components. To do so, go to Help → Software Updates → Find and Install.... Selecting this menu item will load the Install/ Update dialog box. Choose the "Search for new features to install" option and click Next. You will then be presented with a list of "Update sites to visit." Click New Remote Site..., and add a new update site for each new prerequisite. Add a new remote site for each plugin, and then make sure that the remote site is selected. After you click Finish, Eclipse will ask you to select plugins components to install. Select the components you want to install, and Eclipse will download, install, and configure your plugins.

Note that if you are using a recent build of Eclipse 3.4 (Ganymede; see *http://www .eclipse.org/ganymede*), your plugin installation experience may be slightly different. In Ganymede, you will select Help → Software Updates..., which will load the "Software Updates and Add-ons" dialog. In this dialog, choose the Available Software panel and click on Add Site..., which will load the simple "Add Site" dialog. Enter the URL of the update site you wish to add, and click OK. In the "Software Updates and Add-ons" dialog, the available plugins from an update site will appear as soon as the site is added. You can then select the modules you want to install and click the Install... button. Eclipse will then resolve all the dependencies for the selected plugins and will ask you to agree to the plugin license. After Eclipse installs new plugins, it will likely ask you for permission to restart.

Installing Subclipse

To install Subclipse, use the following Eclipse plugin update site:

Subclipse 1.2
   http://subclipse.tigris.org/update_1.2.x

For other versions of Subclipse, and for more information about the Subclipse plugin, please see the Subclipse project's web site at *http://subclipse.tigris.org/*.

Installing Mylyn

To install JIRA integration with Mylyn, add the Mylyn extras Eclipse update URL. You'll want to do this if your organization uses Atlassian's JIRA (*http://www.atlassian .com/software/jira/*) for issue tracking. To install Mylyn, use the following update sites:

Mylyn (Eclipse 3.3)
   http://download.eclipse.org/tools/mylyn/update/e3.3

Mylyn (Eclipse 3.4)
   http://download.eclipse.org/tools/mylyn/update/e3.4

Mylyn extras (JIRA support)
   http://download.eclipse.org/tools/mylyn/update/extras

For more information about the Mylyn project, see the project's web site at *http://www .eclipse.org/mylyn/*.

Installing AspectJ Development Tools (AJDT)

If you are installing the 0.9.4 release of m2eclipse, you may also want to install both the Web Tools Platform (WTP) and the AspectJ Development Tools (AJDT). To install the AJDT, use one of the following update URLs in Eclipse:

AJDT (Eclipse 3.3)
   http://download.eclipse.org/tools/ajdt/33/update

AJDT (Eclipse 3.4)
   http://download.eclipse.org/tools/ajdt/34/dev/update

For more information about the AJDT project, see the project's web site at *http://www .eclipse.org/ajdt/*.

Installing the Web Tools Platform (WTP)

To install the Web Tools Platform (WTP), use one of the following update URLs in Eclipse, or just look for the Web Tools Project in the Discovery Site, which should already be in your Eclipse remote update sites list:

WTP

    http://download.eclipse.org/webtools/updates/

For more information about the Web Tools Platform project, see the project's web site at *http://www.eclipse.org/webtools/*.

Installing m2eclipse

Once you've installed the prerequisites, you can install the m2eclipse plugin from the following Eclipse update URL:

m2eclipse plugin

    http://m2eclipse.sonatype.org/update/

If you would like to install the latest snapshot development version of the plugin, you should use the *update-dev* URL instead:

m2eclipse plugin (development snapshot)

    http://m2eclipse.sonatype.org/update-dev/

To install m2eclipse, just add the appropriate update site for m2eclipse. Go to Help → Software Updates → Find and Install.... Selecting this menu item will load the Install/Update dialog box. Choose the "Search for new features to install" option, and click Next. You will then be presented with a list of "Update sites to visit." Click New Remote Site..., and add a new update site for m2eclipse. Add a new remote site for m2eclipse, and then make sure that the remote site is selected. After you click Finish, Eclipse will ask you to select plugins components to install. Select the components you want to install, and Eclipse will download, install, and configure m2eclipse.

If you've installed the plugin successfully, you should see a Maven option in the list of preferences options when you go to Window → Preferences....

Enabling the Maven Console

Before we begin to examine the features of m2eclipse, let's first enable the Maven console. Open the Console View by going to Window → Show View → Console. Then, click on the little arrow on the righthand side of the Open Console icon and select Maven Console, as shown in Figure 14-1.

Maven Console shows the Maven output that normally appears on the console when running Maven from the command line. It is useful to be able to see what Maven is doing and to work with Maven debug output to diagnose issues.

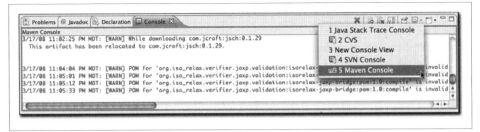

Figure 14-1. Enabling the Maven console in Eclipse

Creating a Maven Project

When using Maven, project creation takes place through the use of a Maven archetype. In Eclipse, project creation takes place via the new project wizard. The new project wizard inside of Eclipse offers a plethora of templates for creating new projects. The m2eclipse plugin improves on this wizard to provide the following additional capabilities:

- Checking out a Maven project from a SCM repository
- Creating a Maven project using a Maven archetype
- Creating a Maven POM file

As shown in Figure 14-2, all three of these options are important to developers using Maven. Let's take a look at each option in the sections that follow.

Figure 14-2. Creating a new project with m2eclipse wizards

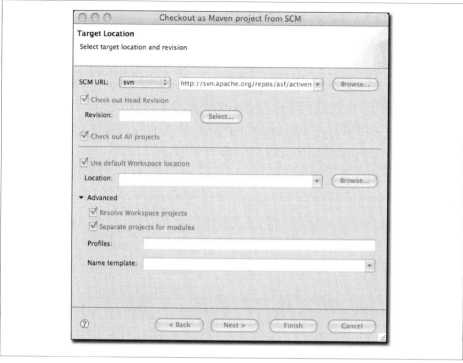

Figure 14-3. Checking out a new project from Subversion

Checking Out a Maven Project from SCM

m2eclipse provides the ability to check out a project directly from a SCM repository. Simply enter the SCM information for a project, and it will check it out for you to a location of your choice, as shown in Figure 14-3.

This dialog offers additional options for specifying a particular revision, either by browsing the revisions in a Subversion repository or simply by entering the revision number manually. These features reuse of some of the features in the Subclipse plugin to interact with the Subversion repository. In addition to Subversion, the m2eclipse plugin also supports the following SCM providers:

- Bazaar
- Clearcase
- CVS
- git
- hg
- Perforce
- Starteam

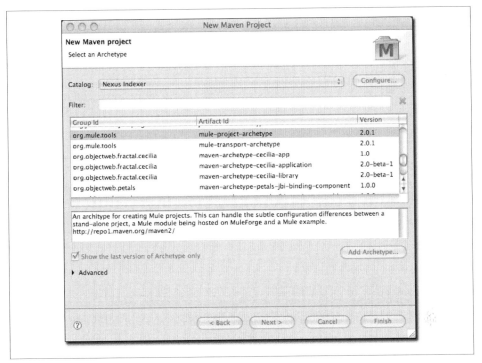

Figure 14-4. Creating a new project with a Maven archetype

- Subversion
- Synergy
- Visual SourceSafe

Creating a Maven Project from a Maven Archetype

m2eclipse offers the ability to create a Maven project using a Maven archetype. There are many Maven archetypes provided in the list that comes with m2eclipse, as shown in Figure 14-4.

The list of archetypes in Figure 14-4 is generated by something called the Nexus Indexer. Nexus is a repository manager that will be introduced in Chapter 16. The Nexus Indexer is a file that contains an index of the entire Maven repository, and m2eclipse uses it to list all of the available archetypes in the entire Maven repository. At the time of this writing, m2eclipse has approximately 90 archetypes in this archetype dialog. Highlights of this list include:

- Standard Maven archetypes to create
  —Maven Plugins
  —Simple Web Applications

—Simple Projects

—New Maven Archetypes

- Databinder (*http://databinder.net/site/show/overview*) archetypes (data-driven Wicket applications) under `net.databinder`
- Apache Cocoon (*http://cocoon.apache.org*) archetypes under `org.apache.cocoon`
- Apache Directory Server (*http://directory.apache.org*) archetypes under `org.apache.directory.server`
- Apache Geronimo (*http://geronimo.apache.org*) archetypes under `org.apache.geronimo.buildsupport`
- Apache MyFaces (*http://myfaces.apache.org*) archetypes under `org.apache.myfaces.buildtools`
- Apache Tapestry (*http://tapestry.apache.org*) archetypes under `org.apache.tapestry`
- Apache Wicket (*http://wicket.apache.org*) archetypes under `org.apache.wicket`
- AppFuse (*http://appfuse.org/display/APF/Home*) archetypes under `org.appfuse.archetypes`
- Codehaus Cargo (*http://cargo.codehaus.org*) archetypes under `org.codehaus.cargo`
- Codehaus Castor (*http://castor.codehaus.org*) archetypes under `org.codehaus.castor`
- Groovy-based (*http://groovy.codehaus.org/GMaven*) Maven plugin archetypes (deprecated)[*] under `org.codehaus.mojo.groovy`

- Jini archetypes
- Mule (*http://mule.mulesource.org/display/MULE/Home*) archetypes under `org.mule.tools`
- Objectweb Fractal (*http://fractal.objectweb.org/index.html*) archetypes under `org.objectweb.fractal`
- Objectweb Petals (*http://petals.objectweb.org/index.html*) archetypes under `org.objectweb.petals`
- ops4j archetypes under `org.ops4j`
- Parancoe (*http://www.parancoe.org*) under `org.parancoe`
- slf4j archetypes under `org.slf4j`
- Spring Framework (*http://www.springframework.org*) OSGI and Web Services archetypes under `org.springframework`

---

[*] Don't use the Groovy Maven plugin in Codehaus' Mojo project. Jason Dillon has moved the Groovy Maven integration to the Groovy project in Codehaus. For more information, see *http://groovy.codehaus.org/GMaven*.

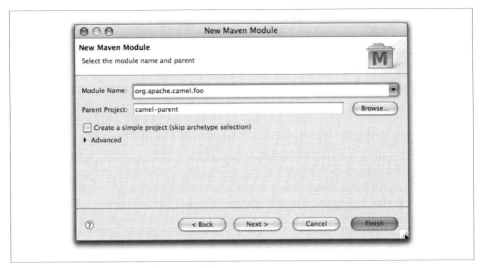

Figure 14-5. Creating a new Maven module

- Trails Framework (*http://www.trailsframework.org*) archetypes under `org.trails
framework`

And these were just the archetypes that were listed under the Nexus Indexer catalog, if you switch catalogs, you'll see other archetypes. Though your results may vary, the following additional archetypes were available in the Internal catalog:

- Atlassian Confluence (*http://www.atlassian.com*) plugin archetype under `com.atlassian.maven.archetypes`
- Apache Struts (*http://struts.apache.org*) archetypes under `org.apache.struts`
- Apache Shale archetypes under `org.apache.shale`

A catalog is simply a reference to a repository index. You can manage the set of catalogs that the m2eclipse plugin knows about by clicking on the Configure... button next to the catalog drop-down. If you have your own archetypes to add to this list, you can click on Add Archetype... and add them.

Once you choose an archetype, Maven will retrieve the appropriate artifact from the Maven repository and create a new Eclipse project with the selected archetype.

Creating a Maven Module

m2eclipse provides the ability to create a Maven module, as shown in Figure 14-5. Creating a Maven module is almost identical to creating a Maven project, as it also creates a new Maven project using a Maven archetype. However, a Maven module is a subproject of another Maven project typically known as a parent project.

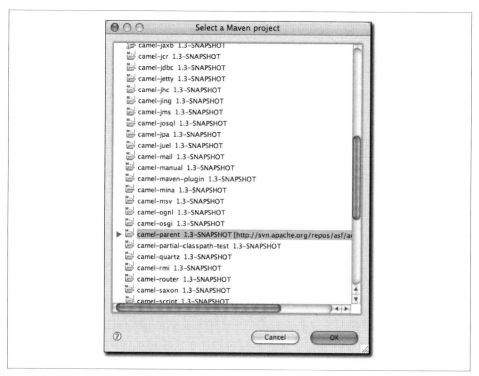

Figure 14-6. Selecting a parent project for a new Maven module

When creating a new Maven module you must select a parent project that already exists inside of Eclipse. Clicking the browse button displays a list of projects that already exist, as shown in Figure 14-6.

After selecting a parent project from the list, you are returned to the New Maven Module window, and the Parent Project field is populated as shown in Figure 14-5. Clicking Next will display the standard list of archetypes described earlier in the section "Creating a Maven Project from a Maven Archetype" so you can choose which one should be used to create the Maven module.

Create a Maven POM File

Another important feature that m2eclipse offers is the ability to create a new Maven POM file. m2eclipse provides a wizard that helps you easily create a new POM file inside a project that is already in Eclipse. This POM creation wizard is shown in Figure 14-7.

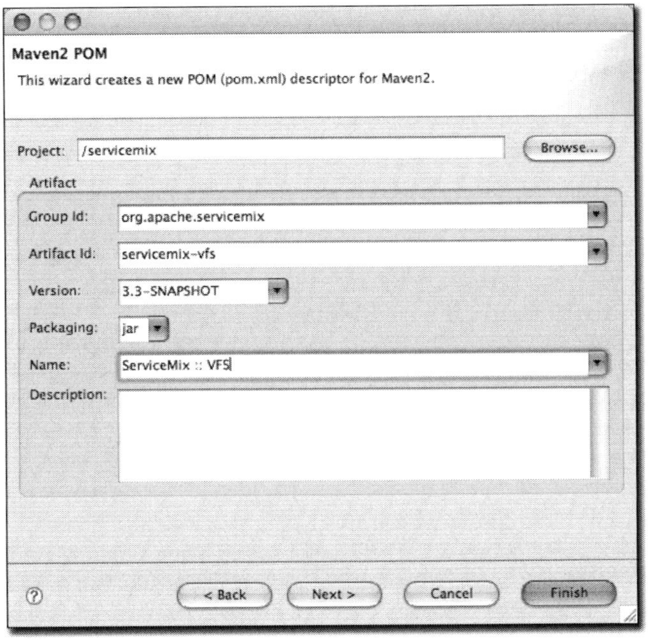

Figure 14-7. Creating a new POM

Creating a new Maven POM is just a matter of selecting a project, entering the Group ID, Artifact ID, Version, choosing the Packaging type, and providing a Name in the fields provided by m2eclipse. Click the Next button to start adding dependencies, as shown in Figure 14-8.

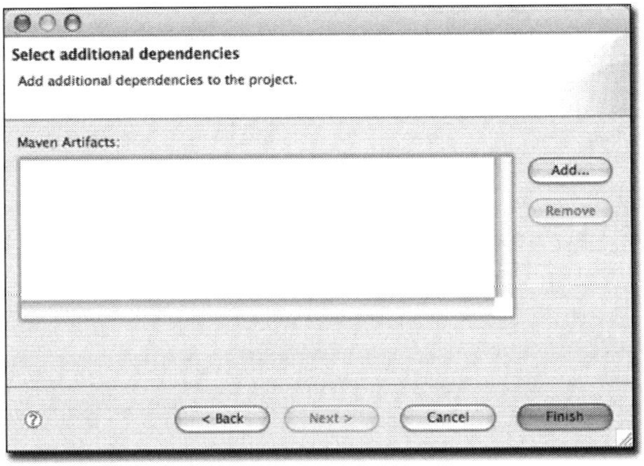

Figure 14-8. Adding dependencies to a new POM

Figure 14-9. Querying the central repository for dependencies

As you can see, no dependencies are in the POM yet. Just click the Add button to query the central Maven repository for dependencies, as shown in Figure 14-9.

Querying for dependencies is as easy as entering the `groupId` for the artifact you need. Figure 14-9 shows a query for `org.apache.commons` with `commons-vfs` expanded to see which versions are available. Highlighting the `1.1-SNAPSHOT` version of `commons-vfs` and clicking OK takes you back to the dependency selection where you can either query for more artifacts or just click finish to create the POM. When you search for dependencies, m2eclipse is making use of the same Nexus repository index that is used in the Nexus Repository Manager from Chapter 16.

Now that the you've seen the m2eclipse features for creating a new project, let's look at a similar set of features for importing projects into Eclipse.

Importing Maven Projects

m2eclipse provides three options for importing a Maven project into Eclipse, including:

- Import an existing Maven project
- Check out a Maven project from SCM
- Materialize a Maven project

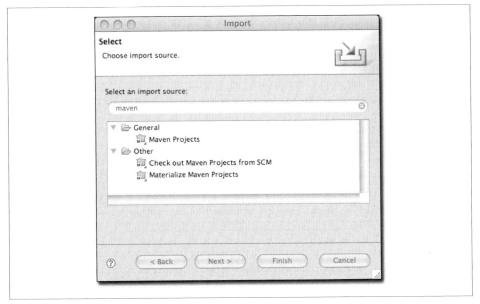

Figure 14-10. Importing a Maven project

Figure 14-10 shows the wizard for importing projects with the options for Maven provided by m2eclipse.

The dialog in Figure 14-10 is displayed when you use the File → Import command in Eclipse and then filter the options by entering the word "maven" in the filter field. As noted earlier, three options are available for importing a Maven project into Eclipse, including: Maven Projects, Check out Maven Project from Subversion, and Materialize Maven Projects.

Importing a Maven project from Subversion is identical to creating a Maven project from Subversion, as discussed in the previous section, so discussion of it here would be redundant. Let's move on now to review the other two options for importing a Maven project into Eclipse.

Importing a Maven Project

m2eclipse can import a Maven project with an existing *pom.xml*. By pointing at the directory where a Maven project is located, m2eclipse detects all the Maven POMs in the project and provides a hierarchical list of them as shown in Figure 14-11.

Figure 14-11 displays the view of the project being imported. Notice that all the POMs from the project are listed in a hierarchy. This allows you to easily select which POMs (and therefore which projects) you want to be imported into Eclipse. Once you select the project you would like to import, m2eclipse will import and build the project(s) using Maven.

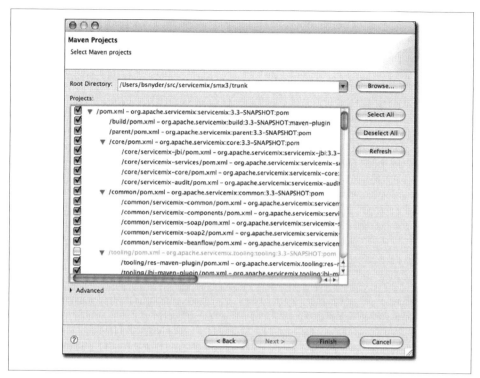

Figure 14-11. Importing a multimodule Maven project

Materializing a Maven Project

m2eclipse also offers the ability to "materialize" a Maven project. Materialization is similar to the process of checking out a Maven project from Subversion, but instead of manually entering the URL to the project's Subversion repository, the Subversion URL is discovered from the project's root POM file. You can use this feature to "materialize" projects from nothing more than a POM file if the POM file has the appropriate elements to specify the location of a source repository. Using this feature, you can browse the central Maven repository for projects and materialize them into Eclipse projects. This comes in handy if your project depends on a third-party open source library and you need to get your hands on the source code. Instead of tracking down the project web site and figuring out how to check it out of Subversion, just use the m2eclipse project to magically materialize the Eclipse project.

Figure 14-12 shows the wizard after choosing to materialize Maven projects.

Figure 14-12. Materializing a Maven project

Notice that the dialog box for Maven artifacts in Figure 14-12 is empty. This is because no projects have been added yet. To add a project, you must click the Add button on the right side and select a dependency to add from the central Maven repository. Figure 14-13 shows how to add a project.

Upon entering a query, candidate dependencies will be located in the local Maven repository. After a few seconds of indexing the local Maven repository, the list of candidate dependencies appears. Select the dependency to add and click OK so that they are added to the list, as shown in Figure 14-14.

Upon adding a dependency, you have the option of telling the m2eclipse plugin to check out all projects for the artifact.

Running Maven Builds

m2eclipse modifies the Run As... and Debug As... menus to allow you to run a Maven build within Eclipse. Figure 14-15 shows the Run As... menu for an m2eclipse project. From this menu you can run one of the more common lifecycle phases such as `clean`, `install`, or `package`. You can also load up the Run configuration dialog window and configure a Maven build with parameters and more options.

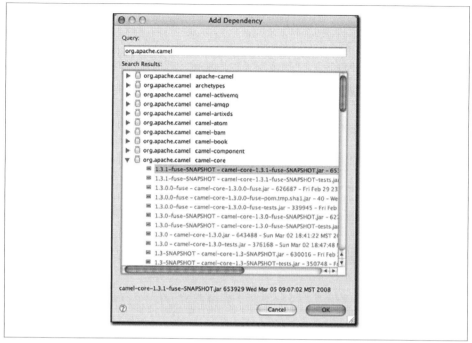

Figure 14-13. Selecting artifact to materialize

If you need to configure a Maven build with more options, you can choose Run Configurations... and create a new Maven build. Figure 14-16 shows the Run dialog for configuring a Maven build.

The Run configuration dialog allows you to specify multiple goals and profiles. It exposes options such as "skip tests" and "update snapshots" and allows you to customize everything from the project to the JRE to the environment variable. You can use this dialog to support any custom Maven build that you wish to launch with m2eclipse.

Working with Maven Projects

The m2eclipse plugin also provides a set of features for working with Maven projects once they are inside Eclipse. Many features make Maven in Eclipse easier to use, so let's dive right into them. In the previous section, I materialized a Maven project and selected a subproject from the Apache Camel project named `camel-core`. We'll use that project to demonstrate these features.

By right-clicking on the `camel-core` project and selecting the Maven menu item, you can see the available Maven features. Figure 14-17 shows a screenshot of this.

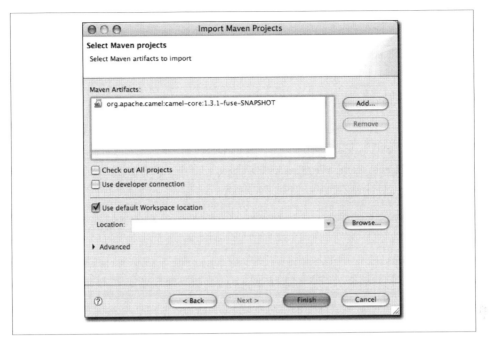

Figure 14-14. Materializing Apache Camel

Notice in Figure 14-17 the available Maven features for the `camel-core` project, including:

- Adding dependencies and plugins
- Updating dependencies, snapshots and source folders
- Creating a Maven module
- Downloading the source
- Opening Project URLs such as the Project Web Page, Issue Tracker, Source Control, and Continuous Integration tool
- Enabling/disabling workspace resolution, nested Maven modules and dependency management

These features are also big timesavers, so let's review them briefly.

Adding and Updating Dependencies and Plugins

Let's say we'd like to add a dependency or a plugin to the `camel-core` POM. For the sake of demonstration, we're going to add `commons-lang` as a dependency. (Please note that the functionality for adding a dependency and a plugin is exactly the same, so we'll demonstrate it by adding a dependency.)

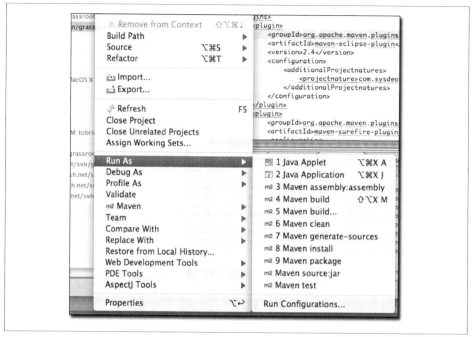

Figure 14-15. Running an Eclipse build with Run As...

m2eclipse offers two options for adding dependencies to a project. The first option is manually editing the POM file to type in the XML to add the dependency. The downside to manually editing the POM file to add a dependency is that you must already know the information about the artifact, or use the features discussed in the next section to manually locate the artifact information in the repository indexes. The upside is that after manually adding the dependency and saving the POM, the project's Maven Dependencies container will be automatically updated to include the new dependency. Figure 14-18 shows how I added a dependency for `commons-lang` to the `camel-console` POM and the Maven Dependencies container was automatically updated to included it.

Manually adding a dependency works well, but it requires more work than the second approach. Upon manually adding the `dependency` element to the POM, the Eclipse progress in the lower righthand corner of the Eclipse workbench reflects the action, as shown in Figure 14-19.

The second option for adding a dependency is much easier because you don't have to know any information about the artifact other than its `groupId`. Figure 14-20 shows this functionality.

By simply entering a `groupId` into the query field, m2eclipse queries the repository indexes and even shows a version of the artifact that is currently in your local Maven repository. This option is preferred because it is such a tremendous timesaver. With

Figure 14-16. Configuring a Maven build as a run configuration

m2eclipse, you no longer need to hunt through the central Maven repository for an artifact version.

Creating a Maven Module

m2eclipse makes it very easy to create a series of nested projects in a multimodule Maven project. If you have a parent project, and you want to add a module to the project, just right click on the project, go the Maven menu, and choose New Maven Module Project. m2eclipse will walk you through the project creation process to create a new project, then it will update the parent project's POM to include the module reference. Before m2eclipse came along it was very difficult to use a hierarchy of Maven projects within Eclipse. With m2eclipse, the details of the underlying relationships between parent and child projects are integrated into the development environment.

Downloading Source

If the central Maven repository contains a source artifact for a particular project, you can download the source from the repository and expose it to the Eclipse environment. When you are trying to debug a complex issue in Eclipse, nothing can be easier than being able to right-click on a third-party dependency and drill into the

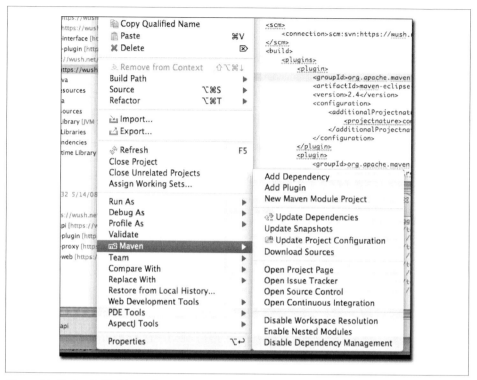

Figure 14-17. Available Maven features

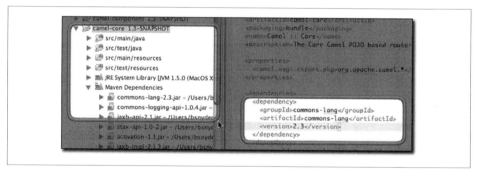

Figure 14-18. Manually adding a dependency to the project's POM

code in the Eclipse debugger. Select this option, and m2eclipse will attempt to download the source artifact from the Maven repository. If it is unable to retrieve this source artifact, you should ask the maintainers of the project in question to upload the appropriate Maven source bundle to the central Maven repository.

Figure 14-19. Updating Maven dependencies

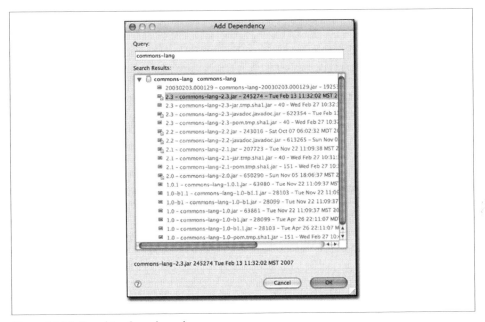

Figure 14-20. Searching for a dependency

Opening Project Pages

A Maven POM contains some valuable URLs that a developer may need to consult. These are the project's web page, the URL for the source code repository, a URL for a continuous integration system such as Hudson, and a URL for an issue tracker. If these URLs are present in a project's POM, m2eclipse will open these project pages in a browser.

Resolving Dependencies

You can configure a project to resolve dependencies from a workspace. This has the effect of altering the way that Maven locates dependency artifacts. If a project is configured to resolve dependencies from the workspace, these artifacts do not need to be present in your local repository. Assume that project-a and project-b are both in the same Eclipse workspace, and that project-a depends on project-b. If workspace resolution is disabled, the m2eclipse Maven build for project-a will succeed only if `project-b`'s artifact is present in the local repository. If workspace resolution is enabled, m2eclipse will resolve the dependency via the eclipse workspace. In other words, when workspace resolution is enabled, project's don't have to be installed in the local repository to relate to one another.

You can also disable dependency management. This has the effect of telling m2eclipse to stop trying to manage your project's classpath, and it will remove the Maven Dependencies classpath container from your project. If you do this, you are essentially on your own when it comes to managing your project's classpath.

Working with Maven Repositories

m2eclipse also provides some tools to make working with Maven repositories a bit easier. These tools provide functionality for:

- Searching for artifacts
- Searching for Java classes
- Indexing Maven repositories

Searching For Maven Artifacts and Java classes

m2eclipse adds a couple of items to the Eclipse navigation menu that make searching for Maven artifacts and Java classes easy work. Each option is available by clicking on the Navigate menu, as shown in Figure 14-21.

Notice the available options in Figure 14-21 under the Eclipse Navigate menu named Open Maven POM... and Open Type from Maven.... The Open Maven POM... option allows you to search the Maven repository for a given POM, as shown in Figure 14-22.

Upon selecting an artifact and clicking OK, the POM for that artifact is opened in Eclipse for browsing or editing. This is handy when you need to take a quick look at the POM for a given artifact.

The second m2eclipse option in the Navigate menu is named Open Type from Maven.... This feature allows you to search for a Java class by name in a remote repository. Upon opening this dialog, simply type "factorybean" and you'll see many classes with the name FactoryBean in them, as shown in Figure 14-23.

This is a big timesaving feature because it means that manually searching through artifacts in a Maven repository for a particular class is a thing of the past. If you need to use a specific class, just fire up Eclipse, go to the Navigate menu, and search for the class. m2eclipse will show you the list of artifacts in which it appears.

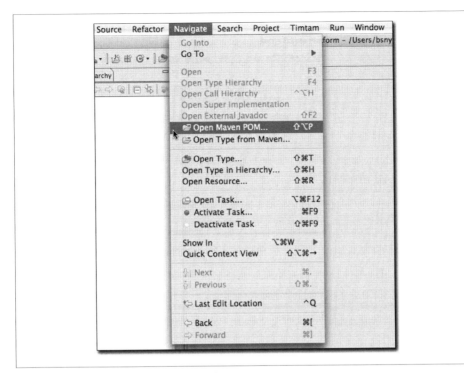

Figure 14-21. Searching for artifacts and classes

Indexing Maven Repositories

The Maven Indexes view allows you to manually navigate to POMs in a remote repository and open them in Eclipse. To see this view, go to View → Show View → Other, type the word "maven" into the search box, and you should see a view named Maven Indexes, as shown in Figure 14-24.

Select this view, and click OK. This will show the Maven Indexes view, as shown in Figure 14-25.

Additionally, Figure 14-26 shows the Maven Indexes view after you manually navigate to locate a POM.

After finding the `apache-camel` artifact, double-clicking on it will open it in Eclipse for browsing or editing.

These features make working with remote repositories from inside of Eclipse so much easier and faster. After all the hours you may have spent doing these types of tasks by manually over the last few years—visiting repositories through a web browser, downloading artifacts, and grepping through them for classes and POMs—you'll find that m2eclipse is a welcome improvement.

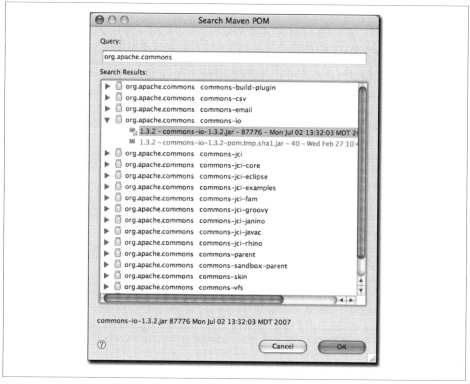

Figure 14-22. Searching for a POM

Using the Form-Based POM Editor

The latest release of the m2eclipse plugin has a form-based POM editor that allows you to edit every part of a project's *pom.xml* with an easy-to-use GUI interface. To open the POM editor, click on a project's *pom.xml* file. If you have customized the editors for a *pom.xml* file, and the POM editor is not the default editor, you may need to right-click on the file and choose Open With... → Maven POM Editor. The POM editor will then display the Overview tab, as shown in Figure 14-27.

One common complaint about Maven is that it forces a developer to confront large and often overwhelming XML documents in a highly complex multimodule project build. Although the authors of this book believe this is a small price to pay for the flexibility of a tool such as Maven, the graphical POM editor is a tool that makes it possible for people to use Maven without ever having to know about the XML structure behind a Maven POM.

The project shown in Figure 14-27 is a project with an `artifactId` of `idiom-core`. You'll notice that most of the fields in this `idiom-core` project are blank. There is no `groupId` or `version`, and there is no SCM information supplied in the POM editor. This is

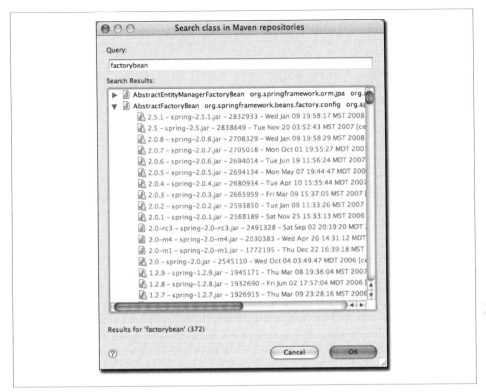

Figure 14-23. Searching the repository for a class

because `idiom-core` inherits most of this information from a parent project named `idiom`. If we open the *pom.xml* for the parent project in the POM editor, we'll see the Overview tab shown in Figure 14-28.

That "open folder" icon on the various list entries throughout the POM editor indicate that the corresponding entry is present in the Eclipse workspace, and the "jar" icon indicates artifacts that are referenced from the Maven repository. You can double-click those entries to open their POMs in the POM editor. This works for modules, dependencies, plugins, and other elements that have corresponding Maven artifacts. Underlined labels in several POM editor sections represent hyperlinks that can be used to open the POM editor for corresponding Maven artifacts.

In this parent POM, we see that the `groupId` and `version` are defined and that the parent POM supplies much of the information that was missing in the `idiom-core` project. The POM editor will show you the contents of the POM that you are editing, and it will not show you any of the inherited values. If you want to look at the `idiom-core` project's effective POM in the POM editor, you can use the Show Effective POM action in the tool bar in the upper-righthand corner of the POM editor, which shows a left bracket

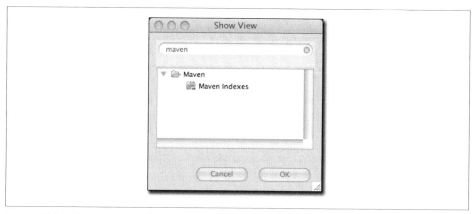

Figure 14-24. Show Maven Indexes view

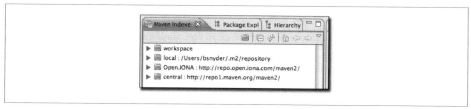

Figure 14-25. Maven Indexes view

and an equals sign on a page with a blue M. It will load the effective POM for `idiom-core` in the POM editor, as shown in Figure 14-29.

This effective view of the POM merges the `idiom-core` POM with the ancestor POMs (the parent, the grandparent, etc.)—similar to the *mvn help:effective-pom* command—and displays the POM editor with the effective values. Because the POM editor displays a composite view of many different merged POMs, this effective POM editor is read-only, and you will not be able to update any of the fields in this effective POM view.

If you are looking at the POM editor for the `idiom-core` project as shown in Figure 14-27, you can also navigate to the parent POM using the Open Parent POM action from the POM editor tool bar in the upper-righthand corner of the POM editor.

The POM editor shows a number of tabs displaying various information from the POM. The final tab exposes the *pom.xml* as an XML document. The Dependencies tab, shown in Figure 14-30, exposes an easy-to-use interface for adding and editing dependencies to your project, as well as for editing the `dependencyManagement` section of the POM. This dependency management screen is also integrated with the artifact searching facilities in the m2eclipse plugin. You can use actions from the editor sections as well as Ctrl-Space typing assistance for the fields in the Dependency Details section.

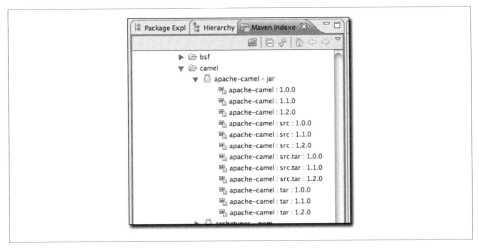

Figure 14-26. Locating a POM from the Indexes view

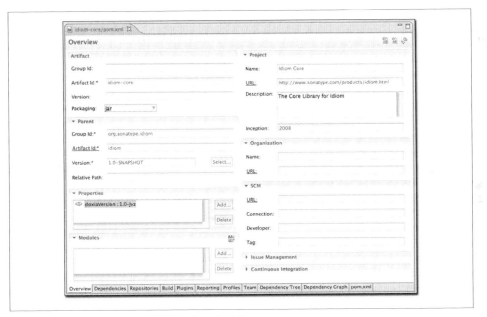

Figure 14-27. Overview tab of POM editor for idiom-core

If you need to know more about one of the artifacts, you can use Open Web Page action from the Dependency Details section tool bar to check the project web page.

The Build tab shown in Figure 14-31 provides access to the contents of the `build` element. From this tab you can customize source directories, add extensions, change the default goal name, and add resources directories.

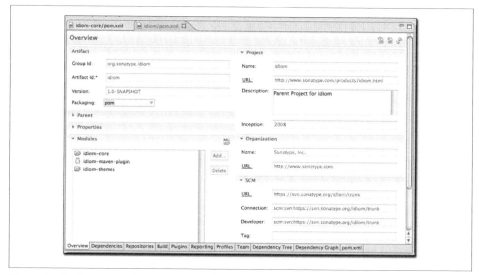

Figure 14-28. Overview tab of POM editor for idiom parent project

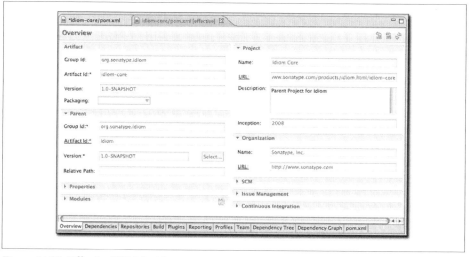

Figure 14-29. Effective POM for idiom-core

We have shown only a small subset of the POM editor here. If you are interested in seeing the rest of the tabs, please download and install the m2eclipse plugin.

Analyzing Project Dependencies in m2eclipse

The latest release of m2eclipse contains a POM editor that provides some dependency analysis tools. These tools promise to change the way users maintain and monitor a

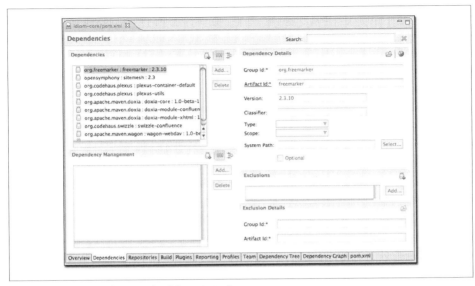

Figure 14-30. Dependencies tab of the POM editor

project's transitive dependencies. One of Maven's main attractions is the fact that it manages a project's dependencies. If you are writing an application that depends on the Spring Framework's Hibernate3 integration, all you need to do is depend on the `spring-hibernate3` artifact from the central Maven repository. Maven then reads this artifact's POM and adds all of the necessary transitive dependencies. Although this is a great feature that attracts people to Maven in the first place, it can become confusing when a project depends on tens of dependencies, each with tens of transitive dependencies.

Problems begin to occur when you depend on a project with a poorly crafted POM that fails to flag dependencies as optional, or when you start encountering conflicts between transitive dependencies. If one of your requirements is to exclude a dependency such as `commons-logging` or the `servlet-api`, or if you need to find out why a certain dependency is showing up under a specific scope you will frequently need to invoke the `dependency:tree` and `dependency:resolve` goals from the command-line to track down the offending transitive dependencies.

This is where the POM editor in m2eclipse comes in handy. If you open a project with many dependencies, you can open the Dependency Tree tab and see a two-column display of dependencies, as shown in Figure 14-32. The lefthand side of the panel displays a tree of dependencies. The first level of the tree consists of direct dependencies from your project, and each subsequent level lists the dependencies of each dependency. This lefthand side is a great way to figure out how a specific dependency made its way into your project's resolved dependencies. The righthand side of this panel displays the resolved dependencies. This is the list of effective dependencies after all

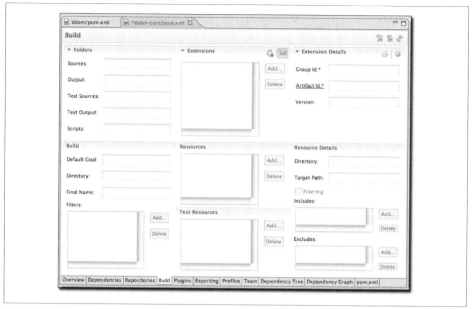

Figure 14-31. Build tab of the POM editor

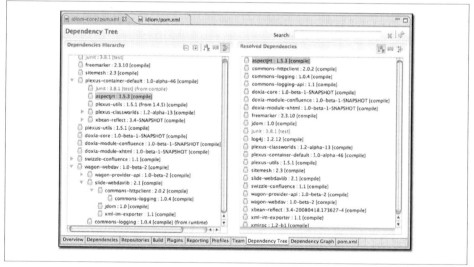

Figure 14-32. Dependency Tree tab of the POM editor

conflicts and scopes have been applied, and it is the effective list of dependencies that your project will use for compilation, testing, and packaging.

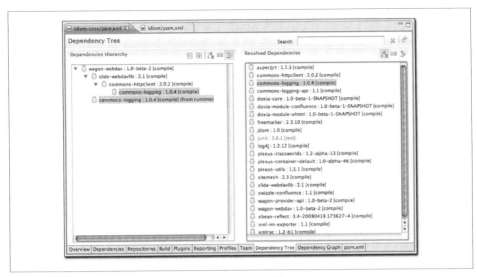

Figure 14-33. Locating dependencies in the Dependency Tree

The feature that makes the Dependency Tree tab so valuable is that it can be used as an investigative tool to figure out how a specific dependency made it into the list of resolved dependencies. Searching and filtering functionality available in the editor makes it really easy to search and browse through the project dependencies. You can use Search entry field from the editor tool bar and the Sort and Filter actions from the Dependency Hierarchy and Resolved Dependencies sections to navigate through dependencies. Figure 14-33 shows what happens when you click on commons-logging in the Resolved Dependencies list. When filtering is enabled in the Dependencies Hierarchy section, clicking on a resolved dependency filters the hierarchy on the lefthand side of the panel to show all of the nodes that contributed to the resolved dependency. If you are trying to get rid of a resolved dependency, you can use this tool to find out which dependencies (and which transitive dependencies) are contributing the artifact to your resolved dependencies. In other words, if you are trying to get rid of something like commons-logging from your dependency set, the Dependency Tree tab is the tool you will likely want to use.

m2eclipse also provides you with the ability to view your project's dependencies as a graph. Figure 14-34 shows the dependencies of idiom-core. The topmost box is the idiom-core project, and the other dependencies are shown below it. Direct dependencies are linked from the top box, and the transitive dependencies are linked from those. You can select a specific node in the graph to highlight the linked dependencies, or you can use the Search field at the top of the page to find matching nodes.

Note that the "open folder" icon on each graph node indicates that the corresponding artifact is present in the Eclipse workspace, and the "jar" icon indicates that the node's artifact is referenced from the Maven repository.

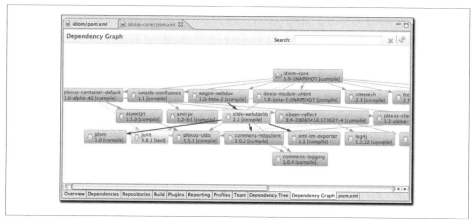

Figure 14-34. Viewing the dependencies of a project as a graph

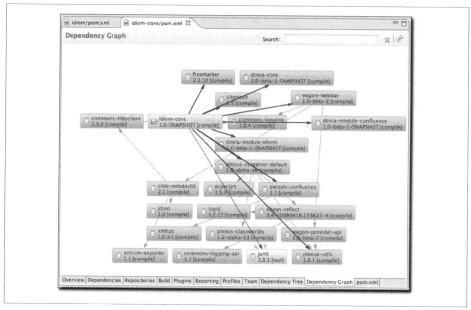

Figure 14-35. Radial layout of dependency graph

The graph presentation can be changed by right-clicking in the editor. You can choose to show artifact IDs, group IDs, versions, scopes, or whether you want to wrap node text or show icons. Figure 14-35 shows the same graph from Figure 14-34 but with a radial layout.

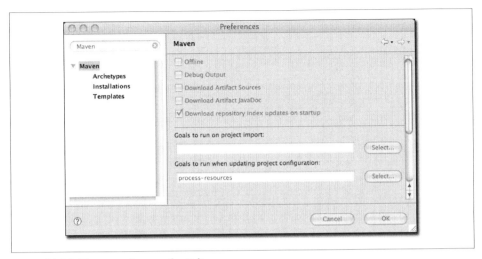

Figure 14-36. Maven preferences for Eclipse

Maven Preferences

The ability to adjust the Maven preferences and some Maven options is an important aspect of developing with Maven, and m2eclipse offers the ability to tweak these items via the Maven preferences page inside of Eclipse. Typically, when using Maven on the command line, such preferences and options are available from files in your *~/.m2* directory and as command-line options. m2eclipse provides access to some of the most important preferences and options from the Eclipse IDE. Figure 14-36 shows the Maven preferences page in Eclipse.

The checkboxes in the top section of Figure 14-36 provide you with the ability to:

- Run Maven in offline mode, disabling any downloads from remote repositories
- Enable debug output in the Maven console
- Download source JARs for artifacts from remote Maven repositories
- Download Javadoc JARs for artifacts from remote Maven repositories
- Download and update local indexes for remote repositories on startup

The next section offers a pop-up menu to select which goal you'd like to be executed when a project is imported and when the source folders for a given project are updated. The default goal is named `process-resources`, which copies and process the resources for the project into the destination directory to make the project ready for packaging. Customizing this list of goals can come in handy if you need to run any custom goals that process resources or generate supporting configuration.

Figure 14-37. Maven Goals dialogs

If you need help selecting a goal, click the Select... button to see the Goals dialog. The dialog on the lefthand side ofFigure 14-37 shows the Goals dialog with a list of all the phases in the default Maven lifecycle.

When you see the Goals dialog for the first time, you might be overwhelmed by the number of goals it lists. There are literally hundreds of Maven plugins, for everything from generating a database to running integration tests to performing static analysis to generating web services with XFire. Over 200 plugins with selectable goals are listed in the Goals dialog. The dialog on the righthand side of Figure 14-37 shows the Goals dialog with the Tomcat Maven plugin's goals highlighted. You can always narrow down the list of goals shown in this dialog by typing some text in the search field. As you type in text, m2eclipse reduces the list of available goals to those that contain the text in the search field.

Another Maven preference page is the Maven installations configuration page, shown in Figure 14-38.

This page allows you to add other Maven installations to the Eclipse environment. If you want to use a different version of Maven with the m2eclipse plugin, you can configure multiple installations of Maven from this configuration page. This is very similar to the ability to add more than one Java Virtual Machine to be run inside of Eclipse. An embedded version of the Maven known as the Maven Embedder is already specified. This is what is used to execute Maven inside of Eclipse. If you have another

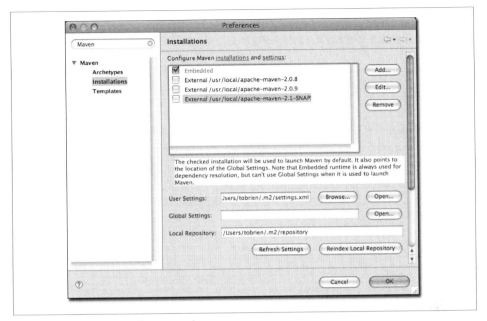

Figure 14-38. Maven installations preference page

installation of Maven that you want to use instead of the Maven Embedder, you can add another Maven runtime by clicking on the Add... button. Figure 14-38 shows a configuration page that lists the Maven Embedder, Maven 2.0.9, and an installation of Maven 2.1-SNAPSHOT.

The installations configuration page also allows you to specify the location of the global Maven settings file. If you do not specify the location of this file on the configuration page, Maven will use the default global settings file found in *conf/settings.xml* of the selected Maven installation. You can also customize the location of your user settings file from the default location of *~/.m2/settings.xml*, and you can customize the location of your local Maven repository from the default location of *~/.m2/repository*.

Also available in the Eclipse preferences is the ability to enable a decorator called the Maven Version Decorator. This preference provides a given project's current version on the Eclipse Package Explorer and is shown in Figure 14-39.

To enable this preference, simply check the Maven Version Decorator option that is highlighted in Figure 14-39. If the Maven Version Decorator is not enabled, a project will list only its name and relative path in the Package Explorer, as shown in Figure 14-40.

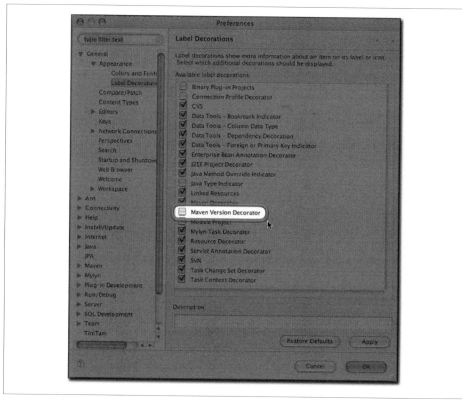

Figure 14-39. Enabling the Maven Version Decorator

Upon enabling the Maven Version Decorator, the project name will include the current project version, as shown in Figure 14-41.

This is a helpful feature that provides you with the project version at a glance instead of requiring you to open the POM to locate the `version` element.

Summary

m2eclipse is more than just a simple plugin that adds Maven support to Eclipse; it is a comprehensive integration that will make everything from creating new projects to locating third-party dependencies orders of magnitude easier. m2eclipse is the first step toward an IDE that is aware of the rich semantic treasure that is the central Maven repository. As more people come to use m2eclipse, more projects are going to be releasing Maven archetypes, and more projects are going to see value in publishing

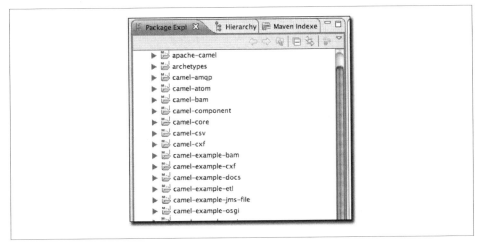

Figure 14-40. Package Explorer without Maven Version Decorator

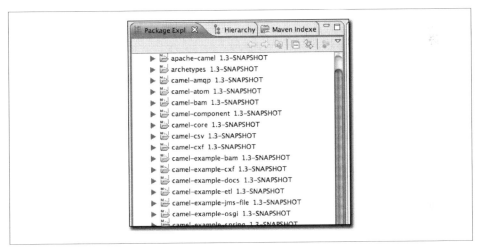

Figure 14-41. Package Explorer with Maven Version Decorator enabled

source artifacts to the Maven repository. If you've tried to use Eclipse and Maven together without a tool that can comprehend the hierarchical project relationships that are central to any multimodule Maven project, you will know that the ability to work with nested projects is essential to smooth integration between the Eclipse IDE and Maven.

## CHAPTER 15

Site Generation

Introduction

Successful software applications are rarely produced by a team of one. When we're talking about any software worth writing, we're usually dealing with teams of collaborating developers ranging anywhere in size from a handful of programmers working in a small team to hundreds or thousands of programmers working in a large distributed environment. Most open source projects (such as Maven) succeed or fail based on the presence or absence of well-written documentation for a widely distributed, ad hoc collection of users and developers. In all environments, it is important for projects to have an easy way to publish and maintain online documentation. Software development is primarily an exercise in collaboration and communication, and publishing a Maven site is one way to make sure that your project is communicating with your end users.

A web site for an open source project is often the foundation for both the end user and developer communities alike. End users look to a project's web site for tutorials, user guides, API documentation, and mailing list archives, and developers look to a project's web site for design documents, code reports, issue tracking, and release plans. Large open source projects may be integrated with wikis, issue trackers, and continuous integration systems that help augment a project's online documentation with material that reflects the current status of ongoing development. If a new open source project has an inadequate web site that fails to convey basic information to prospective users, if often is a sign that the project in question will fail to be adopted. In other words, for an open source project, the site and the documentation are as important to the formation of a community as the code itself.

Maven can be used to create a project web site to capture information that is relevant to both the end user and the developer audience. Out of the box, Maven can generate reports on everything from unit test failures to package coupling to code quality. Maven provides you with the ability to write simple web pages and render those pages against a consistent project template. Maven can publish site content in multiple formats, including XHTML and PDF. Maven can be used to generate API documents and can also be used to embed Javadoc and source code in your project's binary release archive. Once you've used Maven to generate all of your project's end user and developer documentation, you can then use Maven to publish your web site to a remote server.

Building a Project Site with Maven

To illustrate the process of building a project web site, let's create a sample Maven project with the Archetype plugin:

```
$ mvn archetype:create -DgroupId=org.sonatype.mavenbook -DartifactId=sample-project
```

This creates the simplest possible Maven project with one Java class in *src/main/java* and a simple POM. You can then build a Maven site by simply running *mvn site*. To build the site and preview the result in a browser, you can run *mvn site:run*. This will build the site and start an embedded instance of Jetty:

```
$ cd sample-project
$ mvn site:run
[INFO] Scanning for projects...
[INFO] Searching repository for plugin with prefix: 'site'.
[INFO] ------------------------------------------------------------------------
[INFO] Building sample-project
[INFO]     task-segment: [site:run] (aggregator-style)
[INFO] ------------------------------------------------------------------------
[INFO] Setting property: classpath.resource.loader.class =>
           'org.codehaus.plexus.velocity.ContextClassLoaderResourceLoader'.
[INFO] Setting property: velocimacro.messages.on => 'false'.
[INFO] Setting property: resource.loader => 'classpath'.
[INFO] Setting property: resource.manager.logwhenfound => 'false'.
[INFO] [site:run]
2008-04-26 11:52:26.981::INFO:  Logging to STDERR via org.mortbay.log.StdErrLog
[INFO] Starting Jetty on http://localhost:8080/
2008-04-26 11:52:26.046::INFO:  jetty-6.1.5
2008-04-26 11:52:26.156::INFO:  NO JSP Support for /, did not find
           org.apache.jasper.servlet.JspServlet
2008-04-26 11:52:26.244::INFO:  Started SelectChannelConnector@0.0.0.0:8080
```

Once Jetty starts and is listening to port 8080, you can see the project's site when you go to *http://localhost:8080/* in a web browser. You can view the results in Figure 15-1.

If you click around on this simple site, you'll see that it isn't very helpful as a real project site. There's just nothing there (and it doesn't look very good). Since the sample-project hasn't configured any developers, mailing lists, issue tracking providers, or source code repositories, all of these pages on the project site will have no information. Even the index page of the site states, "There is currently no description associated with this project." To customize the site, you'll have to start adding content to the project and to the project's POM.

If you are going to use the Maven Site plugin to build your project's site, you'll want to customize it. You will want to populate some of the important fields in the POM that tell Maven about the people participating in the project, and you'll want to

Figure 15-1. Simple generated Maven site

customize the lefthand navigation menu and the links visible in the header of the page. To customize the contents of the site and affect the contents of the lefthand navigation menu, you will need to edit the site descriptor.

Customizing the Site Descriptor

When you add content to the site, you are going to want to modify the lefthand navigation menu that is generated with your site. The site descriptor shown in Example 15-1 customizes the logo in the upper-lefthand corner of the site. In addition to customizing the header of the site, this descriptor adds a menu section to the lefthand navigation menu under the heading "Sample Project." This menu contains a single link to an overview page.

Example 15-1. An initial site descriptor

```
<project name="Sample Project">
  <bannerLeft>
    <name>Sonatype</name>
    <src>images/logo.png</src>
    <href>http://www.sonatype.com</href>
  </bannerLeft>
  <body>
    <menu name="Sample Project">
      <item name="Overview" href="index.html"/>
    </menu>
    <menu ref="reports"/>
  </body>
</project>
```

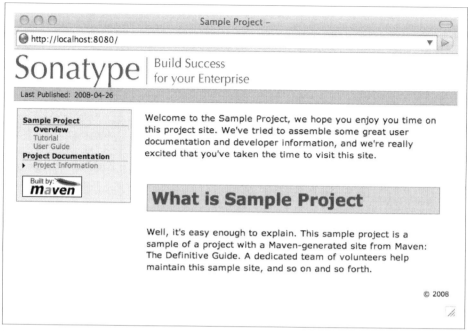

Figure 15-2. Customized sample project web site

This site descriptor references one image. This *logo.png* image should be placed in *${basedir}/src/site/resources/images*. In addition to the change to the site descriptor, you'll want to create a simple *index.apt* page in *${basedir}/src/site/apt*. Put the following content in *index.apt*; it will be transformed to the *index.html* and serve as the first page a user sees when they come to your project's Maven-generated web site:

```
Welcome to the Sample Project, we hope you enjoy your time
on this project site. We've tried to assemble some
great user documentation and developer information, and
we're really excited that you've taken the time to visit
this site.

What is Sample Project

Well, it's easy enough to explain. This sample project is
a sample of a project with a Maven-generated site from
Maven: The Definitive Guide. A dedicated team of volunteers
help maintain this sample site, and so on and so forth.
```

To preview the site, run *mvn clean site* followed by *mvn site:run*:

```
$ mvn clean site
$ mvn site:run
```

Once you do this, load the page in a browser by going to *http://localhost:8080*. You should see something similar to the screenshot in Figure 15-2.

Customizing the Header Graphics

To customize the graphics that appear in the upper lefthand and righthand corners of the page, you can use the `bannerLeft` and `bannerRight` elements in a site descriptor, as shown in Example 15-2.

Example 15-2. Adding a bannerLeft and bannerRight to a site descriptor

```
<project name="Sample Project">

  <bannerLeft>
    <name>Left Banner</name>
    <src>images/banner-left.png</src>
    <href>http://www.google.com</href>
  </bannerLeft>

  <bannerRight>
    <name>Right Banner</name>
    <src>images/banner-right.png</src>
    <href>http://www.yahoo.com</href>
  </bannerRight>
  ...
</project>
```

Both the `bannerLeft` and `bannerRight` elements take `name`, `src`, and `href` child elements. In the site descriptor just shown, the Maven Site plugin will generate a site with *banner-left.png* in the lefthand corner of the page and *banner-right.png* in the righthand corner of the page. Maven is going to look in *${basedir}/src/site/resources/images* for these images.

Customizing the Navigation Menu

To customize the contents of the navigation menu, use the `menu` element with `item` child elements. The `menu` element adds a section to the lefthand navigation menu. Each item is rendered as a link in that menu. See Example 15-3.

Example 15-3. Creating menu items in a site descriptor

```
<project name="Sample Project">
  ...
  <body>

    <menu name="Sample Project">
      <item name="Introduction" href="index.html"/>
      <item name="News" href="news.html"/>
      <item name="Features" href="features.html"/>
      <item name="Installation" href="installation.html"/>
      <item name="Configuration" href="configuration.html"/>
      <item name="FAQ" href="faq.html"/>
    </menu>
    ...
```

```
    </body>
  </project>
```

Menu items can also be nested. If you nest items, you will be creating a collapsible menu in the lefthand navigation menu. Example 15-4 adds a "Developer Resources" link, which links to */developer/index.html*. When a user is looking at the Developer Resources page, the menu items below the Developer Resources menu item will be expanded.

Example 15-4. Adding a link to the site menu

```
<project name="Sample Project">
  ...
  <body>
    ...
    <menu name="Sample Project">
      ...
      <item name="Developer Resources" href="/developer/index.html" collapse="true">
        <item name="System Architecture" href="/developer/architecture.html"/>
        <item name="Embedder's Guide" href="/developer/embedding.html"/>
      </item>
    </menu>
    ...
  </body>
</project>
```

When an item has the `collapse` attribute set to `true`, Maven will collapse the item until a user is viewing that specific page. In Example 15-4, when the user is not looking at the Developer Resources page, Maven will not display the System Architecture and Embedder's Guide links; instead, it will display an arrow pointing to the Developer Resources link. When the user is viewing the Developer Resources page, it will show these links with an arrow pointing down.

Site Directory Structure

Maven places all site document under *src/site*. Documents of similar format are placed in subdirectories of *src/site*. All Almost Plain Text (APT) documents should be in *src/site/apt*, all FAQ Markup Language (FML) documents should be in *src/site/fml*, and XDoc documents should be in *src/site/xdoc*. The site descriptor should be in *src/site/site.xml*, and all resources should be stored under *src/site/resources*. When the Maven Site plugin builds a web site, it will copy everything in the resources directory to the root of the site. If you store an image in *src/site/resources/images/test.png*, you would refer to the image from your site documentation using the relative path *images/test.png*.

The following example shows the location of all files in a project that contains APT, FML, HTML, XHTML, and some XDoc. Note that the XHTML content is simply stored in the *resources/* directory. The *architecture.html* file will not be processed by Doxia; it will simply be copied to the output directory. You can use this approach if you want to include unprocessed HTML content and you don't want to take advantage of the templating and formatting capabilities of Doxia and the Maven Site plugin:

```
sample-project
+- src/
   +- site/
      +- apt/
      |  +- index.apt
      |  +- about.apt
      |  |
      |  +- developer/
      |       +- embedding.apt
      |
      +- fml/
      |  +- faq.fml
      |
      +- resources/
      |  +- images/
      |  |  |  +- banner-left.png
      |  |  |  +- banner-right.png
      |  |  |
      |  +- architecture.html
      |  +- jira-roadmap-export-2007-03-26.html
      |
      +- xdoc/
      |  +- xml-example.xml
      |
      +- site.xml
```

Note that the developer documentation is stored in *src/site/apt/developer/embedding.apt*. This extra directory below the *apt* directory will be reflected in the location of the resulting HTML page on the site. When the Site plugin renders the contents of the *src/site/apt* directory, it will produce HTML output in directories relative to the site root. If a file is in the *apt* directory, it will be in the root directory of the generated web site. If a file is in the *apt/developer* directory, it will be generated in the *developer/* directory of the web site.

Writing Project Documentation

Maven uses a documentation-processing engine called Doxia that reads multiple source formats into a common document model. Doxia can then manipulate documents and render the result in several output formats, such as PDF or XHTML. To write documentation for your project, you will need to write your content in a format that can be parsed by Doxia. Doxia currently has support for Almost Plain Text (APT), XDoc (a Maven 1.x documentation format), XHTML, and FML (useful for FAQ documents) formats.

This chapter provides only a cursory introduction to the APT format. For a deeper understanding of the APT format, or for an in-depth introduction to XDoc or FML, please see the following resources:

APT reference
   http://maven.apache.org/doxia/format.html

XDoc reference
   http://jakarta.apache.org/site/jakarta-site2.html

FML reference
   http://maven.apache.org/doxia/references/fml-format.html

APT Example

Example 15-5 shows a simple APT document with an introductory paragraph and a simple list. Note that the list is terminated by the pseudoelement [ ].

Example 15-5. APT document

```
---
Introduction to Sample Project
---
Brian Fox
---
26-Mar-2008
---

Welcome to Sample Project

  This is a sample project, welcome! We're excited that you've decided to read the
  index page of this Sample Project. We hope you enjoy the simple sample project
  we've assembled for you.

  Here are some useful links to get you started:

  * {{{news.html}News}}

  * {{{features.html}Features}}

  * {{{faq.html}FAQ}}

  []
```

If the APT document from this example is placed in *src/site/apt/index.apt*, the Maven Site plugin will parse the APT using Doxia and produce XHTML content in *index.html*.

FML Example

Many projects maintain a Frequently Asked Questions (FAQ) page. Example 15-6 shows an example of an FML document.

Example 15-6. FAQ markup language document

```
<?xml version="1.0" encoding="UTF-8"?>
<faqs title="Frequently Asked Questions">
  <part id="General">
```

```
  <faq id="sample-project-sucks">
    <question>Sample project doesn't work. Why does sample project suck?</question>
    <answer>
      <p>
        We resent that question. Sample wasn't designed to work, it was designed to
        show you how to use Maven. If you really think this project sucks, then
        keep it to yourself. We're not interested in your pestering questions.
      </p>
    </answer>
  </faq>
  <faq id="sample-project-source">
    <question>I want to put some code in Sample Project, how do I do this?</question>
    <answer>
      <p>
        If you want to add code to this project, just start putting Java source in
        src/main/java. If you want to put some source code in this FAQ, use the
        source element:
      </p>
      <source>
        for( int i = 0; i < 1234; i++ ) {
          // do something brilliant
          }
      </source>
    </answer>
  </faq>
  </part>
</faqs>
```

Deploying Your Project Web Site

Once your project's documentation has been written and you've created a site to be
proud of, you will want to deploy it a server. To deploy your site, you'll use the Maven
Site plugin, which can take care of deploying your project's site to a remote server using
a number of methods, including File Transfer Protocol (FTP), Secure Copy (SCP), and
Distributed Authoring and Versioning (DAV). To deploy the site using DAV, configure
the site entry of the `distributionManagement` section in the POM, as shown in Example 15-7.

Example 15-7. Configuring site deployment

```
<project>
  ...
  <distributionManagement>
    <site>
      <id>sample-project.website</id>
      <url>dav:https://dav.sample.com/sites/sample-project</url>
    </site>
  </distributionManagement>
  ...
</project>
```

The `url` in distribution management has a leading indicator `dav`, which tells the Maven Site plugin to deploy the site to a URL that is able to understand WebDAV. Once you have added the `distributionManagement` section to the `sample-project` POM, you can try deploying the site:

```
$ mvn clean site-deploy
```

If you have a properly configured server that can understand WebDAV, Maven will deploy your project's web site to the remote server. If you are deploying this project to a site and server visible to the public, you are going to want to configure your web server to access for credentials. If your web server asks for a username and password (or other credentials), you can configure these values in your ~/.m2/settings.xml.

Configuring Server Authentication

To configure a username and password combination for use during the site deployment, we'll include the code shown in Example 15-8 in $HOME/.m2/settings.xml.

Example 15-8. Storing server authentication in user-specific settings

```
<settings>
  ...
  <servers>
    <server>
      <id>sample-project.website</id>
      <username>jdcasey</username>
      <password>b@dp@sswOrd</password>
    </server>
    ...
  </servers>
  ...
</settings>
```

The server authentication section can contain a number of authentication elements. In the event that you're using SCP for deployment, you may wish to use public-key authentication. To do this, specify the `publicKey` and `passphrase` elements instead of the `password` element. You may still want to configure the `username` element, depending on your server's configuration.

Configuring File and Directory Modes

If you are working with a large group of developers, you'll want to make sure that your web site's files end up with the proper user and group permissions after they are published to the remote server. To configure specific file and directory modes for use during the site deployment, include the code shown in Example 15-9 in $HOME/.m2/settings.xml.

Example 15-9. Configuring file and directory modes on remote servers

```
<settings>
  ...
  <servers>
    ...
    <server>
      <id>hello-world.website</id>
      ...
      <directoryPermissions>0775</directoryPermissions>
      <filePermissions>0664</filePermissions>
    </server>
  </servers>
  ...
</settings>
```

These settings will make any directories readable and writable by either the owner or members of the owner's primary group; the anonymous users will have access only to read and list the directory. Similarly, the owner or members of the owner's primary group will have access to read and write any files, with the rest of the world restricted to read-only access.

Customizing Site Appearance

The default Maven template leaves much to be desired. If you wish to customize your project's web site beyond simply adding content, navigational elements, and custom logos, Maven offers several mechanisms for customizing your web site that allow successively deeper access to content decoration and web site structure. For small, per-project tweaks, providing a custom *site.css* is often enough. However, if you want your customizations to be reusable across multiple projects, or if your customizations involve changing the XHTML that Maven generates, you should consider creating your own Maven web site skin.

Customizing the Site CSS

The easiest way to affect the look and feel of your project's web site is through the project's *site.css*. Just like any images or XHTML content you provide for the web site, the *site.css* file goes in the *src/site/resources* directory. Maven expects this file to be in the *src/site/resources/css* subdirectory. With CSS, it is possible to change text styling properties, layout properties, and even add background images and custom bullet graphics. For example, if we decided to make the menu heading stand out a little more, we might try the following style in *src/site/resources/css/site.css*:

```
#navcolumn h5 {
    font-size: smaller;
    border: 1px solid #aaaaaa;
    background-color: #bbb;
    margin-top: 7px;
    margin-bottom: 2px;
```

```
    padding-top: 2px;
    padding-left: 2px;
    color: #000;
}
```

When you regenerate the web site, the menu headers should be framed by a gray background and separated from the rest of the menu by some extra margin space. Using this file, any structure in the Maven-generated web site can be decorated with custom CSS. When you change *site.css* in a specific Maven project, the changes will apply to that specific project. If you are interested in making changes that will apply to more than one Maven project, you can create a custom skin for the Maven Site plugin.

 No good reference exists for the structure of the default Maven site template. If you are attempting to customize the style of your Maven project, you should use a Firefox extension such as Firebug as a tool to explore the Document Object Model (DOM) for your project's pages.

Create a Custom Site Template

If the default Maven Site structure just doesn't do it for you, you can always customize the Maven site template. Customizing the Maven Site template gives you complete control over the ultimate output of the Maven plugin, and it is possible to customize your project's site template to the point where it hardly resembles the structure of a default Maven site template.

The Site plugin uses a rendering engine called Doxia, which in turn uses a Velocity template to render the XHTML for each page. To change the page structure that is rendered by default, we can configure the site plugin in our POM to use a custom page template. The site template is fairly complex, and you'll need to have a good starting point for your customization. Start by copying the default Velocity template from Doxia's Subversion repository, *default-site.vm* (see *http://svn.apache.org/viewvc/maven/ doxia/doxia-sitetools/trunk/doxia-site-renderer/src/main/resources/org/apache/maven/ doxia/siterenderer/resources/default-site.vm?revision=595592*) to *src/site/site.vm*. This template is written in a templating language called Velocity. Velocity is a simple templating language that supports simple macro definition and allows you to access an object's methods and properties using simple notation. A full introduction is beyond the scope of this book; for more information about Velocity and a full introduction, please go to the Velocity project site at *http://velocity.apache.org*.

The *default-site.xml* template is fairly involved, but the change required to customize the lefthand menu is relatively straightforward. If you are trying to change the appearance of a menuItem, locate the menuItem macro. It resides in a section that looks like this:

```
#macro ( menuItem $item )
  ...
#end
```

If you replace the macro definition with the following macro definition, you will inject JavaScript references into each menu item, which will allow the reader to expand or collapse the menu tree without suffering through a full page reload:

```
#macro ( menuItem $item $listCount )
  #set ( $collapse = "none" )
  #set ( $currentItemHref = $PathTool.calculateLink( $item.href, $relativePath ) )
  #set ( $currentItemHref = $currentItemHref.replaceAll( "\\", "/" ) )

  #if ( $item && $item.items && $item.items.size() > 0 )
    #if ( $item.collapse == false )
      #set ( $collapse = "collapsed" )
    #else
      ## By default collapsed
      #set ( $collapse = "collapsed" )
    #end

    #set ( $display = false )
    #displayTree( $display $item )

    #if ( $alignedFileName == $currentItemHref || $display )
      #set ( $collapse = "expanded" )
    #end
  #end
  <li class="$collapse">
    #if ( $item.img )
      #if ( ! ( $item.img.toLowerCase().startsWith("http") ||
              $item.img.toLowerCase().startsWith("https") ) )
        #set ( $src = $PathTool.calculateLink( $item.img, $relativePath ) )
        #set ( $src = $item.img.replaceAll( "\\", "/" ) )
        <img src="$src"/>
      #else
        <img src="$item.img" align="absbottom" style="border-width: 0"/>
      #end
    #end
    #if ( $alignedFileName == $currentItemHref )
      <strong>$item.name</strong>
    #else
      #if ( $item && $item.items && $item.items.size() > 0 )
      <a onclick="expand('list$listCount')" style="cursor:pointer">$item.name</a>
      #else
      <a href="$currentItemHref">$item.name</a>
      #end
    #end
  #if ( $item && $item.items && $item.items.size() > 0 )
    #if ( $collapse == "expanded" )
    <ul id="list$listCount" style="display:block">
    #else
    <ul id="list$listCount" style="display:none">
    #end
    #foreach( $subitem in $item.items )
      #set ( $listCounter = $listCounter + 1 )
      #menuItem( $subitem $listCounter )
    #end
    </ul>
```

```
    #end
  </li>
#end
```

This change adds a new parameter to the `menuItem` macro. For the new functionality to work, you will need to change references to this macro, or the resulting template may produce unwanted or internally inconsistent XHTML. To finish changing these references, make a similar replacement in the `mainMenu` macro. Find this macro by looking for something similar to the following template snippet:

```
#macro ( mainMenu $menus )
  ...
#end
```

Replace the `mainMenu` macro with the following implementation:

```
#macro ( mainMenu $menus )
  #set ( $counter = 0 )
  #set ( $listCounter = 0 )
  #foreach( $menu in $menus )
    #if ( $menu.name )
    <h5 onclick="expand('menu$counter')">$menu.name</h5>
    #end
    <ul id="menu$counter" style="display:block">
      #foreach( $item in $menu.items )
        #menuItem( $item $listCounter )
        #set ( $listCounter = $listCounter + 1 )
      #end
    </ul>
    #set ( $counter = $counter + 1 )
  #end
#end
```

This new `mainMenu` macro is compatible with the new `menuItem` macro just shown, and it also provides support for a JavaScript-enabled top-level menu. Clicking on a top-level menu item with children will expand the menu and allow users to see the entire tree without waiting for a page to load.

The change to the `menuItem` macro introduced an `expand()` JavaScript function. This method needs to be added to the main XHTML template at the bottom of this template file. Find the section that looks similar to the following:

```
<head>
  ...
  <meta http-equiv="Content-Type" content="text/html;
      charset=${outputEncoding}" />
  ...
</head>
```

and replace it with this:

```
<head>
  ...
  <meta http-equiv="Content-Type" content="text/html;
      charset=${outputEncoding}" />
```

```
<script type="text/javascript">
  function expand( item ) {
    var expandIt = document.getElementById( item );
    if( expandIt.style.display == "block" ) {
      expandIt.style.display = "none";
      expandIt.parentNode.className = "collapsed";
    } else {
      expandIt.style.display = "block";
      expandIt.parentNode.className = "expanded";
    }
  }
</script>
#if ( $decoration.body.head )
  #foreach( $item in $decoration.body.head.getChildren() )
    #if ( $item.name == "script" )
      $item.toUnescapedString()
    #else
      $item.toString()
    #end
  #end
#end
</head>
```

After modifying the default site template, you'll need to configure your project's POM to reference this new site template. To customize the site template, you'll need to use the `templateDirectory` and template configuration properties of the Maven Site plugin. See Example 15-10.

Example 15-10. Customizing the page template in a project's POM

```
<project>
  ...
  <build>
    <plugins>
      <plugin>
        <artifactId>maven-site-plugin</artifactId>
        <configuration>
          <templateDirectory>src/site</templateDirectory>
          <template>site.vm</template>
        </configuration>
      </plugin>
    </plugins>
  </build>
  ...
</project>
```

Now you should be able to regenerate your project web site. When you do, you may notice that the resources and CSS for the Maven site are missing. When a Maven project customizes the site template, the Site plugin expects the project to supply all of the default images and CSS. To seed your project's resources, you may want to copy the resources from the default Doxia site renderer project to your own project's resources directory by executing the following commands:

```
$ svn co \
        http://svn.apache.org/repos/asf/maven/doxia/doxia-sitetools/trunk/\
        doxia-site-renderer
$ rm \
        doxia-site-renderer/src/main/resources/org/apache/maven/doxia/\
        siterenderer/resources/css/maven-theme.css
$ cp -rf \
        doxia-site-renderer/src/main/resources/org/apache/maven/doxia/\
        siterenderer/resources/*sample-project/src/site/resources
```

Check out the **doxia-site-renderer** project, remove the default *maven-theme.css* file, and then copy all the resources to your project's *src/site/resources* directory.

When you regenerate the site, you'll notice that a few menu items look like regular unstyled text. This is caused by a quirky interaction between the site's CSS and the new custom page template. It can be fixed by modifying the *site.css* to restore the proper link color for these menus. Simply add this:

```
li.collapsed, li.expanded, a:link {
  color:#36a;
}
```

After regenerating the site, the menu's link color should be corrected. If you applied the new site template to the same **sample-project** from this chapter, you'll notice that the menu now consists of a tree. Clicking on "Developer Resources" no longer takes you to the "Developer Resources" page; instead, it expands the submenu. Since you've turned the Developer Resources menu item into a dynamically folding submenu, you have lost the ability to reach the *developer/index.apt* page. To address this change, you should add an Overview link to the submenu that references the same page, as shown in Example 15-11.

Example 15-11. Adding a menu item to a site descriptor

```
<project name="Hello World">
  ...
  <menu name="Main Menu">
    ...
    <item name="Developer Resources" collapse="true">
      <item name="Overview" href="/developer/index.html"/>
      <item name="System Architecture" href="/developer/architecture.html"/>
      <item name="Embedder's Guide" href="/developer/embedding.html"/>
    </item>
  </menu>
  ...
</project>
```

Reusable Web Site Skins

If your organization has created many Maven project sites, you will likely want to reuse site template and CSS customizations throughout an organization. If you want 30 projects to share the same CSS and site template, you can use Maven's support for skinning. Maven Site skins allow you to package up resources and templates that can be reused by other projects in lieu of duplicating your site template for each project that needs to be customized.

Although you can define your own skin, you may want to consider using one of Maven's alternate skins. You can choose from several skins. These each provide their own layout for navigation, content, logos, and templates:

Maven classic skin
> `org.apache.maven.skins:maven-classic-skin:1.0`

Maven default skin
> `org.apache.maven.skins:maven-default-skin:1.0`

Maven stylus skin
> `org.apache.maven.skins:maven-stylus-skin:1.0.1`

You can find an up-to-date and comprehensive listing in the Maven repository: *http://repo1.maven.org/maven2/org/apache/maven/skins/*.

Creating a custom skin is a simple matter of wrapping your customized *maven-theme.css* in a Maven project so that it can be referenced by `groupId`, `artifactId`, and `version`. It can also include resources, such as images, and a replacement web site template (written in Velocity) that can generate a completely different XHTML page structure. In most cases, custom CSS can manage the changes you desire. To demonstrate, let's create a designer skin for the `sample-project` project, starting with a custom *maven-theme.css*.

Before we can start writing our custom CSS, we need to create a separate Maven project to allow the `sample-project` site descriptor to reference it. First, use Maven's archetype plugin to create a basic project. Issue the following command from the directory above the `sample-project` project's root directory:

```
$ mvn archetype:create -DartifactId=sample-site-skin -DgroupId=com.sonatyp.maven
```

This will create a project (and a directory) called `sample-site-skin`. Change directories to the new *sample-site-skin* directory, remove all of the source code and tests, and create a directory to store your skin's resources:

```
$ cd sample-site-skin
$ rm -rf src/main/java src/test
$ mkdir src/main/resources
```

Creating a Custom Theme CSS

Next, write a custom CSS for the custom skin. The CSS file in a Maven site skin should be placed in *src/main/resources/css/maven-theme.css*. Unlike the *site.css* file, which goes in the site-specific source directory for a project, the *maven-theme.css* will be bundled in a JAR artifact in your local Maven repository. In order for the *maven-theme.css* file to be included in the skin's JAR file, it must reside in the main project resources directory, *src/main/resources*.

As with the default site template, you will want to start customizing your new skin's CSS from a good starting point. Copy the CSS file used by the default Maven skin to your project's *maven-theme.css*. To get a copy of this theme file, save the contents of *maven-theme.css* (see *http://svn.apache.org/viewvc/maven/skins/trunk/maven-default -skin/src/main/resources/css/maven-theme.css?view=co*) from the `maven-default-skin` project to *src/main/resources/css/maven-theme.css* in our new skin project.

Now that we have the base theme file in place, customize it using the CSS from our old *site.css* file. Replace the `#navcolumn h5` CSS block with the following:

```
#navcolumn h5 {
  font-size: smaller;
  border: 1px solid #aaaaaa;
  background-color: #bbb;
  margin-top: 7px;
  margin-bottom: 2px;
  padding-top: 2px;
  padding-left: 2px;
  color: #000;
}
```

Once you've customized the *maven-theme.css*, build and install the `sample-site-skin` JAR artifact to your local Maven repository by running:

```
$ mvn clean install
```

Once the installation is complete, switch back to the *sample-project* project directory; if you already customized the *site.css* earlier in this chapter, move *site.css* to *site.css.bak* so it no longer affects the output of the Maven Site plugin:

```
$ mv src/site/resources/css/site.css src/site/resources/css/site.css.bak
```

To use the `sample-site-skin` in the `sample-project` site, you'll need to add a reference to the `sample-site-skin` artifact in the `sample-project`'s site descriptor. A site references a skin in the site descriptor using the skin element, as shown in Example 15-12.

Example 15-12. Configuring a custom site skin in site descriptor

```
<project name="Sample Project">
  ...
  <skin>
    <groupId>org.sonatype.mavenbook</groupId>
    <artifactId>sample-site-skin</artifactId>
  </skin>
  ...
</project>
```

You can think of a Maven site skin as a site dependency. Site skins are referenced as artifacts with a `groupId` and an `artifactId`. Using a site skin allows you to consolidate site customizations to a single project, and makes reusing custom CSS and site templates as easy as reusing build logic through a custom Maven plugin.

Customizing Site Templates in a Skin

Just as you can customize the site CSS in a Maven site skin, you can also customize the site template. Doxia's site-rendering tools will expect to find a file called *META-INF/maven/site.vm* inside the skin JAR. To incorporate a custom page template, copy the template file into the correct location within the `sample-site-skin`. Copy the custom site template developed earlier in the chapter to *src/main/resources/META-INF/maven* in `sample-site-skin`:

```
$ mv sample-project/src/site/site.vm \
    sample-site-skin/src/main/resources/META-INF/maven
```

If you already customized the site template in `sample-project`, remove the Site plugin configuration that pointed to this site template. The Site plugin will render the site using the site template referenced in the site skin:

```
<plugin>
  <artifactId>maven-site-plugin</artifactId>
  <configuration>
    <templateDirectory>src/site</templateDirectory>
    <template>site.vm</template>
  </configuration>
</plugin>
```

A Maven site skin is expected to include all of the resources it depends on. This includes CSS, images, and logos. If you already customized the site template earlier in this chapter, you've already copied the default `doxia-site-renderer` resources to the `sample-project`'s *src/site/resources* directory. You'll need to move those files out of the `sample-project` project and into the new `sample-site-skin` project by executing the following commands:

```
$ cd ..
$ mkdir -p sample-site-skin/src/main/resources/css
$ mv sample-project/src/site/resources/css/maven-base.css \
    sample-site-skin/src/main/resources/css
$ mkdir -p sample-site-skin/src/main/resources/images
$ mv sample-project/src/site/resources/images/logos \
    sample-site-skin/src/main/resources/images
$ mv sample-project/src/site/resources/images/expanded.gif \
    sample-site-skin/src/main/resources/images
$ mv sample/src/site/resources/images/collapsed.gif \
    sample-site-skin/src/main/resources/images
```

You've changed the `sample-site-skin`, so you'll need to install this skin into your local Maven repository. Once you install the skin locally and rebuild the `sample-project` web site, you'll see that the skin's custom site template was applied to the `sample-project`'s web site. You'll notice that the color of the menu items may be a little off because you haven't added the necessary CSS to the collapsed and expanded menu items. To do this, modify *src/main/resources/css/maven-theme.css*. That is, change this:

```
a:link {
    ...
}
```

to this:

```
li.collapsed, li.expanded, a:link {
    ...
}
```

Rebuild the skin, then regenerate the web site, and you'll see that the menu items have returned to normal. You've successfully created a Maven theme that can be used to apply CSS and templates to a set of projects.

Tips and Tricks

This section lists some useful tips and tricks you can use when creating a Maven site.

Inject XHTML into HEAD

To inject XHTML into the HEAD element, add a head element to the body element in your project's Site descriptor. Example 15-13 adds a feed link to every page in the sample-project web site.

Example 15-13. Injecting HTML into the HEAD element

```
<project name="Hello World">
  ...
  <body>
    <head>
      <link href="http://sample.com/sites/sample-project/feeds/blog"
            type="application/atom+xml"
            id="auto-discovery"
            rel="alternate"
            title="Sample Project Blog" />
    </head>
    ...
  </body>
</project>
```

Add Links Under Your Site Logo

If you are working on a project that is being developed by an organization, you may want to add links under your project's logo. Assuming that your project is a part of the Apache Software Foundation, you might want to add a link to the Apache Software Foundation web site right below your logo, and you might want to add a link to a parent project as well. To add links below your site logo, just add a links element to the body element in the Site descriptor. Each item element in the links element will be rendered as a link in a bar directly below your project's logo. Example 15-14 will add a link to the Apache Software Foundation followed by a link to the Apache Maven project.

Example 15-14. Adding links under your site logo

```
<project name="Hello World">
  ...
  <body>
    ...
    <links>
      <item name="Apache" href="http://www.apache.org"/>
      <item name="Maven" href="http://maven.apache.org"/>
    </links>
    ...
  </body>
</project>
```

Add Breadcrumbs to Your Site

If your hierarchy exists within a logical hierarchy, you may want to place a series of breadcrumbs to give the user a sense of context and to give them a way to navigate up the tree to projects that might contain the current project as a subproject. To configure breadcrumbs, add a `breadcrumbs` element to the `body` element in the site descriptor. Each `item` element will render a link, and the items in the `breadcrumbs` element will be rendered in order. The breadcrumb items should be listed from the highest level to the lowest level. In the site descriptor shown in Example 15-15, the Codehaus item would be seen to contain the Mojo item.

Example 15-15. Configuring the site's breadcrumbs

```
<project name="Sample Project">
  ...
  <body>
    ...
    <breadcrumbs>
      <item name="Codehaus" href="http://www.codehaus.org"/>
      <item name="Mojo" href="http://mojo.codehaus.org"/>
    </breadcrumbs>
    ...
  </body>
</project>
```

Add the Project Version

When you are documenting a project that has multiple versions, it is often very helpful to list the project's version number on every page. To display your project's version on the web site, simply add the `version` element to your site descriptor, as shown in Example 15-16.

Example 15-16. Positioning the version information

```
<project name="Sample Project">
  ...
  <version position="left"/>
  ...
</project>
```

This will position the version (in the case of the `sample-project` project, it will say "Version: 1.0-SNAPSHOT") in the upper lefthand corner of the site, just next to the default "Last Published" date. Valid positions for the project version are:

left
> Left side of the bar just below the site logo

right
> Right side of the bar just below the site logo

navigation-top
> Top of the menu

navigation-bottom
> Bottom of the menu

none
> Suppress the version entirely

Modify the Publication Date Format and Location

In some cases, you may wish to reformat or reposition the "Last Published" date for your project web site. Just like the project version tip, you can specify the position of the publication date by using one of the following (see Example 15-17):

left
> Left side of the bar just below the site logo

right
> Right side of the bar just below the site logo

navigation-top
> Top of the menu

navigation-bottom
> Bottom of the menu

none
> Suppress the publication entirely

Example 15-17. Positioning the publish date

```
<project name="Sample Project">
  ...
  <publishDate position="navigation-bottom"/>
```

```
    ...
</project>
```

By default, the publication date will be formatted using the date format string `MM/dd/yyyy`. You can change this format by using the standard notation found in the Javadocs for `java.text.SimpleDateFormat` (see the Javadoc for SimpleDateFormat at *http://java.sun.com/j2se/1.5.0/docs/api/java/text/SimpleDateFormat.html* for more information). To reformat the date using `yyyy-MM-dd`, use the `publishDate` element as shown in Example 15-18.

Example 15-18. Configuring the publish date format

```
<project name="Sample Project">
  ...
  <publishDate position="navigation-bottom" format="yyyy-MM-dd"/>
  ...
</project>
```

Using Doxia Macros

In addition to its advanced document rendering features, Doxia also provides a macro engine that allows each input format to trigger injection of dynamic content. An excellent example of this is the snippet macro, which allows a document to pull a code snippet out of a source file that's available via HTTP. Using this macro, a small fragment of APT can be rendered into XHTML. The following APT code calls out to the snippet macro. Please note that this code should be on a single continuous line; the backslash character is inserted to denote a line break so that this code will fit on the printed page (see Example 15-19 for the output):

```
%{snippet|id=modello-model|url=http://svn.apache.org/repos/asf/maven/archetype/\
trunk/maven-archetype/maven-archetype-model/src/main/mdo/archetype.mdo}
```

Example 15-19. Output of the snippet macro in XHTML

```
<div class="source"><pre>

<model>
  <id>archetype</id>
  <name>Archetype</name>
  <description><![CDATA[Maven's model for the archetype descriptor.]]></description>
  <defaults>
    <default>
      <key>package</key>
      <value>org.apache.maven.archetype.model</value>
    </default>
  </defaults>
  <classes>
    <class rootElement="true" xml.tagName="archetype">
      <name>ArchetypeModel</name>
      <description>Describes the assembly layout and packaging.</description>
      <version>1.0.0</version>
      <fields>
```

```
    <field>
      <name>id</name>
      <version>1.0.0</version>
      <required>true</required>
      <type>String</type>
    </field>
    ...
  </fields>
</class>
</classes>
</model>
```

</pre></div>

 Doxia macros *must not* be indented in APT source documents. Doing
so will result in the APT parser skipping the macro altogether.

For more information about defining snippets in your code for reference by the snippet
macro, see the "Guide to the Snippet Macro" on the Maven web site at *http://maven
.apache.org/guides/mini/guide-snippet-macro.html*.

## CHAPTER 16

Repository Manager

Introduction

Repository managers serve two purposes: they act as highly configurable proxies between your organization and the public Maven repositories, and they also provide an organization with a deployment destination for your own generated artifacts.

Proxying a Maven repository brings a number of benefits. Proxying speeds up builds throughout your organization by installing a local cache for all artifacts from the central Maven repository. If a developer in your organization needs to download version 2.5 of the Spring Framework and you are using Nexus, the dependencies (and the dependencies' dependencies) need to be downloaded from the remote repository only once. With a high-speed connection to the Internet, this might seem like a minor concern, but if you are constantly asking your developers to download hundreds of megabytes of third-party dependencies, the real cost savings are going to be the time it takes Maven to check for new versions of dependencies and to download them. Serving Maven dependencies from a local repository can save you hundreds of requests over HTTP, and in very large multiproject builds, this can shave minutes from a build.

If your project is relying on a number of snapshot dependencies, Maven will need to check for updated version of these snapshots. Depending on the configuration of your remote repositories, Maven will check for snapshot updates periodically, or it might check for snapshot updates on every build. When Maven checks for a snapshot update, it needs to interrogate the remote repository for the latest version of the snapshot dependency. Depending on your connection to the public Internet and the load on the central Maven repository, a snapshot update can add seconds to your project's build for each snapshot update. When you host a local repository proxy with a repository like Nexus, your repository manager is going to check for snapshot updates on a regular schedule, and your applications will be able to interact with a local repository. If you develop software with a lot of snapshot dependencies, using a local repository manager can often shave minutes from a large multimodule project build. Your 5–10 second snapshot update checks against the public central repository are going to execute in hundreds of milliseconds (or less).

In addition to the simple savings in time and bandwidth, a repository manager provides an organization with control over what is downloaded by Maven. You can include or exclude specific artifacts from the public repository. Having this level of control over what is downloaded from the central Maven repository is a prerequisite for organizations that need strict control over which dependencies are used throughout an organization. An organization that wants to standardize on a specific version of a dependency such as Hibernate or Spring can enforce this standardization by providing access to only a specific version of an artifact in a repository manager such as Nexus. Other organizations might be concerned with making sure that every external dependency has a license compatible with the legal standards of that organization. If a corporation is producing an application that is distributed, it might want to make sure that no one inadvertently adds a dependency on a third-party library that is covered under a copyleft license such as the GNU General Public License (GPL). Repository managers provide for the level of control that an organization needs to make sure that overall architecture and policy can be enforced.

Aside from the benefits of mediating access to remote repositories, a repository manager also provides something essential to full adoption of Maven. Unless you expect every member of your organization to download and build every single internal project, you will want to provide a mechanism for developers and departments to share both snapshots and releases for internal project artifacts. Nexus provides your organization with such a deployment target. Once you install Nexus, you can start using Maven to deploy snapshots and releases to a custom repository managed by Nexus. Over time, this central deployment point for internal projects becomes the fabric for collaboration between different development teams.

History of Nexus

Tamás Cservenák started working on Proximity in December 2005 as he was trying to find a way to isolate his own systems from an incredibly slow ADSL connection provided by a Hungarian ISP. Proximity started as a simple web application to proxy artifacts for a small organization with connectivity issues. Creating a local on-demand cache for Maven artifacts from the central Maven repository gave an organization access to the artifacts on the central Maven repository, but it also made sure that these artifacts weren't downloaded over a very slow ADSL connection used by a number of developers. In 2007, Sonatype asked Tamas to help create a similar product named Nexus. Nexus is currently considered the logical next step from Proximity. Nexus currently has an active development team, and portions of the indexing code from Nexus are also being used in m2eclipse.

Installing Nexus

The following subsections explain how to download, install, run, configure, and upgrade Nexus on your system.

Downloading Nexus from Sonatype

You can find information about Nexus at *http://nexus.sonatype.org*. To download Nexus, go to *http://nexus.sonatype.org/downloads/*. Click on the Download link and download the appropriate archive for your platform. Nexus is available as a ZIP and a GZipped TAR file.

Installing Nexus

Installing Nexus is straightforward: unpack the Nexus archive in a directory. If you are installing Nexus on a local workstation to give it a test run, you can install it in your home directory or wherever else you like. Nexus doesn't have any hardcoded directories; it will run from any directory. If you download the ZIP archive, run this:

```
$ unzip nexus-1.0.0-bundle.zip
```

And if you download the GZipped TAR archive, run this:

```
$ tar xvzf nexus-1.0.0-bundle.tgz
```

 There are some known incompatibilities with the version of TAR provided by Solaris and the GZip TAR format. If you are installing Nexus on Solaris, you must use the GNU *tar* application or you will end up with corrupted files. Please see *http://sunsolarisadmin.blogspot.com/ 2007/03/how-to-install-gnu-tar-in-solaris.html*.

If you are installing Nexus on a server, you might want to use a directory other than your home directory. On a Unix machine, this could be under */usr/local/nexus-1.0.0* with a symbolic link */usr/local/nexus* to the *nexus* directory. Using a generic symbolic link *nexus* to a specific version is a common practice that makes it easier to upgrade when a newer version of Nexus is made available:

```
$ sudo cp nexus-1.0.0-bundle.tgz /usr/local
$ cd /usr/local
$ sudo tar xvzf nexus-1.0.0-bundle.tgz
$ ln -s nexus-1.0.0 nexus
```

Although it isn't required for Nexus to run, you may want to set an environment variable NEXUS_HOME in your environment that points to the installation directory of Nexus. This chapter will refer to this location as ${NEXUS_HOME}.

Running Nexus

When you start Nexus, you are starting a web server on the default port of localhost: 8081. Nexus runs within a servlet container called Jetty and is started with a native service wrapper called the Tanuki Java Service Wrapper (*http://wrapper.tanukisoftware .org/doc/english/introduction.html*). This service wrapper can be configured to run

Nexus as a Windows service or a Unix daemon. To start Nexus, you will need to find the appropriate startup script for your platform. To see the list of available platforms, list the contents of the *${NEXUS_HOME}/bin/jsw* directory.

The following example code starts Nexus using the script for Mac OS X. First we list the contents of the *${NEXUS_HOME}/bin/jsw* to show you the available platforms, then we make the contents of the bin directory executable with *chmod*. The Mac OS X wrapper is started with a call to *app start*, and after that we tail the *wrapper.log* in *${NEXUS_HOME}/container/logs*. Nexus will initialize itself and print a message that it is listening on `localhost:8081`:

```
$ cd Nexus
$ ls ./bin/jsw/
aix-ppc-32/          linux-ppc-64/          solaris-sparc-32/
aix-ppc-64/          linux-x86-32/          solaris-sparc-64/
hpux-parisc-32/      linux-x86-64/          solaris-x86-32/
hpux-parisc-64/      macosx-universal-32/   windows-x86-32/
$ chmod -R a+x bin
$ ./bin/jsw/macosx-universal-32/nexus start
Nexus Repository Manager...
$ tail -f container/logs/wrapper.log
INFO  ... [ServletContainer:default] - SelectChannelConnector@0.0.0.0:8081
```

At this point, Nexus will be running and listening on port 8081. To use Nexus, fire up a web browser and type in the URL *http://localhost:8081/nexus*. Click on the "Log In" link in the upper-righthand corner of the web page, and you should see the login dialog shown in Figure 16-1.

 The default Nexus username and password are "admin" and "admin123".

Post-Install Checklist

Nexus ships with some default passwords and settings for repository indexing that need to be changed for your installation to be useful (and secure). After installing and running Nexus, you need to make sure to complete the following tasks:

Change the administrative password and email address
> The administrative password defaults to "admin123". The first thing you should do to your new Nexus installation is change this password. To change the administrative password, log in as "admin" with the password "admin123", and click on Change Password under the Security menu in the lefthand side of the browser window.

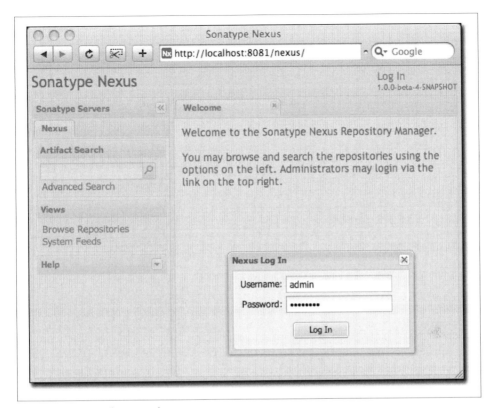

Figure 16-1. Nexus login window

Configure the SMTP settings

Nexus can send username and password recovery emails. To enable this feature, you need to configure Nexus with an SMTP host and port, as well as any necessary authentication parameters that Nexus needs to connect to a mail server. To configure the SMTP settings, load the server configuration dialog shown in "Customizing Server Configuration."

Enable remote index downloads

Nexus ships with three important proxy repositories: the central Maven repository, the Apache snapshot repository, and the Codehaus snapshot repository. Each of these repositories contains thousands (or tens of thousands) of artifacts, and it would be impractical to download the entire contents of each. To that end, most repositories maintain a Lucene index that catalogs the entire contents and provides for fast and efficient searching. Nexus uses these remote indexes to search for artifacts, but index downloads are disabled as a default setting. To download remote indexes:

1. Click on Repositories under the Administration menu, and change Download Remote Indexes to "true" for the three proxy repositories. You'll need to load the dialog shown in "Managing Repositories" for each of the three repositories.

2. Right-click on each proxy repository and select "Re-index." This will trigger Nexus to download the remote index files.

It might take Nexus a few minutes to download the entire index, but once you have it, you'll be able to search the entire contents of the Maven repository.

Once you've enabled remote index downloads, you still won't be able to browse the complete contents of a remote repository. Downloading the remote index allows you to search for artifacts in a repository, but until you download those artifacts from the remote repository, they will not show in the repository tree when you are browsing a repository. When browsing a repository, you will be shown only artifacts that have been downloaded from the remote repository.

Startup Scripts for Linux

You can configure Nexus to start automatically by copying the *app* script to the */etc/init.d* directory. On a Linux system (tested with Red Hat, Fedora, Ubuntu, or CentOS), perform the following operations as the root user:

1. Copy either *${NEXUS_HOME}/bin/jsw/linux-ppc-64/app*, *${NEXUS_HOME}/bin/jsw/linux-x86-32/app*, or *${NEXUS_HOME}/bin/jsw/linux-x86-64/app* to */etc/init.d/nexus*.

2. Make the */etc/init.d/nexus* script executable: *chmod 755 /etc/init.d/nexus*.

3. Edit this script changing the following variables:

   - Change `APP_NAME` to "nexus"
   - Change `APP_LONG_NAME` to "Sonatype Nexus"
   - Add a variable `NEXUS_HOME` that points to your Nexus installation directory
   - Add a variable `PLATFORM` that contains either `linux-x86-32`, `linux-x86-64`, or `linux-ppc-64`
   - Change `WRAPPER_CMD` to *${NEXUS_HOME}/bin/jsw/${PLATFORM}/wrapper*
   - Change `WRAPPER_CONF` to *${NEXUS_HOME}/conf/wrapper.conf*
   - Change `PIDDIR` to */var/run*
   - Add a `JAVA_HOME` variable that points to your local Java installation
   - Add a *${JAVA_HOME}/bin* to the `PATH`

4. (Optional.) Set the `RUN_AS_USER` to "nexus". If you do this, you will need to:

   - Create a Nexus user
   - Change the owner and group of your Nexus install directory to "nexus"

At the end of this, you should have a file in */etc/init.d/nexus* that starts with a series of configuration properties that look something like this (assuming you've installed Nexus in */usr/local/nexus* and Java in */usr/java/latest*):

```
JAVA_HOME=/usr/java/latest
PATH=${PATH}:${JAVA_HOME}/bin
APP_NAME="nexus"
APP_LONG_NAME="Sonatype Nexus"
NEXUS_HOME=/usr/local/nexus
PLATFORM=linux-x86-64
WRAPPER_CMD="${NEXUS_HOME}/bin/jsw/${PLATFORM}/wrapper"
WRAPPER_CONF="${NEXUS_HOME}/conf/wrapper.conf"
PRIORITY=
PIDDIR="/var/run"
#RUN_AS_USER=nexus
```

Add Nexus as a service on Red Hat, Fedora, and CentOS

This script has the appropriate *chkconfig* directives, so all you need to do to add Nexus as a service is run the following commands:

```
$ cd /etc/init.d
$ chkconfig --add nexus
$ chkconfig --levels 345 nexus on
$ service nexus start
Starting Sonatype Nexus...
$ tail -f /usr/local/nexus/logs/wrapper.log
```

The second command adds Nexus as a service to be started and stopped with the *service* command and managed by *chkconfig* command. *chkconfig* manages the symbolic links in */etc/rc[0-6].d* that control the services that are started and stopped when the operating system restarts or transitions between run-levels. The third command adds Nexus to run-levels 3, 4, and 5. The *service* command starts Nexus, and the last command tails the *wrapper.log* to verify that Nexus has been started successfully. If Nexus has started successfully, you should see a message notifying you that Nexus is listening for HTTP connections on a port.

Add Nexus as a service on Ubuntu

The process for setting up Nexus as a service on Ubuntu differs slightly from the process used on a Red Hat variant. Instead of running *chkconfig*, you should run the following sequence of commands once you've configured the startup script in */etc/init.d*:

```
$ cd /etc/init.d
$ update-rc.d nexus defaults
$ service nexus start
Starting Sonatype Nexus...
$ tail -f /usr/local/nexus/logs/wrapper.log
```

Running Nexus Behind a Proxy

This section is entirely optional. Nexus is based on Jetty, which is a very high-performance servlet container based on Java NIO. From a performance perspective, there is no reason for you not to run Nexus by itself without a proxy. Yet, more often than not, organizations run applications behind a proxy for security concerns and to consolidate multiple disparate applications using tools such as mod_rewrite and mod_proxy. For this reason, we've included some brief instructions for configuration mod_proxy in Apache HTTPd. We assume that you've already installed Apache 2 and that you are using a virtual host for *www.somecompany.com*.

Let's assume that you want to host Nexus behind Apache HTTPd at the URL *http:// www.somecompany.com*. To do this, you'll need to change the context path that Nexus is served from:

1. Edit *plexus.xml* in *${NEXUS_HOME}/conf*. You'll see an element named webappInfos that contains the relevant elements. Change the contextPath element from "/nexus" to "/"

2. Restart Nexus and verify that it is available on *http://localhost:8081/*.

3. Clear the Base URL in Nexus as shown in "Customizing Server Configuration" under Application Server Settings.

At this point, edit the HTTPd configuration file for the *www.somecompany.com* virtual host. Include the following to expose Nexus via mod_proxy at *http://www.somecompany.com*:

```
ProxyRequests Off
ProxyPreserveHost On

<VirtualHost *:80>
  ServerName www.somecompany.com
  ServerAdmin admin@somecompany.com
  ProxyPass / http://localhost:8081/
  ProxyPassReverse / http://localhost:8081/
  ErrorLog logs/somecompany/nexus/error.log
  CustomLog logs/somecompany/nexus/access.log common
</VirtualHost>
```

Alternatively, if you just wanted to continue to serve Nexus at the */nexus* context path, you would not change the contextPath in *${NEXUS_HOME}/conf/plexus.xml*, and you would include the context path in your ProxyPass and ProxyPassReverse directives as follows:

```
ProxyPass /nexus/ http://localhost:8081/nexus/
ProxyPassReverse /nexus/ http://localhost:8081/nexus/
```

Apache configuration is going to vary based on your own application's requirements and the way you intend to expose Nexus to the outside world. If you need more details about Apache HTTPd and mod_proxy, please see *http://httpd.apache.org*.

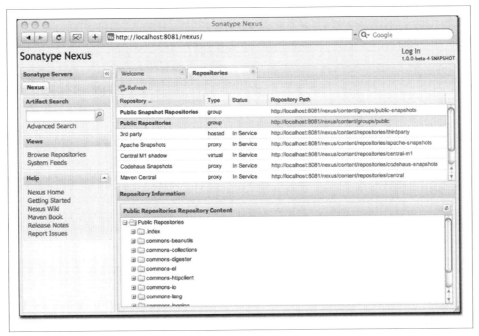

Figure 16-2. Nexus interface for anonymous users

Using Nexus

Nexus provides for anonymous access for users who only need to search repositories, browse repositories, and peruse the system feeds. This anonymous access level changes the navigation menu and some of the options available when you right-click on a repository. This read-only access displays a user interface shown in Figure 16-2.

Browsing Repositories

One of the most straightforward uses of the Nexus is to browse the structure of a Maven repository. If you click on the Browse Repositories menu item in the Views menu, you should see the display shown in Figure 16-3. The top half of the figure shows you a list of groups and repositories along with the type of the repository and the repository status.

When you are browsing a repository, you can right-click on any file and download it directly to your browser. This allows you to retrieve specific artifacts manually or examine a POM file in the browser.

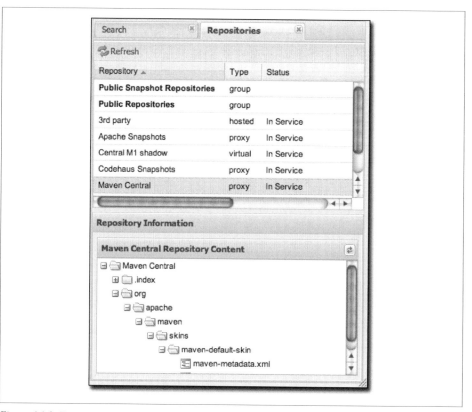

Figure 16-3. Browsing a Nexus repository

When browsing a remote repository, you might notice that the tree doesn't contain all of the artifacts in a repository. When you browse a proxy repository, Nexus is displaying the artifacts that have been cached locally from the remote repository. If you don't see an artifact you expected to see through Nexus, it means only that Nexus has yet to cache the artifact locally. If you have enabled remote repository index downloads, Nexus will return search results that may include artifacts not yet downloaded from the remote repository. Figure 16-3 is just an example, and you may or may not have the `maven-default-skin` artifact available in your installation of Nexus.

Browsing Groups

Nexus contains ordered groups of repositories that allow you to expose a series of repositories through a single URL. More often than not, an organization is going to point Maven at the two default Nexus groups: public repositories and public snapshot repositories. Most end users of Nexus are not going to know which artifacts are being

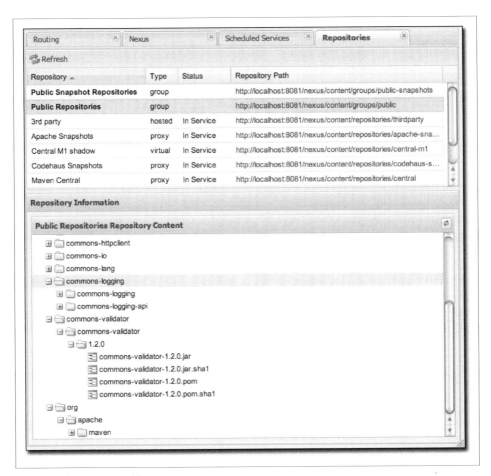

Figure 16-4. Browsing a Nexus group

served from which specific repository, and they are going to want to be able to browse the public repository. To support this use case, Maven allows you to browse the contents of a Nexus group as if it were a single merged repository with a tree structure. Figure 16-4 shows the browsing interface with a Nexus group selected for browsing. The user experience of browsing a Nexus group is no different from that of browsing a Nexus repository.

Searching for Artifacts

In the lefthand navigation area, there is an Artifact Search text field next to a magnifying glass. To search for an artifact by `groupId` or `artifactId`, type in some text and click the magnifying glass. Typing in the search term "maven" and clicking the magnifying glass should yield a search result similar to Figure 16-5.

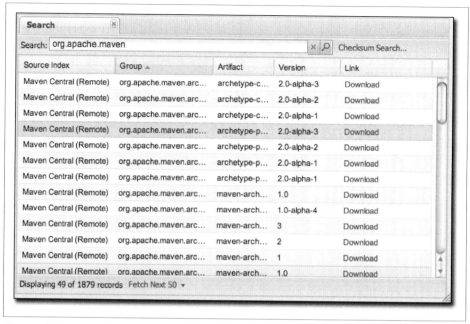

Figure 16-5. Results of an Artifact Search for "maven"

Once you've located the artifact you were looking for, you can click on the Download link to download the artifact. Nexus shows you 50 results at a time and provides links on the bottom of the search result panel for you to navigate through the results. If you would prefer to see a list of all of the matching artifacts, you can select Fetch All from the drop-down at the bottom of the search result panel.

In addition to searching by a `groupId` or an `artifactId`, Nexus has a feature that allows you to search for an artifact by a checksum.

 Let me guess—you installed Nexus, ran to the search box, typed in the name of a group or an artifact, clicked the magnifying glass, and saw absolutely nothing. No results. Why? Nexus won't retrieve the remote repository indexes by default; you need to activate downloading of remote indexes for the three proxy repositories that Nexus ships with. Without these indexes, Nexus has nothing to search. Find instructions for activating index downloads in "Post-Install Checklist."

Browsing System Feeds

Nexus provides feeds that capture system events. You can browse these feeds by clicking on System Feeds under the View menu. This will show the panel in Figure 16-6. You can use this simple interface to browse the most recent reports of artifact

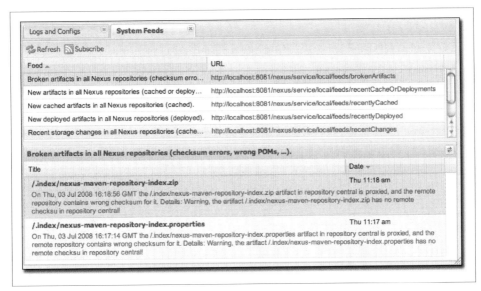

Figure 16-6. Browsing Nexus system feeds

deployments, cached artifacts, broken artifacts, and storage changes that have occurred in Nexus.

These feeds can come in handy if you are working at a large organization with multiple development teams deploying to the same instance of Nexus. In such an arrangement, all developers in an organization can subscribe to the RSS feeds for New Deployed Artifacts as a way to ensure that everyone is aware when a new release has been pushed to Nexus. Exposing these system events as RSS feeds also opens the door to other, more creative uses of this information, such as connecting Nexus to external automated testing systems. To access the RSS feeds for a specific feed, select the feed in the System Feeds view panel and then click on the Subscribe button. Nexus will load the RSS feed in your browser and you can subscribe to the feed in your favorite RSS reader.

Six system feeds are available in the System Feeds view, and each has a URL that resembles the following:

```
http://localhost:8081/nexus/service/local/feeds/recentChanges
```

where `recentChanges` would be replaced with the identifier of the feed you were attempting to read. Available system feeds are shown in Table 16-1.

Table 16-1. Available system feeds

Feed Identifier	Description
brokenArtifacts	Checksum mismatch, missing checksums, invalid POMs
recentCacheOrDeployments	New artifacts in all repositories (cached or deployed)
recentlyCached	New cached artifacts in all repositories

Feed Identifier	Description
recentlyDeployed	New deployed artifacts in all repositories
recentChanges	All caches, deployments, or deletions
systemRepositoryStatusChanges	Automatic or user-initiated status changes (out-of-service and blocked proxies)
systemChanges	Booting Nexus, changing configuration, re-indexing, and rebuilding of attributes

Browsing Log Files and Configuration

"Logs and Config Files" under the Views menu is visible only to administrative users. Clicking on this option brings up the dialog shown in Figure 16-7. From this screen, you can view the following log and configuration files by clicking on the drop-down selection next to the Download button:

nexus.log

Think of this as the general application log for Nexus. Unless you are an administrative user, you might not have much interest in the information in this log. If you are trying to debug an error, or if you have uncovered a bug in Nexus, you'll use this log viewer to diagnose problems with Nexus.

nexus.xml

This XML file contains most of the configuration data for your instance of Nexus. It is stored in *${NEXUS_HOME}/runtime/apps/nexus/conf/nexus.xml*.

Changing Your Password

If you have the appropriate security privilege, you will see an option to change your password in the lefthand side of the browser. To change your password, click on Change Password, supply your current password, and choose a new password. When you click on Change Password at the bottom, as shown in Figure 16-8, your Nexus password will be changed.

Configuring Maven to Use Nexus Repositories

To use Nexus, you will configure Maven to check Nexus instead of the public repositories. To do so, you'll need to edit your mirror settings in your *~/.m2/settings.xml* file. First, we're going to demonstrate how to configure Maven to consult your Nexus installation instead of retrieving artifacts directly from the central Maven repository. After we override the central repository and demonstrate that Nexus is working, we'll circle back to provide a more sensible set of settings that will cover both releases and snapshots.

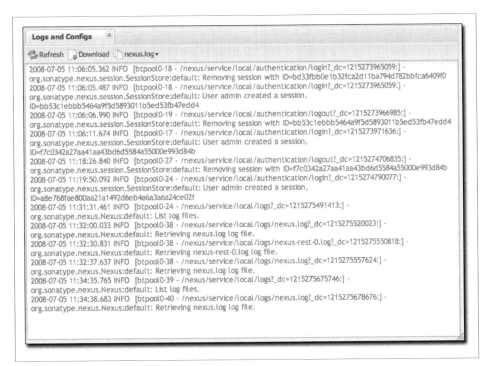

Figure 16-7. Browsing Nexus logs and configuration

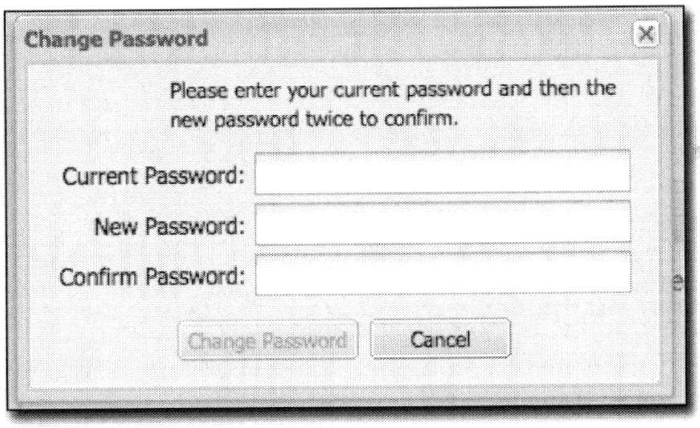

Figure 16-8. Changing your Nexus password

Using the Nexus Central Proxy Repository

To configure Maven to consult Nexus instead of the central Maven repository, add the mirror settings from Example 16-1 to your *~/.m2/settings.xml* file.

Example 16-1. Configuring Maven settings for Nexus (~/.m2/settings.xml)

```xml
<?xml version="1.0"?>
<settings>
  ...
  <mirrors>
    <mirror>
      <id>Nexus</id>
      <name>Nexus Public Mirror</name>
      <url>http://localhost:8081/nexus/content/groups/public</url>
      <mirrorOf>central</mirrorOf>
    </mirror>
  </mirrors>
  ...
</settings>
```

Once you've configured Nexus to be the mirror for all repositories, Maven will now consult the local installation of Nexus instead of going out to the central Maven repository. If Nexus has the artifact requested, the artifact will be served from the local Nexus installation. If Nexus does not have the artifact, Nexus will retrieve it from the remote repository and then add it to the local mirror of that remote repository.

To test how Nexus is working, try deleting a directory from your local Maven repository and then running a Maven build. If you delete *~/.m2/repository/org*, you'll be deleting a large number of dependencies (including Maven plugins). The next time you run Maven, you should see the following:

```
$ mvn clean install
...
Downloading: http://localhost:8081/nexus/content/groups/public/...
3K downloaded
```

This output should convince you that Maven is communicating with your local installation of Nexus instead of going out to the central Maven repository to retrieve an artifact. After you've run a few builds against your local Nexus installation, you can start to browse the contents cached in your local instance of Maven.

Using Nexus for Snapshot Repositories

The Maven settings described earlier in "Using the Nexus Central Proxy Repository" will allow you to use the Nexus public group. This resolves artifacts from four repositories managed by Nexus, but it won't allow you to reference the `public-snapshots` group that includes the Apache and Codehaus snapshots. To configure Maven to use Nexus for both releases and plugins, you will have to configure Maven to reference the Nexus groups by adding the mirror configuration shown in Example 16-2 to your Maven settings in *~/.m2/settings.xml*.

Example 16-2. Configuring Maven to use Nexus for releases and snapshots

```
<settings>
  <mirrors>
    <mirror>
      <!--This is used to direct the public snapshots repo in the
          profile below over to a different nexus group -->
      <id>nexus-public-snapshots</id>
      <mirrorOf>public-snapshots</mirrorOf>
      <url>http://localhost:8081/nexus/content/groups/public-snapshots</url>
    </mirror>
    <mirror>
      <!--This sends everything else to /public -->
      <id>nexus</id>
      <mirrorOf>*</mirrorOf>
      <url>http://localhost:8081/nexus/content/groups/public</url>
    </mirror>
  </mirrors>
  <profiles>
    <profile>
      <id>development</id>
      <repositories>
        <repository>
          <id>central</id>
          <url>http://central</url>
          <releases><enabled>true</enabled></releases>
          <snapshots><enabled>true</enabled></snapshots>
        </repository>
      </repositories>
      <pluginRepositories>
        <pluginRepository>
          <id>central</id>
          <url>http://central</url>
          <releases><enabled>true</enabled></releases>
          <snapshots><enabled>true</enabled></snapshots>
        </pluginRepository>
      </pluginRepositories>
    </profile>
    <profile>
      <!--this profile will allow snapshots to be searched when activated-->
      <id>public-snapshots</id>
      <repositories>
        <repository>
          <id>public-snapshots</id>
          <url>http://public-snapshots</url>
          <releases><enabled>false</enabled></releases>
          <snapshots><enabled>true</enabled></snapshots>
        </repository>
      </repositories>
      <pluginRepositories>
        <pluginRepository>
          <id>public-snapshots</id>
          <url>http://public-snapshots</url>
          <releases><enabled>false</enabled></releases>
          <snapshots><enabled>true</enabled></snapshots>
        </pluginRepository>
```

```
        </pluginRepositories>
      </profile>
    </profiles>
    <activeProfiles>
      <activeProfile>development</activeProfile>
    </activeProfiles>
</settings>
```

In this example, we have defined two profiles: `development` and `public-snapshots`. The
`development` profile is configured to download from the central repository with a bogus
URL of `http://central`. The `public-snapshots` profile is configured to download from
the public-snapshots repository with a bogus URL of `http://public-snapshots`. These
bogus URLs are overridden by two mirror settings in the same *settings.xml* file. The
first mirror is configured to override the public-snapshots repository to the public-
snapshots Nexus group. The second mirror overrides all other repositories to the public
Nexus group. With these settings, all builds will include the public Nexus group. If you
want to include the public-snapshots group, you would have to add the
`public-snapshots` profile by using the -*P* flag on the command line as follows:

```
$ mvn -Ppublic-snapshots clean install
```

Adding Custom Repositories for Missing Dependencies

If you've configured your Maven *settings.xml* to list Nexus as a mirror for all public
repositories and all public-snapshot repositories, you might encounter projects that are
unable to retrieve artifacts from your local Nexus installation. This usually happens
because you are trying to build a project that has defined a custom set of
`repositories` and `snapshotRepositories` in a *pom.xml*. This is definitely going to happen
if you are building open source projects or if you've added custom third-party Maven
repositories to your configuration.

As an example, let's try to build Apache Shindig from source we've checked out of the
Apache Incubator. What is Apache Shindig? It doesn't matter to this example; all we
need is an example project we can easily check out from source control and build. If
you really want to know, Shindig is a project in the Apache Incubator that revolves
around the OpenSocial API from Google. Shindig aims to provide a container that will
allow people to execute OpenSocial gadgets. It provides us with an interesting example
project because it depends on some custom Maven repositories for components that
have yet to be added to the central Maven repository. Using Shindig, we can show you
what happens when Nexus doesn't have your artifacts and what steps you can take to
add repositories to Nexus.

The following example assumes that you have Subversion installed and that you are
running Subversion from the command line. Let's check out Apache Shindig from the
Apache Incubator with Subversion and attempt to build it from source. To do this,
execute the following commands:

```
$ svn co http://svn.apache.org/repos/asf/incubator/shindig/trunk shindig
... Subversion will checkout the trunk of Apache Shindig ...
$ cd shindig
$ mvn install
... Maven will build Shindig ...
Downloading: http://localhost:8081/nexus/content/groups/public/\
    caja/caja/r2178/caja-r2178.jar
...
[INFO] ------------------------------------------------------------------
[ERROR] BUILD ERROR
[INFO] ------------------------------------------------------------------
[INFO] Failed to resolve artifact.

Missing:
----------
1) caja:caja:jar:r2178

  Try downloading the file manually from the project website.


...
----------
3 required artifacts are missing.

for artifact:
  org.apache.shindig:shindig-gadgets:jar:1-SNAPSHOT

from the specified remote repositories:
  nexus (http://localhost:8081/nexus/content/groups/public)
```

The build fails because it is unable to download three artifacts. One of the artifacts
Maven tries to download has a group identifier of caja, an artifact identifier of caja,
and a version of r2178. It is an artifact that is hosted on a custom repository: *http://
google-caja.googlecode.com/svn/maven*. Maven fails to download this artifact because
your *settings.xml* is configured to direct all mirrors to the public and public-snapshots
groups hosted on our Nexus installation. Even though the *pom.xml* for Apache Shindig
defines a repository and points it to *http://google-caja.googlecode.com/svn/maven*,
Nexus won't retrieve an artifact from a repository it doesn't know about, and you've
configured all requests for remote artifacts to pass through Nexus. In fact, there are
two repositories that Nexus doesn't know about in this build: caja and oauth. Caja
(*http://code.google.com/p/google-caja/*) and OAuth (*http://code.google.com/p/oauth/*)
are two libraries that are still in development. Both projects have been "released," and
the versions that Shindig depends on are certainly not snapshot releases, but these
projects have not been published to the central Maven repository. We need to find a
way to let Nexus know about these repositories before we can build this project.

There are two ways to fix this problem. First, you can change your *settings.xml* to
override specific repository identifiers. Instead of listing the Nexus public group as a
mirrorOf all repositories, you can change the mirrorOf element in your *settings.xml* to
"central". If you do this, Maven will then attempt to download the dependencies directly from the oauth and caja repositories at the URLs listed in the previous code

listing. This will work because Maven will only consult Nexus for repositories that match those specified in the `mirrorOf` element in *settings.xml*. If Maven sees the repositories identifier `caja` or `oauth`, and doesn't see a mirror configured in your *settings.xml*, it will attempt to connect to the repository directly.

The second, more interesting option is to add both of these repositories to Nexus and then add these repositories to the public group. You'll see how to do this in the next sections.

Adding a New Repository

To add the caja repository, log into Nexus as an administrator and click on the Repositories link in the lefthand navigation menu in the Configuration section. Clicking on this link should bring up a window that lists all the repositories Nexus knows about. You'll then want to create a new proxy repository. To do this, click on the Add link that is directly above the list of repositories. When you click this button, click the down arrow directly to the right of the word Add; this will show a drop-down that has the options Hosted, Proxy, and Virtual. Since you are creating a proxy repository, click on Proxy. Once you do so, you will see a screen resembling Figure 16-9. Populate the required fields Repository ID and Repository Name with "caja" and "Google Caja". Set the Repository Policy to "Release" and the Remote Storage Location to *http://google -caja.googlecode.com/svn/maven*.

Once you've filled out this screen, click on the Save button. Nexus will then be configured with the caja proxy repository. Do the same thing for the oauth repository. Create a repository with a Repository ID of "oauth", a Release policy, and a Remote Storage Location of *http://oauth.googlecode.com/svn/code/maven*.

Adding a Repository to a Group

Next, you will need to add both of these new repositories to the public Nexus group. To do so, click on the Groups link in the lefthand navigation menu in the Configuration section. When you see the Group management screen, click on the public group. Clicking on the public group should bring up a screen which resembles Figure 16-10.

To add the two new repositories to the public Nexus group, find the repositories in the Available Repositories list on the right, click on the repository you want to add, and drag it to the left to the Ordered Group Repositories list. Once the repository is in that list, you can click and drag the repository within the list to alter the order in which it will be searched for a matching artifact. Once the Google Caja and Google OAuth project repositories are added to the public Nexus group, you should be able to build Apache Shindig and watch Maven download the Caja and OAuth artifacts from the respective repositories.

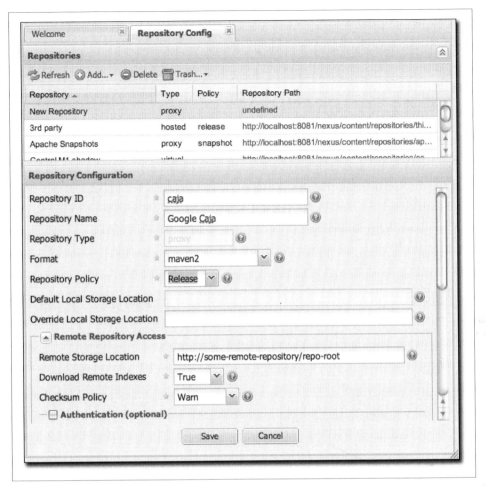

Figure 16-9. Adding a Nexus repository

Nexus makes use of an interesting JavaScript widget library called ExtJS (*http://extjs.com/*). ExtJS provides for a number of interesting UI widgets that allow for rich interaction such as the drag-and-drop UI for adding repositories to a group and reordering the contents of a group.

In the last few sections, you encountered a situation where you needed to add two custom repositories to a build in order to download two libraries (Google Caja and Google OAuth) that are not available in the central Maven repository. If you were not using a repository manager, you would have added these repositories to the `repository` element of your project's POM, or you would have asked all of your developers to modify *~/.m2/settings.xml* to reference two new repositories. Instead, you used the Nexus repository manager to add the two repositories to the public group. If all of

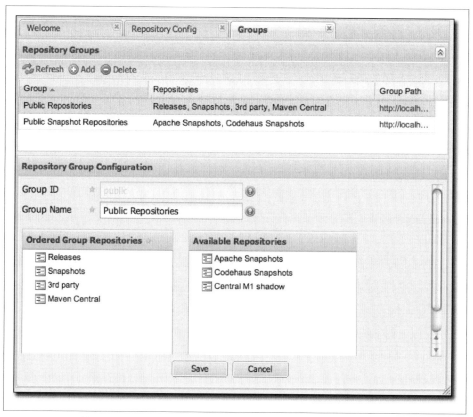

Figure 16-10. Adding new repositories to a Nexus group

the developers are configured to point to the public group in Nexus, you can freely swap in new repositories without asking your developers to change local configurations, and you've gained a certain amount of control over which repositories are made available to your development team.

Configuring Nexus

Many of the configuration screens shown in this section are available only to administrative users. Nexus allows the admin user to customize the list of repositories, create repository groups, customize server settings, and create routes or "rules" that Maven will use to include or exclude artifacts from a repository.

Customizing Server Configuration

In a real installation of Nexus, you'll probably want to customize the administrative password to something other than "admin123", and you might want to override the

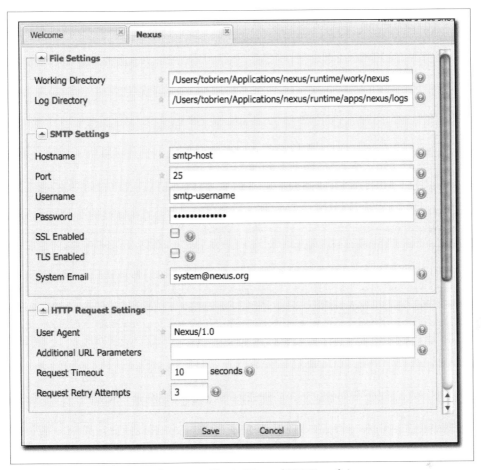

Figure 16-11. Nexus server configuration (file, SMTP, and HTTP config)

default directories that Nexus uses to store repository data. To do this, log in as the administrative user and click on Server under Configuration in the lefthand navigation menu. The server configuration screen is shown in Figures 16-11 and 16-12.

This screen allows you to change:

Working directory

Under the File Settings group, you can customize the working directory. You may wish to customize the working directory if your Nexus installation is going to be mirroring very large repositories and you want to put your working directory on another partition.

Log directory

You can change where Nexus looks for logs. On a Unix machine, a common practice is to place all log files under */var/log*. If you wanted to follow this practice, you could create a */var/log/nexus* directory with the appropriate permissions. Note that

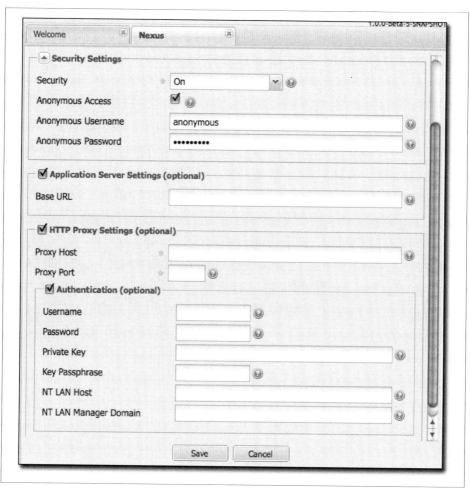

Figure 16-12. Nexus server configuration (security, app server, and HTTP proxy config)

this setting does not change the logging directory used by Nexus; it simply tells Nexus where to look for the logs. To change the location of the logs, you will need to change the *jul-logging.properties* and *log4j.properties* files in the *runtime/apps/nexus/conf* directory of your Nexus installation.

SMTP settings

Nexus sends email to users who need to recover usernames and password. To set this up, you'll need to configure the SMTP server settings in this dialog. This section of the form takes an SMTP host and port as well as other parameters relating to SMTP authentication and encryption. You can also change the *From:* header of an email from Nexus.

User agent

> This is the identifier Nexus uses when it is making an HTTP request. You may want to change this if Nexus needs to use an HTTP proxy, and the proxy will work only if the user agent is set to a specific value.

Additional URL parameters

> This is a list of extra parameters to place on a GET request to a remote repository. You could use this to add identifying information to requests.

Request timeout

> The amount of time Nexus will wait for a request to succeed when interacting with an external, remote repository.

Request retry attempts

> The number of times Nexus will retry a failed HTTP request.

Security settings

> You can choose to enable or disable security, enable or disable anonymous access, and set the username and password for anonymous access. If you choose to enable security, you are telling Nexus to enforce role-based access control to enforce read and write access to repositories.

> The anonymous username and password is used to integrate with other realms that may need a special username for anonymous access. In other words, the username and password here are what we attempt to authorize when someone makes an anonymous request. You would change the anonymous username to "guest" if you wanted to integrate Nexus with Microsoft's Active Directory.

Application server settings

> This section allows you to change the Base URL for your Nexus installation. It is used when generating links in emails and RSS feeds. The Sonatype Nexus repository is available on *http://respository.sonatype.org*, and it makes use of this Base URL field to ensure that links in emails and RSS feeds point to the correct URL.

HTTP proxy settings

> A number of HTTP proxy settings for Nexus installations need to be configured to use an HTTP Proxy. You can specify a host, port, and a number of authentication options that might be required by your proxy server.

Managing Repositories

To manage Nexus repositories, log in as the administrative user and click on Repositories in the Configuration menu in the lefthand navigation menu. Nexus provides for three different kinds of repositories:

Proxy repository

> A proxy repository is a proxy of a remote repository. By default, Nexus ships with the following configured proxy repositories:

Apache Snapshots

This repository contains snapshot releases from the Apache Software Foundation: *http://people.apache.org/repo/m2-snapshot-repository*

Codehaus snapshots

This repository contains snapshot releases from Codehaus: *http://snapshots .repository.codehaus.org/*

Central Maven repository

This is the central Maven repository (for releases): *http://repo1.maven.org/ maven2/*

Hosted repository

A hosted repository is a repository that is hosted by Nexus. Maven ships with the following configured hosted repositories:

3rd party

This hosted repository should be used for third-party dependencies not available in the public Maven repositories. Examples of these dependencies could be commercial, proprietary libraries such as an Oracle JDBC driver that may be referenced by your organization.

Releases

This hosted repository is where your organization will publish internal releases.

Snapshots

This hosted repository is where your organization will publish internal snapshots.

Virtual repository

This serves as an adapter to and from different types of repositories. Currently Nexus supports conversion to and from Maven 1 repositories and Maven 2 repositories.

Figure 16-13 shows the Repository configuration screen for a proxy repository in Nexus. From this screen, you can manage the settings for proxying an external repository. You can configure:

Repository ID

The repository ID is the identifier that will be used in the Nexus URL. For example, the central proxy repository has an ID of "central", which means Maven can access the repository directly at *http://localhost:8081/nexus/content/repositories/central*. The Repository ID must be unique in a given Nexus installation. An ID is required.

Repository name

The display name for a repository. A name is required.

Repository type

The type of repository (proxy, hosted, or virtual). You can't change the type; it is selected when you create a repository.

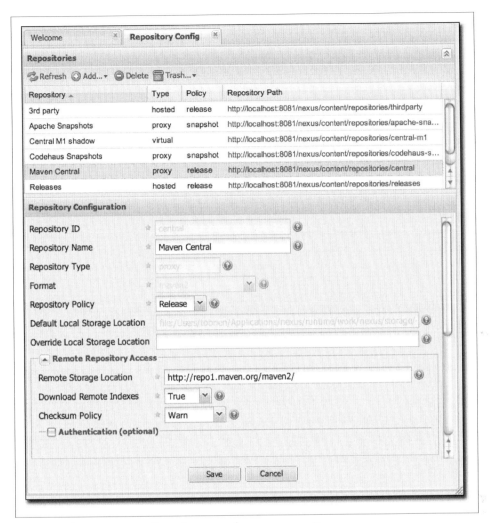

Figure 16-13. Repository configuration screen for a proxy repository

Repository policy

> If a proxy repository has a policy of release, it will only access released versions from the remote repository. If a proxy repository has a policy of snapshot, it will download snapshots from the remote repository.

Default storage location

> Not editable; shown only for reference. This is the default storage location for the local cached contents of the repository.

Override storage location

> You can choose to override the storage location for a specific repository. You would do this if you were concerned about storage and wanted to put the contents of a specific repository (such as central) in a different location.

Remote repository access

> This section tells Nexus where to look for and how to interact with the remote Maven repository being proxied:

Remote storage location

> This is the URL of the remote Maven repository.

Download remote indexes (not shown in figure)

> This field controls the downloading of the remote indexes. Currently, only central has an index at *http://repo1.maven.org/maven2/.index*. If enabled, Nexus will download the index and use that for its searches as well as serve it up to any clients that ask for the index (such as m2eclipse). The default for new proxy repositories is enabled, but all of the default repositories included in Nexus have this option disabled. To change this setting for one of the proxy repositories that ship with Nexus, change the option, save the repository, and then re-index the repository. Once this is done, artifact search will return every artifact available in the central Maven repository. The section "Managing Repositories," earlier in this chapter, details the process for re-indexing a repository.

Checksum policy

> Sets the checksum policy for a remote repository. This option is set to Warn by default. The possible values of this setting are:

Ignore

> Ignore the checksums entirely.

Warn

> Print a warning in the log if a checksum is not correct.

StrictIfExists

> Refuse to cache an artifact if the calculated checksum is inconsistent with a checksum in the repository. Perform this check only if the checksum file is present.

Strict

> Refuse to cache an artifact if the calculated checksum is inconsistent or if there is no checksum for an artifact.

Authentication

> This section allows you to set a username, password, private key, key passphrase, NT LAN host, and NT LAN manager domain for a remote repository.

Access settings

> This section configures access settings for a repository:

Allow deployment

> If set to true, Nexus will allow Maven to deploy artifacts to this repository. This option is visible for hosted repositories.

Allow file browsing

> When set to true, users can browse the contents of the repository with a web browser.

Include in search

> When set to true, this repository is searched when you perform an artifact search in Nexus. If this setting is false, the contents of the repository are excluded from a search.

Expiration settings

> Nexus maintains a local cache of artifacts and metadata. You can configure expiration parameters for a proxy repository. The expiration settings are:

Not found cache TTL

> If Nexus fails to locate an artifact, it will cache this result for a given number of minutes. In other words, if Nexus can't find an artifact in a remote repository, it will not repeatedly attempt to resolve this artifact until the Not Found Cache TTL time has been exceeded. The default for this setting is 1440 minutes (or 24 hours).

Artifact max age

> Tells Nexus when that maximum age of an artifact is before it retrieves a new version from the remote repository. The default for this setting is –1 for a repository with a release policy and 1440 for a repository with snapshot policy.

Metadata max age

> Nexus retrieves metadata from the remote repository. It will retrieve updates to metadata only after the Metadata Max Age has been exceeded. The default value for this setting is 1440 minutes (or 24 hours).

HTTP request settings

> This section lets you change the properties of the HTTP request to the remote repository. You can configure the user agent of the request, add parameters to a request, and set the timeout and retry behavior. This section refers to the HTTP request made from Nexus to the remote Maven repository being proxied.

HTTP proxy settings

> This section lets you configure the HTTP proxy for the request from Nexus to the remote repository. You can configure a proxy host and port plus any authentication settings you need to tell Nexus to use an HTTP proxy for all requests to a remote repository.

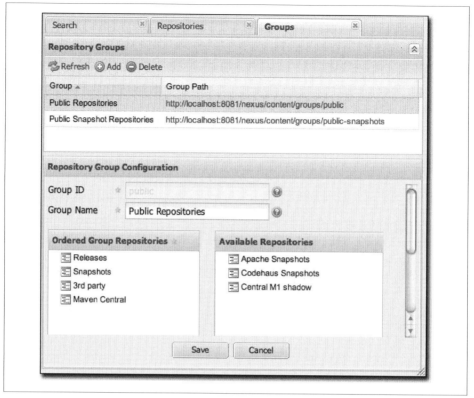

Figure 16-14. Group configuration screen in Nexus

Managing Groups

Groups are a powerful feature of Nexus—they allow you to combine multiple repositories in a single URL. Nexus ships with two groups: public and public-snapshots. The public group combines the three hosted repositories: 3rd party, releases, and snapshots with the central Maven repository. The public-snapshots repository combines the Apache snapshots and Codehaus snapshots repositories. In "Configuring Maven to Use Nexus Repositories," earlier in this chapter, we configured Maven via the *set tings.xml* to look for artifacts in the public group managed by Nexus. Figure 16-14 shows the group configuration screen in Nexus; you can see the contents of the public group.

Note that the order of the repositories listed in Order Group Repositories is important. When Nexus searches for an artifact in a group of repositories, it returns the first match. To reorder a repository in this list, click and the drag the repositories in the Ordered Group Repositories selection list.

The order of repositories in a group can be used to influence the effective metadata that will be retrieved by Maven from a Nexus repository group. We recommend placing release repositories higher in the list than snapshot repositories so that LATEST and RELEASE versions are merged appropriately. We also recommend placing repositories with a higher probability of matching the majority of artifacts higher in this list. If most of your artifacts are going to be retrieved from the central Maven repository, putting the central repository higher in this list than a smaller, more focused repository will be better for performance, as Nexus will not interrogate the smaller remote repository for as many missing artifacts.

Managing Routes

Nexus routes are like filters you can apply to Nexus groups; they allow you to configure Nexus to include or exclude repositories from a particular artifact search when Nexus is trying to locate an artifact in a Nexus group. There are a number of different scenarios in which you might configure a route in Nexus. The most common is when you want to make sure that you are retrieving artifacts in a particular group ID from a particular repository. This is especially useful when you want to make sure that you are trying to retrieve your own organization's artifacts from the hosted release and snapshot repositories. Nexus routes are applicable when you are trying to resolve an artifact from a Nexus group; using routes allows you to modify the repositories Nexus will consult when it tries to resolve an artifact from a group of repositories.

Figure 16-15 shows the route configuration screen. Clicking on a route will bring up a screen that allows you to configure the properties of the route. The configuration options available are:

URL Pattern
This is the pattern that Nexus will use to match a request to Nexus. If the regular expression in this pattern is matched, Nexus will either include or exclude the listed repositories from a particular artifact query. In Figure 16-15, the two patterns are:

.*/(com|org)/somecompany/.*
This pattern would match all of the paths that included either "/com/some-company/" or "/org/somecompany". The expression in the parentheses matches either com or org, and the .* matches one or more characters. You would use a route like this to match your own organization's artifacts and map these requests to the hosted Nexus releases and snapshots repositories.

.*/org/some-oss/.*
This pattern is used in an exclusive route. It matches every path that contains "/org/some-oss/". This particular exclusive route excludes the local hosted releases and snapshots directory for all artifacts that match this path. When Nexus tries to resolve artifacts that match this path, it will exclude the releases and snapshots repositories.

Rule Type
Rule type can be either "inclusive" or "exclusive." An inclusive rule type defines the set of repositories that should be searched for artifacts when the URL pattern

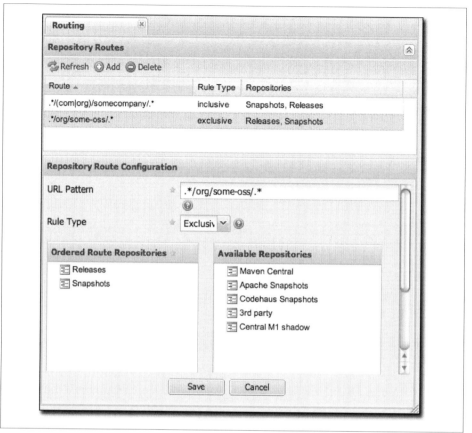

Figure 16-15. Routes configuration screen in Nexus

has been matched. An exclusive rule type defines repositories which should not be searched for a particular artifact.

Ordered Route Repositories

This is an ordered list of repositories which Nexus will search to locate a particular artifact. Nexus searches top to bottom; if it's looking for an artifact, it will return the first match. When Nexus is looking for metadata, all repositories in a group are checked and the results are merged. The merging gives preference to the earlier repositories. This is relevant when a project is looking for a LATEST or a RELEASE version. Within a Nexus group, you should define the release repositories before the snapshot repositories; otherwise, LATEST may incorrectly resolve to a snapshot version.

In Figure 16-15, you can see the two dummy routes that Nexus has as default routes. The first route is an inclusive route; it is provided as an example of a custom route that an organization might use to make sure that internally generated artifacts are resolved from the releases and snapshots repositories. If your organization's group IDs all start with `com.somecompany`, and if you deploy internally generated artifacts to the releases and snapshots repositories, this route will make sure that Nexus doesn't waste time trying to resolve these artifacts from public Maven repositories such as the central Maven repository or the Apache snapshots repository.

The second dummy route is an exclusive route. This route excludes the releases and snapshots repositories when the request path contains "/org/some-oss". This example might make more sense if we replaced "some-oss" with "apache" or "codehaus". If the pattern were "/org/apache", this rule would be telling Nexus to exclude the internal releases and snapshots repositories when it is trying to resolve these dependencies. In other words, don't bother looking for an Apache dependency in your organization's internal repositories.

What if there is a conflict between two routes? Nexus will process inclusive routes before it will process the exclusive routes. Remember that Nexus routes only affect Nexus' resolution of artifacts when it is searching a group. When Nexus starts to resolve an artifact from a Nexus group, it will start with the list of repositories in a group. If there are matching inclusive routes, Nexus will then take the intersection of the repositories in the group and the repositories in the inclusive Nexus route. The order as defined in the Nexus group will not be affected by the Inclusive routes. Nexus will then take the result of applying the inclusive routes and apply the exclusive routes to this new group. The resulting list is then searched for a matching artifact.

One straightforward use of routes is to create one that excludes the central Maven repository from all searches for your own organization's hosted artifacts. If you are deploying your own artifacts to Nexus under a `groupId` of `org.mycompany`, and if you are not deploying these artifacts to a public repository, you can create a rule that tells Nexus not to interrogate central for your own organization's artifacts. This will improve performance because Nexus will not need to communicate with a remote repository when it serves your own organization's artifacts. In addition to the performance benefits, excluding central from searches for your own artifacts will reduce needless queries to the public repositories.

To summarize, there are creative possibilities with routes that the designers of Nexus may not have anticipated, but we advise you to proceed with caution if you start relying on conflicting or overlapping routes. Use routes sparingly, and use course URL patterns. As Nexus evolves, there will be more features that allow for more fine-grained rules to allow you to prohibit requests for specific artifacts and specific versions of artifacts. Remember that routes are applied only to Nexus groups, and that routes are not used when an artifact is requested from a specific repository.

Managing Scheduled Services

Nexus allows you to schedule tasks that will be applied to all repositories or to specific repositories on a configurable schedule. You can create the following kinds of scheduled services:

Remove snapshots from a repository

Often, you will want to remove snapshots from a snapshot repository to preserve storage space. When you create a scheduled service to remove snapshots, you can specify:

- Minimum snapshots to preserve in a repository
- Snapshot retention (in days)
- Whether snapshots should be removed if an artifact has been released

Clear repository caches

Nexus maintains information about a proxied remote repository to avoid unnecessary network traffic. Clear cache simply expires the artifacts so that the next time they are requested, Nexus will recheck the remote. This scheduled job clears all cached information about a remote repository stored in your installation of Nexus and forces Nexus to retrieve artifacts and information from the remote repository.

Evict unused proxied items from repository caches

Use it or lose it. This scheduled service tells Nexus to get rid of all proxied items that haven't been "used" (referenced or retrieved by a client). This can be a good job to run if you are try to conserve storage space. In this service, you can specify the number of days over which Nexus will look for activity before making the decision to evict an artifact. (See the upcoming note about deletion.)

Publish indexes

Just as Maven downloads an index from a remote repository, Nexus can publish an index in the same format. This will make it easier for people using m2eclipse or Nexus to interact with your repositories.

Purge nexus timeline

Nexus maintains a lot of data that relates to the interaction between itself, proxied remote repositories, and clients on Nexus. While this information can be important for purposes of auditing, it can also take up storage space. Using this scheduled service, you can tell Nexus to periodically purge this information. (See the upcoming note about deletion.)

Rebuild repository attributes

This scheduled service tells Nexus to walk every file in a repository and gather information such as checksums and file contents for every file.

Re-index repositories

This service tells Nexus to re-index a repository.

The evict and purge actions do not delete data from the Nexus working directory. They simply move data to be cleared or evicted to a trash directory under the Nexus work directory. If you want to reclaim disk space, you need to clear the trash on the Browse Repositories screen. If something goes wrong with an evict or clear service, you can move the data back to the appropriate storage location from the trash.

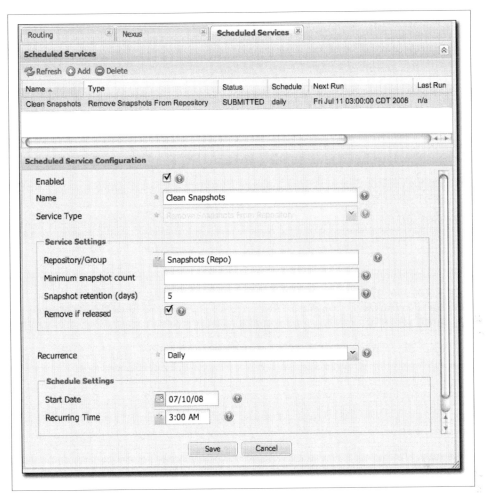

Figure 16-16. Managing Nexus scheduled services

When you create a new service, you can configure it to apply to all repositories, the repositories in a Nexus group, or a specific Nexus repository. A service can be scheduled to run once at a specific date and time, or periodically once every day, week, or month. If none of these options suit your specific needs, you can select a recurrence of "Advanced" that will allow you to supply your own cron expression to specify when the job should execute.

To create a new scheduled service, click on Scheduled Services under the Administration menu, and click on the Add button. This will bring up the screen shown in Figure 16-16.

Managing Security

The latest release of Nexus has role-based access control (RBAC), which gives administrators very fine-grained control over who can read from a repository (or a subset of repositories), who can administer the server, and who can deploy to repositories. The security model in Nexus is also so flexible that it allows you to specify that only certain users or roles can deploy and manage artifacts in a specific repository under a specific groupId or asset class. The default configuration of Nexus ships with three roles and three users with a standard set of permissions that will make sense for most users. As your security requirements evolve, you'll likely need to customize security settings to create protected repositories for multiple departments or development groups. Nexus provides a security model that can adapt to almost anything.

Nexus' RBAC system is designed around the following four security concepts:

Privileges

Privileges are rights to read, update, create, or manage resources and perform operations. Nexus ships with a set of core privileges that cannot be modified, and you can create new privileges to allow for fine-grained targeting of role and user permissions for specific repositories.

Targets

Privileges are usually associated with resources or targets. In the case of Nexus, a target can be a specific repository or a set of repositories grouped in something called a repository target. A target can also be a subset of a repository or a specific asset class within a repository. Using a target you can apply to a specific privilege to apply to a single groupId.

Roles

Collections of privileges can be grouped into roles to make it easier to define collections of privileges common to certain classes of users. For example, deployment users will all have similar sets of permissions. Instead of assigning individual privileges to individual users, you use roles to make it easier to manage users with similar sets of privileges. A role has one or more privilege and/or one or more roles.

Users

Users can be assigned roles and privileges, and model the individuals who will be logging into Nexus and read, deploying, or managing repositories.

Managing privileges

Nexus has two types of privileges: application privileges, which cover actions a user can execute in Nexus, and repository-target privileges, which govern the level of access a user has to a particular repository or repository target. Behind the scenes, a privilege is related to a single REST operation and method such as create, update, delete, or read. See Figure 16-17.

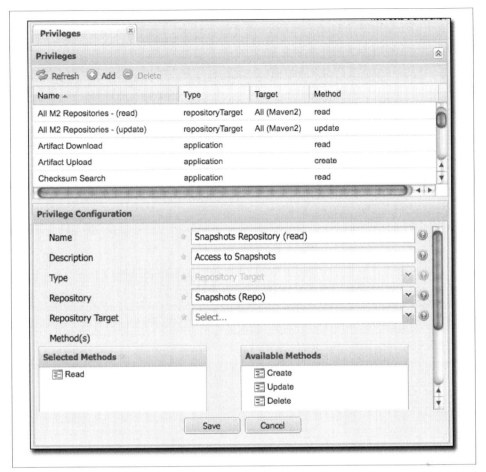

Figure 16-17. Managing security privileges

Repository target privileges can apply to individual repositories or repository targets. All of the permissions that ship with Nexus target repository targets. To create a new repository target privilege that targets a specific repository, click on the Add button and select a repository from the repository drop-down. Application permissions correspond to areas of the application to which a user has a specific level of access (method). The available methods are create, read, update, and delete (CRUD). The list of application permissions are as follows:

- Administrator privilege (ALL)
- Artifact download
- Artifact upload
- Checksum search
- Clear repository cache

- Configuration file
- Login to UI
- Logs
- Nexus remote control
- Read repository metadata
- Read repository status
- Rebuild repository attributes
- Re-index
- Repositories
- Repository groups
- Repository routes
- Repository targets
- Repository templates
- RSS feeds
- Scheduled tasks
- Search repositories
- Server settings
- Server status
- Status
- User change password
- User forgot password
- User forgot user ID
- User privileges
- User reset password
- User roles
- Users
- Wastebasket

Managing repository targets

A target is a set of regular expressions to match on a path (exactly how the route rules work now). This allows you to define, for example, a target called Apache Maven that is `org/apache/maven/.*` You can then add a new privilege that relates to the target and controls the CRUD operations for artifacts matching that path (the privilege can span multiple repositories if you want). You could thus delegate all control of `org.apache.maven` targets to a "Maven" team. In this way, you don't need to create separate repositories for each logical division of your artifacts. See Figure 16-18.

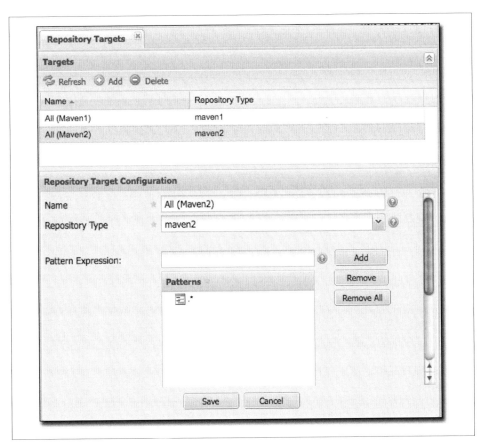

Figure 16-18. Managing repository targets

Managing security roles

Nexus ships with three roles: Nexus administrator role, Nexus anonymous role, and Nexus deployment role. The administrator role grants all privileges, the anonymous role grants read-only privileges, and the deployment role grants read and update permissions for all repositories. See Figure 16-19.

With the repository targets, you have fine-grained control over every action in the system. For example, you could make a target that includes everything except sources (`.*(?!-sources)\.*`) and assign that to one group while giving yet another group access to everything. This means that you can host your public and private artifacts in a single repository without giving up control of your private artifacts.

Managing users

Nexus ships with three users: admin, anonymous, and deployment. The admin user has all privileges, the anonymous user has read-only privileges, and the deployment

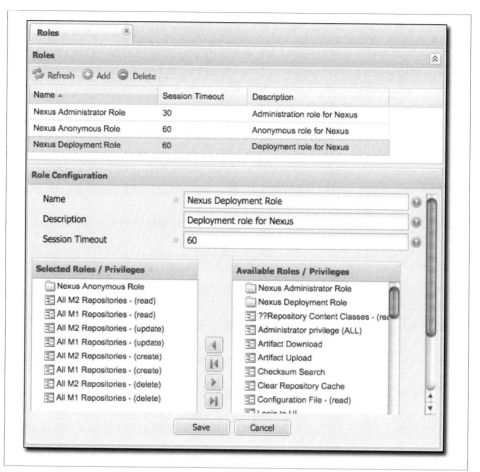

Figure 16-19. Managing security roles

user can both read and deploy to repositories. If you need to create users with a more focused set of permissions, you can click on Users under Security in the lefthand navigation menu. Once you see the list of users, you can click on a user to edit that specific user ID, name, email, or status. You can also assign or revoke specific roles or permissions for a particular user. See Figure 16-20.

Network Configuration

By default, Nexus listens on port 8081. You can change this port by changing the value in *${NEXUS_HOME}/conf/plexus.properties*; this file is shown in Example 16-3. To change the port, stop Nexus, change the value of `applicationPort` in this file, and then

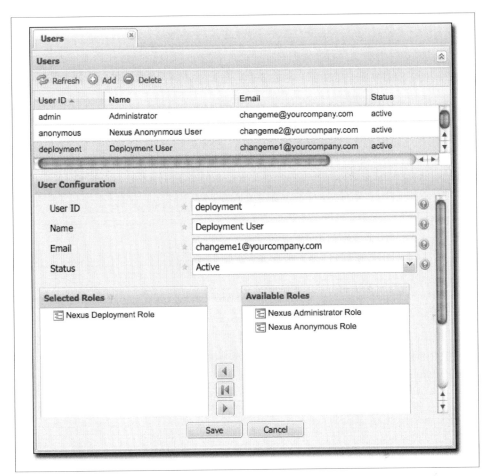

Figure 16-20. Managing users

restart Nexus. Once you do this, you should see a log statement in *${NEXUS_HOME}/logs/wrapper.log* telling you that Nexus is listening on the altered port.

Example 16-3. Contents of ${NEXUS_HOME}/conf/plexus.properties

```
applicationPort=8081
runtime=${basedir}/runtime
apps=${runtime}/apps
work=${runtime}/work
webapp=${runtime}/apps/nexus/webapp
nexus.configuration=${runtime}/apps/nexus/conf/nexus.xml
```

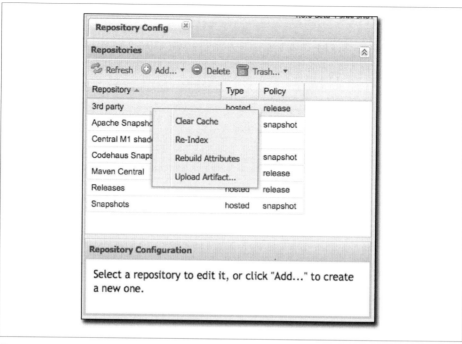

Figure 16-21. Repository options (right-click on a repository)

Maintaining Repositories

Once you've set up a series of repositories and grouped those repositories into Nexus groups, users will be able to see a list of repositories in the Nexus UI by clicking on the Repositories link in the lefthand navigation menu in the Maintenance section. This will bring up a list of repositories. This list will show you the status of the remote repository. To test this, edit one of your repositories to have a garbage remote storage location URL; you will then notice that the status of this repository will change on the Manage Repositories screen. Clicking on a repository will bring up a tree view that provides users with a way to navigate through the contents of a repository.

Right-clicking on a repository will bring up a series of actions that can be applied to a repository. The available actions for each repository are as follows (some are shown in Figure 16-21):

Clear Cache
> Clears the cache for the repository. This causes Nexus to check the remote repository for new updates or snapshots. It also resets the Not Found Cache.

Re-Index
> Causes Maven to re-index a repository. Nexus will recreate the index it uses to search for a request artifact. If the repository has been configured to download the remote index, this option will cause Nexus to download the remote index from

the remote repository. Note that if you have enabled the remote index download, the remote index may take some time to download from the remote repository. You will know that the remote repository has been updated for a large remote repository, such as the central Maven repository, when the artifact search results start showing artifacts that haven't been cached or requested.

Rebuild Attributes
Rebuilds the attributes for a given repository. This will cause Nexus to go through the entire repository and process every file, updating attributes such as checksums.

Upload Artifact...
(Only visible for hosted repositories.) You can use this option to upload an artifact to a hosted repository.

Put Out of Service
In the Browse Repositories view, you have the option of putting a repository "out of service." When a hosted repository is put out of service, no artifacts can be served from that repository.

Block Proxy
In the Browse Repositories view, you have the option of blocking a proxy for a proxy repository. Blocking a proxy repository has the side effect of cutting communication between Nexus and the remote repository. Although this is a rather blunt instrument for controlling the contents of a repository, you can use this feature to make certain that no new artifacts are downloaded from a remote repository.

Uploading Artifacts to Hosted Repositories

If you are using Nexus hosted repositories, the best way to deploy an artifact is to use the procedure details covered in the upcoming section "Deploying Artifacts to Nexus." But there may be times when you just need to upload an artifact to Nexus manually for a number of reasons. One frequent reason for uploading an artifact manually is that a vendor or proprietary software vendor has left you with a single JAR file for something like a commercial database and they haven't bothered to publish this driver's JAR file in a public Maven repository. In this case, you'll want to upload a JAR artifact and supply the Maven coordinates so that Nexus can serve it from your third-party hosted repository just like any other artifact.

To upload an artifact, select the repository in either the Browse Repositories list or the list that is displayed when clicking on Repositories in the Administration menu. Right-click on a hosted repository, and select Upload Artifact.... You should then see the Artifact Upload form shown in Figure 16-22.

When you upload an artifact, you must choose a file to upload, and then you must either supply a POM file or populate the Maven coordinates by selecting Attributes. If you upload a JAR file such as *test.jar*, and then you supply a group ID, artifact ID, version, and packaging of `org.test`, `test`, `1.0`, and `jar`, Nexus will upload the file to

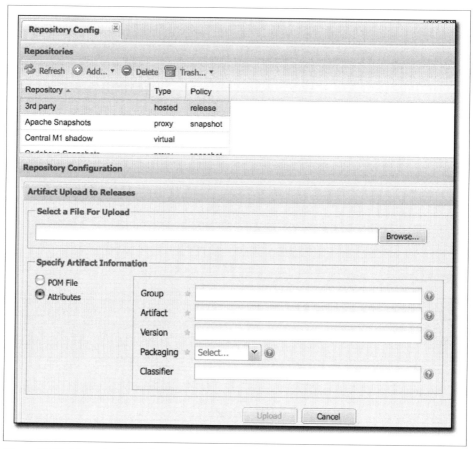

Figure 16-22. Manual upload of an artifact to a hosted repository

the appropriate directory and create a POM and a few checksums for the artifact. If you choose to upload a *pom.xml*, Nexus will use the group ID, artifact ID, version, and packaging of the upload POM to find the appropriate location for your manually uploaded artifact.

Deploying Artifacts to Nexus

Different organizations have different reasons for deploying artifacts to an internal repository. In large organizations with hundreds (or thousands) of developers, an internal Maven repository can be an efficient way for different departments to share releases and development snapshots with one another. Most organizations that use Maven will eventually want to start deploying both releases and artifacts to a shared, internal repository. Using Nexus, it is easy to deploy artifacts to Nexus hosted repositories.

To deploy artifacts to Nexus, supply the repository URL in `distributionManagement` and run *mvn deploy*. Maven will push project POMs and artifacts to your Nexus installation with a simple HTTP PUT. No extra wagon extension is needed in your project's POM. Nexus works with Maven's built-in `wagon-http-lightweight`.

Configuring Deployment Security

Nexus ships with a deployment user that has a default password of `deployment123`. For this chapter, we'll assume that you are using the default deployment password. To configure Maven to deploy to Nexus, add the following server elements to your *~/.m2/ settings.xml* file:

```
<settings>
  ...
  <servers>
    <server>
      <id>releases</id>
      <username>deployment</username>
      <password>deployment123</password>
    </server>
    <server>
      <id>snapshots</id>
      <username>deployment</username>
      <password>deployment123</password>
    </server>
    <server>
      <id>thirdparty</id>
      <username>deployment</username>
      <password>deployment123</password>
    </server>
  </servers>
  ...
</settings>
```

You supply security credentials in your own Maven settings file in the form of a server name, a username, and a password. When you attempt to deploy to a server with an identifier of `releases` or `snapshots`, Maven will consult your *settings.xml* to find these credentials.

Deploying Releases

To deploy a release artifact to Nexus, you need to configure a `repository` in the `distributionManagement` section of your project's POM. Example 16-4 shows an example of a release deployment repository that is configured to point to the releases repository at *http://localhost:8081/nexus/content/repositories/releases*. This is one of the default hosted repositories that comes configured in Nexus.

Example 16-4. Configuring release repository for deployment

```
<project>
  ...
  <distributionManagement>
    ...
    <repository>
      <id>releases</id>
      <name>Internal Releases</name>
      <url>http://localhost:8081/nexus/content/repositories/releases</url>
    </repository>
    ...
  </distributionManagement>
  ...
</project>
```

You would replace localhost:8081 with the host and port of your Nexus installation. Once your project has this configuration, you can deploy an artifact by executing *mvn deploy*:

```
$ mvn deploy
[INFO] Scanning for projects...
[INFO] Reactor build order:
[INFO]   Sample Project
[INFO] ------------------------------------------------------------
[INFO] Building Sample Project
[INFO]   task-segment: [deploy]
[INFO] ------------------------------------------------------------
[INFO] [site:attach-descriptor]
[INFO] [install:install]
[INFO] Installing ~/svnw/sample/pom.xml to ~/.m2/repository/sample/sample\
                                       /1.0/sample-1.0.pom
[INFO] [deploy:deploy]
altDeploymentRepository = null
[INFO] Retrieving previous build number from snapshots
Uploading: http://localhost:8081/nexus/content/repositories/releases/\
          sample/sample/1.0/sample-1.0.pom
24K uploaded
```

Note that Nexus can support multiple hosted repositories; you don't need to stick with the default releases and snapshots repositories. You can create different hosted repositories for different departments and then combine multiple repositories into a single Nexus group.

Deploying Snapshots

To deploy a snapshot artifact to Nexus, you need to configure a snapshotRepository in the distributionManagement section of your project's POM. Example 16-5 shows an example of a snapshot deployment repository that is configured to point to the snapshots repository at *http://localhost:8081/nexus/content/repositories/snapshots*.

Example 16-5. Configuring snapshot repository for deployment

```
<project>
  ...
  <distributionManagement>
    ...
    <snapshotRepository>
      <id>snapshots</id>
      <name>Internal Snapshots</name>
      <url>http://localhost:8081/nexus/content/repositories/snapshots</url>
    </snapshotRepository>
    ...
  </distributionManagement>
  ...
</project>
```

You would replace localhost:8081 with the host and port of your Nexus installation. Once your project has this configuration, you can deploy an artifact by executing *mvn deploy*. Maven will deploy to the snapshotRepository if your project has a snapshot version (i.e., 1.0-SNAPSHOT):

```
$ mvn deploy
[INFO] Scanning for projects...
[INFO] Reactor build order:
[INFO]    Sample Project
[INFO] ------------------------------------------------------------------
[INFO] Building Sample Project
[INFO]    task-segment: [deploy]
[INFO] ------------------------------------------------------------------
[INFO] [site:attach-descriptor]
[INFO] [install:install]
[INFO] Installing ~/svnw/sample/pom.xml to ~/.m2/repository/sample/sample\
        /1.0-SNAPSHOT/sample-1.0-20080402.125302.pom
[INFO] [deploy:deploy]
altDeploymentRepository = null
[INFO] Retrieving previous build number from snapshots
Uploading: http://localhost:8081/nexus/content/repositories/releases/\
        sample/sample/1.0-SNAPSHOT/sample-1.0-20080402.125302.pom
24K uploaded
```

Deploying Third-Party Artifacts

Your Maven projects may start depending on artifacts that are not available from the central Maven repository or any other public Maven repository. This can happen for a number of reasons; perhaps the artifact in question is a JDBC driver for a proprietary database such as Oracle, or perhaps you are depending on another JAR that is neither open source nor freely available. In these cases, you will have to get your hands on the artifact in question and publish it to your own repository. Nexus provides a hosted "third-party" repository for just this purpose.

To illustrate the process of publishing an artifact to the third-party repository, we will use a real artifact: the Oracle JDBC drivers. Oracle publishes a widely used commercial database product that has a JDBC driver that is not present in the central Maven repository. Although the central Maven repository maintains some POM information for the Oracle JDBC driver at *http://repo1.maven.org/maven2/com/oracle/ojdbc14/10.2.0.3.0/*, there is only a POM that references the Oracle site. Let's say you add the dependency shown in Example 16-6 to your project.

Example 16-6. Oracle JDBC JAR dependency

```
<project>
  ...
  <dependencies>
    ...
    <dependency>
      <groupId>com.oracle</groupId>
      <artifactId>ojdbc14</artifactId>
      <version>10.2.0.3.0</version>
    </dependency>
    ...
  </dependencies>
  ...
</project>
```

Running a Maven build with this dependency will produce the following output:

```
$ mvn install
...
[INFO] ------------------------------------------------------------------
[ERROR] BUILD ERROR
[INFO] ------------------------------------------------------------------
[INFO] Failed to resolve artifact.

Missing:
----------
1) com.oracle:ojdbc14:jar:10.2.0.3.0

  Try downloading the file manually from:
      http://www.oracle.com/technology/software/tech/java/sqlj_jdbc/index.html

  Then, install it using the command:
      mvn install:install-file -DgroupId=com.oracle -DartifactId=ojdbc14 \
          -Dversion=10.2.0.3.0 -Dpackaging=jar -Dfile=/path/to/file

  Alternatively, if you host your own repository you can deploy the file there:
      mvn deploy:deploy-file -DgroupId=com.oracle -DartifactId=ojdbc14 \
              -Dversion=10.2.0.3.0 -Dpackaging=jar -Dfile=/path/to/file \
              -Durl=[url] -DrepositoryId=[id]

  Path to dependency:
      1) sample:sample:jar:1.0-SNAPSHOT
      2) com.oracle:ojdbc14:jar:10.2.0.3.0

----------
1 required artifact is missing.
```

The Maven build fails because it can't find the Oracle JDBC driver in the Maven repository. To remedy this situation, you need to publish the Oracle JDBC artifact to your Nexus third-party repository. To do so, download the Oracle JDBC driver from *http: //www.oracle.com/technology/software/tech/java/sqlj_jdbc/index.html* and save it to the file *ojdbc.jar*.

Once you have downloaded the file for this third-party asset, we recommend that you use the UI-based upload that was shown in the section "Uploading Artifacts to Hosted Repositories," earlier in this chapter. Uploading via the UI is easier and less error-prone than calling the `deploy:deploy-file` goal from the command line. If you prefer to upload this third-party from the command line, execute the following command:

```
$ mvn deploy:deploy-file -DgroupId=com.oracle -DartifactId=ojdbc14 \
> -Dversion=10.2.0.3.0 -Dpackaging=jar -Dfile=ojdbc.jar \
> -Durl=http://localhost:8081/nexus/content/repositories/thirdparty \
> -DrepositoryId=thirdparty
...
[INFO] [deploy:deploy-file]
Uploading: http://localhost:8081/nexus/content/repositories/thirdparty/\
               com/oracle/ojdbc14/10.2.0.3.0/ojdbc14-10.2.0.3.0.jar
330K uploaded
[INFO] Retrieving previous metadata from thirdparty
[INFO] Uploading repository metadata for: 'artifact com.oracle:ojdbc14'
[INFO] Retrieving previous metadata from thirdparty
[INFO] Uploading project information for ojdbc14 10.2.0.3.0
```

After you run *mvn deploy:deploy-file*, this artifact will be published to the third-party repository in Nexus.

## CHAPTER 17

Writing Plugins

Introduction

Although this chapter covers an advanced topic, don't let the idea of writing a Maven plugin intimidate you. For all of the theory and complexity of this tool, the fundamental concepts are easy to understand and the mechanics of writing a plugin are straightforward. After you read this chapter, you will have a better grasp of what is involved in creating a Maven plugin.

Programming Maven

Most of this book has dealt with using Maven, though you haven't yet seen many code examples dealing with Maven customization. In fact, you haven't seen any. This is by design, since 99 out of 100 Maven users will never need to write a custom plugin to customize Maven. There is an abundance of configurable plugins, and unless your project has particularly unique requirements, you will have to work to find a reason to write a new plugin. And a very small percentage of people who end up writing custom plugins will ever need to crack open the source code for Maven and customize a core Maven component. If you really needed to customize the behavior of Maven, you would then write a plugin. Modifying the core Maven code is as far out of scope for most developers as modifying the TCP/IP stack on an operating system; it is that abstract for most Maven users.

On the other hand, if you *are* going to start writing a custom plugin, you will have to learn a bit about the internals of Maven: How does it manage software components? What does a plugin do? How can I customize the lifecycle? This section answers some of those questions and introduces a few concepts at the core of Maven's design. Learning how to write a custom Maven plugin is the gateway to customizing Maven itself. If you were wondering how to begin understanding the code behind Maven, you've found the proper starting place.

What Is Inversion of Control?

At the heart of Maven is an Inversion of Control (IoC) container called Plexus. What does it do? It is a system for managing and relating components. Although Martin Fowler wrote a canonical essay about IoC, the concept and term have been so heavily overloaded in the past few years that it is tough to find a good definition of the concept that isn't a self-reference (or just a lazy reference to the aforementioned essay). Instead of resorting to a Wikipedia quote, we'll summarize Inversion of Control and Dependency Injection (DI) with an analogy.

Suppose you have a series of components that need to be wired together. When you think about components, think stereo components, not software components. Imagine several stereo components hooked up to a PlayStation 3 and a TiVo that have to interface with an Apple TV box as well as a 50" flat panel LCD TV. You bring everything home from the electronics store, and you purchase a series of cables that you will use to connect it all. You unpack all of these components, put them in their right places, and then get to the job of hooking up 50,000 coaxial cables and stereo jacks to 50,000 digital inputs and network cables. Step back from your home entertainment center and turn on the TV; you've just performed Dependency Injection, and you've just been using an IoC container.

So, what does that have to do with anything? Your PlayStation 3 and a Java bean both provide an interface. The PlayStation 3 has two inputs—power and network—and one output to the TV. Your Java bean has three properties: `power`, `network`, and `tvOutput`. When you open the box of your PlayStation 3, it doesn't provide you with detailed pictures and instructions for how to connect it to every different kind of TV that might be in every different kind of house, and when you look at your Java bean, it just provides a set of properties, not an explicit recipe for creating and managing an entire system of components. In an IoC container such as Plexus, you are responsible for declaring the relationships between a set of components that simply provide an interface of inputs and outputs. You don't instantiate objects; Plexus does. Your application's code isn't responsible for managing the state of components; Plexus is. Although it sounds cheesy, when you start up Maven, it starts Plexus and manages a system of related components just like your stereo system does.

What are the advantages of using an IoC container? Well, what is the advantage of buying discrete stereo components? If one component breaks, you can drop in a replacement for your PlayStation 3 without having to spend $20,000 on the entire system. If you are unhappy with your TV, you can swap it out without affecting your CD player. Most important to you, your stereo components cost less and are more capable and reliable because manufacturers can build to a set of known inputs and outputs and can focus on building individual components. IoC containers and DI encourage disaggregation and the emergence of standards. The software industry likes to imagine itself as the font of all new ideas, but DI and IoC are really just new terms for the concepts of disaggregation and interchangeable machinery. If you really want to know about DI and IoC, learn about the Model T, the cotton gin, and the emergence of a railroad standard in the late 19th century.

Introduction to Plexus

The most important feature of an IoC container implemented in Java is the mechanism of Dependency Injection. The basic idea of IoC is that the control of creating and managing objects is removed from the code itself and placed into the power of an IoC framework. Using DI in an application that has been programmed to interfaces, you can create components that are not bound to specific implementations of these interfaces. Instead, you program to interfaces and then configure Plexus to connect the appropriate implementation to the appropriate component. While your code deals with interfaces, you can capture the dependencies between classes and components in an XML file that defines components, implementation classes, and the relationships between your components. In other words, you can write isolated components, and then you can wire them together using an XML file that defines how the components are wired together. In the case of Plexus, system components are defined with an XML document that is found in *META-INF/plexus/components.xml*.

In a Java IoC container, several methods exist for injecting dependencies values into a component object: constructor, setter, or field injections. Although Plexus is capable of all three Dependency Injection techniques, Maven uses only two types—field and setter injection:

Constructor Injection
> Constructor Injection is populating an object's values through its constructor when an instance of the object is created. For example, if you had an object of type `Person` that had the constructor `Person(String name, Job job)`, you could pass in values for both `name` and `job` via this constructor.

Setter Injection
> Setter Injection is using the setter method of a property on a Java bean to populate object dependencies. For example, if you were working with a `Person` object with the properties `name` and `job`, an IoC container that uses Setter Injection would create an instance of `Person` using a no-arg constructor. Once it had an instance of `Person`, it would proceed to call the `setName()` and `setJob()` methods.

Field Injection
> Both Constructor and Setter Injection rely on a call to a public method. Using Field Injection, an IoC container populates a component's dependencies by setting an object's fields directly. For example, if you were working with a `Person` object that had two fields `name` and `job`, your IoC container would populate these dependencies by setting these fields directly (i.e., `person.name = "Thomas"; person.job = job;`).

Why Plexus?

Spring happens to be the most popular IoC container at the moment, and there's a good argument to be made that it has affected the Java "ecosystem" for the better, forcing companies such as Sun Microsystems to yield more control to the open source community and helping open up standards by providing a pluggable, component-oriented "bus." But Spring isn't the only IoC container in open source. There are many IoC containers (such as PicoContainer; see *http://www.picocontainer.org/*).

Years and years ago, when Maven was created, Spring wasn't a mature option. The initial team of committers on Maven were more familiar with Plexus because they had invented it, so they decided to use it as an IoC container. Although it might not be as popular as the Spring Framework, it is no less capable. And the fact that it was created by the same person who created Maven makes it a perfect fit. After reading this chapter, you will have an idea of how Plexus works. If you already use an IoC container, you'll notice similarities and differences between Plexus and the container you currently use.

> Just because Maven is based on Plexus doesn't mean that the Maven community is "anti-Spring" (we've included a whole chapter with a Spring example in this book; portions of the Spring project are moving to Maven as a build platform). We get the question "Why didn't you use Spring?" often enough that it makes sense for us to address it here. We know—Spring is a rock star, we don't deny it, but it is on our continual to-do list to introduce people to (and document) Plexus. Choice in the software industry is always a good thing.

What Is a Plugin?

A Maven plugin is a Maven artifact that contains a Plugin descriptor and one or more Mojos. A Mojo can be thought of as a goal in Maven, and every goal corresponds to a Mojo. The `compiler:compile` goal corresponds to the `CompilerMojo` class in the Maven Compiler plugin, and the `jar:jar` goal corresponds to the `JarMojo` class in the Maven Jar plugin. When you write your own plugin, you are simply grouping together a set of related Mojos (or goals) in a single plugin artifact.

> Mojo? What is a Mojo? The word *mojo* is defined as "a magic charm or spell," "an amulet, often in a small flannel bag containing one or more magic items," and "personal magnetism; charm."[*] Maven uses the term *Mojo* because it is a play on the word Pojo (Plain-Old Java Object).

A Mojo is much more than just a goal in Maven; it is a component managed by Plexus that can include references to other Plexus components.

---

[*] *The American Heritage Dictionary of the English Language*

Plugin Descriptor

A Maven plugin contains a road map for Maven that tells Maven about the various Mojos and plugin configurations. This plugin descriptor is present in the plugin JAR file in *META-INF/maven/plugin.xml*. When Maven loads a plugin, it reads this XML file, and instantiates and configures plugin objects to make the Mojos contained in a plugin available to Maven.

When you are writing custom Maven plugins, you will almost never need to think about writing a plugin descriptor. In Chapter 10, the lifecycle goals bound to the `maven-plu gin` packaging type show that the `plugin:descriptor` goal is bound to the `generate-resources` phase. This goal generates a plugin descriptor off the annotations present in a plugin's source code. Later in this chapter, you will see how Mojos are annotated, and you will also see how the values in these annotations end up in the *META-INF/maven/plugin.xml* file.

Example 17-1 shows a plugin descriptor for the Maven Zip plugin. This plugin is a contrived plugin that simply zips up the output directory and produces an archive. Normally, you wouldn't need to write a custom plugin to create an archive from Maven; you could simply use the Maven Assembly plugin that is capable of producing a distribution archive in multiple formats. Read through the plugin descriptor in this example to get an idea of the content it contains.

Example 17-1. Plugin descriptor

```
<plugin>
  <description></description>
  <groupId>com.training.plugins</groupId>
  <artifactId>maven-zip-plugin</artifactId>
  <version>1-SNAPSHOT</version>
  <goalPrefix>zip</goalPrefix>
  <isolatedRealm>false</isolatedRealm>
  <inheritedByDefault>true</inheritedByDefault>
  <mojos>
    <mojo>
      <goal>zip</goal>
      <description>Zips up the output directory.</description>
      <requiresDirectInvocation>false</requiresDirectInvocation>
      <requiresProject>true</requiresProject>
      <requiresReports>false</requiresReports>
      <aggregator>false</aggregator>
      <requiresOnline>false</requiresOnline>
      <inhcritedByDefault>true</inheritedByDefault>
      <phase>package</phase>
      <implementation>com.training.plugins.ZipMojo</implementation>
      <language>java</language>
      <instantiationStrategy>per-lookup</instantiationStrategy>
      <executionStrategy>once-per-session</executionStrategy>
      <parameters>
        <parameter>
          <name>baseDirectory</name>
```

```
        <type>java.io.File</type>
        <required>false</required>
        <editable>true</editable>
        <description>Base directory of the project.</description>
      </parameter>
      <parameter>
        <name>buildDirectory</name>
        <type>java.io.File</type>
        <required>false</required>
        <editable>true</editable>
        <description>Directory containing the build files.</description>
      </parameter>
    </parameters>
    <configuration>
      <buildDirectory implementation="java.io.File">
          ${project.build.directory}</buildDirectory>
      <baseDirectory implementation="java.io.File">
          ${basedir}</baseDirectory>
    </configuration>
    <requirements>
      <requirement>
        <role>org.codehaus.plexus.archiver.Archiver</role>
        <role-hint>zip</role-hint>
        <field-name>zipArchiver</field-name>
      </requirement>
    </requirements>
  </mojo>
</mojos>
<dependencies>
  <groupId>org.apache.commons</groupId>
  <artifactId>commons-io</artifactId>
  <version>1.3.2</version>
</dependencies>
</plugin>
```

A plugin descriptor has three parts: the top-level configuration of the plugin that contains elements such as groupId and artifactId, the declaration of Mojos, and the declaration of dependencies. Let's examine each of these sections in more detail.

Top-Level Plugin Descriptor Elements

The top-level configuration values in the plugin element are:

description

> This element contains a short description of the plugin. In the case of the Zip plugin, this description is empty.

groupId, artifactId, version

> Just like everything else in Maven, a plugin needs to have a unique coordinate. The groupId, artifactId, and version are used to locate the plugin artifact in a Maven repository.

goalPrefix

This element controls the prefix used to reference goals in a particular plugin. If you were to look at the Compiler plugin's descriptor, you would see that goalPrefix has a value of compile, and if you look at the descriptor for the Jar plugin, it would have a goalPrefix of jar. It is important that you choose a distinct goal prefix for your custom plugin.

isolatedRealm (*deprecated*)

This is a legacy property that is no longer used by Maven. It is still present in the system to provide for backward compatibility with older plugins. Earlier versions of Maven provided a mechanism to load a plugin's dependencies in an isolated ClassLoader. Maven makes extensive use of a project called ClassWorlds (*http:// classworlds.codehaus.org/*) from the Codehaus community to create hierarchies of ClassLoader objects that are modeled by a ClassRealm object. Feel free to ignore this property and always set it to false.

inheritedByDefault

If inheritedByDefault is set to true, any Mojo in this plugin that is configured in a parent project will be configured in a child project. If you configure a Mojo to execute during a specific phase in a parent project, and the plugin has inheritedByDefault set to true, this execution will be inherited by the child project. If inheritedByDefault is not set to true, a goal execution defined in a parent project will not be inherited by a child project.

Mojo Configuration

Next is the declaration of each Mojo. The plugin element contains an element named mojos that contains a mojo element for each Mojo present in the plugin. Each mojo element contains the following configuration elements:

goal

This is the name of the goal. If you were running the compiler:compile goal, then compiler would be the plugin's goalPrefix and compile would be the name of the goal.

description

This contains a short description of the goal to display to the users when they use the Help plugin to generate plugin documentation.

requiresDirectInvocation

If you set this to true, the goal can be executed only if it is explicitly executed from the command line by the user. If someone tries to bind this goal to a lifecycle phase in a POM, Maven will print an error message. The default for this element is false.

requiresProject

This specifies that a given goal cannot be executed outside of a project. The goal requires a project with a POM. The default value for this requiresProject is true.

requiresReports

> If you were creating a plugin that relies on the presence of reports, you would need to set `requiresReports` to `true`. For example, if you were writing a plugin to aggregate information from a number of reports, you would set `requiresReports` to `true`. The default for this element is `false`.

aggregator

> A Mojo descriptor with `aggregator` set to `true` is supposed to run only once during the execution of Maven. It was created to give plugin developers the ability to summarize the output of a series of builds; for example, to create a plugin that summarizes a report across all projects included in a build. A goal with `aggregator` set to `true` should be run against only the top-level project in a Maven build. The default value of `aggregator` is `false`. `aggregator` is slated for deprecation in a future release of Maven.

requiresOnline

> This specifies that a given goal cannot be executed if Maven is running in offline mode (e.g., the -o command-line option). If a goal depends on a network resource, you would specify a value of `true` for this element and Maven would print an error if the goal were executed in offline mode. The default for `requiresOnline` is `false`.

inheritedByDefault

> If `inheritedByDefault` is set to `true`, a Mojo that is configured in a parent project will be configured in a child project. If you configure a Mojo to execute during a specific phase in a parent project and the Mojo descriptor has `inheritedByDefault` set to `true`, this execution will be inherited by the child project. If `inheritedByDefault` is not set to `true`, then a goal execution defined in a parent project will not be inherited by a child project.

phase

> If you don't bind this goal to a specific phase, this element defines the default phase for this Mojo. If you do not specify a `phase` element, Maven will require the user to explicitly specify a phase in a POM.

implementation

> This element tells Maven which class to instantiate for this Mojo. This is a Plexus component property (defined in Plexus `ComponentDescriptor`).

language

> The default language for a Maven Mojo is `java`. This controls the Plexus `ComponentFactory` used to create instances of this Mojo component. This chapter focuses on writing Maven plugins in Java, but you can also write Maven in a number of alternative languages such as Groovy, BeanShell, and Ruby. If you were writing a plugin in one of these languages, you would use a language element value other than `java`.

instantiationStrategy

> This property is a Plexus component configuration property; it tells Plexus how to create and manage instances of the component. In Maven, all mojos are going to

be configured with an `instantiationStrategy` of `per-lookup`; a new instance of the component (`mojo`) is created every time it is retrieved from Plexus.

executionStrategy

The execution strategy tells Maven when and how to execute a Mojo. The valid values are `once-per-session` and `always`. In truth, the valid values can be anything. This particular property doesn't do a thing; it is a holdover from an early design of Maven. This property is slated for deprecation in a future release of Maven.

parameters

This element describes all of the parameters for this Mojo. What is the name of the parameter? What is the type of parameter? Is it required? Each parameter has the following elements:

name

This is the name of the parameter (i.e., `baseDirectory`).

type

This is the type (Java class) of the parameters (i.e., `java.io.File`).

required

Is the parameter required? If `true`, the parameter must be nonnull when the goal is executed.

editable

If a parameter is not editable (if `editable` is set to `false`), the value of the parameter cannot be set in the POM. For example, if the plugin descriptor defines the value of `buildDirectory` to be `${basedir}` in the descriptor, a POM cannot override this value to be another value in a POM.

description

This is a short description to use when generating plugin documentation (using the Help plugin).

configuration

This element provides default values for all of the Mojo's parameters using Maven property notation. This example provides a default value for the `baseDir` Mojo parameter and the `buildDirectory` Mojo parameter. In the `parameter` element, the implementation specifies the type of the parameter (in this case, `java.io.File`). The value in the `parameter` element contains either a hardcoded default or a Maven property reference.

requirements

This is where the descriptor gets interesting. A Mojo is a component that is managed by Plexus, and because of this, it has the opportunity to reference other components managed by Plexus. This element allows you to define dependencies on other components in Plexus.

Although you should know how to read a plugin descriptor, you will almost never need to write one of these descriptor files by hand. Plugin descriptor files are generated automatically off a set of annotations in the source for a Mojo.

Plugin Dependencies

Lastly, the plugin descriptor declares a set of dependencies, just like a Maven project. When Maven uses a plugin, it will download any required dependencies before it attempts to execute a goal from this plugin. In this example, the plugin depends on Jakarta Commons IO version 1.3.2.

Writing a Custom Plugin

When you write a custom plugin, you are going to be writing a series of Mojos (goals). Every Mojo is a single Java class that contains a series of annotations that tell Maven how to generate the plugin descriptor described in the previous section. Before you can start writing Mojo classes, you will need to create a Maven project with the appropriate packaging and POM.

Creating a Plugin Project

To create a plugin project, you should use the Maven Archetype plugin. The following command line will create a plugin with a groupId of org.sonatype.mavenbook.plugins and an artifactId of first-maven-plugin:

```
$ mvn archetype:create \
   -DgroupId=org.sonatype.mavenbook.plugins \
   -DartifactId=first-maven-plugin \
   -DarchetypeGroupId=org.apache.maven.archetypes \
   -DarchetypeArtifactId=maven-archetype-mojo
```

The Archetype plugin will create a directory named *my-first-plugin*, which contains the POM shown in Example 17-2.

Example 17-2. A plugin project's POM

```xml
<?xml version="1.0" encoding="UTF-8"?><project>
  <modelVersion>4.0.0</modelVersion>
  <groupId>org.sonatype.mavenbook.plugins</groupId>
  <artifactId>first-maven-plugin</artifactId>
  <version>1.0-SNAPSHOT</version>
  <packaging>maven-plugin</packaging>
  <name>first-maven-plugin Maven Mojo</name>
  <url>http://maven.apache.org</url>
  <dependencies>
    <dependency>
      <groupId>org.apache.maven</groupId>
      <artifactId>maven-plugin-api</artifactId>
      <version>2.0</version>
    </dependency>
    <dependency>
      <groupId>junit</groupId>
      <artifactId>junit</artifactId>
      <version>3.8.1</version>
```

```
      <scope>test</scope>
    </dependency>
  </dependencies>
</project>
```

The most important element in a plugin project's POM is the packaging element that has a value of maven-plugin. This packaging element customizes the Maven lifecycle to include the necessary goals to create a plugin descriptor. The plugin lifecycle was introduced in the section "Maven Plugin" in Chapter 10. It is similar to the JAR lifecycle, with three exceptions: plugin:descriptor is bound to the generate-resources phase, plugin:addPluginArtifactMetadata is added to the package phase, and plugin:updateRegistry is added to the install phase.

The other important piece of a plugin project's POM is the dependency on the Maven plugin API. This project depends on version 2.0 of the maven-plugin-api, and it also adds in JUnit as a test-scoped dependency.

A Simple Java Mojo

In this chapter, we will introduce a Maven Mojo written in Java. Each Mojo in the project will implement the org.apache.maven.plugin.Mojo interface. The Mojo implementation shown in the upcoming example implements the Mojo interface by extending the org.apache.maven.plugin.AbstractMojo class. Before we dive into the code for this Mojo, let's take some time to explore the methods on the Mojo interface. Mojo provides the following methods:

void setLog(org.apache.maven.monitor.logging.Log log)
> Every Mojo implementation has to provide a way for the plugin to communicate the progress of a particular goal. Did the goal succeed? Or was there a problem during goal execution? When Maven loads and executes a Mojo, it will call the setLog() method and supply the Mojo instance with a suitable logging destination to be used in your custom plugin.

protected Log getLog()
> Maven will call setLog() before your Mojo is executed, and your Mojo can retrieve the logging object by calling getLog(). Instead of printing out status to standard output or the console, your Mojo is going to invoke methods on the Log object.

void execute() throws org.apache.maven.plugin.MojoExecutionException
> This method is called by Maven when it is time to execute your goal.

The Mojo interface is concerned with two things: logging the results of goal execution and executing a goal. When you are writing a custom plugin, you'll be extending AbstractMojo. AbstractMojo takes care of handling the setLog() and getLog() implementations and contains an abstract execute() method. When you extend AbstractMojo, all you need to do is implement the execute() method. Example 17-3 shows a trivial Mojo implement that simply prints out a message to the console.

Example 17-3. A simple EchoMojo

```
package org.sonatype.mavenbook.plugins;

import org.apache.maven.plugin.AbstractMojo;
import org.apache.maven.plugin.MojoExecutionException;
import org.apache.maven.plugin.MojoFailureException;

/**
 * Echos an object string to the output screen.
 * @goal echo
 * @requiresProject false
 */
public class EchoMojo extends AbstractMojo
{
    /**
     * Any Object to print out.
     * @parameter expression="${echo.message}" default-value="Hello Maven World..."
     */
    private Object message;

    public void execute()
        throws MojoExecutionException, MojoFailureException
    {
        getLog().info( message.toString() );
    }
}
```

If you create this Mojo in ${basedir} under *src/main/java* in *org/sonatype/mavenbook/mojo/EchoMojo.java* in the project created in the previous section and run *mvn install*, you should be able to invoke this goal directly from the command line with:

```
$ mvn org.sonatype.mavenbook.plugins:first-maven-plugin:1.0-SNAPSHOT:echo
```

That large command is *mvn* followed by the *groupId:artifactId:version:goal*. When you run this command, you should see output that contains the output of the echo goal with the default message: "Hello Maven World...." If you want to customize the message, you can pass the value of the message parameter with the following command:

```
$ mvn org.sonatype.mavenbook.plugins:first-maven-plugin:1.0-SNAPSHOT:echo \
      -Decho.message="The Eagle has Landed"
```

This command will execute the EchoMojo and print out the message "The Eagle has Landed".

Configuring a Plugin Prefix

Specifying the groupId, artifactId, version, and goal on the command line is cumbersome. To address this, Maven assigns a plugin a prefix. Instead of typing:

```
$ mvn org.apache.maven.plugins:maven-jar-plugin:2.2:jar
```

You can use the plugin prefix jar and turn the command into *mvn jar:jar*. How does Maven resolve something like jar:jar to org.apache.mven.plugins:maven-jar:2.3?

Maven looks at a file in the Maven repository to obtain a list of plugins for a specific groupId. By default, Maven is configured to look for plugins in two groups: `org.apache.maven.plugins` and `org.codehaus.mojo`. When you specify a new plugin prefix such as *mvn hibernate3:hbm2ddl*, Maven will scan the repository metadata for the appropriate plugin prefix. First, Maven will scan the `org.apache.maven.plugins` group for the plugin prefix `hibernate3`. If it doesn't find the plugin prefix `hibernate3` in the `org.apache.maven.plugins` group, it will scan the metadata for the `org.code haus.mojo` group.

When Maven scans the metadata for a particular `groupId`, it is retrieving an XML file from the Maven repository that captures metadata about the artifacts contained in a group. This XML file is specific for each repository referenced; if you are not using a custom Maven repository, you will be able to see the Maven metadata for the `org.apache.maven.plugins` group in your local Maven repository (*~/.m2/repository*) under *org/apache/maven/plugins/maven-metadata-central.xml*. Example 17-4 shows a snippet of the *maven-metadata-central.xml* file from the `org.apache.maven.plugin` group.

Example 17-4. Maven metadata for the Maven plugin group

```xml
<?xml version="1.0" encoding="UTF-8"?>
<metadata>
  <plugins>
    <plugin>
      <name>Maven Clean Plugin</name>
      <prefix>clean</prefix>
      <artifactId>maven-clean-plugin</artifactId>
    </plugin>
    <plugin>
      <name>Maven Compiler Plugin</name>
      <prefix>compiler</prefix>
      <artifactId>maven-compiler-plugin</artifactId>
    </plugin>
    <plugin>
      <name>Maven Surefire Plugin</name>
      <prefix>surefire</prefix>
      <artifactId>maven-surefire-plugin</artifactId>
    </plugin>
    ...
  </plugins>
</metadata>
```

As you can see in this example, this *maven-metadata-central.xml* file in your local repository is what makes it possible for you to execute *mvn surefire:test*. Maven scans `org.apache.maven.plugins` and `org.codehaus.mojo`. Plugins from `org.apache.maven.plu gins` are considered core Maven plugins, and plugins from `org.codehaus.mojo` are considered extra plugins. The Apache Maven project manages the `org.apache.maven.plugins` group, and a separate independent open source community manages the Codehaus Mojo project. If you would like to start publishing plugins to your own `groupId`, and you would like Maven to automatically scan your own groupId for plugin prefixes, you can customize the groups that Maven scans for plugins in your Maven settings.

If you want to be able to run the first-maven-plugin's echo goal by running first:echo, add the org.sonatype.mavenbook.plugins groupId to your ~/.m2/set tings.xml, as shown in Example 17-5. This will prepend the org.sonatype.maven book.plugins to the list of groups that Maven scans for Maven plugins.

Example 17-5. Customizing the plugin groups in Maven settings

```
<settings>
  ...
  <pluginGroups>
    <pluginGroup>org.sonatype.mavenbook.plugins</pluginGroup>
  </pluginGroups>
</settings>
```

You can now run *mvn first:echo* from any directory and see that Maven will properly resolve the goal prefix to the appropriate plugin identifiers. This works because the project adheres to a naming convention for Maven plugins. If your plugin project has an artifactId that follows the pattern maven-first-plugin or first-maven-plugin, Maven will automatically assign a plugin goal prefix of first to your plugin. In other words, when the Maven Plugin plugin is generating the plugin descriptor for your plugin and you have not explicitly set the goalPrefix in your project, the plu gin:descriptor goal will extract the prefix from your plugin's artifactId when it matches one of the following patterns:

- ${prefix}-maven-plugin
- maven-${prefix}-plugin

If you would like to set an explicit plugin prefix, you'll need to configure the Maven Plugin plugin. This is plugin is responsible for building the plugin descriptor and per- forming plugin-specific tasks during the package and load phases. The Maven Plugin plugin can be configured just like any other plugin in the build element. To set the plugin prefix for your plugin, add the build element shown in Example 17-6 to the first-maven-plugin project's *pom.xml*.

Example 17-6. Configuring a plugin prefix

```
<?xml version="1.0" encoding="UTF-8"?><project>
  <modelVersion>4.0.0</modelVersion>
  <groupId>org.sonatype.mavenbook.plugins</groupId>
  <artifactId>first-maven-plugin</artifactId>
  <version>1.0-SNAPSHOT</version>
  <packaging>maven-plugin</packaging>
  <name>first-maven-plugin Maven Mojo</name>
  <url>http://maven.apache.org</url>
  <build>
    <plugins>
      <plugin>
        <artifactId>maven-plugin-plugin</artifactId>
```

```
        <version>2.3</version>
        <configuration>
          <goalPrefix>blah</goalPrefix>
        </configuration>
      </plugin>
    </plugins>
  </build>
  <dependencies>
    <dependency>
      <groupId>org.apache.maven</groupId>
      <artifactId>maven-plugin-api</artifactId>
      <version>2.0</version>
    </dependency>
    <dependency>
      <groupId>junit</groupId>
      <artifactId>junit</artifactId>
      <version>3.8.1</version>
      <scope>test</scope>
    </dependency>
  </dependencies>
</project>
```

This example sets the plugin prefix to blah. If you've added the org.sonatype.maven book.plugins to the pluginGroups in your *~/.m2/settings.xml*, you should be able to execute the EchoMojo by running *mvn echo:blah* from any directory.

Logging from a Plugin

Maven takes care of connecting your Mojo to a logging provider by calling setLog() prior to the execution of your Mojo. It supplies an implementation of org.apache.maven.monitor.logging.Log. This class exposes methods that you can use to communicate information back to the user. This Log class provides multiple levels of logging similar to that API provided by Log4J (*http://logging.apache.org/*). Those levels are captured by a series of methods available for each level—debug, info, error, and warn. To save trees, we will list only the methods for a single logging level—debug:

void debug(CharSequence message)
> Prints a message to the debug logging level

void debug(CharSequence message, Throwable t)
> Prints a message to the debug logging level that includes the stack trace from the Throwable (either Exception or Error)

void debug(Throwable t)
> Prints out the stack trace of the Throwable (either Exception or Error)

Each of the four levels exposes the same three methods. The four logging levels serve different purposes. The debug level exists for debugging purposes and for people who want to see a very detailed picture of the execution of a Mojo. You should use the debug logging level to provide as much detail on the execution of a Mojo, but you should never assume that a user is going to see the debug level. The info level is for general informational messages that should be printed as a normal course of operation. If you're building a plugin that compiles code using a compiler, you might want to print the output of the compiler to the screen.

The `warn` logging level is used for messages about unexpected events and errors that your Mojo can cope with. If you are trying to run a plugin that compiles Ruby source code and there is no Ruby source code available, you might want to just print a warning message and move on. Warnings are not fatal, but errors are usually build-stopping conditions. For the completely unexpected error condition, there is the `error` logging level. You would use `error` if you couldn't continue executing a Mojo. If you are writing a Mojo to compile some Java code and the compiler isn't available, you'd print a message to the `error` level and possibly pass along an exception that Maven can print out for the user. You should assume that a user is going to see most of the messages in `info` and all of the messages in `error`.

Mojo Class Annotations

In the `first-maven-plugin` example, you didn't write the plugin descriptor yourself; you relied on Maven to generate the plugin descriptor from your source code. The descriptor was generated using your plugin project's POM information and a set of annotations on your `EchoMojo` class. `EchoMojo` specifies only the `@goal` annotation. Here is a list of other annotations you can place on your `Mojo` implementation:

`@goal <goalName>`
> The only required annotation that gives a name to this goal that is unique to this plugin.

`@requiresDependencyResolution <requireScope>`
> Flags this Mojo as requiring the dependencies in the specified scope (or an implied scope) to be resolved before it can execute. Supports `compile`, `runtime`, and `test`. If this annotation had a value of `test`, it would tell Maven that the Mojo cannot be executed until the dependencies in the `test` scope had been resolved.

`@requiresProject (true|false)`
> Marks that this goal must be run inside of a project. The default is `true`. This is opposed to plugins such as archetypes that do not.

`@requiresReports (true|false)`
> If you were creating a plugin that relied on the presence of reports, you would need to set `requiresReports` to `true`. The default value of this annotation is `false`.

`@aggregator (true|false)`
> A Mojo with `aggregator` set to `true` is supposed to run only once during the execution of Maven. It was created to give plugin developers the ability to summarize the output of a series of builds; for example, to create a plugin that summarizes a report across all projects included in a build. A goal with `aggregator` set to `true`

should be run against only the top-level project in a Maven build. The default value of aggregator is false.

@requiresOnline (true|false)

When set to true, Maven must not be running in offline mode when this goal is executed. Maven will throw an error if you attempt to execute this goal offline. The default is false.

@requiresDirectInvocation

When set to true, the goal can be executed only if it is explicitly executed from the command line by the user. Maven will throw an error if someone tries to bind this goal to a lifecycle phase. The default for this annotation is false.

@phase <phaseName>

This annotation specifies the default phase for this goal. If you add an execution for this goal to a *pom.xml* and do not specify the phase, Maven will bind the goal to the phase specified in this annotation by default.

@execute [goal=goalName|phase=phaseName [lifecycle=lifecycleId]]

This annotation can be used in a number of ways. If a phase is supplied, Maven will execute a parallel lifecycle ending in the specified phase. The results of this separate execution will be made available in the Maven property ${executedProperty}.

The second way of using this annotation is to specify an explicit goal using the prefix:goal notation. When you specify only a goal, Maven will execute this goal in a parallel environment that will not affect the current Maven build.

The third way of using this annotation is to specify a phase in an alternate lifecycle using the identifier of a lifecycle:

```
@execute phase="package" lifecycle="zip"
@execute phase="compile"
@execute goal="zip:zip"
```

If you look at the source for EchoMojo, you'll notice that Maven is not using the standard annotations available in Java 5. Instead, it is using Commons Attributes (*http://com mons.apache.org/attributes/*). Commons Attributes provided a way for Java programmers to use annotations before annotations were a part of the Java language specification. Why doesn't Maven use Java 5 annotations? Because Maven is designed to target pre-Java 5 JVMs. Because Maven has to support older versions of Java, it cannot use any of the newer features available in Java 5.

When a Mojo Fails

The execute() method in Mojo throws two exceptions: MojoExecutionException and MojoFailureException. The difference between these two exceptions is both subtle and important, and it relates to what happens when a goal execution "fails." A MojoExecutionException is a fatal exception: it means something unrecoverable happened. You will throw a MojoExecutionException if something happens that warrants a complete stop in a build: you are trying to write to disk, but there is no space left, or you are trying to publish to a remote repository, but you can't connect to it. Throw a `MojoExecutionException` if there is no chance of a build continuing: that is, something terrible has happened, and you want the build to stop and the user to see a "BUILD ERROR" message.

A `MojoFailureException` is something less catastrophic: a goal can fail, but it might not be the end of the world for your Maven build. A unit test can fail, or an MD5 checksum can fail; both of these are potential problems, but you don't want to return an exception that is going to kill the entire build. In this situation, you would throw a `MojoFailureException`. Maven provides for different "resiliency" settings when it comes to project failure. These are described next.

When you run a Maven build, it can involve a series of projects, each of which can succeed or fail. You have the option of running Maven in three failure modes:

`mvn -ff`
> Fail-fast mode: Maven will fail (stop) at the first build failure.

`mvn -fae`
> Fail-at-end: Maven will fail at the end of the build. If a project in the Maven reactor fails, Maven will continue to build the rest of the builds and report a failure at the end of the build.

`mvn -fn`
> Fail never: Maven won't stop for a failure and won't report a failure.

You might want to ignore failures if you are running a continuous integration build and you want to attempt a build, regardless of the success or failure of an individual project build. As a plugin developer, you'll have to make a call as to whether a particular failure condition is a `MojoExecutionException` or a `MojoFailureExeception`.

Mojo Parameters

Just as important as the `execute()` method and the Mojo annotations is the fact that a Mojo is configured via parameters. This section deals with some configuration and topics surrounding Mojo parameters.

Supplying Values for Mojo Parameters

In EchoMojo, we declare the message parameter with the following annotations:

```
/**
 * Any Object to print out.
 * @parameter
 *      expression="${echo.message}"
 *      default-value="Hello Maven World"
 */
private Object message;
```

The default expression for this parameter is ${echo.message}. This means that Maven will try to use the value of the echo.message property to set the value for message. If the value of the echo.message property is null, the default-value attribute of the @parameter annotation will be used instead. Instead of using the echo.message property, we can configure a value for the message parameter of the EchoMojo directly in a project's POM.

We can populate the message parameter in the EchoMojo in a few ways. First, we can pass in a value from the command line like this (assuming that you've added org.sonatype.mavenbook.plugins to your pluginGroups):

```
$ mvn first:echo -Decho.message="Hello Everybody"
```

We can also specify the value of this message parameter by setting a property in our POM or in our *settings.xml*:

```
<project>
  ...
  <properties>
    <echo.message>Hello Everybody</echo.message>
  </properties>
</project>
```

This parameter can also be configured directly as a configuration value for the plugin. If we wanted to customize the message parameter directly, we could use the following build configuration, which bypasses the echo.message property and populates the Mojo parameter in plugin configuration:

```
<project>
  ...
  <build>
    <plugins>
      <plugin>
        <groupId>org.sonatype.mavenbook.plugins</groupId>
        <artifactId>first-maven-plugin</artifactId>
        <version>1.0-SNAPSHOT</version>
        <configuration>
          <message>Hello Everybody!</message>
        </configuration>
      </plugin>
    </plugins>
  </build>
</project>
```

If we wanted to run the EchoMojo twice at difference phases in a lifecycle, and if we wanted to customize the message parameter for each execution separately, we could configure the parameter value at the execution level in a POM like this:

```
<build>
  <build>
    <plugins>
      <plugin>
        <groupId>org.sonatype.mavenbook.plugins</groupId>
        <artifactId>first-maven-plugin</artifactId>
```

```
        <version>1.0-SNAPSHOT</version>
        <executions>
          <execution>
            <id>first-execution</id>
            <phase>generate-resources</phase>
            <goals>
              <goal>echo</goal>
            </goals>
            <configuration>
              <message>The Eagle has Landed!</message>
            </configuration>
          </execution>
          <execution>
            <id>second-execution</id>
            <phase>validate</phase>
            <goals>
              <goal>echo</goal>
            </goals>
            <configuration>
              <message>${project.version}</message>
            </configuration>
          </execution>
        </executions>
      </plugin>
    </plugins>
  </build>
</build>
```

Although this last configuration example seems very verbose, it illustrates the flexibility of Maven. In the previous configuration example, you bound the EchoMojo to both the validate and generate-resources phases in the default Maven lifecycle. The first execution is bound to generate-resources; it supplies a string value to the message parameter of "The Eagle has Landed!". The second execution is bound to the validate phase; it supplies a property reference to ${project.version}. When you run *mvn install* for this project, you'll see that the first:echo goal executes twice and prints out two different messages.

Multivalued Mojo Parameters

Plugins can have parameters that accept more than one value. Take a look at the ZipMojo shown in Example 17-7. Both the includes and excludes parameters are multivalued String arrays that specify the inclusion and exclusion patterns for a component that creates a ZIP file.

Example 17-7. A plugin with multivalued parameters

```
package org.sonatype.mavenbook.plugins
/**
 * Zips up the output directory.
 * @goal zip
 * @phase package
 */
```

```java
public class ZipMojo extends AbstractMojo
{
    /**
     * The Zip archiver.
     * @parameter expression="${component.org.codehaus.plexus.archiver.Archiver#zip}"
     */
    private ZipArchiver zipArchiver;

    /**
     * Directory containing the build files.
     * @parameter expression="${project.build.directory}"
     */
    private File buildDirectory;

    /**
     * Base directory of the project.
     * @parameter expression="${basedir}"
     */
    private File baseDirectory;

    /**
     * A set of file patterns to include in the zip.
     * @parameter alias="includes"
     */
    private String[] mIncludes;

    /**
     * A set of file patterns to exclude from the zip.
     * @parameter alias="excludes"
     */
    private String[] mExcludes;

    public void setExcludes( String[] excludes ) { mExcludes = excludes; }

    public void setIncludes( String[] includes ) { mIncludes = includes; }

    public void execute()
        throws MojoExecutionException
    {
        try {
            zipArchiver.addDirectory( buildDirectory, includes, excludes );
            zipArchiver.setDestFile( new File( baseDirectory, "output.zip" ) );
            zipArchiver.createArchive();
        } catch( Exception e ) {
            throw new MojoExecutionException( "Could not zip", e );
        }
    }
}
```

To configure a multivalued Mojo parameter, you use a series of elements for each value. If the name of the multivalued parameter is `includes`, you would use an element `includes` with child elements `include`. If the multivalued parameter is `excludes`, you would use an element `excludes` with child elements `exclude`. To configure the `ZipMojo` to ignore all files ending in *.txt* and all files ending in a tilde, you would use the following plugin configuration:

```xml
<project>
...
  <build>
    <plugins>
      <plugin>
        <groupId>org.sonatype.mavenbook.plugins</groupId>
        <pluginId>zip-maven-plugin</pluginId>
        <configuration>
          <excludes>
            <exclude>**/*.txt</exclude>
            <exclude>**/*~</exclude>
          </excludes>
        </configuration>
      </plugin>
    </plugins>
  </build>
</project>
```

Depending on Plexus Components

A Mojo is a component managed by an IoC container called Plexus. A Mojo can depend on other components managed by Plexus by declaring a Mojo parameter and using the `@parameter` or the `@component` annotation. Example 17-8 shows a `ZipMojo` that depends on a Plexus component using the `@parameter` annotation. This dependency could be declared using the `@component` annotation.

Example 17-8. Depending on a Plexus component

```
/**
 * The Zip archiver.
 * @component role="org.codehaus.plexus.archiver.Archiver" roleHint="zip"
 */
private ZipArchiver zipArchiver;
```

When Maven instantiates this Mojo, it will then attempt to retrieve the Plexus component with the specified role and role hint. In this example, the Mojo will be related to a `ZipArchiver` component that will allow the `ZipMojo` to create a ZIP file.

Mojo Parameter Annotations

Unless you insist on writing your plugin descriptors by hand, you'll never have to write that XML. Instead, the Maven Plugin plugin has a `plugin:descriptor` goal bound to the `generate-resources` phase. This goal generates the plugin descriptor from annotations on your Mojo. To configure a Mojo parameter, you should use the following annotations on the private member variables for each of your Mojo's parameters. You can also use these annotations on public setter methods, but the most common convention for Maven plugins is to annotate private member variables directly:

@parameter   [alias="*someAlias*"]   [expression="${*someExpression*}"]   [default-value="*value*"]

> Marks a private field (or a setter method) as a parameter. The alias provides the name of the parameter. If alias is omitted, Maven will use the name of the variable as the parameter name. The expression is an expression that Maven will evaluate to obtain a value. Usually the expression is a property reference such as ${echo.message}. default-value is the value that this Mojo will use if no value can be derived from the expression or if a value was not explicitly supplied via plugin configuration in a POM.

@required

> If this annotation is present, a valid value for this parameter is required prior to Mojo execution. If Maven tries to execute this Mojo and the parameter has a null value, Maven will throw an error when it tries to execute this goal.

@readonly

> If this annotation is present, the user cannot directly configure this parameter in the POM. You would use this annotation with the expression attribute of the parameter annotation. For example, if you wanted to make sure that a particular parameter always had the value of the finalName POM property, you would list an expression of ${build.finalName} and then add the @readOnly annotation. If this were the case, the user could change the value of this parameter only by changing the value of finalName in the POM.

@component

> Tells Maven to populate a field with a Plexus component. A valid value for the @component annotation would be:

> @component role="org.codehaus.plexus.archiver.Archiver" roleHint="zip"

> This would have the effect of retrieving the ZipArchiver from Plexus. The ZipArchiver is the archiver that corresponds to the role hint zip. Instead of component, you could also use the @parameter annotation with an expression attribute of:

> @parameter expression="${component.org.codehaus.plexus.archiver.Archiver#zip}"

> Although the two annotations are effectively the same, the @component annotation is the preferred way to configure dependencies on Plexus components.

@deprecated

> The parameter will be deprecated. Users can continue configuring this parameter, but a warning message will be displayed.

Plugins and the Maven Lifecycle

In Chapter 10, you learned that lifecycles can be customized by packaging types. A plugin can both introduce a new packaging type and customize the lifecycle. In this section, you will learn how you can customize the lifecycle from a custom Maven plugin. You will also see how you can tell a Mojo to execute a parallel lifecycle.

Executing a Parallel Lifecycle

Let's assume you write some goal that depends on the output from a previous build. Maybe the `ZipMojo` goal can run only if there is output to include in an archive. You can specify something like a prerequisite goal by using the `@execute` annotation on a Mojo class. This annotation will cause Maven to spawn a parallel build and execute a goal or a lifecycle in a parallel instance of Maven that isn't going to affect the current build. Maybe you wrote some Mojo that you can run once a day that runs *mvn install* and then packages up all of the output in some sort of customized distribution format. Your Mojo descriptor could tell Maven that before you execute your `CustomMojo`, you'd like it to execute the default lifecycle up to the `install` phase and then expose the results of that project to your Mojo as the property `${executedProject}`. You could then reference properties in that project before some sort of postprocessing.

Another possibility is that you have a goal that does something completely unrelated to the default lifecycle. Let's consider something completely unexpected. Maybe you have a goal that turns a WAV file into an MP3 using something like LAME, but before you do that, you want to step through a lifecycle that turns a MIDI file to a WAV. (You can use Maven for anything; this example isn't that "far out.") You've created a midi-sound lifecycle, and you want to include the output of the `midi-sound` lifecycle's `install` phase in your web application project, which has a `war` packaging type. Since your project is running in the `war` packaging lifecycle, you'll need to have a goal that effectively forks off an isolated build and runs through the `midi-source` lifecycle. You would do this by annotating your mojo with `@execute lifecycle="midi-source" phase="install"`:

`@execute goal="<goal>"`
> This will execute the given goal before the execution of this one. The goal name is specified using the `prefix:goal` notation.

`@execute phase="<phase>"`
> This will fork an alternate build lifecycle up to the specified phase before continuing to execute the current one. If no lifecycle is specified, Maven will use the lifecycle of the current build.

`@execute lifecycle="<lifecycle>" phase="<phase>"`
> This will execute the given alternate lifecycle. A custom lifecycle can be defined in *META-INF/maven/lifecycle.xml*.

Creating a Custom Lifecycle

A custom lifecycle must be packaged in the plugin under the *META-INF/maven/lifecy cle.xml* file. You can include a lifecycle under *src/main/resources* in *META-INF/maven/ lifecycle.xml*. The *lifecycle.xml* shown in Example 17-9 declares a lifecycle named zipcycle that contains only the zip goal in a package phase.

Example 17-9. Define a custom lifecycle in lifecycle.xml

```
<lifecycles>
  <lifecycle>
    <id>zipcycle</id>
    <phases>
      <phase>
        <id>package</id>
        <executions>
          <execution>
            <goals>
              <goal>zip</goal>
            </goals>
          </execution>
        </executions>
      </phase>
    </phases>
  </lifecycle>
</lifecycles>
```

If you wanted to execute the zipcycle phase within another build, you could then create a ZipForkMojo that uses the @execute annotation to tell Maven to step through the zipcycle phase to package when the ZipForkMojo is executed. See Example 17-10.

Example 17-10. Forking a customer lifecycle from a Mojo

```
/**
 * Forks a zip lifecycle.
 * @goal zip-fork
 * @execute lifecycle="zipcycle" phase="package"
 */
public class ZipForkMojo extends AbstractMojo
{
  public void execute()
    throws MojoExecutionException
  {
    getLog().info( "doing nothing here" );
  }
}
```

Running the ZipForkMojo will fork the lifecycle. If you've configured your plugin to execute with the goal prefix zip, running zip-fork should produce something similar to the following output:

```
$ mvn zip:zip-fork
[INFO] Scanning for projects...
[INFO] Searching repository for plugin with prefix: 'zip'.
```

```
[INFO] ------------------------------------------------------------------------
[INFO] Building Maven Zip Forked Lifecycle Test
[INFO]    task-segment: [zip:zip-fork]
[INFO] ------------------------------------------------------------------------
[INFO] Preparing zip:zip-fork
[INFO] [site:attach-descriptor]
[INFO] [zip:zip]
[INFO] Building zip: ~/maven-zip-plugin/src/projects/zip-lifecycle-test/\
           target/output.zip
[INFO] [zip:zip-fork]
[INFO] doing nothing here
[INFO] ------------------------------------------------------------------------
[INFO] BUILD SUCCESSFUL
[INFO] ------------------------------------------------------------------------
[INFO] Total time: 1 second
[INFO] Finished at: Sun Apr 29 16:10:06 CDT 2007
[INFO] Final Memory: 3M/7M
[INFO] ------------------------------------------------------------------------
```

Calling `zip-fork` spawns another lifecycle. Maven executes the `zipcycle` lifecycle, and then it prints out the message from `ZipFormMojo`'s execute method.

Overriding the Default Lifecycle

Once you've created your own lifecycle and spawned it from a Mojo, the next question you might have is: How do you override the default lifecycle? How do you create custom lifecycles and then attach them to projects? In Chapter 10, we saw that the packaging of a project defines the lifecycle of a project. There's something different about almost every packaging type: `war` attaches different goals to package, custom lifecycles such as `swf` from the Israfil Flex 3 plugin attach different goals to the `compile` phase. When you create a custom lifecycle, you can attach that lifecycle to a packaging type by supplying some Plexus configuration in your plugin's archive.

To define a new lifecycle for a new packaging type, you'll need to configure a `LifecycleMapping` component in Plexus. In your plugin project, create a *META-INF/ plexus/components.xml* under *src/main/resources*. In *components.xml*, add the content from Example 17-11. Set the name of the packaging type under `role-hint`, and the set of phases containing the coordinates of the goals to bind (omit the version). Multiple goals can be associated with a phase using a comma delimited list.

Example 17-11. Overriding the default lifecycle

```xml
<component-set>
  <components>
    <component>
      <role>org.apache.maven.lifecycle.mapping.LifecycleMapping</role>
      <role-hint>zip</role-hint>
      <implementation>org.apache.maven.lifecycle.mapping.DefaultLifecycleMapping
          </implementation>
      <configuration>
        <phases>
```

```
        <process-resources>org.apache.maven.plugins:maven-resources-plugin:resources
            </process-resources>
        <compile>org.apache.maven.plugins:maven-compiler-plugin:compile</compile>
        <package>org.sonatype.mavenbook.plugins:maven-zip-plugin:zip</package>
      </phases>
    </configuration>
  </component>
 </components>
</component-set>
```

If you create a plugin that defines a new packaging type and a customized lifecycle, Maven won't know anything about it until you add the plugin to your project's POM and set the extensions element to true. Once you do this, Maven will scan your plugin for more than just Mojos to execute; it will look for the *components.xml* under *META-INF/plexus*, and it will make the packaging type available to your project. See Example 17-12.

Example 17-12. Configuring a plugin as an extension

```
<project>
  ...
  <build>
    ...
    <plugins>
      <plugin>
        <groupId>com.training.plugins</groupId>
        <artifactId>maven-zip-plugin</artifactId>
        <extensions>true</extensions>
      </plugin>
    </plugins>
  </build>
</project>
```

Once you add the plugin with the extensions element set to true, you can use the custom packaging type and your project will be able to execute the custom lifecycle associated with that packaging type.

## CHAPTER 18

Writing Plugins in Alternative Languages

You can write a Mojo in Java, or you can write a Mojo in an alternative language. Maven has support for a number of implementation languages, and this chapter will show you how to create plugins in three languages: Ant, Ruby, and Groovy.

Writing Plugins in Ant

Ant isn't a language as much as it is a build tool that allows you to describe a build as a set of tasks grouped into build targets. Ant then allows you to declare dependencies between build targets; for example, in Ant you are essentially creating your own life-cycle. An Ant *build.xml* might have an install target that depends on a test target that depends on a compile target. Ant is something of an ancestor to Maven; it was the ubiquitous procedural build tool that almost every project used before Maven introduced the concept of wide-scale reusability of common build plugins and the concept of a universal lifecycle.

Although Maven is an improvement on Ant, Ant can still be useful when describing parts of the build process. Ant provides a set of tasks that can come in handy when you need to perform file operations or XSLT transformations or any other operation you can think of. There is a large library of available Ant tasks for everything from running JUnit tests to transforming XML to copying files to a remote server using SCP. An overview of available Ant tasks can be found online in the Apache Ant Manual (*http://ant.apache.org/manual/tasksoverview.html*). You can use these tasks as a low-level build customization language, and you can also write a Maven plugin where, instead of a Mojo written in Java, you can pass parameters to a Mojo that is an Ant build target.

Creating an Ant Plugin

To create a Maven plugin using Ant, you need to have a *pom.xml* and a single Mojo implemented in Ant. To get started, create a project directory named *firstant-maven-plugin*. Place the *pom.xml* shown in Example 18-1 in this directory.

Example 18-1. POM for an Ant Maven plugin

```xml
<project>
  <modelVersion>4.0.0</modelVersion>
  <groupId>org.sonatype.mavenbook.plugins</groupId>
  <artifactId>firstant-maven-plugin</artifactId>
  <name>Example Ant Mojo - firstant-maven-plugin</name>
  <packaging>maven-plugin</packaging>
  <version>1.0-SNAPSHOT</version>
  <dependencies>
    <dependency>
      <groupId>org.apache.maven</groupId>
      <artifactId>maven-script-ant</artifactId>
      <version>2.0.9</version>
    </dependency>
  </dependencies>
  <build>
    <plugins>
      <plugin>
        <artifactId>maven-plugin-plugin</artifactId>
        <version>2.4</version>
        <dependencies>
          <dependency>
            <groupId>org.apache.maven.plugin-tools</groupId>
            <artifactId>maven-plugin-tools-ant</artifactId>
            <version>2.4</version>
          </dependency>
        </dependencies>
      </plugin>
    </plugins>
  </build>
</project>
```

Next, you will need to create your Ant Mojo. An Ant Mojo consists of two parts: the Ant tasks in an XML file, and a file that supplies Mojo descriptor information. The Ant plugin tools will look for both of these files in *${basedir}/src/main/scripts*. One file will be named *echo.build.xml* and will contain the Ant XML. See Example 18-2.

Example 18-2. Echo Ant Mojo

```xml
<project>
  <target name="echotarget">
    <echo>${message}</echo>
  </target>
</project>
```

The other file will describe the Echo Ant Mojo and will be in the *echo.mojos.xml* file, also in *${basedir}/src/main/scripts*. See Example 18-3.

Example 18-3. Echo Ant Mojo descriptor

```
<pluginMetadata>
  <mojos>
    <mojo>
      <goal>echo</goal>
      <call>echotarget</call>
      <description>Echos a Message</description>
      <parameters>
        <parameter>
          <name>message</name>
          <property>message</property>
          <required>false</required>
          <expression>${message}</expression>
          <type>java.lang.Object</type>
          <defaultValue>Hello Maven World</defaultValue>
          <description>Prints a message</description>
        </parameter>
      </parameters>
    </mojo>
  </mojos>
</pluginMetadata>
```

This *echo.mojos.xml* file configures the Mojo descriptor for this plugin. It supplies the goal name "echo", and it tells Maven which Ant task to call in the call element. In addition to configuring the description, this XML file configures the message parameter to use the expression ${message} and to have a default value of "Hello Maven World."

If you've configured your plugin groups in *~/.m2/settings.xml* to include org.sona type.mavenbook.plugins, you can install this Ant plugin by executing the following command at the command line:

```
$ mvn install
[INFO] ------------------------------------------------------------------------
[INFO] Building Example Ant Mojo - firstant-maven-plugin
[INFO]    task-segment: [install]
[INFO] ------------------------------------------------------------------------
[INFO] [plugin:descriptor]
[INFO] Using 3 extractors.
[INFO] Applying extractor for language: java
[INFO] Extractor for language: java found 0 mojo descriptors.
[INFO] Applying extractor for language: bsh
[INFO] Extractor for language: bsh found 0 mojo descriptors.
[INFO] Applying extractor for language: ant
[INFO] Extractor for language: ant found 1 mojo descriptors.
...
[INFO] ------------------------------------------------------------------------
[INFO] BUILD SUCCESSFUL
[INFO] ------------------------------------------------------------------------
```

Note that the `plugin:descriptor` goal finds a single Ant mojo descriptor. To run this goal, execute the following command:

```
$ mvn firstant:echo
...
[INFO] [firstant:echo]

echotarget:
    [echo] Hello Maven World
[INFO] ------------------------------------------------------------------------
[INFO] BUILD SUCCESSFUL
[INFO] ------------------------------------------------------------------------
```

The `echo` goal executes and prints out the default value of the `message` parameter. If you are used to Apache Ant build scripts, you will notice that Ant prints out the name of the target executed and then adds a logging prefix to the output of the echo Ant task.

Writing Plugins in JRuby

Ruby is an object-oriented scripting language that provides a rich set of facilities for metaprogramming and reflection. Ruby's reliance on closures and blocks make for a programming style that is both compact and powerful. Although Ruby has been around since 1993, most people came to know Ruby after it was made popular by a Ruby-based web framework known as Ruby on Rails. JRuby is a Ruby interpreter written in Java. For more information about the Ruby language, see *http://www.ruby-lang.org/*, and for more information about JRuby, see *http://jruby.codehaus.org/*.

Creating a JRuby Plugin

To create a Maven plugin using JRuby, you need to have a *pom.xml* and a single Mojo implemented in Ruby. To get started, create a project directory named *firstruby-maven-plugin*. Place the *pom.xml* shown in Example 18-4 in this directory.

Example 18-4. POM for a JRuby Maven plugin

```
<project>
  <modelVersion>4.0.0</modelVersion>
  <groupId>org.sonatype.mavenbook.plugins</groupId>
  <artifactId>firstruby-maven-plugin</artifactId>
  <name>Example Ruby Mojo - firstruby-maven-plugin</name>
  <packaging>maven-plugin</packaging>
  <version>1.0-SNAPSHOT</version>
  <dependencies>
    <dependency>
      <groupId>org.codehaus.mojo</groupId>
      <artifactId>jruby-maven-plugin</artifactId>
      <version>1.0-beta-4</version>
      <scope>runtime</scope>
    </dependency>
  </dependencies>
```

```
<build>
  <plugins>
    <plugin>
      <artifactId>maven-plugin-plugin</artifactId>
      <version>2.4</version>
      <dependencies>
        <dependency>
          <groupId>org.codehaus.mojo</groupId>
          <artifactId>jruby-maven-plugin</artifactId>
          <version>1.0-beta-4</version>
        </dependency>
      </dependencies>
    </plugin>
  </plugins>
</build>
</project>
```

Next, you will need to create a Mojo implemented in Ruby. Maven will look for a Ruby Mojo in *${basedir}/src/main/scripts*. Put the Ruby class shown in Example 18-5 in *${basedir}/src/main/scripts/echo.rb*.

Example 18-5. The Echo Ruby Mojo

```
# Prints a message
# @goal "echo"
# @phase "validate"
class Echo < Mojo

  # @parameter type="java.lang.String" default-value="Hello Maven World" \
    expression="${message}"
  def message
  end

  def execute
    info $message
  end

end

run_mojo Echo
```

The Echo class must extend Mojo, and it must override the execute() method. At the end of the *echo.rb* file, you will need to run the mojo with run_mojo Echo. To install this plugin, run *mvn install*:

```
$ mvn install
[INFO] Scanning for projects...
[INFO] ------------------------------------------------------------------------
[INFO] Building Example Ruby Mojo - firstruby-maven-plugin
[INFO]    task-segment: [install]
[INFO] ------------------------------------------------------------------------
...
[INFO] [plugin:descriptor]
...
[INFO] Applying extractor for language: jruby
```

```
[INFO] Ruby Mojo File: /echo.rb
[INFO] Extractor for language: jruby found 1 mojo descriptors.
...
[INFO] ------------------------------------------------------------------------
[INFO] BUILD SUCCESSFUL
[INFO] ------------------------------------------------------------------------
```

During the build, you should see that the Maven Plugin plugin's `descriptor` goal applies the JRuby extractor to create a *plugin.xml* that captures the annotations in the Echo class. If you've configured your default plugin groups to include `org.sonatype.maven book.plugins`, you should be able to run this `echo` goal with the following command:

```
$ mvn firstruby:echo
...
[INFO] [firstruby:echo]
[INFO] Hello Maven World
...
```

Ruby Mojo Implementations

Ruby Mojos are annotated using comments in Ruby source files. A single annotation such as `@parameter` takes a number of attributes, and each of these attributes must be specified on the same line. There can be no line breaks between an annotations attribute in the Ruby source. Both classes and parameters are annotated. Parameters are annotated with four annotations: `@parameter`, `@required`, `@readonly`, and `@deprecated`. The `@parameter` attribute takes the following attributes:

alias
> An alias for the parameter; an alternate name that can be used to populate the same parameter.

default-value
> Provides a default value to the parameter if the supplied value or the parameter expression produces a null result. In *echo.rb*, we specify the default as "Hello Maven World".

expression
> Contains an expression that can resolve to a Maven property or a System property.

type
> The fully qualified Java type of the parameter. If the type is not specified, it will default to `java.lang.String`.

In addition to the `@parameter` annotation, a parameter can take the following annotations:

@required "<true|false>"
> Marks the parameter as being required. The default value is `false`.

`@readonly "<true|false>"`

Marks the parameter as read-only. If this is `true`, you may not override the default value or the value from the expression from the command line. The default value is `false`.

`@deprecated "<true|false>"`

Marks the parameter as deprecated. The default value is `false`.

Putting this all together, a fully annotated message parameter from *echo.rb* would look like the following code:

```
# @parameter type="java.lang.String" default-value="Hello Maven World" \
  expression="${message}"
# @readonly true
# @required false
# @deprecated false
def message
end
```

Ruby Mojo classes are annotated with the following attributes:

`@goal`

Specifies the name of the goal.

`@phase`

The default phase to bind this goal to.

`@requiresDependencyResolution`

True if the Mojo requires that dependencies be resolved before execution.

`@aggregator`

Marks this mojo as an aggregator.

`@execute`

Provides the opportunity to execute a goal or lifecycle phase before executing this Mojo. The `@execute` annotation takes the following attributes:

`goal`

Name of the goal to execute

`phase`

Name of the lifecycle phase to execute

`lifecycle`

Name of the lifecycle (if other than default)

For an example of an annotated Mojo class, consider the following code example:

```
# Completes some build task
# @goal custom-goal
# @phase install
# @requiresDependencyResolution false
# @execute phase=compile
class CustomMojo < Mojo
   ...
end
```

Mojo parameters can reference Java classes and Maven properties. Example 18-6 shows you how to get access to the Maven Project object from a Ruby Mojo.

Example 18-6. Referencing a Maven Project from a Ruby Mojo

```
# This is a mojo description
# @goal test
# @phase validate
class Test < Mojo
  # @parameter type="java.lang.String" default-value="nothing" alias="a_string"
  def prop
  end

  # @parameter type="org.apache.maven.project.MavenProject" \
    expression="${project}"
  # @required true
  def project
  end

  def execute
    info "The following String was passed to prop: '#{$prop}'"
    info "My project artifact is: #{$project.artifactId}"
  end
end


run_mojo Test
```

In the example just shown, we can access properties on the `Project` class using standard Ruby syntax. If you put *test.rb* in `firstruby-maven-plugin`'s *src/main/scripts* directory, install the plugin, and then run it, you will see the following output:

```
$ mvn install
...
[INFO] [plugin:descriptor]
[INFO] Using 3 extractors.
[INFO] Applying extractor for language: java
...
[INFO] Applying extractor for language: jruby
[INFO] Ruby Mojo File: /echo.rb
[INFO] Ruby Mojo File: /test.rb
[INFO] Extractor for language: jruby found 2 mojo descriptors.
...
$ mvn firstruby:test
...
[INFO] [firstruby:test]
[INFO] The following String was passed to prop: 'nothing'
[INFO] My project artifact is: firstruby-maven-plugin
```

Logging from a Ruby Mojo

To log from a Ruby Mojo, call the `info()`, `debug()`, and `error()` methods with a message:

```
# Tests Logging
# @goal logtest
```

```
# @phase validate
class LogTest < Mojo

  def execute
    info "Prints an INFO message"
    error "Prints an ERROR message"
    debug "Prints to the Console"
  end

end

run_mojo LogTest
```

Raising a MojoError

If there is an unrecoverable error in a Ruby Mojo, you will need to raise a MojoError. Example 18-7 shows you how to raise a MojoError. This example Mojo prints out a message and then raises a MojoError.

Example 18-7. Raising a MojoError from a Ruby Mojo

```
# Prints a Message
# @goal error
# @phase validate
class Error < Mojo

  # @parameter type="java.lang.String" default-value="Hello Maven World" \
    expression="${message}"
  # @required true
  # @readonly false
  # @deprecated false
  def message
  end

  def execute
    info $message
    raise MojoError.new( "This Mojo Raised a MojoError" )
  end

end

run_mojo Error
```

Running this Mojo produces the following output:

```
$ mvn firstruby:error
...
INFO] [firstruby:error]
[INFO] Hello Maven World
[ERROR] This Mojo Raised a MojoError
```

Referencing Plexus Components from JRuby

A Ruby Mojo can depend on a Plexus component. To do this, you would use the expression attribute of the @parameter annotation to specify a role and a hint for Plexus. The Ruby Mojo shown in Example 18-8 depends on an Archiver component that Maven will retrieve from Plexus.

Example 18-8. Depending on a Plexus component from a Ruby Mojo

```
# This mojo tests plexus integration
# @goal testplexus
# @phase validate
class TestPlexus < Mojo

  # @parameter type="org.codehaus.plexus.archiver.Archiver" \
expression="${component.org.codehaus.plexus.archiver.Archiver#zip}"
  def archiver
  end

  def execute
    info $archiver
  end
end

run_mojo TestPlexus
```

Please note that the attributes for an annotation in a Ruby Mojo cannot span multiple lines. If you were to run this goal, you would see Maven attempt to retrieve a component from Plexus with a role of `org.codehaus.plexus.arhiver.Archiver` and a hint of `zip`.

Writing Plugins in Groovy

Groovy is a dynamic language based on the Java Virtual Machine that compiles to Java bytecode. Groovy is a project in the Codehaus community. If you are fluent in Java, Groovy will seem like a natural choice for a scripting language. Groovy takes the features of Java, pares down the syntax a bit, and adds features such as closures, duck-typing, and regular expressions. For more information about Groovy, please see the Groovy web site at *http://groovy.codehaus.org*.

Although it is possible to create a Groovy plugin using the techniques described in this section, there is a newer project devoted to Groovy–Maven integration called GMaven (*http://groovy.codehaus.org/GMaven*), which is scheduled to have a 1.0 release in September 2008. The authors of this book encourage you to look into this project as an alternative to the methods described in this section.

Creating a Groovy Plugin

To create a Maven plugin using Groovy, you need only two files: a *pom.xml* and a single Mojo implemented in Groovy. To get started, create a project directory named *first groovy-maven-plugin*. Place the *pom.xml* shown in Example 18-9 in this directory.

Example 18-9. POM for a Groovy Maven plugin

```xml
<?xml version="1.0" encoding="UTF-8"?>
<project>
  <modelVersion>4.0.0</modelVersion>
  <groupId>org.sonatype.mavenbook.plugins</groupId>
  <artifactId>firstgroovy-maven-plugin</artifactId>
  <name>Example Groovy Mojo - firstgroovy-maven-plugin</name>
  <packaging>maven-plugin</packaging>
  <version>1.0-SNAPSHOT</version>
  <dependencies>
    <dependency>
      <groupId>org.codehaus.mojo.groovy</groupId>
      <artifactId>groovy-mojo-support</artifactId>
      <version>1.0-beta-3</version>
    </dependency>
  </dependencies>
  <build>
    <plugins>
      <plugin>
        <artifactId>maven-plugin-plugin</artifactId>
        <version>2.4</version>
      </plugin>
      <plugin>
        <groupId>org.codehaus.mojo.groovy</groupId>
        <artifactId>groovy-maven-plugin</artifactId>
        <version>1.0-beta-3</version>
        <extensions>true</extensions>
        <executions>
          <execution>
            <goals>
              <goal>generateStubs</goal>
              <goal>compile</goal>
              <goal>generateTestStubs</goal>
              <goal>testCompile</goal>
            </goals>
          </execution>
        </executions>
      </plugin>
    </plugins>
  </build>
</project>
```

What's going on in this POM? First, notice that the packaging of the POM is maven-plugin because we are creating a project that will package a Maven plugin. Next, note that the project depends on the groovy-mojo-support artifact in the org.code haus.mojo.groovy group.

Then, under *src/main/groovy* in the directory *org/sonatype/mavenbook/plugins*, create a file named *EchoMojo.groovy* that contains the EchoMojo class, as shown in Example 18-10.

Example 18-10. EchoMojo.groovy

```
package org.sonatype.mavenbook.plugins

import org.codehaus.mojo.groovy.GroovyMojo

/**
 * Example goal which echos a message
 *
 * @goal echo
 */
class EchoMojo extends GroovyMojo {

    /**
     * Message to print
     *
     * @parameter expression="${echo.message}"
     *            default-value="Hello Maven World"
     */
    String message

    void execute() {
      log.info( message )
    }
}
```

## PART IV

Appendixes

This section contains two appendixes for Maven reference: Appendix A, *Settings Details*, and Appendix B, *Sun Specification Alternatives*.

Settings Details

Quick Overview

The settings element in the *settings.xml* file contains elements used to define values that configure Maven execution. Settings in this file are settings that apply to many projects and should not be bundled to any specific project or distributed to an audience. These include values such as the local repository location, alternate remote repository servers, and authentication information. There are two locations where a *settings.xml* file may live:

Maven installation directory
   $M2_HOME/conf/settings.xml

User-specific settings file
   ~/.m2/settings.xml

Example A-1 shows an overview of the top elements under settings.

Example A-1. Overview of top-level elements in settings.xml

```
<settings xmlns="http://maven.apache.org/POM/4.0.0"
  xmlns:xsi="http://www.w3.org/2001/XMLSchema-instance"
  xsi:schemaLocation="http://maven.apache.org/POM/4.0.0
                    http://maven.apache.org/xsd/settings-1.0.0.xsd">
  <localRepository/>
  <interactiveMode/>
  <usePluginRegistry/>
  <offline/>
  <pluginGroups/>
  <servers/>
  <mirrors/>
  <proxies/>
  <profiles/>
  <activeProfiles/>
</settings>
```

Settings Details

Simple Values

Half of the top-level settings elements are simple values, representing a range of values that configure core behavior of Maven. These are shown in Example A-2.

Example A-2. Simple top-level elements in settings.xml

```
<settings xmlns="http://maven.apache.org/POM/4.0.0"
  xmlns:xsi="http://www.w3.org/2001/XMLSchema-instance"
  xsi:schemaLocation="http://maven.apache.org/POM/4.0.0
                      http://maven.apache.org/xsd/settings-1.0.0.xsd">
  <localRepository>${user.dir}/.m2/repository</localRepository>
  <interactiveMode>true</interactiveMode>
  <usePluginRegistry>false</usePluginRegistry>
  <offline>false</offline>
  <pluginGroups>
    <pluginGroup>org.codehaus.mojo</pluginGroup>
  </pluginGroups>
  ...
</settings>
```

The simple top-level elements are:

localRepository

> This value is the path of this build system's local repository. The default value is *${user.dir}/.m2/repository*.

interactiveMode

> `true` if Maven should attempt to interact with the user for input; `false` if not. Defaults to `true`.

usePluginRegistry

> `true` if Maven should use the *${user.dir}/.m2/plugin-registry.xml* file to manage plugin versions. Defaults to `false`.

offline

> `true` if this build system should operate in offline mode. Defaults to `false`. This element is useful for build servers that cannot connect to a remote repository, either because of network setup or for security reasons.

pluginGroups

> This element contains a list of `pluginGroup` elements. Each contains a `groupId`. The list is searched when a plugin is used and the `groupId` is not provided in the command line. This list contains `org.apache.maven.plugins` by default.

Servers

The `distributionManagement` element of the POM defines the repositories for deployment. However, certain settings such as security credentials should not be distributed along with the *pom.xml*. This type of information should exist on the build server in the *settings.xml*. See Example A-3.

Example A-3. Server configuration in settings.xml

```
<settings xmlns="http://maven.apache.org/POM/4.0.0"
  xmlns:xsi="http://www.w3.org/2001/XMLSchema-instance"
  xsi:schemaLocation="http://maven.apache.org/POM/4.0.0
                      http://maven.apache.org/xsd/settings-1.0.0.xsd">
  ...
  <servers>
    <server>
      <id>server001</id>
      <username>my_login</username>
      <password>my_password</password>
      <privateKey>${usr.home}/.ssh/id_dsa</privateKey>
      <passphrase>some_passphrase</passphrase>
      <filePermissions>664</filePermissions>
      <directoryPermissions>775</directoryPermissions>
      <configuration></configuration>
    </server>
  </servers>
  ...
</settings>
```

The elements under the server are:

id
> This is the `id` of the server (not of the user to log in as) that matches the `distributionManagement` repository element's `id`.

username, password
> These elements appear as a pair denoting the login and password required to authenticate to this server.

privateKey, passphrase
> Like the previous two elements, this pair specifies a path to a private key (the default is *${user.home}/.ssh/id_dsa*) and a passphrase, if required. The `passphrase` and `password` elements may be externalized in the future, but for now they must be set in plain text in the *settings.xml* file.

filePermissions, directoryPermissions
> When a repository file or directory is created on deployment, these are the permissions to use. The legal values of each is a three-digit number corresponding to *nix file permissions, i.e., 664 or 775.

Mirrors

See Example A-4.

Example A-4. Mirror configuration in settings.xml

```
<settings xmlns="http://maven.apache.org/POM/4.0.0"
  xmlns:xsi="http://www.w3.org/2001/XMLSchema-instance"
  xsi:schemaLocation="http://maven.apache.org/POM/4.0.0
                      http://maven.apache.org/xsd/settings-1.0.0.xsd">
  ...
  <mirrors>
    <mirror>
      <id>planetmirror.com</id>
      <name>PlanetMirror Australia</name>
      <url>http://downloads.planetmirror.com/pub/maven2</url>
      <mirrorOf>central</mirrorOf>
    </mirror>
  </mirrors>
  ...
</settings>
```

The elements are:

id, name

>   The unique identifier of this mirror. The id is used to differentiate between mirror
>   elements.

url

>   The base URL of this mirror. The build system will use this URL to connect to a
>   repository rather than the default server URL.

mirrorOf

>   The ID of the server that this is a mirror of. For example, to point to a mirror of
>   the Maven central server (*http://repo1.maven.org/maven2*), set this element to
>   central. This must not match the mirror id.

Proxies

See Example A-5.

Example A-5. Proxy configuration in settings.xml

```
<settings xmlns="http://maven.apache.org/POM/4.0.0"
  xmlns:xsi="http://www.w3.org/2001/XMLSchema-instance"
  xsi:schemaLocation="http://maven.apache.org/POM/4.0.0
                      http://maven.apache.org/xsd/settings-1.0.0.xsd">
  ...
  <proxies>
    <proxy>
      <id>myproxy</id>
      <active>true</active>
      <protocol>http</protocol>
```

```
          <host>proxy.somewhere.com</host>
          <port>8080</port>
          <username>proxyuser</username>
          <password>somepassword</password>
          <nonProxyHosts>*.google.com|ibiblio.org</nonProxyHosts>
     </proxy>
  </proxies>
  ...
</settings>
```

The elements are:

id
> The unique identifier for this proxy. This is used to differentiate between proxy elements.

active
> true if this proxy is active. This is useful for declaring a set of proxies, but only one may be active at a time.

protocol, host, port
> The protocol://host:port of the proxy, separated into discrete elements.

username, password
> These elements appear as a pair denoting the login and password required to authenticate to this proxy server.

nonProxyHosts
> This is a list of hosts that should not be proxied. The delimiter of the list is the expected type of the proxy server; Example A-5 is pipe-delimited, and comma-delimited is also common.

Profiles

The profile element in the *settings.xml* is a truncated version of the *pom.xml* profile element. It consists of the activation, repositories, pluginRepositories, and properties elements. The profile elements include only these four elements because they concern themselves with the build system as a whole (which is the role of the *settings.xml* file), not with individual Project Object Model settings.

If a profile is active from settings, its values will override any equivalent profiles with matching identifiers in a POM or *profiles.xml* file.

Activation

Activations are the key of a profile. Like the POM's profiles, the power of a profile comes from its ability to modify some values only under certain circumstances; those circumstances are specified via an activation element. See Example A-6.

Example A-6. Defining activation parameters in settings.xml

```
<settings xmlns="http://maven.apache.org/POM/4.0.0"
  xmlns:xsi="http://www.w3.org/2001/XMLSchema-instance"
  xsi:schemaLocation="http://maven.apache.org/POM/4.0.0
                      http://maven.apache.org/xsd/settings-1.0.0.xsd">
  ...
  <profiles>
    <profile>
      <id>test</id>
      <activation>
        <activeByDefault>false</activeByDefault>
        <jdk>1.5</jdk>
        <os>
          <name>Windows XP</name>
          <family>Windows</family>
          <arch>x86</arch>
          <version>5.1.2600</version>
        </os>
        <property>
          <name>mavenVersion</name>
          <value>2.0.3</value>
        </property>
        <file>
          <exists>${basedir}/file2.properties</exists>
          <missing>${basedir}/file1.properties</missing>
        </file>
      </activation>
      ...
    </profile>
  </profiles>
  ...
</settings>
```

Activation occurs when all specified criteria have been met, though not all are required at once. These are the elements:

jdk

> Activation has a built in, Java-centric check in the jdk element. This will activate if the test is run under a jdk version number that matches the prefix given. In Example A-6, 1.5.0_06 will match.

os

> The os element can define some operating system-specific properties, shown previously.

property

> The profile will activate if Maven detects a property (a value that can be dereferenced within the POM by ${name}) of the corresponding name-value pair.

file

> Finally, a given filename may activate the profile by the existence of a file, or if it is missing.

The activation element is not the only way that a profile may be activated. The *settings.xml* file's activeProfile element may contain the profile's id. They may also be activated explicitly through the command line via a comma-separated list after the -P flag (e.g., -P test).

To see which profile will activate in a certain build, use the maven-help-plugin:

```
mvn help:active-profiles
```

Properties

Maven properties are value placeholders, like properties in Ant. Their values are accessible anywhere within a POM by using the notation ${*X*}, where *X* is the property. They come in five different styles, all accessible from the *settings.xml* file:

env.*X*
> Prefixing a variable with env. will return the shell's environment variable. For example, ${env.PATH} contains the $path environment variable. (%PATH% in Windows.)

project.*x*
> A dot-notated (.) path in the POM will contain the corresponding elements value.

settings.*x*
> A dot-notated (.) path in the *settings.xml* will contain the corresponding elements value.

Java system properties
> All properties accessible via java.lang.System.getProperties() are available as POM properties, such as ${java.home}.

x

> Set within a properties element or an external file, the value may be used as ${someVar}.

See Example A-7.

Example A-7. Setting the ${user.install} property in settings.xml

```
<settings xmlns="http://maven.apache.org/POM/4.0.0"
  xmlns:xsi="http://www.w3.org/2001/XMLSchema-instance"
  xsi:schemaLocation="http://maven.apache.org/POM/4.0.0
                      http://maven.apache.org/xsd/settings-1.0.0.xsd">
  ...
  <profiles>
    <profile>
      ...
      <properties>
        <user.install>${user.dir}/our-project</user.install>
      </properties>
      ...
    </profile>
  </profiles>
```

```
    ...
  </settings>
```

The property ${user.install} is accessible from a POM if this profile is active.

Repositories

Repositories are remote collections of projects that Maven uses to populate the local repository of the build system. It is from this local repository that Maven calls its plugins and dependencies. Different remote repositories may contain different projects, and under the active profile they may be searched for a matching release or snapshot artifact. See Example A-8.

Example A-8. Repository configuration in settings.xml

```
<settings xmlns="http://maven.apache.org/POM/4.0.0"
  xmlns:xsi="http://www.w3.org/2001/XMLSchema-instance"
  xsi:schemaLocation="http://maven.apache.org/POM/4.0.0
                      http://maven.apache.org/xsd/settings-1.0.0.xsd">
  ...
  <profiles>
    <profile>
      ...
      <repositories>
        <repository>
          <id>codehausSnapshots</id>
          <name>Codehaus Snapshots</name>
          <releases>
            <enabled>false</enabled>
            <updatePolicy>always</updatePolicy>
            <checksumPolicy>warn</checksumPolicy>
          </releases>
          <snapshots>
            <enabled>true</enabled>
            <updatePolicy>never</updatePolicy>
            <checksumPolicy>fail</checksumPolicy>
          </snapshots>
          <url>http://snapshots.maven.codehaus.org/maven2</url>
          <layout>default</layout>
        </repository>
      </repositories>
      <pluginRepositories>
        ...
      </pluginRepositories>
      ...
    </profile>
  </profiles>
  ...
</settings>
```

These are the elements:

releases, snapshots
These are the policies for each type of artifact, `release` or `snapshot`. With these two sets, a POM has the power to alter the policies for each type independent of the other within a single repository. For example, one may decide to enable only snapshot downloads, possibly for development purposes.

enabled
`true` or `false` for whether this repository is enabled for the respective type (`releases` or `snapshots`).

updatePolicy
This element specifies how often updates should attempt to occur. Maven will compare the local POMs timestamp to the remote. The choices are: `always`, `daily` (default), `interval:X` (where *X* is an integer in minutes), or `never`.

checksumPolicy
When Maven deploys files to the repository, it also deploys corresponding checksum files. Your options are to `ignore`, `fail`, or `warn` on missing or incorrect checksums.

layout
In the earlier description of repositories, we mentioned that they all follow a common layout. This is mostly correct. Maven 2 has a default layout for its repositories; however, Maven 1.x had a different layout. Use this element to specify whether it is default or legacy.

Plugin Repositories

Repositories are home to two major types of artifacts. The first are artifacts that are used as dependencies of other artifacts. These are the majority of plugins that reside within central. The other type of artifact is plugins. Maven plugins are themselves a special type of artifact. Because of this, plugin repositories are separated from other repositories. The structure of the `pluginRepositories` element block is similar to the `repositories` element. The `pluginRepository` elements each specify a remote location where Maven can find new plugins.

Active Profiles

See Example A-9.

Example A-9. Setting active profiles in settings.xml

```
<settings xmlns="http://maven.apache.org/POM/4.0.0"
  xmlns:xsi="http://www.w3.org/2001/XMLSchema-instance"
  xsi:schemaLocation="http://maven.apache.org/POM/4.0.0
                      http://maven.apache.org/xsd/settings-1.0.0.xsd">
  ...
  <activeProfiles>
    <activeProfile>env-test</activeProfile>
```

```
    </activeProfiles>
</settings>
```

The final piece of the *settings.xml* puzzle is the `activeProfiles` element. This contains a set of `activeProfile` elements, which each have a value of a profile `id`. Any profile `id` defined as an `activeProfile` will be active, regardless of any environment settings. If no matching profile is found, nothing will happen. For example, if `env-test` is an `activeProfile`, a `profile` in a *pom.xml* (or *profile.xml* with a corresponding `id`), it will be active. If no such profile is found, execution will continue as normal.

Sun Specification Alternatives

The Apache Geronimo project maintains implementations of various enterprise Java specifications. Table B-1 lists the `artifactId` and artifact version for all of the specifications implemented by the Geronimo project. To use one of these dependencies, use a `groupId` of `org.apache.geronimo.specs`, locate the version of the specification you want to use, and reference the dependency with the `artifactId` and artifact version listed in Table B-1.

 All artifacts in Table B-1 have a `groupId` of `org.apache.geronimo.specs`.

Table B-1. Alternate spec implementations artifacts

Specification	Spec version	Artifact ID	Artifact version
Activation	1.0.2	geronimo-activation_1.0.2_spec	1.2
Activation	1.1	geronimo-activation_1.1_spec	1.0.1
Activation	1.0	geronimo-activation_1.0_spec	1.1
CommonJ	1.1	geronimo-commonj_1.1_spec	1.0
Corba	2.3	geronimo-corba_2.3_spec	1.1
Corba	3.0	geronimo-corba_3.0_spec	1.2
EJB	2.1	geronimo-ejb_2.1_spec	1.1
EJB	3.0	geronimo-ejb_3.0_spec	1.0
EL	1.0	geronimo-el_1.0_spec	1.0
Interceptor	3.0	geronimo-interceptor_3.0_spec	1.0
J2EE Connector	1.5	geronimo-j2ee-connector_1.5_spec	1.1.1
J2EE Deployment	1.1	geronimo-j2ee-deployment_1.1_spec	1.1
J2EE JACC	1.0	geronimo-j2ee-jacc_1.0_spec	1.1.1

Specification	Spec version	Artifact ID	Artifact version
J2EE Management	1.0	`geronimo-j2ee-management_1.0_spec`	1.1
J2EE Management	1.1	`geronimo-j2ee-management_1.1_spec`	1.0
J2EE	1.4	`geronimo-j2ee_1.4_spec`	1.1
JACC	1.1	`geronimo-jacc_1.1_spec`	1.0
JEE Deployment	1.1MR3	`geronimo-javaee-deployment_1.1MR3_spec`	1.0
JavaMail	1.3.1	`geronimo-javamail_1.3.1_spec`	1.3
JavaMail	1.4	`geronimo-javamail_1.4_spec`	1.2
JAXR	1.0	`geronimo-jaxr_1.0_spec`	1.1
JAXRPC	1.1	`geronimo-jaxrpc_1.1_spec`	1.1
JMS	1.1	`geronimo-jms_1.1_spec`	1.1
JPA	3.0	`geronimo-jpa_3.0_spec`	1.1
JSP	2.0	`geronimo-jsp_2.0_spec`	1.1
JSP	2.1	`geronimo-jsp_2.1_spec`	1.0
JTA	1.0.1B	`geronimo-jta_1.0.1B_spec`	1.1.1
JTA	1.1	`geronimo-jta_1.1_spec`	1.1
QName	1.1	`geronimo-qname_1.1_spec`	1.1
SAAJ	1.1	`geronimo-saaj_1.1_spec`	1.1
Servlet	2.4	`geronimo-servlet_2.4_spec`	1.1.1
Servlet	2.5	`geronimo-servlet_2.5_spec`	1.1.1
STaX API	1.0	`geronimo-stax-api_1.0_spec`	1.0.1
WS Metadata	2.0	`geronimo-ws-metadata_2.0_spec`	1.1.1

The version numbers in the artifact version column may be out of date by the time you read this book. To check on the version number, visit *http://repo1.maven.org/maven2/org/apache/geronimo/specs/* in a web browser and click on the `artifactId` you want to add. Choose the highest version of the spec you want to depend on.

To illustrate how to use this table, if we wanted to write some code in our project that interacted with the JTA 1.0.1B specification, we would need to add the dependency shown in Example B-1 to our project.

Example B-1. Adding JTA 1.0.1B to a Maven project

```
<dependency>
  <groupId>org.apache.geronimo.specs</groupId>
  <artifactId>geronimo-jta_1.0.1B_spec</artifactId>
  <version>1.1.1</version>
</dependency>
```

Notice how the version of the artifact isn't going to line up with the version of the specification—the previous dependency configuration adds version 1.0.1B of the JTA specification using the artifact version of 1.1.1. Be aware of this when depending on the alternate Geronimo implementations, and always double-check that you are using the latest artifact version number for your specifications.

Index

We'd like to hear your suggestions for improving our indexes. Send email to *index@oreilly.com*.

authentication, project web site, 318

G

generate-resources phase (default lifecycle), 184

generate-sources phase (default lifecycle), 184

generate-test-resources phase (default lifecycle), 184

generate-test-sources phase (default lifecycle), 184

Geronimo project (see Apache Geronimo project)

getLog() method (Mojo interface), 393

global settings profiles, 207, 208

@goal annotation (Mojo), 398

goal element (Mojo declarations), 389

goalPrefix element, plugins, 389

goals, 30

    (see also plugins)

    about, 26

    attaching to lifecycle phases, 32

    defined, 30

    triggering on pre-clean phase, 182

graphical POM editor, 294

graphics for project web site, 313

group identifiers, about, 168

    (see also groupId attribute)

group permissions, project web site, 318

groupId attribute (pom.xml), 29, 36, 168

    built-in, to avoid dependency duplication, 133

    determining for dependencies, 47

        Apache Geronimo implementation of Servlet API, 73

    referencing, 262

groupId element (plugins), 388, 394–397

grouping dependencies (best practice), 173

<groupVersionAlignments> flag (assembly repositories), 250

H

HEAD element, XHTML in (project web sites), 328

header graphics, project web site, 313

Help plugin, 18

    help:describe goal, 19–21

help with Maven, getting, 17

Help:active-profiles goal, 209

Hibernate, 90

Hibernate annotations, 92

Hibernate plugin, 108

hibernate.cfg.xml file, 104

Hibernate3 plugin, 104, 108

    building database using, 116

HOME environment variable, 264

<host> element (<proxy> element), 429

HQL (Hibernate Query Language), 94

hyperlinks at project web site, 328

I

<id> element, 427

    assembly descriptions, 228

    <mirror> element, 428

    <profiles> element, 201

implementation element (Mojo declarations), 390

implicit variables, list of, 158

importing projects into Eclipse, 282–285

    materializing projects, 284–285

in-house portability, 198

<includeDependencies> flag (module sets), 248

<includeMetadata> flag (assembly repositories), 250

<includes> section (<fileSets> element), 231

<includeSubModules> flag (module sets), 244, 248

inclusive boundaries (version ranges), 163

incremental versions (projects), 156

indexing repositories with m2eclipse, 293

inheritance between projects or modules, 171

    choosing multimodule projects instead of, 175

inheritedByDefault element (Mojo declarations), 390

inheritedByDefault element, plugins, 389

install phase (default lifecycle), 185, 196

Install plugin, 196

installation directory

    contents of, 16

    identifying, 264

installing Maven, 13–17

    details about, 16

    on FreeBSD or OpenBSD, 15

    on Linux, 15

    on Mac OS X, 14

    on Microsoft Windows, 15

    testing the installation, 16

    upgrade an installation, 17

simple-parent project, 90–91
simple-persist module of, 99–105
simple-weather module of, 95–99
simple-webapp, 105–115
running, 85
simple-parent project, 77
simple-weather submodule, 79–81
simple-webapp submodule, 81–82
multimodule projects, in general, 169
inheritance versus, 175
module sets for assemblies, 227, 243–249
multimodule projects, optimizing POMs for, 130
multivalued Mojo parameters, 402–404
mvn install command, 27
mvn script, 16
Mylyn
installing, 273
Mylyn plugin, 271

N

name attribute (pom.xml), referencing, 263
name element (Mojo parameters), 391
<name> element (<mirror> element), 428, 429
@NamedQueries annotation (Hibernate), 94
@NamedQuery annotation (Hibernate), 94
navigation menu, project web site, 313
new project wizard, Eclipse, 275
nonportable builds, 198, 199
<nonProxyHosts> element (<proxy> element), 429
NOTICE.txt file, 16

O

object model (see POM; pom.xml file)
ObjectWeb ASM toolkit, 138
obtaining example programs for this book, 25
obtaining Maven, 14
<offline> element (settings.xml), 426
open source generation, web site for (see site generation)
OpenBSD, installing Maven on, 15
opening project pages with m2eclipse, 291
optimizing POMs, 129–147
about cleaning up POMs, 130
dependency optimization, 130–134
Maven Dependency plugin, 136–139

plugin optimization, 134–135
optional dependencies, 161
ordering of version qualifiers, 156
organizational information (project information), 150
adding to project, 45
organizational portability, 198
<os> element (<activation> element), 430
<outputDirectory> element (assembly descriptors), 231
<outputDirectory> flag (module sets), 248
<outputDirectoryMapping> element (assembly descriptors), 235
interpolation of, in module sets, 246
<outputFileNameMapping> element (assembly descriptors), 235
overriding with profiles (see build profiles)

P

package phase (default lifecycle), 185
package-specific lifecycle, 185–189
packages
custom packaging types, 188
EARs as, 188
EJBs (Enterprise JavaBeans) as, 187
JAR files (see JAR files)
plugins as, 186
(see also plugins)
POM files (see POM; pom.xml file)
types of, 185
WAR files as (see WAR files)
packaging applications, 27
command-line applications, 65–66
packaging attribute (pom.xml), 29, 37
<packaging> element (pom.xml), 186
parallel lifecycles for plugins, 406
@parameter annotation (Mojo parameters), 405
parameters element (Mojo declarations), 391
parent POM, 26, 80
(see also POM)
configuring project assembly in, 223
dependency management in, 166
inheritance from (see project inheritance)
module sets and, 249
prototype parent projects, 179
resolving dependency duplication, 130
<passphrase> element, 427
<password> element, 427, 429

for writing plugins, 392
properties, 261–266
    activating profiles upon absence of, 205
    configuration in settings.xml, 431
    project properties, 262–264
    referencing in assembly descriptors, 228
    referencing in pom.xml, 157
    resource filtering, 266–269
    settings properties, 264
    user-defined, 265
properties file, 190
<property> element (<activation> element),
    430
<protocol> element (<proxy> element), 429
prototype parent projects, 179
provided dependencies, 160
<proxies> element (settings.xml), 428
publication date format, project web site, 330

Q

qualifiers for project versions, 156
    ordering of, 156

R

ranges for dependency versions, 162
README.txt file, 16
@readonly annotation (Mojo parameters),
    405
real POMs, 155
refactoring POMs (see optimizing POMs)
references to properties, in pom.xml, 157
relationships, project, 168–173
<releases> element (<repository> element),
    433
replacing transitive dependencies, 164
replicated dependencies, 130
report generation, 41
repositories, 37
    central, 154
    configuration in settings.xml, 432
    dependency management, 39–40
    m2eclipse tools for, 292–293
        indexing repositories, 293
        searching for artifacts and Java classes,
            292
repository directory, 17
<repository> element (settings.xml), 432

repository information section (assembly
        descriptors), 227, 249–250
@required annotation (Mojo parameters), 405
required element (Mojo parameters), 391
requirements element (Mojo declarations),
    391
@requiresDependencyResolution annotation
        (Mojo), 398
@requiresDirectInvocation annotation (Mojo),
    399
requiresDirectInvocation element (Mojo
        declarations), 389
@requiresOnline annotation (Mojo), 399
requiresOnline element (Mojo declarations),
    390
requiresProject element (Mojo declarations),
    389
@requiresProjet annotation (Mojo), 398
@requiresReports annotation (Mojo), 398
requiresReports element (Mojo declarations),
    390
resolving dependencies with m2eclipse, 291
resolving dependency conflicts, 164
resource filtering, 190, 266–269
resources
    adding to packages, 53–54
    adding to unit tests, 61–62
resources directory, 61, 191
    creating, 53
resources for programs, where stored, 27
Resources plugin
    resources goal, 32
    testResources goal, 34
reusable assembly descriptors, 252–255
root directory, assemblies, 250
    componentDescriptors and
            containerDescriptorHandlers,
            251
runtime dependencies, 160

S

<scope> element (<dependency> element),
    60
scope, dependency, 40, 160
    excluding dependencies from assemblies by,
        237–238
    transitive dependencies and, 164
searching for dependency attributes, 47
security of project web site, 317–319

About the Author

The primary contributor to this book is **Tim O'Brien**, online editor of O'Reilly News, and author of three other O'Reilly titles: *Harnessing Hibernate*, *Maven: A Developer's Notebook*, and *Jakarta Commons Cookbook*.

Colophon

The animal on the cover of *Maven: The Definitive Guide* is a giant anteater (*Myrmecophaga tridactyla*), the largest species of anteater. It grows to an average length of seven feet and weighs about 85 pounds—the size of a German shepherd dog. Its head tapers to a long, narrow snout, and its tail is nearly as large as the rest of its body and covered with bristly hair. Despite its species name, *tridactyla* (Greek for "three fingers"), the anteater has five digits on each foot, but the middle three have extra-long claws. The anteater uses these claws to break open insect mounds and defend itself against predators. It walks on its knuckles to protect the claws, causing it to walk with a shuffle.

Giant anteaters live in grasslands and tropical forests in Central and South America, where ants and termites are plentiful. They prefer to eat soft-bodied insects because anteaters are edentate animals, meaning they have no teeth; instead of chewing, they crush their food against hard growths on the inside of their mouths. The anteater first tears an opening in a tree trunk or an anthill with its claws, and then it uses its snout and tongue to collect the insects inside. It has the longest tongue in proportion to body size of any mammal—more than two feet long—and can scoop up thousands of insects in minutes. A single anteater can eat up to 30,000 ants and termites each day.

Being solitary creatures, giant anteaters tend not to stay in one spot for long. They are not aggressive, but they can be fierce and will use their claws to fight off pumas or jaguars (their main natural predators). When threatened, the giant anteater stands on its hind legs, using its tail for balance, and either strikes or hugs its attackers like a bear—hence it is sometimes called the "ant bear." Anteaters are frequently killed by humans, whether hunted or hit by cars, and habitat destruction is the primary threat to their survival. They are listed as "vulnerable" by the International Union for Conservation of Nature and Natural Resources.

The cover image is from the *Dover Pictorial Archive*. The cover font is Adobe ITC Garamond. The text font is Linotype Birka; the heading font is Adobe Myriad Condensed; and the code font is LucasFont's TheSansMonoCondensed.

Made in the USA
San Bernardino, CA
06 December 2013